WRITING THE NORTH OF ENGLAND IN THE MIDDLE AGES

Writing the North of England in the Middle Ages offers a literary history of the North–South divide, examining the complexities of the relationship – imaginative, material, and political – between North and South in a wide range of texts. Through sustained analysis of the North–South divide as it emerges in the literature of medieval England, this study illustrates the convoluted dynamic of desire and derision of the North by the rest of the country. Joseph Taylor dissects England's problematic sense of nationhood as one which must be negotiated and renegotiated from within, rather than beyond, national borders. Providing fresh readings of texts such as Chaucer's *Canterbury Tales*, the fifteenth-century Robin Hood ballads, and the Towneley plays, this book argues for the North's vital contribution to processes of imagining nation in the Middle Ages and shows that that regionalism is both contained within and constitutive of its apparent opposite, nationalism.

JOSEPH TAYLOR is Associate Professor of English at the University of Alabama in Huntsville, where he teaches courses in medieval literature and history of the English language. He is the co-editor (with Randy P. Schiff) of *The Politics of Ecology: Land, Life and Law in Medieval Britain* (2016).

CAMBRIDGE STUDIES IN MEDIEVAL LITERATURE

Founding Editor
Alastair Minnis, *Yale University*

General Editor
Daniel Wakelin, *University of Oxford*

Editorial Board
Anthony Bale, *Birkbeck, University of London*
Zygmunt G. Barański, *University of Cambridge*
Christopher C. Baswell, *Barnard College and Columbia University*
Mary Carruthers, *New York University*
Rita Copeland, *University of Pennsylvania*
Roberta Frank, *Yale University*
Marissa Galvez, *Stanford University*
Alastair Minnis, *Yale University*
Jocelyn Wogan-Browne, *Fordham University*

This series of critical books seeks to cover the whole area of literature written in the major medieval languages – the main European vernaculars, and medieval Latin and Greek – during the period *c.*1100–1500. Its chief aim is to publish and stimulate fresh scholarship and criticism on medieval literature, special emphasis being placed on understanding major works of poetry, prose, and drama in relation to the contemporary culture and learning which fostered them.

Recent titles in the series
Mark Faulkner *A New Literary History of the Long Twelfth Century: Language and Literature Between Old and Middle English*
Mark Chinca and Christopher Young Literary Beginnings in the European Middle Ages
Andrew M. Richmond Landscape in Middle English Romance: The Medieval Imagination and the Natural World
David G. Lummus The City of Poetry: Imagining the Civic Role of the Poet in Fourteenth-Century Italy
Richard Matthew Pollard Imagining the Medieval Afterlife
Christiania Whitehead The Afterlife of St Cuthbert: Place, Texts and Ascetic Tradition, 690–1500
Orietta Da Rold Paper in Medieval England: From Pulp to Fictions
Jonathan Morton and Marco Nievergelt (eds.) The Roman de la Rose and Thirteenth-Century Thought
George Corbett Dante's Christian Ethics: Purgatory and Its Moral Contexts
Andrew Kraebel Biblical Commentary and Translation in Later Medieval England: Experiments in Interpretation

Robert J. Meyer-Lee Literary Value and Social Identity in the Canterbury Tales
Glenn D. Burger and Holly A. Crocker (eds.) Medieval Affect, Feeling, and Emotion
Lawrence Warner Chaucer's Scribes: London Textual Production, 1384–1432

A complete list of titles in the series can be found at the end of the volume.

WRITING THE NORTH OF ENGLAND IN THE MIDDLE AGES

Regionalism and Nationalism in Medieval English Literature

JOSEPH TAYLOR
University of Alabama in Huntsville

Shaftesbury Road, Cambridge CB2 8EA, United Kingdom

One Liberty Plaza, 20th Floor, New York, NY 10006, USA

477 Williamstown Road, Port Melbourne, VIC 3207, Australia

314–321, 3rd Floor, Plot 3, Splendor Forum, Jasola District Centre, New Delhi – 110025, India

103 Penang Road, #05–06/07, Visioncrest Commercial, Singapore 238467

Cambridge University Press is part of Cambridge University Press & Assessment, a department of the University of Cambridge.

We share the University's mission to contribute to society through the pursuit of education, learning and research at the highest international levels of excellence.

www.cambridge.org
Information on this title: www.cambridge.org/9781009182096

DOI: 10.1017/9781009182102

© Joseph Taylor 2023

This publication is in copyright. Subject to statutory exception and to the provisions of relevant collective licensing agreements, no reproduction of any part may take place without the written permission of Cambridge University Press & Assessment.

First published 2023
First paperback edition 2025

A catalogue record for this publication is available from the British Library

ISBN 978-1-009-18211-9 Hardback
ISBN 978-1-009-18209-6 Paperback

Cambridge University Press & Assessment has no responsibility for the persistence or accuracy of URLs for external or third-party internet websites referred to in this publication and does not guarantee that any content on such websites is, or will remain, accurate or appropriate.

For Laura
'Something in the way she knows,
And all I have to do is think of her.'

Contents

Acknowledgments	page x
1. Introduction: Region and Nation in England's North–South Divide	1
2. William of Malmesbury, Bede, and the Problem of the North	32
3. The North–South Divide in the Medieval English Universities	63
4. Chaucer's Northern Consciousness in the *Reeve's Tale*	88
5. Centralization, Resistance, and the North of England in *A Gest of Robyn Hode*	113
6. The Towneley Plays, the Pilgrimage of Grace, and Northern Messianism	137
7. Conclusion: A Medieval and Modern North–South Divide	173
Notes	190
Works Cited	232
Index	251

Acknowledgments

This book is the product of many years' conversations with numerous kind scholars and thinkers, as well as significant financial support from various institutions. I want to thank the Department of English at the University of Texas at Austin for travel and research support, as well as a dissertation fellowship, that afforded me opportunities to both perform initial research on this book and present it at various conferences. I also want to thank the University of Alabama in Huntsville's (UAH) College of Arts, Humanities, and Social Sciences, the UAH Provost's office, and the UAH Humanities Center for extensive travel monies that allowed me to visit archives in the UK as the final manuscript took shape. So much of the secondary scholarship that I read for this book came into my hands – in quick fashion – from the excellent inter-library loan staffs at Texas' Perry-Castañeda Library and UAH's Salmon Library; I am grateful for their labors. I owe much gratitude to the wonderful folks at the British Library for help with both manuscripts and rare print texts that informed several chapters of the present book, and I am doubly indebted to the patient staff at both the Manchester City Archives and the Lancashire Archives in Preston, UK. I have heard in the past from colleagues about the wonderful people at Cambridge University Press, and I can sing their praises further here. Editor Emily Hockley was kind and thorough in reviewing and sending out my manuscript, and always quick in response to my inquiries. George Laver has been so very helpful as the manuscript transitioned to a real book! I am grateful to Dan Wakelin, as series editor, for his attention to the work and his encouraging words. The anonymous reviewers offered significant and substantive feedback on the project and I am grateful for their time and attention. Portions of Chapters 3 and 4 of this book appear, respectively, in the *Journal of English and Germanic Philology* (University of Illinois Press) and *Modern Philology* (University of Chicago Press). I thank the editors and presses of these journals for permission to use this work here.

This project grew out of my doctoral dissertation, which I wrote within the vibrant graduate program at the University of Texas at Austin. I feel lucky to have had, as my dissertation advisors, Elizabeth Scala and Daniel Birkholz, both of whom provided tremendous guidance, encouragement, and sheer attention to my education and to the project. Liz was a patient and thorough teacher whose disciplined practice of instruction and scholarship continues to inform my being today. Dan was an energetic champion, prolific in suggestions to move and expand the project, and his thought-energy-fission continues to inform my research process. I find myself uncannily repeating their maxims and even their pedagogic subtleties every day with my own students. Jorie Woods was a quintessential advisor and friend throughout my graduate career, and she, further, afforded me an impactful opportunity to see (and work with) a scholar-in-process as she completed her magnum opus on the *Poetria Nova*. Mary Blockely hooked me on medieval dialects, and thus afforded the birth of this project in her always-fun and rigorous classroom. Geraldine Heng made timely suggestions for texts and ideas as the project developed, and I owe Chapter 4 of this book to her. Many other important teachers impacted my learning, including Janine Barchas, Doug Bruster, Linda Ferreira-Buckley, Tom Cable, Diane Davis, Jacqueline Henkel, Trish Roberts-Miller, Wayne Rebhorn, John Riszkiewicz, and the late Wayne Lesser. At Virginia Tech, I was fortunate to have two outstanding advisors. Tony Colaianne made me want to study medieval literature in the first place, with his dynamic in-class readings of *Piers Plowman*, while Dan Mosser introduced me to Chaucer's *oeuvre* in several classes, piquing my interest in medieval studies for the better (or worse, depending on how you feel about the book!). I also want to thank David Radcliffe for his honest and encouraging words when I was stumbling around as an aspirant graduate student. I was fortunate to be part of a cohort of graduate students at the University of Texas that I would pit against any group of thinkers/scholars in the world. Jon Lamb and Greg Foran were brothers in scholarly arms, and I owe so much success to the fact that I was able to share intellectual space with them for five years. They read significant portions of this work in its early stages and allowed me to bounce ideas repeatedly, which they then shaped for the better. Brooke Hunter's dazzling intellect challenged me to step up my game as a medievalist, and her humble demeanor reminded us all that you can be a gifted thinker without telling everyone about it. Other student colleagues were consummate interlocutors and provided significant commentary and suggestions to improve the early project in reading groups or simple conversation.

These wonderful people include Meghan Andrews, Chris Bradley, Nick D'Alessio, Donna Hobbs, Brad Irish, Jason Leubner, Kevin Psonak, and Tim Turner. And, though I will inevitably and unintentionally exclude someone (for which I'm sorry), I express immense gratitude to my colleagues in English and friends at UAH with whom I've conversed about this project, including Angela Balla, Laurel Bollinger Dylan Baun, Ryan Brown, Joseph Conway, Anna Foy, Alanna Frost, Andrei Gandila, Rolf Goebel, Gaines Hubbell, Holly Jones, Seth Lee, Bill Munson, David Neff, Jeff Nelson, Daniel Schenker, Eric Smith, Chad Thomas, and Ryan Weber.

I am fortunate to count Randy Schiff as a friend. His conversations on all things, his professional advice, and his readings and commentaries on drafts of my work over the years has proved immensely helpful to my development as a scholar. Several medievalists have allowed me to be part of programs, whether presenting or organizing, that afforded venues for this work, so I want to thank Jeffrey Cohen, George Edmondson, Patty Ingham, Jessica Rosenfeld, and Matthew Giancarlo. I must acknowledge Marion Turner for asking me one particularly tough question about the complexities of "the North" many years ago, when I was a graduate student, and her words resonated with me to the very completion of this book. I will also shout out to Rob Barrett for directing me toward the right scholarship on the Towneley Manuscript before I began Chapter 6, and that direction was timely and crucial. I am grateful to John Ganim, James Goldstein, Jonathan Hsy, Patty Ingham (again), Kathy Lavezzo, and Kelly Robertson for their willingness to evaluate my work in my tenure year. Their scholarship significantly inspired this project and continues to inform new work, so I'm very appreciative of their time.

I want to acknowledge my supportive family, who have always cheered me on as I undertook a career in academia. My older sisters Monica and Crystie have always been a loving force in my life, and, through them, I'm thankful to know or have known Joey Davenport, John Beattie, Will Beattie, and George Beattie. I want to recognize my late father, William Earl Taylor, who passed when I was seven but who will always inform my identity, and I want to further thank my late grandparents George and Helen McDonough, and Joseph and Elizabeth Taylor. My parents were behind my education, working hard to assure me success. I express love and immense thanks to my stepfather Douglas Blackwell for his persistence and to my mother Patsy, who planted literary seeds by reading to me every day, including a child-friendly version of *Sir Gawain and the Green Knight*, when I was six!

My greatest love and thanks are reserved for my girls, Ellie and Anna, and my wife, Laura. No professional or publication success compares with being part of our family. Each day my kids teach me about humor and humanity. They are beautiful souls and I'm so blessed to have them in my life. My darling wife encouraged me to pursue this work, recognizing my unhappiness in the business world. She supported me both emotionally and, let's be honest, financially, as I moved through graduate school and into a professional academic career, and, further, as we moved around the country. I would need another book to write of her immense love, encouragement, and sheer presence, all of which make my life joyful. I am so very lucky to have her in my life.

CHAPTER 1

Introduction: Region and Nation in England's North–South Divide

Near Lamesley, UK, where Durham Road intersects with the A1, the largest sculpture in Britain stares southeast down the motorway. Built of 200 tons of steel and sitting atop the old Team Valley colliery pithead baths in order to honor mineworkers, the Angel of the North welcomes motorists to Gateshead just before they might veer northeast to Newcastle or remain on the A1 and travel all the way to Berwick. Artist Antony Gormley designed the sculpture, which was erected in February 1998, but the Angel's beginnings were contentious. While its emplacement was championed by the local council as a sign of the region's productive turn from old industry to the information age, even today, as a "catalyst to the cultural regeneration of Gateshead Quays," it was also parodied as the "Gateshead Flasher" for its outstretched wings[1] and, further, derided as a "potential death trap for passing motorists," who might be distracted by its substantial height (20 m or 54 ft) or the massive span (54 m or 175 ft) of those wings.[2] For this threat, Gormley recalled, in an interview, that some critics labeled it "Hell's Angel" or the "Angel of Death."[3] Yet the sculpture has become a beloved icon of the region. As Martin Roberts claims in his recent survey of County Durham architecture, the Angel of the North as a community project "posed the greatest risk yet delivered the greatest reward" and it is further revered as a daring work of art.[4] Given its existence as both a damning image and a salvific icon of the region, the Angel of the North provesa fitting point of departure for this book's examination of the origins of northern consciousness and the English North–South divide. The hulking steel giant that is Gateshead's Angel, called by some the largest angel sculpture in the world, has a fitting precursor in medieval biblical typology.

1

In Passus 1 of the C-text of *Piers Plowman* the radical fourteenth-century poet and preacher William Langland offers a joke on the North of England. The dreamer asks:

> Lord! why wolde he tho, þat wykkede Lucifer,
> Luppen alofte in þe north syde
> Thenne sitten in þe sonne (sun's) syde þere þe day roweth?
> (111–13)[5]

This passage specifically alludes to *Isaiah 14*, which imagines the return of exiles from Babylonian captivity and also satirises the fall of their oppressors, comparing Babylonian rulers to the fallen angel, Lucifer himself. Verse 13, to which Langland refers here, recalls the rebellious Lucifer's arrogant claims: *"in caelum conscendam super astra Dei axaltabo solium meum sedebo in monte testament in lateribus"* (I will ascend into heaven, I will exalt my throne above the stars of God, I will sit in the mountain of the covenant, in the sides of the north). In the context of Lucifer's proclamations, *Piers Plowman*'s dreamer asks, in effect, "why would that wicked Lucifer take up his seat in the North?" Lady Holy Church responds to the dreamer playfully: "Ne were it for northerne men a-non ich wolde telle" (115). While evoking a patristic aspect of northern-ness in medieval theology – that is, the North as the space wherein we find the Devil, Lucifer, at his most defiant – Langland acknowledges a second view of the North more closely akin to the cultural and political landscapes of England. Lady Holy Church's joke – that she will pass over any further explanation of diabolic northern-ness so as not to offend England's northerners ("Ne were it for northerne men...") – is extended playfully and purposefully in the lines that follow. She continues: "Hit is sykerer by soothe where the sonne regneth / Than in the north by meny notes, all men know" (116–17). For Lady Holy Church, the South is more desirable than the North because the sun reigns there in its warmth (*sonne regneth*) and, by allusion, Christ (the *sone*) reigns there in his glory.[6] Beyond these reasons are "meny notes" more. It is, thus, quite possible to hear in Langland's allusion a sarcasm born of the North–South divide: that his readers, fellow non-northerners – and, more specifically, the Londoners in whose circles Langland moved – know exactly why one would place Lucifer in the culturally-backward and often-rebellious frontier of the North of England rather than in the South, where it is safer (*sykerer*).

Although he represses any explicit desire for the North in his disparaging humor, Langland nonetheless intimates his own awareness of the region's complex character as both derided *and* desired throughout

England's political and cultural history. In a Latin declarative that precedes these lines in the C-text, Langland quotes Augustine's own exegetical reading of *Isaiah 14*: "*Ponam pedem meum in aquiline, et ero similis altissimo*" (I will put my foot in the North and I will be like the Most High).[7] This particular note, from which Langland quotes, is part of Augustine's long discussion on the coming together of Jews and Gentiles as two mountains flanking Zion or, per *Psalm 118:22*, as two walls that meet at the cornerstone of Christ in order to form the new Zion. In Augustine's explanation, the "North" signifies anyone possessed by the Devil ("serving images, adoring demons") because "North," here, signifies Lucifer. Augustine explains, "The North is wont to be contrary to [Z]ion: [Z]ion forsooth is in the South, the North over against the South," for, he continues, "Who is the North, but He who said, *I will sit in the sides of the North, I will be like the Most High*?"[8] But as Lucifer's monstrations imply, he aims to take the place of God, to "be like" God, and that place is *in* the North. Yet, he will fail in his rebellion. Lady Holy Church notes that "as the fend flegh to set his foot there / He faileth and fell and his felawes with him" (119–20). Indeed, Augustine finds in *Job 37:22* that God will re-inscribe the North as his own domain: "Therefore also in another Scripture is it said, *Out of the North come clouds of golden colour: great is the glory and honour of the Almighty*" (editor's emphasis). For Augustine, then, the North is that place of God that has been usurped by the Devil, but it will be remade through the forthcoming return of the Almighty. On His return, God will descend from the North, illuminating the bleak clouds with gold, undoing the Devil's work through His own presence and in His own likeness: "and the sides of the North will be joined to the city of the great king." The image of two walls coming together in this biblical typology is compelling for thinking about the English nation with its North–South divide. The biblical North provokes both disdain and longing, a place both frightening through Lucifer's presence and his rebellion against God, and yet intimate in Christ's salvific return. Thus, we can understand how Augustine's exegesis explains the duality of the North for medieval English writers. Langland's clever use of *Isaiah 14:13* in the C-text of *Piers Plowman*, with its winking nod to Augustine's theology and all in a regionalist frame, captures the complex nature of the North as both destructive and salvific. Langland's contemporary, Geoffrey Chaucer, will play upon this typology in the *Friar's Tale* with a devil-in-disguise who claims to be from "fer in the north contree" (III, 1413) and who rids the local population of a criminous summoner.[9]

In medieval England, the North is not simply "other"; rather, the broad region comprises a liminal space, both within and without a national frame. In the North, English national identity confronts strong regional cultures and politics. Anxiety stemming from the North's haunting presence is not merely the product of southern-derived stereotypes and superstitions. As Dave Russell notes, scholarship on the North–South divide "often underestimates the extent to which the region has been active in its own making."[10] Numerous rebellions by northerners against the crown and its South-centered government contribute to a negative northern consciousness and provoke negative characterizations of the region in literature and culture. In 1069, for example, the northern populace aligned with King Swein II of Denmark and the exiled English claimant to the throne, Edgar Ætheling, in order to rebel against the new Norman ruler, William I (the Conqueror). The revolt elicited from William a crushing military response, the "Harrying of the North," in the winter of 1069–70 that set the region back for decades. In 1214, northern barons refused to fight in King John's Poitevin campaign, and these men later brought the monarch to the table at Runnymeade to sign Magna Carta. Late historian J.C. Holt captures the regional identity of these men in the title of his study on the period, *The Northerners*.[11] In the early fourteenth century, Richard II cultivated the powerful marcher families of the North, including the Percys, Cliffords, and Nevilles, in order to systematically address the Scottish threat, but in 1399 these wardens of the march assisted in Richard's overthrow. Almost as quickly, the Percys rebelled against Henry IV before the younger Percy (Hotspur) met his fate at the Battle of Shrewsbury in 1403. Beyond these major revolts, the North has always evoked suspicion and derision from non-northerners. To many Englishmen who lived and thrived elsewhere, the North of England loomed as a cultural and political bogeyman over the rest of the realm for much of the Middle Ages. Unlike the Irish, the Welsh, and even the Scots, northerners remained within the borders of England while at the same time far-flung from the ideological heart of the realm in the South.[12]

At the same time, we cannot paint the North of England solely as a region of rebellion and angst against the crown and its government. The North was a staging ground for English historical writing and religious devotional life, as well as a central factor in English politics and national defense. The remote monastery of St Peter's at Jarrow was home to the Venerable Bede, the "Father of English History," whose eighth-century *Historia Ecclesiastica Gentis Anglorum* became the touchstone for later historiographers writing their revisions of English history after the

Norman Conquest. Northern devotional practice, including Cistercian monasticism or the affective piety described in the writings of celebrated hermit Richard Rolle of Hampole, were profoundly popular and influential throughout England in the Middle Ages. The Lindisfarne monk Cuthbert (634–687 CE) was England's preeminent saint and his shrine at Durham arguably the most visited pilgrimage site in England up until the martyrdom of Thomas Becket in 1170.[13] From the 1160s, Cuthbert's banner was carried by an array of peoples and, with the advent of the Anglo-Scottish wars in 1296, the banner proved "a vital talisman accompanying English campaigns against the Scots."[14] This was never more evident than when, in 1346, it was marched into the fray against the Scots at Neville's Cross, just outside Durham. There, an army of local levies lead by the Archbishop of York, William le Zouche, defeated the Scottish army of King David II, who was captured during the battle. This victory was a significant national moment that erased, at least briefly, years of Scottish military success against the English. King Edward III clarified this erasure when he ordered Scotland to pay David's ransom annually on 24 June, the anniversary of the Scottish victory at Bannockburn in 1314.[15]

In this long war, England's second city, York, became an intermittent capital, wherein one might find the royal household, the exchequer, the chancery, and parliament from the late thirteenth century to the end of the fourteenth century. Indeed, Richard II moved the government to York in 1392–3 for the express purpose of spiting London. Given the convoluted relationship of the North to the rest of the realm as either a seat for rebellion or the seat of the king, we are not surprised that William Langland found a parallel in the imagery of *Isaiah 14*. The present study proposes to analyze the complexities of northern consciousness extant in the literature of medieval England, wherein we witness the North–South divide with its interplay of regionalism and nationalism.

In spite of abundant evidence of a North–South divide extant in – or, arguably, emerging in – medieval England, most discussions of the great rift see the Industrial Revolution as a definitive point of origin. In *The Road to Wigan Pier* (1937), George Orwell declares confidently that "it was the industrialization of the North that gave the North–South antithesis its peculiar slant."[16] One would imagine that Orwell's views are shaped in part by the Victorian novels that bore witness to the Industrial Revolution in England, the most famous of which are Benjamin Disraeli's *Sybil, or The Two Nations* (1845) and Elizabeth Gaskell's *North and South* (1855). In *Sybil*, Disraeli posits a distinct division between rich and poor "who are as ignorant of each other's habits, thoughts, and feelings, as if they were dwellers in different zones, or inhabitants of different planets" (BK 2, Ch. 2), but the book's focus on the industrial North unquestionably broaches a geographic divide – truly "dwellers in different zones" – between the North and South. Gaskell's novel is more explicit. Her heroine, Margaret Hale, begins the novel as a lady-in-training at the London home of her wealthy aunt before moving back to her beloved cottage in the rural hamlet of Helstone, by the New Forest in Hampshire. Her world is upended quickly when her father moves both she and her mother to the industrial muck of the northern town Milton (a fictionalized version of Manchester), where she is made to confront the awful conditions and the tragedies of the northern poor in the face of exploitive labor. While Gaskell was gravely concerned over the plight of industrial workers, as her previous novels *Mary Barton* (1848) and the scandalous *Ruth* (1853) expressed, it was her editor Charles Dickens, at the magazine *Household Words* in which Gaskell published the novel in serial, who suggested the title *North and South*.[17] These works illustrate the cultural and economic differences between industrial North and agrarian South and accentuate the impact of the Industrial Revolution on England from the late eighteenth century.

Scholars have tended to follow Orwell's lead in declaring the Industrial Revolution as a root cause of the divide. Sociologist Rob Shields points specifically to the work of Disraeli and Gaskell when he claims:

> The contemporary dichotomous North and South view came into focus with nineteenth-century literary works which responded to the rapid industrialization of the North (and the emergence of an urbanized industrial elite which challenged the social status of the landed aristocracy largely centered in the Home Counties around London).[18]

Shields arguments are echoed in recent examinations of the North–South divide by other sociologists, historians, and literary scholars. Dave Russell's *Looking North* and Neville Kirk's essay collection *Northern Identities* focus almost exclusively on the nineteenth and twentieth centuries, analyzing various examples of music, stage and film, sport, tourism, and language that proffer and affirm the North's discrete identity within England.[19] Remarkably, even when scholars have attended to the North–South divide before the Industrial Age, they find it difficult to admit the rift's cultural or political prominence. Allan Baker and Mark Billinge's essay collection *Geographies of England: The North–South Divide, Material and Imagined* traces the division backwards from the present day to the Norman Invasion of 1066. Historian Bruce M.S. Campbell, whose contribution analyzes the medieval period from 1066 to 1550, acknowledges that in the Middle Ages "differences between the North and South are not hard to find," but he questions whether these differences really divided the realm. He argues that by the thirteenth century, "there is nothing to suggest that there was any contemporary concept of a '"North–South divide"'; rather, the period is notable for the "emergence of a growing sense of national consciousness, which overrode older regional identities."[20] While Campbell is right to view the period as one of emergent nationalism, his conclusion—that "the one North–South divide that was as real as it was imagined was that between England and Scotland" – fails to account for the ways in which the tenuous relationship between the North and the rest of the England informs, if not enables, the emergence of a national consciousness in the period. If we return briefly to Orwell, we recognize that such modern commentaries on industrialization and the North–South divide betray medieval foundations. Orwell, for example, observes:

> when you go to the industrial North you are conscious, quite apart from the unfamiliar scenery, of entering a strange country. This is partly because of certain real differences which do exist, but still more because of the North–South antithesis which has been rubbed into us for such a long time past .... The Northerner has "grit," he is grim, "dour," plucky, warm-hearted, and democratic; the Southerner is snobbish, effeminate, and lazy – that at any rate is the theory. Hence, the Southerner goes north ... for the first time, with the vague inferiority-complex of a civilised man venturing among savages, while the Yorkshireman, like the Scotchman, comes to London in the spirit of a barbarian out for loot. And feelings of this kind, which are the result of tradition, are not affected by visible facts.[21]

Orwell speaks, here, of a cultural inertia that continues to inform representations of the North and an understanding of the divide in the present. His "long time past," however, is far longer than he might recognize because his allusion to "savages" and to the "spirit of a barbarian out for loot," as well as his juxtaposition of the "Yorkshireman" with the "Scotchman," betray premodern anxieties and recall disparaging remarks made by southern writers as far back as the twelfth century about the "strange country" north of the Humber, with its barbarous tongue and rebellious people.

The present study seeks to add to long-running conversations about the English North by attending to a perceived North–South divide, and, specifically, to examples of northern consciousness, in premodern England. In the pages that follow, I will argue, in part, that the North–South divide was a central point of tension in premodern England and that northern consciousness is, in fact, a necessary condition for an emergent English national consciousness in the Middle Ages. Such inquiry, of course, risks falling into what Patricia Yeager has called the "dead-end binarism" that undermines cultural studies.[22] Indeed, northern England – whether one now locates this region above the River Trent, the Humber Estuary, or even Watford Gap – is a heterogeneous space, and so it was in medieval England. York was not Carlisle and to hail from Holderness was not to hail from Newcastle; rather, we find a multiplicity of identities including the legal palatinates in Cheshire and Durham, the duchy of Lancaster, the border fortress at Berwick, all of which maintain significant – and different – political personas and a distinct consciousness of place. But what emerges nevertheless is that the broader region's many spaces, places, and peoples are reproduced frequently in monochrome – "THE North" – at the surface-level of medieval literature. Yeager claims that "materiality is not just solid but also imaginary – that place only persuades us because it is made out of reiterated stories and objects that produce a constant, pervasive sense of locatability."[23] My task in this study is to understand the cultural politics informing popular reiterations of a North–South divide in premodern England, while, at the same time, I analyze how this reductionist logic betrays far more complex relationships that move beyond a center–periphery model, deeper desires and derisions tied to imagining a greater English collective, an English nation.

What is Nation?

The question of a North–South divide in the Middle Ages is crucial to scholarly debate concerning a medieval English nation. For over twenty years, historians and literary critics have sought and debated forms of medieval nationhood. There has been an almost rhythmic strain to scholarly work in medieval literary studies since Thorlac-Turville Petre's *England the Nation* was published in 1996. Michelle Warren's *History on the Edge* (2000), Patricia Clare Ingham's *Sovereign Fantasies* (2001), Geraldine Heng's *Empire of Magic* (2003), Kathy Lavezzo's *Angels on the Edge of the World* (2006), Robert Barrett's *Against All England* (2008), Ardis Butterfield's *The Familiar Enemy* (2009), Randy P. Schiff's *Revivalist Fantasy* (2011), Lynn Staley's *The Island Garden* (2012), and Susan Nakely's *Living in the Future* (2017) have all contributed wonderfully compelling arguments on the relationships between medieval authors and English identity, as well as medieval concepts of nation. These books have often contested Benedict Anderson's view that the nation-state emerges only in the sixteenth century and that it is largely a modern phenomenon. Anderson's view irks medievalists because it speaks to a larger sentiment, at least, about medieval Europe. This involves, as Andrea Ruddick explains

> the claim that medieval people were unable to think in terms of the nation, because the medieval mind (itself a questionable concept) was dominated by submission to the universal Catholic Church, on the one hand, and by provincial loyalties, on the other. In addition, features of the modern states, such as a defined territory, widespread political participation and a commercialised economy are deemed to have been absent or underdeveloped in medieval kingdoms and other political entities.[24]

But medievalists have been quick to distinguish their own discussions of medieval nations from modern ones. Ruddick continues, "This refusal to draw straight lines from medieval ideas about nationhood to modern nationalisms has been accomplished by a conviction that national identity in the middle ages needs to be investigated on its own terms, rather than trying to shoehorn medieval concepts of nationhood into modernists definitions."[25] As far back as 1984, Susan Reynolds qualified Anderson's then-recent arguments: "The trouble about all this for the medieval historian is not that the idea of the permanent and objectively real nation is foreign to the middle ages, as so many historians of nationalism assume, but that it closely resembles the medieval idea of the kingdom as comprising a people with a similarly permanent and objective reality."[26] R.R. Davies built on Reynolds work in one of his last essays, arguing that medieval England's "self-identification as a separate and unified people, its 'regnal solidarity' as a tightly-textured kingdom, and its effective cultivation of its own historical mythology ... were woven tightly together to create a credible 'nation state'."[27] Even the concept of the *regnum* is compelling, in its political use, for medieval concepts of nation. As Ruddick's recent study shows, this term was deployed in the government discourse of the later thirteenth and fourteenth centuries to refer to England rather than the expanse of all English-held territory.[28]

It is clear then: if Anderson's concept of "imagined communities" of nations seems to exclude the Middle Ages, then it has offered nevertheless astounding utility for critical demonstrations of nationalism in medieval texts and cultures.[29] Heng explains, "[k]ey to the notion of an imagined community ... is self-identification by a national grouping ... against large communities of others in oppositional confrontations over territory, political jurisdiction and dominion, and in warfare."[30] Such large-scale identification is evident in Lavezzo's *Angels on the Edge of the World*, which illustrates how English writers and cartographers across the Middle Ages "actively participated in the construction of England as a global borderland," and, in so doing, employed England's "geographic remoteness" as a "means to articulate national fantasy."[31] Similarly, Staley's *Island Garden* relates the complexity of communitarian fantasy in her exploration of England's "language of place," one deeply pervaded by the concept of "enclosure" and, in particular, England as an island territory set against the world.[32] In this formulation, as Staley demonstrates through numerous literary examples, the island of Britain was made to denote "England." In her recent study of the *Canterbury Tales*, Nakely contends that "as a formation, the nation depends upon internationalism, the expression of relation between comparable but discrete political and cultural groups."[33] And Nakely echoes Butterfield, who, in her own engagement with Chaucer and the nation, finds "[i]f on the French side of nationhood we need to consider the fluidity of territorial acquisition and loss on the continent, on the English side we need to take account of the relations between England and the rest of the peoples of Britain, the Scots, the Irish, and the Welsh."[34] The English nation is best imagined when the realm is set against rival political territories in contestations and negotiations of geography, economy, and religion.

A medieval English nation emerges, however, not only in terms of "England versus the world"; nation is a concept deployed as well to overwrite internal differences. For Davies, England overcomes foreign invasion, civil strife, and a remarkable conflation of different peoples (Angle, Saxon, Jute, Dane, Norman, Fleming, and more) with what he calls "civic ethnicity" – a term similar to Reynolds "regnal solidarity." For Davies, this is the broad acceptance of common rule and allegiance to a single king.[35] Turville-Petre posits that "[c]oncepts of nationhood become dominant when the nation is perceived to be under threat from outside attack or influence," but that they are asserted even more "when the nation is tearing itself apart" and, thus, when "national unity is the good that can be set against the evil of internal strife, of brother against brother."[36] Ingham, for example, looks to England's "celtic fringe," the Welsh marches, in order to argue that "medieval community is imagined not through homogenous stories of a singular 'people,' but through narratives of sovereignty as a negotiation of differences, of ethnicity, region, language, class, and gender."[37] Thus, she finds that concepts of nation were necessary for covering over "psychic and political instabilities" in a national collective.[38] Attention to particular moments of internal conflict provokes examination of local and regional frames broadly in the history of medieval England, frames that help us clarify the crucial interplay of region and nation in English identity. Emily Dolmans argues that a consideration of various regional identities emergent in medieval England allow us to see a "multinucleated country where the plurality of England's regional identities adds complexity – and instability – to English 'national' identity in this period."[39] In his study of medieval and early modern Cheshire, Barrett considers the fallacy of thinking too broadly about nation and the region's role, for example, in periodization: "the historical changes we identify as period markers do not take place inside a single homogeneous space, but within a heterogeneous England divided into an assemblage of 'parcellized sovereignties.'"[40] For Barrett, the bigness of "nation" ultimately "eclipses the equally necessary concept of the local," so that, in recent medievalist scholarship on nation, England "maintains its national coherence because its intranational spaces escape sustained analysis."[41] Daniel Birkholz's important study on English *mappamundi* and *mapparegni* reminds us that, though we date objects like the Gough Map (Bodleian Library, MS. Gough Gen. Top. 16) to a specific moment (in this case, 1360), their compositions "stretch" across decades within which English nationalism is cultivated by the monarchy. The extant Gough Map illustrates local knowledge of South Yorkshire and Lincolnshire and, as Birkholz explains, such national maps were likely posited in regional centers, as symbolic reminders of the interplay of region and nation.[42] As more studies of regional literature in medieval England emerge, we find not that we must choose between the local and the "national"; rather, we must recognize a polyphony of competing political voices and concepts that at times conflict and otherwise intertwine in a multifaceted political theater that nevertheless falls under the larger imagined community of England. Butterfield's incisive arguments on the French language in medieval England map nicely onto concepts of political territory and identity, onto concepts of "Englishness": "Work on dialect, code-switching, and multilingualism is in its infancy in relation to medieval language use, but the more it proceeds the more we are reminded that languages do not function autonomously in multilingual environments, but rather form a shifting set of relationships in which meanings are produced through a constant process of contrast, discrimination, overlap, and rivalry."[43] Butterfield's explanation of the French tongue in England befits the entity of the region as well. Cheshire was a palatinate, a legally autonomous territory, but its role in the machinations of national politics, particularly during the rule of Richard II, illustrates the "constant process of contrast, discrimination, overlap, and rivalry" of which Butterfield speaks.

Rather than focusing on a specific, politically demarcated region, such as the county palatines of Cheshire, Lancaster, or Durham, this study proposes to examine the North as a regional concept in the literature of medieval England. To that end, I will engage both the northern consciousness of southern authors as well as the regionalist character of northern texts. The works examined by this book can only be snapshots of regional consciousness rather than that they carry the weight of illustrating North–South rivalries for the whole of the century in which they are produced. Nevertheless, these texts demonstrate what I think is a consistency in ideas about a medieval North–South divide that should not be reduced to either linguistic awareness over dialect or regionalist comedy. Indeed, one of the motivations for selecting literature like Chaucer's *Reeve's Tale* or the Towneley Plays is that these narratives have been repeatedly trotted out by scholars as evidence of regionalist discourse without much sustained or in-depth analyses that might better expose the intricacies of regional relationships in medieval England. For writers such as the Wiltshire monk William of Malmesbury or the London poet Chaucer, the North is not simply a pariah to the English cause; rather, the North proves a liminal figure in English politics and culture that exists both within and without an English national frame. For the anonymous authors of the Robin Hood ballads or the Towneley Plays, literary regionalism may have been a means to express a sense of limited regional autonomy and solidarity, as well as – and within – desires for national identity. Exploring the complexities of these narratives, I will argue that the outlying North actually operates as a necessary, if not sufficient, condition for the processes of imagining nation; that regionalism is both contained within and constitutive of its apparent opposite, nationalism. My study aims to uncover the emerging dialectic of region and nation within the medieval North–South divide and hopes to reveal how England's nationalist impulse found its greatest expression when it was confronted with the uncanny figure of the North. Throughout the Middle Ages, the North of England proves an object of derision and desire within England's national politics, a figure that threatens to destroy the English nation and, yet, always seems to promise its salvation at the same time.

Critical discourse on medieval English political communities often reduces the multifaceted political and cultural machinations of the period to a binary: whether to use the term "nation" or not. This study does not aim to simplify difficult social, cultural, or political relations through the concept of the North–South divide; rather, it explores the manner by which simplification and complexity are actually deployed at different times and by different parties – by the monarch or by regional lords, by southern writers or by northern factions – in order to contest or to affirm "regnal solidarity" in medieval England. As geographer David Harvey concludes, "Places are, in short, always contingent on the relational processes that create, sustain, and dissolve them."[44] The North of England and the medieval English nation are constructed by discourses that comprise, and pass through, the literary.

Where *is* the North?

In order to discuss the medieval North–South divide, we must begin by locating the North in premodern England, a task more difficult than it may seem. For much of the later Middle Ages, the River Trent served as a legal boundary between North and South for a variety of government purposes, including the division of forest administration, the deployment of royal escheators, the marking of assize circuits, and, as will be discussed in Chapter 3, the segregation of students at the Oxford colleges.[45] But there are other lines, also natural, that enable this division in Britain's early history and, later, as an English realm begins to emerge from the various Celtic, Saxon, and Scandinavian communities of the post–Roman period. Helen Jewell's seminal study of the divide begins, quite literally, with the land, that is, a line of Jurassic limestone running roughly from the mouth of the Tees in the northeast to the Exe in the far southwest. This geological formation marks a point of divergence from which we witness the development, to the northwest, of pastoral farming and nomadic settlements, while, to the southeast, we find arable cultivation and nucleated settlement.[46] And if this geological fact dictates the formation of early British cultures in both North and South, then we find later political boundaries veering very little from the land's own ebbs and flows.

The kingdom of Northumbria declared its eponymous boundary at the Humber Estuary, marking what would become a readily accepted line between North and South for centuries to come. And, of course, the Trent emerges from this estuary. In spite of the establishment of a very different border between the so-called Danelaw and his own kingdom of Wessex, King Alfred acknowledges the Humber as a significant line of demarcation between North and South. In his "Preface" to the vernacular translation of Gregory the Great's *Pastoral Care*, written in the 890s, Alfred explains:

> *Swæ clæne hio wæs oðfeallenu on Angelkynne ðætte swiðe feawa wæron behionan Humbre þe hiora ðenunga cuðen understandan on Englisc, oððe furðum an ærendgewrit of Lædene on Englisc areccean; & ic wene ðætte nauht monige begeondan Humbre næren.*
>
> (So complete was learning's decay among the English people that there were very few this side of the Humber who could understand their services in English, or even translate a letter from Latin into English; and I imagine that there were not many beyond the Humber.)[47]

Alfred speaks famously of the decline of Latin learning and writing among the English people (*Angelkynne*) and proposes a translation program that would put Latin works into the English tongue (*Englisc*) as part of a national literary project. But, in so doing, he points to the Humber Estuary as a geographical rift that marks a division between two peoples, North or South of the line, who nevertheless suffer the same linguistic incompetency. Following the Norman Conquest, the early twelfth-century Latin historiographer William of Malmesbury writes at length, in his histories of England, about the people "north of the Humber" (420–21) (*terram Transhumbranam*),[48] this time framing northern difference *through* language. In an oft-cited passage from Book III of his *Gesta Pontificum Anglorum*, William complains, "*Sane tota lingua Nordanhimbrorum, et maxime in Eboraco, ita inconditum stridet ut nichil nos australes intelligere possimus*" (326–27) (Of course, the whole language of the Northumbrians, particularly in York, is so inharmonious and uncouth that we southerners can make nothing of it).[49] The southern monk finds that northern crudity abounds because of the region's distance from the South and the centralized rulers in Winchester and, later, in London. William's comments are taken up again by the Cheshire monk Ranulph Higden in 1322 in his Latin *Polychronicon*, and, just a few decades later, by the Oxford scholar and Berkeley clergyman John Trevisa in his 1387 Middle English translation of Higden: "*Al þe longage of þe Norþhumbres, and specialliche at ȝork, is so scharp, slitting, and frotynge and vnschape, þat we souperne men may þat longage vnneþe vnderstonde.*" (II, 163) (The whole language of the Northumbrians, particularly in York, is so shrill, biting, and grating, that we southern men can barely understand it).[50] As I will discuss in Chapter 3 of this book, William of Malmesbury's ascription of northern uncouthness tied to language resonates in the mimed northern vernacular of Chaucer's *Reeve's Tale*, arguably the first use of dialect in English literature for comedic purposes. And, as I will explore in Chapter 5, it continues well into the sixteenth century in the counterclaims of biblical shepherds in the Towneley *Second Shepherd's Play* (*Secunda Pastorum*), when the performed southern speech of Mak the sheep-stealer is mocked by the northern pastors who would be his victims: "Now take outt that Sothren tothe, / And sett in a torde!" (311–12).[51] As Katie Wales claims, "Northern English (and its speakers) since the fifteenth century is perceived very much in relation to an Other."[52] The presumption here is that, at some point in the fifteenth century, a standard English emerges out of London, rendering northern speech an odd and marginal tongue. But the alienation of northern English in the fifteenth century is the continuation of – rather than the beginning of – centuries of social and political marginalization of the North of England, its people, and its territory.

The southern monk, William of Malmesbury, singles out York "*et maxime in Eboraco*" (particularly in York) in his linguistic diatribe and with good reason. The city, as both ecclesiastical and political center in the North, occasionally rivaled the South politically and economically, and these rivalries contribute to York's standing, in Ralph Hanna's words, as "the quintessentially different place, the centre of Northern Otherness."[53] The archbishops of Canterbury and York engaged for many years in a contest over Canterbury's assertion of ecclesiastical primacy in England. William the Conqueror chose Archbishop of York Ealdred, not the controversial Stigand of Canterbury, to crown him at Westminster in December 1066, and, as Jewell suggests, his appointment of Thomas of Bayeux to the archbishopric of York in 1070 implied that this position was a royal appointment by contrast to Canterbury, which was, at that time, "complicated by the electoral claims of Christchurch, Canterbury, and the southern bishops."[54] But 1070 also marks the consecration of Lanfranc to the seat at Canterbury, just after Thomas' appointment. Lanfranc immediately demanded profession of obedience from the York see, and the ensuing dispute lingered into the early decades of the twelfth century, the very years in which the young William of Malmesbury began to write his *Gesta Regum Anglorum*. In 1116, Archbishop of York Thurstan was denied consecration and Henry I ultimately ruled in Canterbury's favor, yet Thurstan refused to submit to Canterbury and resigned the archbishopric even as his refusal was upheld by Pope Paschal II.[55] This rivalry continued into the 1120s and included spectacular document forgeries by Canterbury to make the case for primacy.[56] In addition to this ecclesiastical rivalry, the Anglo-Scottish wars that began at the end of the thirteenth century made York a strategic location from which the king could orchestrate government while remaining close to his military interests in Scotland. During the period of these wars, as Sarah Reese Jones illustrates, "York was effectively the capital of England, hosting the main offices of state, the exchequer and chancery, as well as meetings or parliament in 1298, 1315, 1322, 1328, 1330, 1332–3, 1334, 1335, and 1336."[57] Mark Ormrod finds, further, that the transfer of royal government to York, including that of Richard II's government in 1392–93, was motivated by a combination of factors reducible to three: a desire to remain close to the King's armies engaged with the Scots: a desire to create an "alternative and perhaps even permanent power base ... away from the focus of so much political activity in the south-east," and, ironically, a desire to "punish the city of London for its lack of co-operation with the crown."[58] If a North–South divide was forged by the land itself, then England's religious and political bodies perpetuated it through policy and practice across the Middle Ages.

While debates over where the territory of the North actually persist into the present, the more vexing question for medieval England is where it ended. Where is the northern border of the English North? William of Malmesbury's derisive claims about northern speech not only recognize the southernmost border of the region as the Humber, but also its northern boundaries with Scotland. In his complaints on the North of England, its language and its restless peoples, William finds at the heart of the issue the region's "proximity to barbaric people" (99) (*propinquitatem ad sequendos barbarico populo*), that is, the North is too close to Scotland.[59] William writes nearly two centuries prior to the outset of the Anglo-Scottish Wars, but even here we find Scotland's presence arguably informing the character of the North more than any other component. In the 1380s, a decade rife with warfare between England and Scotland, Trevisa – via Higden's Latin – translates William's equation into Middle English, but with a similar attention to strangeness: "I trowe þat þat is bycause þat þey beeþ nyh to straunge men and naciouns" (II, 163). The anxieties evident in such claims speak to the fluid spaces at the Anglo-Scottish border, with the borderline itself either frequently moving or repeatedly dissolving into a larger marcher zone that became a sub-region within the North. Only York was shired by the eleventh century, and this created disparities in royal authority within the North in early medieval England, providing grounds for the later distinctions between the march and the rest of the North as the Anglo-Scottish Wars began.[60] The term "march" is defined in the fifteenth-century *Promptorium Parvulorum* as "myddys betwyx ii cuntreys."[61] In this sense, the march is non-territory, lacking clear national ties, and this jibes with other fourteenth- and fifteenth-century illustrations of the Anglo-Scottish border zone where, as Randy Schiff asserts, "expansionist English and Scottish states ... literally bled into one another."[62] Mark Bruce and Katherine Terrell suggest, further, that "the Anglo-Scottish border emerges as a crucial third term in the articulation of English and Scottish national consciousness and cultural identity."[63] But the liminality of the Anglo-Scottish march proves central to depictions of the larger North, a microcosm in conceptions of the greater region. Consequently, for non-northerners, the entire North of England, rather than, simply, the marcher zone, becomes a border community promising to defend England from the foreign incursion while, at the same time, evoking fear as a landscape already, in the words of the Winchester monk Richard Devizes, "full of filthy, treacherous, subhuman Scots." [64]

There were real legal distinctions to be made between North and South and these likely contribute as well to resentment by those who lived elsewhere. During the wars with Scotland, the march maintained its own brand of law apart from the common law. As Cynthia Neville's work has documented, marcher law was repeatedly adapted to the changing state of hostilities between the two nations. It was, Neville explains, "a living law: sensitive, certainly, to the tenor of diplomatic relations between the warring realms of England and Scotland, but subject to conscientious alteration, refinement and improvement."[65] And this marcher law coincided with the enhancement of the positions of the English wardens of the marches in the North. The unique situation at the border forced the crown to support powerful northern magnates in an attempt to harness these lords' own local influence by giving them expansive control to make war, to solicit peace, and to investigate and prosecute those who ignored any armistice.[66] Henry Summerson explains, of the king's dilemma:

> the nature of the war fought on the Border was such that the king could only protect his subjects there by employing the services of just those magnates whose power he needed to restrain, but whose local predominance he was, for all that, obliged to maintain and all too often increase, because the immediate consequences for the north would have been disastrous had he failed to do so.[67]

Neville points to a specific instance of magnate autonomy in 1385. While both kings, Richard II of England and Robert II of Scotland, prepared for war, border lords Henry Percy and the Scotsman Archibald Douglas met at Esk "[acting] entirely on their own initiative ... to seal an indenture of 'special Trewe and Assurance' for the west march."[68] Chronic warfare with Scotland further afforded border counties and towns special economic subsidies and exemptions to compensate for expenses of defense, repair, and loss, and the great magnates also received subsidies to maintain both their vast forces and the local influence that enabled their power in the first place. Sometimes it wasn't enough. Sheriff of Cumberland Peter Tilliol complains in 1348 that many of Carlisle's citizens "being too much burdened with watches and other efforts for the safety of the city, go away and live in Scotland and elsewhere."[69]

As much as marcher law and the offices of wardens of the march distinguished the broader North from the South, so too did they provoke various legal and religious divisions within the North as well. If, as I aim to show, those writers living far-flung from the North of England tended to paint the region with a broad brush, the reality of political and religious relations within the North were fluid. The increased power and financial success of magnate families in the fourteenth century provoked jealousy from those men left out of, or in diminished positions for, the lucrative trade of border warfare. If, for example, John of Coupland won fame and position for his capture of David II at Neville's Cross, then the offices proffered from his service – constable and sheriff of Roxburgh Castle, later keeper of Berwick, and sheriff of Northumberland – and from his deliberate pursuit of power and wealth in the region due to this emboldened status, led to his murder on Bolton Moor in 1363.[70] To take a more sustained example, the liberty status of Durham in the Middle Ages promoted political and religious conflict with other lords, towns, and the archbishopric of York itself. The late historian R.B. Dobson once mused that "it already seems sufficiently obvious, if somewhat ironical, that in any attempt to actually understand the mentality of the inhabitants of the late medieval north, the best prospects lie neither in peasant village nor aristocratic affinity but rather within the great monastic precinct of Durham."[71] One finds in Durham the hallmarks of the larger North–South divide: distinct regional identity, negotiated political contracts with the crown, and intra-regional tensions with other northerners not afforded the same attention. Durham's independence from English law is evident in the bishop's "palatinate seal," made, as Matthew Holford notes, "to emphasise the bishop's regalian powers" and, indeed, made physically to look like the king's own seal.[72] A distinct and local identity emerges among the citizens of the liberty of Durham, who readily identified as the *Haliwerfolk,* that is, the people of St Cuthbert. And Cuthbert's divine aid to English interests only reinforces support for Durham's independence in the fourteenth century. As Holford explains, Edward I viewed himself as a custodian of Cuthbert's lands, with the belief that "God and Cuthbert would come to the aid of those who desired the welfare of the liberty," while his grandson, Edward III, similarly revived the liberty's waning status in 1335 "because of his affection for Cuthbert."[73] But resentment from the towns and counties outside of Durham's boundaries no doubt festered. The Tyne marked the northern border of the liberty and the town of Newcastle fought frequently with Durham over jurisdiction of the river, engaging a tit-for-tat building campaign at Tyne bridge and elsewhere along the river to assert its own increasing economic and political status.[74] Opportunistic magnates within Durham, including the powerful Nevilles, moved from the local bishop's court to crown courts whenever an advantage was to be gained in either jurisdiction. And Durham was exempt from having to provide troops for border defense or northern campaigns – though this is not to say that the bishops of Durham did not often do so voluntarily – and its privileges relative to taxation unquestionably hindered England's larger military interests in the marches. Tensions further abound between the archbishops of York and the bishops of Durham with, perhaps, the most remarkable illustration occurring in 1284 at the translation of York's patron saint, the recently-canonized William of York, to the place of the high altar in York Cathedral. The ceremony was performed not, as we might expect, by Archbishop of York William Wickwane but by the flamboyant bishop-elect of Durham, Antony Bek, who had been consecrated by Wickwane that very same day. Adding insult to Wickwane's injury, the ceremony was attended by King Edward I and Queen Eleanor, with the king himself helping to carry the chest of St William's bones.[75]

The August 1388 Battle of Otterburn affords a nexus point for thinking through the complexities of the North – its proximity with Scotland and the marches, its uncanny relationship with the rest of the English nation, and tensions among its own regional elites. The battle was fought between James, second Earl of Douglas, and the warden of the English east march, Henry Percy ("Hotspur") in the lower Cheviot Hills, where England and Scotland blur together in a mass of barren slopes and occasional woods. While the Scots ultimately claimed victory, capturing Percy in the process, Douglas was killed. Another casualty of the battle's aftermath was the reputation of the Bishop of Durham, John de Fordham. Indeed, the bishop arrived to the battle too late with his army, which might otherwise have turned the tide for the English. Dobson points to John de Fordham's tenuous relationship with the Percys and his impending departure as bishop just after the battle as a possible reason for his slow march to the contest: "If the most powerful magnates of the north were so eager to see Bishop Fordham ejected from his see of Durham in early 1388, perhaps it should occasion no great surprise that Bishop Fordham was so slow to come to Hotspur's support at Otterburn a few months later?"[76] The Bishop's actions illustrate how intra-regional competition sometimes outweighed national interests. Nevertheless, the Westminster chronicler blames all northern parties in his own account of the battle, including the Scots and the young Percy, whose "heady spirit and excessive boldness" (*impetuosum animum et excessivam audaciam*) led to a disorderly engagement. While the Westminster anonymous speaks of the English at Otterburn as "our troops," he unwittingly complicates this assuredness with acculturation: laboring to explain substantial English casualties from the battle as accidental, he notes: "the darkness played such tricks on the English that when they aimed a careless blow at a Scotsman, owing to the chorus of voices *speaking a single language*, it was an Englishmen that they cut down" (*quia nox nostros Anglicos delusit in tantum quando ipsi percuterent Scotum incaute propter unius lingue consonanciam profecto Anglicum ceciderunt*).[77] Neither tongues nor territories (nor loyalties) are clear in the march.

The battle provoked literary responses in addition to the chronicle accounts offered by Jean Froissart, the Percy propagandist John Hardyng, and the Westminster anonymous. An early fifteenth-century ballad known as "The Battle of Otterburn" stands close to these chronicle accounts by beginning with Douglas' raid into Northumberland to pillage and burn. But it is the illustration of the battle offered by a mid-sixteenth-century poem "The Hunting of the Cheviot," found in Bodleian MS Ashmole 48, that proves instructive in spite of its sometimes-fantastical account. The Ashmole "Cheviot" poem, in contrast to the earlier ballad or chronicle accounts, begins with a provocative deer hunt by Hotspur into what is implied to be Douglas' own territory. The poem, thus, augments the hazy political geography of the Cheviot with a romantic forest hunt. Percy, we are told, "an avowe to god mayd ... / That he wold hunte in the mowntayns / off chyviat ... / In the magger of doughte dogles" (2–4).[78] Douglas and his men quickly close in on Percy's party and a battle commences. The greenwoods of marcher literature, such as those in which begin many Arthurian romances like the *Awntyrs off Arthure at the Terne Wathelyn*, or, similarly, "King and Subject" poems such as *Rauf Coilyear*, work repeatedly to muddy political, economic, and legal borders. The "Cheviot" poem romanticizes the complex relationship of English and

Scottish border magnates and relishes the local scene over any national implications. In the "Cheviot" poem, overmighty subjects Percy and Douglas assault – but also acclaim – one another. Douglas calls Percy "the manfullyste man ... / that ever I conqueryd in filde fighttynge" (141–42), and when the Earl is struck and killed by a stray arrow, Percy takes the dead Douglas' hand and cries:

> wo ys me for the
> To have savyde thy lyffe I wolde have partyde
> with my landes for years iii
> For a better man of hart nare hande
> was nat in all the north contre
>   (160–64)

Percy is, then, run through himself by Hugh of Montgomery, an occurrence that is pure fiction but that nevertheless balances the fight-card in the narrative. Ironically, in a poem that should be rife with concerns for national defense, disparities between Englishness and Scottishness are diluted in the fluid mix of local culture, in economic and martial contact and conflict. As Michelle Warren explains of borderlands, "The figure of paradox inhabits all boundary concepts because the line of the limit seeks to institute an absolute difference at the place of most intimate contact between two spaces."[79] After the battle, both kings are said to bewail the loss of such singular commanders as Douglas and Percy, but the final lines recognize the "Old men that knowen the growne well yenoughe" (269) and lament that "Ther was never a tym on the marche-partes / sen the doglas and the perse met" (275–76). The poem remembers Hotspur Percy as a national hero, and yet his actions in the poem are motivated by personal affront and rash action. The poem, further, betrays desire for such bloody contests, and, thus, for Scotland itself as a necessary interlocutor in these encounters within the march. The relationship between the North of England and Scotland, the blurring of identity in the marches, complicates the place of England's borderlands – and, consequently, the North broadly – within a larger English national frame.[80] Certainly, this centuries-long confrontation both bolstered the North's presence on the English national stage and, at the same time, intensified suspicion of the North in the minds of those Englishmen living elsewhere.

Damning and Salvific

We witness a compelling illustration of the push and pull of northern identity in the devotional cultures that emerge from the region and spread into the rest of England across the Middle Ages. A response to northern revolt against his kingship, William I's brutal military campaign, the aforementioned "Harrying of the North" in 1069–70, devastated the region's agriculture and its infrastructure for decades. But this event also, ironically, marks the return of a northern devotional culture that would prove influential for England's religious identity until the Reformation. Indeed, in the midst of the bloody campaign and while camped at York, William I gave consent for the creation of the Benedictine monastery at Selby. Whitby (1078) and St Mary's Abbey, York (1086) were founded in the proceeding decades. As Janet Burton's work shows, Normans who garnered northern estates from the 1069–70 campaign were responsible, largely, for reigniting monasticism there in the eleventh and twelfth centuries.[81] Hugh Fitz Baldric and William de Percy were among the first Normans to settle north of the Humber and they patronized local houses or aided in the transition of monks to new foundations. As Burton explains, "Political conquest and alien settlement marched hand in hand with monastic foundations, and stone abbeys like stone castles became a powerful symbol of the Norman presence in the north, even when – perhaps especially when – they annexed Anglo-Saxon and Northumbrian nostalgia and sentiment."[82] And while Hugh, ironically, was implicated in the 1088 rebellion against William II, monastic foundations in the North under Henry I increased as aristocratic positions within the Norman regime also grew in number. In the latter years of Henry's reign, the Cistercians arrived from the Continent and founded a series of monasteries including Fountains (1132), Furness (1138), and Kirkstall (1147). The so-called White Monks found the remote wastes of the North perfect ground for their return to a primitive Benedictine monasticism. Many of these northern houses, born out of rebellion against the crown, became intimately tied to royal power for the very fact that they were founded in territories where crown authority was weakest. They worked, then, to advocate for the interests of the king and for their own noble patrons, who afforded them monies and protection.[83] The revitalization of northern monasticism springs a devotional culture that significantly impacted England's broader religious identity in the coming centuries.

In the midst of a northern monastic renaissance in the late eleventh and twelfth centuries, the influence of the cult of Saint Cuthbert reached its zenith in national popularity. Cuthbert had always been the North's most prominent religious character. Immediately following his death in 687, Cuthbert was celebrated in texts like Bede's prose and metrical versions of the *Vita Sancti Cuthberti*, and, in the centuries that followed, his shrine became one of the most popular pilgrimage sites in England. Kings such as Aethelstan, Edmund, and Cnut all visited the body of Cuthbert, whether it was at Chester-le-Strete (from 883 to 995) or at Durham (from 995). Cuthbert was a central figure in the monastic reforms of the late tenth and eleventh centuries, particularly in the south and east of England, appearing in works such as Aelfric of Eynsham's *Catholic Homilies*.[84] According to Symeon of Durham, William I also visited the shrine and called into question the incorruptibility of Cuthbert's body, after which the king was struck by an intense fever and fled in fear:

> Hastening to leave the church, he left behind a great feast which had been lavishly prepared for him, and he at once mounted his horse, ceaselessly urging it to a gallop until he reached the river Tees. By this sign he acknowledged that the great confessor of God Cuthbert rests there, and he was not permitted to harm the people because God prohibited him from doing so.
>
> (*Festinan ergo de ecclesia exire, relictoque quod ingenti copia preparatum fuerat conuiuio, equum confestim ascendit, et quousque ad Tesam ueniret, in cursum urgere non cessauit. Quo indicio magnum Dei confessorem Cuthbertum ibi requiescere fatebatur, et populum Deo prohibent ledere non permittebatur.*)[85]

As Dominic Warner points out, by the twelfth century, the cult of St Cuthbert knew an "unchallenged supremacy" among England's saints. In the first version of his *Libellus*, Reginald of Durham offered some 111 miracle stories of Cuthbert, that covered the period from the removal of Cuthbert's body from Lindisfarne in 875, following Viking attacks, to the twelfth century. The 1170 murder of Archbishop of Canterbury, Thomas Becket, however, created a rival national saint almost overnight. Marner explains, "With the assassination of Thomas Becket and the establishment of his cult in the South, Durham, Cuthbert and the North were once again on the defensive."[86] Indeed, Cuthbert's national prominence – and the lucrative economy it bore for the Durham community – is evidenced in the vigorous defense mounted to preserve his status against St Thomas' bourgeoning cult. The Durham community, and the, bishop Hugh du Puiset, responded by producing new Cuthbert texts that included more recent miracles derived from his shrine, while Reginald of Durham seems to have added as many as eighteen additional miracles to his *Libellus* after 1170. Even with the waning of his shrine as the preeminent pilgrimage site in England, Cuthbert's status remained significant, as his appearance in the *South English Legendary* (late thirteenth century) makes clear. When the English defeated the Scots at Neville's Cross, under the banner of Cuthbert, Ralph Neville placed the captured Scottish flag at the shrine in homage to the saint.[87] Thus, the shrine continued to signify nationally, as the tomb of England's most renowned desert father, and regionally as "the symbolic center of the liberty" of Durham.[88]

Like Cuthbert's following, other northern saint cults gained significant traction in the South in the later Middle Ages. The local reputation of John Thweng (d. 1379), prior of Bridlington, was announced in a biography of his life by his successor Hugh and later incorporated by a chronicle written at Kirkstall. Thweng's cult expanded quickly, and, just a few years later, Thomas Walsingham records in his *Historia Anglicana* that "so many miracles were performed at the tomb that nearly all of England was astonished" (*ad tumbam Johannis, quondam Prioris ibidem, tanta, namque manifestata, fiebant miracula, ut pene totam Angliam ducerent in stuporem*).[89] As early as 1388, King Richard II allowed crenallation of the buildings at Bridlington out of reverence for John, and Henry Bolingbroke visited John's tomb in 1391 following his Baltic Crusade. In light of Thweng's immediate and growing reputation, he was canonized in 1401. But if the cults of Thweng and Cuthbert venerated religious fathers from the North of England, other saints' cults emerged for politically polarizing figures. Thomas, Earl of Lancaster rebelled against his nephew, Edward II, but met defeat at the Battle of Boroughbridge in March 1322. Lancaster was summarily executed at Pontefract. Shortly thereafter, the hill on which he died and the Cluniac priory where his remains were interred began drawing pilgrims and boasting miracles. Lancaster's popularity as a "political saint," in Robert Bartlett's words, was aided, no doubt, by the tumultuous events of the 1320s and, particularly, the overthrow of Edward II and the Despensers, who had exploited the king's rule and who were Lancaster's chief targets.[90] His treason translated to sacrifice for the crown and the realm, Thomas of Lancaster's cult garnered national prestige such that we find a biographical plaque for him some years later at St Paul's in London.[91] Though Lancaster failed to be canonized – Archbishop of York John Thoresby presented the case to the papal curia in 1354 – a chapel was built on the site of the execution and the cult remained prominent until the Reformation. A similarly popular cult arose around Archbishop of York Richard Scrope, who was implicated in the Percy rebellion of 1403 and executed in 1405. Only six months after his death, miracles were attested by pilgrims journeying to his tomb and crowds grew to such an extent that John, Duke of Bedford, ordered the site to be clogged with logs and stones to discourage any further assembly. Riots by pilgrims and devotees led

Henry IV, ultimately, to relent and by 1419 the tomb was yielding some 150 pounds per annum in offerings.[92] If the 1069–70 rebellion against William I strangely informs the subsequent prominence of the North as a place of exemplary monasticism, devotional culture, and national saints' cults, then the region's vast and remote wastes – some created by the 1069–70 "Harrying" – additionally aid the contemplative writing of authors like the Cistercian Ailred of Rivalux and the hermit Richard Rolle of Hampole (c.1295–1349), who *"in solitudine sedere incessanter concupiscent"* (desire to sit in solitude).

Northern religious writers no doubt promoted their own local scene. As already discussed, Reginald of Durham's *Libellus* on Cuthbert's miracles aimed to maintain the saint's national profile, yet the book was inspired by Ailred of Rievaulx, himself a "man of the north, who celebrated northern saints, and transmitted their cults for future generations."[93] Certainly, the spiritual practice and exegetical writings of Richard Rolle afforded him a significant local following but the famed mystic's works made him, arguably, the most popular author in England in the late fourteenth and fifteenth centuries. As Denis Renevey contends, Rolle's name in the fifteenth century "generated a reverence equal to that of Bernard of Clairvaux and Augustine."[94] Rolle's works were distributed both within and beyond the North, as evidenced by over 500 surviving manuscripts,[95] and his appeal went well beyond Yorkshire. For example, we find, in Cambridge, Emmanuel College, MS 35, an important anthology of Rolle's work that, according to Hanna, had no northern connections and seems to have made it to London at the outset of the sixteenth century.[96] And Nicholas Watson shows, further, that Rolle's prominence is evident in the direct responses his teaching elicited – not always positive – from other prominent devotional writers like Walter Hilton, Margery Kempe, and the author of *The Cloud of Unknowing*.[97] While he wrote extensively in Latin, Rolle also produced significant texts in English, and, perhaps for this reason and for his subsequent reputation as an exegetical, didactic, and mystical writer, he is seen as the first definitive *auctor* in English literature, preceding poets like Chaucer. Of course, Rolle was not shy about cultivating his own authoritative status in and through his works. Following his death, likely from plague in 1349, Hampole Priory, where Rolle spent many years and near which he is buried, became such a prominent pilgrimage site that the papacy played upon its popularity to aid repairs there, granting indulgences to visitors who offered donations toward the restorative work.[98]

If Rolle is the most prominent northern devotional writer of the Middle Ages, the region produced other significant authors and texts throughout the period who found popular appeal south of the Humber. In the Towneley *Judgment* play, demons race to Doomsday "up Watlin Strete" (185–86), but we might note that northern devotional texts were moving down Watling Street, through the cathedral city of Lichfield, where they were, in Ralph Hanna's words, "revamped for non-Northern consumption."[99] *The Northern Homily Cycle* is, for example, rendered into a Midland dialect in England's largest devotional collection, the so-called Vernon Manuscript (Bodleian Library, MS Eng. Poet.a.1). Hanna claims that "virtually the full canonical range of extensive Yorkshire writing *c.*1290–1375" passed through the city to be consumed by non-northern readers who craved texts such as the *Pricke of Conscience*, which survives in nearly twice the manuscripts of the *Canterbury Tales*.[100] Other writers took matters into their own hands but found similar fame. Nicholas Love, prior of the Carthusian house Mount Grace, in North Yorkshire, took his *Mirror of the Blessed Life of Jesus Christ* to London and eventually submitted the work to Archbishop of Canterbury Thomas Arundel, who authorized it in the first decade of the fifteenth century. Love's *Mirror* became one of the most popular devotional treatises circulating in England, a popularity that Carol Meale pins on its relationship to "the particular form of affective piety most effectively popularised through the writings of the Franciscans" (20).[101] Love's conservative text was timely for Arundel because its conservative theology could be used to combat the Lollardy that stemmed from the writings and protest of another Yorkshire man, the Oxford Theologian John Wyclif (d. 1384). The national prominence of writers like Rolle and Love, and the substantial circulation of works like *Pricke of Conscience* testify to the North's impact on England's spiritual reading and devotional life. Hanna points out that even the most famous Middle English manuscript of the period, the London-produced Auchinleck Manuscript, "relies heavily on texts of northern origin, for example *Horn Child* and *Maiden Riminild*."[102]

It is important, then, to recognize the entanglements of northern autonomy and English religious identity and practice, the way that northern rebellion and sovereign retribution birth a devotional culture that is both peculiarly northern and, yet, significantly revered throughout England. It is perhaps a further irony that the very virtues of northern devotional culture in Catholic England in the Middle Ages will provoke future rebellion against the crown, when Henry VIII drives the country into the Reformation in the early sixteenth century.

Chapters

We come to find in the North of England what the geographer Edward Casey would term a "perdurance," that is a combination of "sameness or permanence over time with a capacity to modify or evolve."[103] This is not an eternally fixed identity of place that persists unchanged in time, what we might conceive, for example, in the philosopher Martin Heidegger's words, as a "lasting" or "mere duration,"[104] nor is it endless flux; the perduring place known as "The North" sits between permanence and flux "providing sameness and difference, motion and rest, at the same time and not just in succession."[105] The sense of the North within England as an uncanny region – both derided and desired, both damning and salvific – persists throughout this book as I examine the regionalist and nationalist sentiments of numerous literary and historical texts and, particularly, how these works come to represent and weigh the North, whether in terms of their northern consciousness or – in the case of northern texts – their regionalism. In Chapter 2, I explore the most profound and lasting example of northern consciousness in the literature of medieval England, that which we find in the Latin historiography of the twelfth century. Bede's eighth-century *Historia Ecclesiastica Gentis Anglorum*, the foundational text of English history and identity and also a chief source for these historiographers, troubles their work as they seek to redefine Englishness in the wake of the Norman Conquest, even as many of these writers are products themselves of English and Norman parentage. I claim that the period's seminal historian, William of Malmesbury, notices a distinct regional undercurrent, a "northern-ness," in Bede's text that provokes provocative responses from the Wiltshire monk as he constructs his own seminal histories of England and its people. I argue that William's derision of the North in his own works – notably his *Gesta Regum Anglorum* and *Gesta Pontificum Anglorum* – informs his desire to both claim Bede as "Father" and to overwrite the intense regionalism of Bede's text. Their relationship reveals the ways in which the regional voice complicates, even undercuts, the ideological force of the national story that aims to suppress it.

In Chapter 3, I examine the conflict between the "nacions" northern and southern within the medieval English universities at Oxford and Cambridge. Segregated by the vague regional descriptors – *boreales et australes* – which referred generally to a student's province of origin relative to the River Trent, students nevertheless demonstrate the intense animosity pervading the English North–South divide. Following an overview of nations in medieval universities and the various regionalist conflicts that haunted English colleges in the thirteenth and early fourteenth centuries, I turn to a particularly turbulent event, the Stamford Schism that began at Oxford in 1333 and lasted until 1335. The Schism started when northern scholars, under oppression by their southern counterparts, fled the town to establish an alternative university in Lincolnshire. Specifically, I analyze two obscure poems that emerge from the Schism written by northern students swept up in the events of that period. The poems defiantly mock both the students' southern enemies and the Oxford chancellor, Richard Fitzralph. While conflict within the halls and colleges of medieval Oxford and Cambridge is a microcosm of larger, intranational tensions, the Stamford Schism illustrates how a local clash between North and South escalates to threaten not only England's intellectual center but, as a consequence, the kingdom's sense of self. In the end, King Edward III and a bevy of legal and clerical officials from across England labored intently to resolve the Schism and restore order.

Chapter 4 of this study demonstrates Chaucer's deft attention to the North's puzzled character in the *Canterbury Tales*. As Marion Turner notes in her recent and expansive biography of Chaucer, while "Scotland and Wales themselves are only briefly mentioned by Chaucer ... the borders – particularly Northumberland ... were central to Chaucer's imagination."[106] Indeed, in the *Canterbury Tales*, the pilgrim's stories rarely take place in England proper, but for those that do, the North is pervasive. In the *Man of Law's Tale*, Constance washes up on the shore "Fer in Northhumberlond" (II, 508), while in the *Friar's Tale*, the yeoman-devil claims to be from "fer in the north contree" (III, 1413). In the *Summoner's Tale*, we find ourselves in "A mersshy contree called Holdernesse" (III, 1710). But it is the *Reeve's Tale*, with its northern clerks from "fer in the North" (I, 4015), that has garnered the most attention from critics for its regionalist bent and, precisely, its use of northern dialect. I will contend, however, that Chaucer's use of dialect in the tale is merely symptomatic of a larger engagement with the region's long-standing cultural identity as an uncanny presence in England's national story. In the tale, the thieving miller and social-upstart Symkyn is put in his place by two Cambridge students, John and Aleyn. But the simple plot of a "gylour ... bigyled" (I, 4321) is complicated by the two bumbling clerks' violent turn in the tale's unsettling finale. What we find in the *Reeve's Tale* is not Chaucer's playful philological humor, but rather the poet's northern consciousness. And this betrays the poet's hope and anxiety for intranational relations within the English nation amidst the turmoil of the late fourteenth century. Such a view complicates the critical tendency to champion Chaucer's "Europeanness" by examining, instead, Chaucer's engagement in the dialectic of region and nation within his most English of works, the *Canterbury Tales*, with its pilgrims "from every shires ende" (I, 15).

The fifteenth-century ballad *A Gest of Robyn Hode* shows how, as Robert Barrett explains, "[r]egional identity is simultaneously oppositional and compliant."[107] In Chapter 5, I read this ballad as resistance literature that dramatizes the North's struggle to come to terms with its fledgling self-rule amidst government centralization in the late fifteenth century. Until that time, the North had maintained a precarious relationship with the rest of England, defending the northern border against emboldened Scots while – through the power of its magnates – remaining largely autonomous from strict control of the central government and the crown. The North's combination of servitude and independence was embodied by these great northern lords, particularly the Earls of Northumberland, the Percys, whose military resources and provincial following nearly rivaled that of the king himself. But centralization wrested self-rule from the North and its magnates. *A Gest of Robyn Hode* offers an intricate commentary on sovereignty and the law that ultimately takes up the convoluted relationship of these magnates as "Kings in the North" with England's king through the confluence of Robin Hood and King Edward in the poem's later episodes.[108]

In Chapter 6, I revisit another collection of texts famous among critics for their regionalist character: the plays in the Towneley Manuscript (Huntington MS HM 1). For nearly two centuries, critics have debated the dating of the plays, their unity, and their intended audience. I propose to read this compilation of plays through the lens of political and religious struggles in the 1530s that lead ultimately to the northern rebellion of 1536–37, the so-called Pilgrimage of Grace. Malcolm Parkes' more recent dating of the manuscript between 1553 and 1558 stems from Towneley's coupling of legal script with elaborate strapwork evident on many of its pages. But this same strapwork is known to have existed as early as 1500, while the narrow window into which Parkes fits Towneley – the reign of a Catholic queen wedged between Protestant monarchs – is, perhaps, too convenient. Furthermore, the late Barbara Palmer's work on the plays and on drama in general in the West Riding suggests that the manuscript is a "Lancashire–Yorkshire compilation,"[109] part of a network of drama centers that included major sites of activity during the 1536–37 revolt. To what extent, then, was religious drama of this sort provocative of rebellion in the

North of England, or to what extent does the turmoil of Reformation in England, and the subsequent rebellions of 1536–37, resonate in the northern religious dramas of the mid-sixteenth century such as those in Towneley? I suggest that the Towneley Manuscript, as a compilation, can be read as protest literature emerging from the Pilgrimage of Grace. Over the course of this chapter, I examine the Towneley Plays alongside other protest literature born of the Pilgrimage of Grace, including poems and testimonies by alleged and convicted rebels. Shared concerns and parallel themes between these many texts suggest that we might consider the Towneley compilation in light of this rebellion that shook Tudor England to its core. The northern rebels of 1536–37 opposed religious and government reform that threatened the North of England's culture and economy, and, as I show, the eclectic collection of plays within the Towneley Manuscript take up a similar regionalist ethos that extends the rebellion's economic and political concerns, and its Catholic dissent further into the sixteenth century.

In this chapter, I return once more to *Isaiah 14* and its use as a peculiar inflection on English regional politics and culture. As Chapter 6 of this study will show, the verses that William Langland deploys for regional jibes in the late fourteenth century become the content of rebel poetry during the 1536–37 Pilgrimage of Grace, a northern rebellion of Catholics in response to the dissolution of the monasteries and other anti-Catholic legislation, which had a profound effect on the North of England. Although this resistance was brief and utterly destroyed by Henry VIII Catholicism remained prevalent in the North. The King witnessed its ubiquitous presence himself on procession through Lincolnshire and Yorkshire in 1541. As Eamon Duffy explains, in particular, "[t]raditionalist feeling was … strong in connection with the cult of the saints, and evidently many 'abused' images and shrines still stood, in defiance of Henry's Injunctions and proclamation."[110] With Elizabeth's rise to the throne and the reinstitution of Catholicism, after the brief reign of the Catholic Mary I, the North's Catholic damning and salvific character lingered, emerging once more in the Northing Rising of 1569 that aimed to restore Catholicism to the realm.

Throughout these chapters, several threads move consistently. If we are to understand the emergence of a medieval English nation, then we must recognise the North's uncanny presence, its status as an intimate stranger that both troubles and affirms the bourgeoning political community of premodern England. William of Malmesbury's derisive claims about northern speech tied to a backward and barbaric northern culture repeat over and again across centuries, and we find these same sentiments informing, comedically or otherwise, the work of Chaucer, as well as the rebuttal to southern antagonism in the Towneley Plays. The biblical typology of the North as home to the Devil also pervades many of these works as well. The texts of my study suggest that a North–South divide abounds in medieval and early modern England well before the Industrial Revolution that is so often seen as the progenitor of the modern divide. My aim is, again, not to simplify the study of regionalist or nationalist voices in the literature of medieval England with what seems like a stripped binary – North and South – over the complexities of many regional characters, whether in the Welsh march, the Anglo-Scottish march, in the cosmopolitan centers of York and London, in the midland territories of Lincolnshire or Herefordshire, or the southern county of Kent, but, rather, to understand how these texts themselves reduce England's regional divides into a North–South dichotomy through a distinct northern consciousness and through regionalist propaganda that continues to inform a North–South rift today. My study aims to show how these texts are conditioned by England's emergence out of the Norman Conquest, its effort to form a distinct national collective by the fourteenth century, during the Hundred Years War, and its shift into the early modern period through its break with the Catholic Church. In all of these episodes, the North of England plays a pronounced role, informing and undermining any clear sense of Englishness and, in so doing, moving Englishness and a sense of the national collective to the center of political and cultural attention.

CHAPTER 2

William of Malmesbury, Bede, and the Problem of the North

In 731 CE, the Northumbrian monk Bede completed his *Historia Eccelsiastica Gentis Anglorum*, and while he wrote during a heptarchy of Angle, Saxon, and Jutish kingdoms, his work nevertheless presents an inherent unity – not merely religious – of a *gens Anglorum*. As Jeffrey Jerome Cohen claims of Bede's labor, "by imagining the island's past as a story heroically accomplished by this putative collective, by distilling a complicated historical field into the chronicle of a single people, Bede breathes life into the collective identity *English* and ... imagines a past, that, despite ample evidence to the contrary, seems monolithic, pure."[1] It is not surprising, then, that Bede's text found renewed popularity in the wake of the Norman invasion of 1066, which, Emily Dolmans contends, "prompted a drastic reassessment of what it meant to be English."[2] A new Norman ruling elite eagerly infiltrated English culture, retaining English laws and promoting a distinct cultural unity wherein they merged into the body English. As Hugh Thomas explains, "though there was no official ideology of assimilation, there clearly was a theoretical policy, stemming from the king."[3] Assimilation inspires the numerous historiographical works that emerge in the twelfth century. Orderic Vitalis, Henry of Huntingdon, Geffrei Gaimar, and Ailred of Rievaulx all labored to fashion English histories that contribute to what Robert Stein has called "[t]he master narrative ... of the rise of the Norman state in England" wherein "an English state is ... both the precursor and preordained outcome of the story."[4] Such a narrative depends on a seamless, if fictitious, genealogy of the English people surviving through centuries of invasion and cultural incursion and culminating in the then-present Anglo-Norman England. For many of these writers the textual source for this narrative was Bede's *Historia*, and it was to Bede that they appealed as *auctor* in their new histories. As Richard Gameson shows in his study of manuscripts in early Norman England, Bede was second only to Augustine in popularity in the early decades of the twelfth century.[5]

The most prolific and, arguably, the most respected of England's historians during this period was William of Malmesbury. William was born in the last decade of the eleventh century, probably in Wiltshire near the abbey of Malmesbury, founded in 675 by Aldhelm. William is explicit in his works that he was of mixed parentage, a Norman father and English mother, who afforded him some education before he moved formally to the abbey's cloister as a young boy. Rodney Thomson speculates, further, that William may have received extensive education beyond Malmesbury, at Glastonbury or Canterbury.[6] From at least the second decade of the twelfth century, William worked on the companion works *Gesta Regum Anglorum* and *Gesta Pontificum Anglorum*, each of which were complete in their first iterations by the middle of the 1120s. As these two texts illustrate in relation to the work of his contemporaries, William was the historian most invested in Bede's work and his legacy. Thomson, for example, compares William with his younger contemporary John of Salisbury. Both writers were moved and motivated by the literary and civic works of Latin antiquity, yet whereas John saw his writings in relation to Seneca and Cicero, William revered Bede as his model and "hero." As Thomson notes, Bede was for William "a model of detached and selfless devotion to Christian learning, to the recovery and promotion of the legacy of the past."[7] Other modern critics follow suit in singling William out as a "second Bede," "Bede's heir," and Bede's "self-appointed successor," ascriptions that intimate a filial association between the Wiltshire monk and the so-called Father of English History.[8]

With his contemporaries, William faced a significant task in writing new histories of the English people. Kirsten Fenton reminds us that "the definition of national groupings was an issue of some importance after 1066 as a process of cross-fertilization and assimilation between the two cultures [Norman and English] began."[9] As the child of Norman and English parentage, similar to Orderic Vitalis, William was positioned to confront this issue's many complexities. That King Henry I's wife, Matilda of Scotland, initially commissioned the *Gesta Regum Anglorum*, perhaps in 1115 and before her death in 1118, suggests that William understood his charge. Sarah Breckenridge Wright suggests, "This patronage required William to promulgate the Norman myth, a fiction that distinguishes the Normans from the Anglo-Saxons while confirming the two peoples common ancestral bonds and applauding the Normans' time-honoured skill of assimilating cultures."[10] And it is this very willingness to assimilate that William finds virtuous in the Normans. Sigbjorn Sønnesyn parses William's use of the disparate terms *gens*, *natio*, and *populus*, noting that

William follows a Latin ecclesiastical pattern of deploying these words interchangebly as markers of group identity – whether ethnic (even biological) or political.[11] In his *Gesta Regum Anglorum*, William's vision of a *gens Angli* appears, most often, to signifiy the imagined community of an English political collective rather than some biologically linked or territorially derived kinship, and this is perhaps most evident in his repeated emphasis on civic harmony and kingship.[12]

To this extent, then, we are not surprised to find William critical of those communities within England who stir discord and who overtly oppose the rule of ordained kingship. Striving explicitly to acknowledge Britain's diversity of peoples and, at the same time, to proffer a unified sense of Englishness, William pays attention to those people beyond the borders of England ever threatening to undo its wholeness. He finds the Welsh "in constant revolt" (*GR*, I, 726–27) (*Walenses ... semper in rebellionem*), the Irish a "poor ... unskillful ... ragged mob of rustic[s]" (*GR*, I, 738–39) (immo pro inscientia cultorum ieiunum ... agrestem et squalidam multitudinem Hibernensium), and the Scots characterized by a "familiarity with fleas" (*GR*, I, 606–7) (*Scottus familaritatem pulicum*). William, thus, defines England as a subject against the many savage *others* within Britain, but in doing so he also runs up against a distinctly different sort of alterity with the North of England. William finds that "land north of the Humber" (*GR*, I, pp. 420–21) (*terram Transhumbranam*) to be "barbaric and cruel" (*GR*, I, p. 499). His many criticisms against the historical kingdom of Northumbria and, later, the North of England, often sound like those leveled against Wales, Ireland, or Scotland. Northumbrian speech is "uncouth" and its people degenerate. But the Northumbrians are, by contrast, intimate to England, nestled within its borders, and, consequently, more perplexing to William and his consummate view that a nation's strength is bound in the political unity of its peoples. William's representation of Northumbria or the North, then, demonstrates the historian's negotiation of this strange intimacy. As Sønnesyn explains, "[t]he separatist tendencies of the Northumbrians are a recurring theme in the two first [*sic*] books of the *Gesta Regum Anglorum*," and, consequently, "the Northumbrians are treated as a *gens* of their own from this point on, albeit as a sub-*gens* of the *Angli*."[13] Thomas similarly remarks, of early Norman England, "there is ample evidence that contemporaries saw all the northern counties as part of England, and their inhabitants as English, albeit Englishness with a difference."[14] Over the course of both the *Gesta Regum Anglorum* and *Gesta Pontificum Anglorum*, William's negative northern consciousness emerges in a series of rhetorical drubbings of Northumbria that connect a turbulent past with the region's sad state in the early twelfth century and that, further, decry the region's tenacious autonomy. In so doing, William lays the foundation for the discourse of an English North–South divide that persists even in the twenty-first-century.

The Northumbria that William first encounters when he sets out to write his histories is, however, not geographic but textual. He must confront the regionalism of his hero and historical model, Bede. As critics have recently pointed out, Bede's history seems driven by a regional imperative rather than any desire to put forward a uniform English identity. Antonia Gransden concludes that "Bede loved the Anglo-Saxon people in general, but he loved the Northumbrians in particular ... devoted a disproportionate amount of space to Northumbria ... [and] in places his work reads like a panegyric on Northumbria."[15] N.J. Higham, similarly, sees the overall design of the *Historia* "inclined ... to the portrayal of characters of greater interest to the author and his immediate, regional audience."[16] Higham claims, further, that "[Bede] was writing both as a biblical scholar and as a Northumbrian, with a preference for the re-establishment of his own immediate *gens* with the full force of divine approbation."[17] The *Historia*'s explicit regionalism complicates our understanding of Bede's reception by twelfth-century historiographers like William of Malmesbury. Eighth-century Britain with its disparate kingdoms was not twelfth-century England under centralized Norman rule, but it is this very post-Conquest context that informs William's relationship to Bede's history. Like many of his contemporaries, William of Malmesbury aims to fashion a distinct English cultural unity born of historical continuity, what R. R. Davies describes as "a sense of historical identity ... which bolsters and justifies [an English] sense of distinctiveness."[18] Bede's reputation as the patriarchal figure of English history, even in the twelfth century, necessitates his inclusion as a source for the many historiographic texts that emerge following the Conquest. As I will show in this chapter, however, when William appropriates Bede's *Historia* to draft a continuous narrative of the English people, he must confront Bede's inherent regionalism, which is bound up in the nefarious past of Northumbria.

The problem of Bede's regionalism is particularly vexing for William of Malmesbury. Bede is always already present in William's *Gesta Regum Anglorum* from the very first sentence: "The history of the English ... has been told ... by Bede, most learned and least proud of men" (*GR*, I, 14–15) (*Anglorum gestas Beda, vir maxime doctus et minime superbus*). But if it seems William must embrace Bede's work in order to reconstitute a seamless genealogy of the English in the wake of the Norman invasion, then William implicitly refuses. While he invokes Bede in his introduction, William disavows him just a few sentences later, conceding that he will "let most [of Bede] go by" (*pluribus valefatiens*). Compare this strategy to his contemporary, Henry of Huntingdon, who claims to use Bede "where [he] could."[19] We might explain this difference as a decision of narrative economy that avoids repetition of the material Bede already wrote; but William's omission of Bede also suggests his desire to negate Bede's text altogether. As I will illustrate in my examination of William's use of Bede, this early example of homage-omission is followed by other distinct moments where William can be seen to overwrite Bede's text, moments that intimate a deeper antagonism underlying any veneration by William for his literary progenitor. I do not dispute in any way Bede's significant influence on William's writing or his understanding of his role as "historicus." Yet, this veneration actually renders Bede's cultural geography all the more problematic for his literary heir. I will argue that a subtle antagonism toward Bede is evident in William's work and that this tension stems from William's recognition of Bede's regionalism – the uncanny northern-ness of his text. In referring to "northern-ness" in Bede's work, I do not mean simply those moments when he writes of Northumbria – its kings and bishops, its geography and its customs. Instead, "northern-ness" refers to the way that Bede's accounts of a Northumbrian past repeatedly signify to William the region's fractious political and cultural presence in the broader theater of English history. At the heart of Bede's *Historia* – the textual centerpiece for medieval concepts of Englishness and the *gentes Anglorum* – lies the very region that most resists English *natio*. Despite his renown as Bede's historical successor, William can be heard in particular moments either to repress Bede's accounts or to rework them in acts of negation that deaden the northern effect of their regionalism. William's confrontation with Bede's northern-ness informs his marked derision of the North throughout his own history and well past the early books of the *Gesta Regum* for which Bede is a source. William views the North, beginning with the kingdom of Northumbria, as a region infused with violence, rebellion, and degeneration. Such a North, as it is represented in Bede's history and as it lurks at the borders of the English realm in the early twelfth century, threatens to undo the national community William and his contemporaries labor to fashion.

The Father of English History?

William of Malmesbury's reverence for Bede as his historical model cannot be missed. For his *Gesta Pontificum Anglorum*, Bede's *Historia Ecclesiastica Gentis Anglorum* was the most obvious model. As Emily Joan Ward notes, William's contemporaries Goscelin of Saint-Bertin, Symeon of Durham, and Henry of Huntingdon "perceived the *Historia Eccelsiastica* as authoritative, primarily because of its presentation of English saints," but William "uniquely engaged with Bede as a writer of history and drew out Bede's portrayal of himself as the truthful historian (*verax historicus* (see *GR*, I, 49.7))."[20] There was also, in this period, a preoccupation with Bede's own biography. Gameson shows that Cuthbert's *Epistola de obitu Bedae* was often found with twelfth-century copies of the *Historia*, which suggests that readers were interested, at least, in the questions of Bede's own sanctity. But this might also draw further attention to the Benedictine monk's cultural geography. Perhaps this was the case for William, who devotes ten chapters of Book I in the *Gesta Regum Anglorum* to Bede's biography. Yet, in the very same moment that he celebrates Bede's life, William also acknowledges the deplorable state of Bede's *patria*. In Book I of the *Gesta Regum Anglorum*, William describes the place of Bede's birth and education,

> in [England's] most distant region, not far from Scotland ... a district once fragrant with religious houses as a garden is with flowers, and brilliant with many cities of the Romans' building; but now made wretched by the Danes of old or Normans in our own day, it offers nothing that can much attract us. (*GR*, I, pp. 82–83)

> (... *in remotissima... Scottiae propinquum. Plaga, olim et suave halantibus monasterirorum floribus dulcis et urbium a Romanis edificatarum frequentia renidens, nunc vel antiquo Danorum vel recenti Normannorum populatu lugubris, nihil quod animos multum allitiat pretendit.*)

Here, William conflates Bede's eighth-century Northumbria in the golden age of monasticism with the twelfth-century wasteland of the North of England, still wasted from the devastation of the William I's horrific winter campaign of 1069–70, the so-called Harrying of the North. Bede's Northumbria, the place from which emerged one of the most remarkable minds of Roman Christianity, now contributes "nothing that can much attract us." William's first-person plural "us" denotes his readers, but the implication of "attraction" implies that he speaks to the rest of England, excluding those northerners who are already familiar with – and perhaps contribute to – the "wretched" territory. For William, then, the North of England is uncannily the place from which the central narrative of a *gentes Anglorum* emerges, and, at the same time, a territory "ever ripe for rebellion" (*GR*, I, p. 499) (*populus semper rebellioni deditus*) that repeatedly resists inclusion in that very same English political community.

William of Malmesbury could not overlook the differences at the heart of Bede's text that threatens to infiltrate his own. Thomson contends that William is keenly aware of "the relationship between texts," especially the relationship between his sources and his own writing.[21] By examining specific intertextual passages between William's *Gesta Regum Anglorum* and Bede's *Historia Ecclesiastica* – those moments for which Bede is William's only, or chief, informant – we see William confront Bede's regionalism. To say that William is sometimes at odds with Bede is not new. Critics have pointed out William's explicit frustrations with Bede's work. Thomson concedes that "the terms in which William habitually refers to Bede illustrate that William did indeed regard his writing as 'authoritative' . . . yet he would not on that account prefer Bede's dating to that given in the [*Anglo-Saxon*] *Chronicle*, and on other occasions felt free to criticise him."[22] In the *Gesta Pontificum Anglorum*, William, for example, calls into question Bede's narrative on the life of Wilifrid, Archbishop of York, in which "many things are missing" (*GP*, I, pp. 326–27) (*multa ex historia Bedae vacant*). But even these local disagreements do not account for the implicit antagonism pertaining to the North of England that emerges over the course of William's *Gesta Regum Anglorum*, an antagonism that has been ignored to this point in analyses of the textual relationship between William and Bede. Despite William's explicit admiration for, and debt to, Bede, I suggest that we can locate within William's history a tension that stems from the inherent regionalism in Bede's text that threatens William's presentation of the mythos of the English people.

This tension is most obvious in Book I of the *Gesta Regum Anglorum*, the part of William's text that covers the fifth to the early ninth centuries and, thus, runs nearly parallel to Bede's *Historia*. Both historians chronicle the most famous story in England's religious history: that of the sixth-century Northumbrian slave-boys in Rome whose beauty indirectly prompts the future Pope Gregory the Great (540–604) to send the missionary Augustine to England in order to Christianize its people. In Bede's account, Gregory wonders from where these children come, with such "fair complexions, handsome faces, and lovely hair." Reshaping the responses to his questions about the pagan children, Gregory interprets a divine mandate. On their race, called "Angli," Gregory replies, "they have the face of angels." On their kingdom of "deiri," he responds, "De ira! good, snatched from the wrath of Christ and called to his mercy." On the name of their king, Ælla, Gregory sings, "Alleluia! the praise of God the Creator must be sung in those parts."[23] The hand of Providence is confirmed for Gregory in his interpretation of these answers. The boys in front of him denote a whole people ripe for awakening. Bede explains, "I have thought it proper to insert this story into this Church History, based as it is on the tradition which we have received from our ancestors" (*HE* pp. 134–35) (*Haec iuxta opinionem, quam ab antiquis accepimus, historiae nostrae ecclesiasticae inserere oportunum duximus*). For Bede, the story constitutes a seminal tale for the origins of English Christianity, but it also implicitly places at its center his own homeland, Northumbria, the kingdom under which the later King Æthelfrith united the two northern kingdoms, Bernicia and Deira – the home Ælla and the slave-boys. Bede's monastery at Monkwearmouth lay almost at the old border between the two realms.

Bede was not the only writer to render this legend. Notably, the tenth-century monk Ælfric offers a similar account in his Old English *Homilies*.[24] As Kathy Lavezzo points out, later versions of the story in Layamon's *Brut* or the *South English Legendary* remove the puns in the story on the kingdom of Deira and its King Ælla. In this way, these later texts eliminate the slave boys' Northumbrian identity, and we might presume that this stems from a desire, in these texts, for the boys to signify all of England rather than Deira or Northumbria. These edited versions void any ambiguity on the celebration of a single region's Christianization and, instead, testify to the foundation of Catholic Christianity in England proper. Ælfric, however, preserves the boys' Northumbrian origins even though he had no ties to the North himself, unlike Bede or the anonymous monk of Whitby who also recounts the story in his so-called earliest *Life of Gregory* (*ca.*704–714). Lavezzo explains that Ælfric's impetus was, nevertheless, concerned with a broader English community and driven, specifically, by church reform, of which Northumbria had been opposed. Lavezzo claims that Ælfric,

> keeps the boys' Deiran identification precisely because of the problematic positioning of the north in the tenth century. The synechdochic role of Deira as a sign of the whole of England in the slave-boy homily, that is, imaginatively resolves the separation of Northumbria from England during Ælfric's lifetime. By representing both Gregory"s Christian interpretation of the Anglian boys and his inadvertent union of these pagans with the rest

of England, the homily symbolically accomplishes what the tenth-century reformers could not – the conversion and incorporation of a region "regressive" in its resistance to the institutional Anglo-Saxon church.[25]

Ælfric's version is concerned specifically with the Benedictine reform of the late tenth century, but his rendering of the Gregory story intimates how this seminal narrative manifests regional and national concerns at the same time.

In Ælfric's period, the kings of England depended on Northumbrian earls to manage the North. Kings Edmund the Elder and Edgar had ceded territories in Cumbria and Lothian to the Scots in 945 and 975, the effect of which increased the importance of extant northern territories in a unified kingdom of England as it headed into the tumultuous eleventh century. As Frank Musgrove contends, as late as 1086, "[the] regality of the ancient earldom of Northumbria was still intact" and because of the effects of Norman attack on northern lands and peoples following the Norman invasion, and, consequently, the devastation to agriculture, "these lands were excluded from the Domesday survey: since nothing went from them to the royal exchequer."[26] Thurstan's appointment as Archbishop of York in 1114 and his contestation of Canterbury's primacy, as well as the subsequent rise of David of Scotland, only enhanced perceived northern separatism in the early twelfth century when William wrote his histories. From tenth-century monastic reform, to eleventh-century political revolt and suppression, to early twelfth-century battles over ecclesiastical supremacy and governance between Canterbury and York, William of Malmesbury could not have missed the North of England's protests of autonomy within the larger English state and primacy over its church. It is within the context of these protests that southern William reacts to Bede's regionalism.

In his own version of Bede's story, William of Malmesbury subtly uncouples the slave-boys from their Northumbrian origins while, at the same time, he derides both ancient Northumbria and the contemporary North of England. William claims of Ælla's Deira:

> It was in his time that the slave-children from Northumbria, by a custom so familiar and almost ingrained among the Northumbrians that, as has been witnessed even in our own day, they did not hesitate to put their nearest and dearest on the market in hopes of some trifling profit – the children from England, as I was saying, taken to Rome for sale, provided the means for the salvation of their fellow-countrymen. Their surprising beauty and graceful forms had attracted the attention of the citizens, when among others appeared by chance the most blessed Gregory. (*GR*, I, pp. 60–63)

(*Huius tempore uenales ex Nothanimbria pueri–familiari scilicet et pene ingenita illi nationi consuetudine, adeo ut, sicut nostra quoque secula uiderunt, no dubitarent arctissimas necessitudines sub pretextu minimorum commodorum distrahere–venales ergo ex Anglia pueri, Romam deducti, saluti omnium compatriotarum occasionem dedere" nam, cum miraculo uultus et liniamentorum gratia oculos ciuitatis inuitassent, affuit forte cum aliis beatissimus Gregorius.*)

If any regional pride lies in Bede's version, William defuses it immediately. The children are, for him, only in Rome because of the barbaric practices of Northumbrians. This region's terrible slavery is not, like the story, "ancient" but rather "ingrained," an inherited practice that William claims his reader might find "even in our own day." Northumbrians ignore the sanctity of kinship, putting their "nearest and dearest" on the auction block for any "trifling profit" that might be garnered. Bede conveys the sense that these children's beauty is undeniable. Yet, before recounting Gregory's fascination with their splendor, William alters the context in which we hear of it. Following a pause, he quickly reconfigures Northumbrian slaves into the "children of England" who "[provide] the means for the salvation of all their fellow-countrymen" (*GR*, I, pp. 62–63) (*saluti omnium compatriotarum occasionem dedere*). Only after purging them of their northern-ness does William re-tell Gregory's recognition of the boys' "surprising beauty." By making this shift explicit with his interjection, "as I was saying," William signals a return from his northern digression to the main story. He ends the whole account by reminding his reader that the Northumbrian King Ælla, though he was "the prime cause of the Christian mission to the English people," was "not worthy ... to hear Christianity himself" (*GR*, I, pp. 62–63) (*qui, quamquam maxima occasio Christianitatis genti Anglorum fuerit, nichil umquam siue Dei consilio siue quodam infortunio de ea audire meruit*). In his revision of Bede's history, William cleanses this pivotal narrative on English Catholic Christianity of any enduring trace of the North.

Contentiousness also mars William's account of the Northumbrian King Æthelfrith, for which Bede was a significant source. In Bede's history, Æthelfrith is "a very brave king and most eager for glory," who "ravaged the Britons more extensively than any other English ruler" (*HE* pp. 116–17) (*rex fortissimus et gloriae cupidissimus Aedilfrid, qui plus omnibus Anglorum primatibus gentem uastauit Brettonum*). Bede compares Æthelfrith to Saul, and cites *Genesis 49* on Saul's martial prowess as the first Israelite king: "Benjamin shall ravin as a wolf; in the morning he shall devour the prey and at night shall divide the spoil" (*HE* p. 117) (*Beniamin lupus rapax; mane comedet praedam et vespere dividet spolia*). Bede, then, links Æthelfrith's victories to Saul's spoils: "no ruler had subjected more land to the English race or settled it, having either exterminated or conquered the natives" (*nemo in regibus plures eorum terras, exterminatis uel suiugatis indigenis, aut tributarias genti Anglorum aut habitabiles fecit*). Though Bede notes Æthelfrith's rash behavior and his notorious persecution of the first Christian King, Edwin, he is seen to conquer lands and put down inferior peoples like the Britons all in the name of the English. His victory at the Battle of Degsastan (*c*.603) over the Scots (to whom Bede refers as the "Irish living in Britain") is so devastating that, Bede claims, "no Irish king in Britain has dared to make war on the English race to this day" (*HE* pp. 116–17) (Neque ex eo tempore quisquam regum Scottorum in Brittania aduersus gentem Anglorum usque ad hanc diem in proelim uenire audebat). We might interpret Bede's account of Æthelfrith in terms of the author's own nationalist impulse: Bede depicts an English king set against Celtic *others*, the Britons and Irish, and hunting new territory to fuse with his own, for the sake of the English people. But I would also argue that Bede's encomium to Æthelfrith is, explicitly, pro-Northumbrian. He discusses several of Æthelfrith's exploits – the Battle of Chester, his persecution of Edwin, his death at the River Idle – but the northern Battle of Degsastan is the only event of Æethlefirth's reign mentioned in Bede's conclusion to the whole *Historia*. According to critics, the brief annalistic recapitulation that comprises Bede's conclusion is meant to highlight important events narrated throughout the main text. Of the whole recapitulation, Higham points out that "the Northumbrians were the first named of any English *gens* here" and that Bede, in recounting his text, "[places] the Northumbrian dynasty in a lead position within Anglo-Saxon England."[27]

William' of Malmesbury's account of Æthelfrith's reign suggests that he recognises the inherent regionalism in Bede's depiction of the Northumbrian King. For William, Æthelfrith is a strong ruler but not one to stand for all of England. Although Æthelfrith "zealously [defends] his own possessions," he also "unjustly invad[es] those of others, inventing on all sides opportunities to shine" (*GR*, I, pp. 64–65) (*Ethelfridus igitur, ut dicere ceperam, regnum natus primo acriter sua defendere, post etiam improbe aliena inuadere, gloriae occasiones undecumque conflar*). What is more, William remarks, incisively, "[Æthelfrith"s] praise indeed and that of his successors earned the attention of Bede, and Bede was particularly concerned with the Northumbrians, his own neighbors [*familiarius*], who were familiar to him because they were so near" (*GR*, I, pp. 64–65) (*et illius quidem in confines sibi Northanimbros eo familiarus quo propinquius prospitiebat intentio*). Here, William seems unwilling to firmly place Bede among Northumbrians like Æthelfrith. Bede is concerned with Æthelfrith and the Northumbrians because he is "near" them and "neighbor" to them. We understand William's equation in strictly geographic – rather than historical – terms, and the effect of Bede's "nearness" both muddies Bede's cultural geography, which Bede claims even for himself, and heads off any implied regionalist impetus in Bede's account of Æthelfrith. William's timely and explicit claim that Bede spends so much energy discussing Northumbrians simply because he lived near them reminds us that the potent King Æthelfrith is *merely* a Northumbrian and, consequently, that Bede is not Northumbrian at all, at least not in a way that links him to the degenerative region William repeatedly illustrates throughout his histories.

William's neutralization of Bede's northern-ness is nowhere more explicit than in his version of the early seventh-century Battle of Chester, a story again involving Æthelfrith. Bede illustrates the battle, in which the pagan Northumbrian Æthelfrith defeats a body of men from the Breton kingdoms of Gwynned and Powys.[28] Prior to combat with the Britons – "that nation of heretics" (*gentis perfidae*), as Bede refers to them – Æthelfrith notices a contingent of monks who arrive to pray for the Britons' army. The monks had come from the nearby Welsh monastery at Bangor Is-Coed (*Bancornaburg*). According to Bede's account in the *Historia*, when Æthelfrith hears of the monks' purpose, he declares, "If they are praying to their God against us, then, even if they do not bear arms, they are fighting against us, assailing us as they do with prayers for our defeat" (*EH* pp. 140–41) (*Ergo si adversum nos ad Deum suum clamant, profecto et ipsi, quamuis arma non ferant, contra nos pugnant, qui adversis nos inprecationibus persequuntur*). Æthelfrith's fears were not without warrant. As Katherine Allen Smith explains, "The earliest leaders of the Church had inherited from pagan antiquity a conviction that prayers and related rituals helped ensure success in battle," thus, "[l]iturgical prayer, as performed by well-trained experts was a potent weapon."[29] Æthelfrith orders his men to massacre the non-combatants, "about twelve hundred" (*mille ducentos*), prior to the battle's start. The monks' own guardsmen, led by a certain Brocmail, flee in the face of the assault leaving the unarmed monks to the charging Northumbrians. Though Bede notes that the Bangor collective was helpless in the assault, he offers little sympathy for their deaths. Their slaughter is, for Bede, the fulfillment of Augustine of Canterbury's prophecy, which Bede explains as a prequel to this account.

Amid strife between the Celtic and Roman churches, Augustine and Celtic representatives, largely from Bangor, agreed to a conference. Bede illustrates the infamous encounter between Augustine and the Britons. As they approach Augustine, the monks aim to judge if he is "meek and lowly of heart" (*mitis et humilis corde*) by whether or not he rises to greet them. Augustine, of course, does not rise, and the enraged brothers consequently "str[i]ve to contradict everything he [says]" (*quae dicebat contradicere laborant*). Augustine implores them to accept and follow the rites of the Holy Roman Church, in favor of their own Celtic practices, and evangelize to the English, but the Bangor contingent refuses.[30] He offers a caveat: "if they refused to accept peace from their brethren, they would have to accept war from their enemies; and if they would not preach the way of life to the English nation, they would one day suffer vengeance at their hands" (*EH* pp. 140–41) (*si pacem cum fratribus accipere nollent, bellum ab hostibus forent accepturi, et si nationi Anglorum nolvisset viam vitae praedicare, per horum manus ultionem essent mortis passuri*). Augustine's prophecy is, thus, realized in their slaughter at Chester.

The fulfillment of Augustine's divination leads to various interpretations of what exactly Bede does here. Gransden supposes that "Bede seems in this instance to prefer heathenism to non-Roman Christianity."[31] Indeed, a great irony lies in Æthelfrith's paganism, that he is, as Bede states "ignorant of the divine religion" (*HE* pp. 116–17) (*quod divinae erat religionis ignarus*), and we might wonder whether the king is concerned at all with the monks' religious practices or their battlefield prayers to a god whom he does not recognize. Placed within the context of Bede's preceding account of the Bangor monks and their denigration of Augustine, the pagan Æthelfrith and his Northumbrians become unwitting instruments of God (and Bede) wielded against the sinful Britons. The Northumbrians are themselves victims of these Celtic monks' indifference to their own ignorance of the Gospel – again the Britons are unwilling to step across borders to minister to them. Bede's account clearly evinces a chronic enmity between the Roman and Celtic (Irish) churches, which culminates in his account of the 664 Synod at Whitby, in Book III of the *Historia*.[32] To this extent, then, we might hear in Bede's account of the Battle of Chester a jingoistic tale of English triumphalism over the Celtic *other*. These pagans' conversion to Roman Christianity is inevitable – again, conversion follows Æthelfrith's reign through Edwin. Bede leaves us with a sense that, though this particular band of Englishmen is pagan at the moment, they will eventually choose Christianity (with no help from the Britons) – and the *right* Christianity at that. Like the Battle of Degsastan, the Britons' death might be read to explicitly serve the cause of Englishness.

Critics have lambasted Bede, nevertheless, for seeming to revel in the deaths of the Bangor monks. Alfred Smyth, for example, labels Bede's justification of the slaughter as "racist," and we might interpret Bede's Chester rendering as a moment where Christian brotherhood takes a backseat to the *gentes Anglorum*.[33] The Chester narrative, however, is also imbued with a regionalist imperative. Gransden argues of the butchery at Chester that Bede's revelry at the Britons' demise is "no doubt ... influenced by his loyalty to the Northumbrians and his belief that a strong Northumbria was ultimately to the church's advantage."[34] Bede concludes of the monks, "those heretics would also suffer the vengeance of temporal death because they had despised the offer of everlasting salvation" (*EH* 142–43) (*ut etiam temporalis interitus ultione / sentirent perfidi, quod oblata sibi perpetuae salutis consilia spreuerant*), but he leaves unsaid what he clearly believes: that the Britons would meet "everlasting" suffering due expressly to their sins. More than simple transgressors, the Britons are bad neighbors. They judge Augustine's Christian earnestness by arbitrary physical mannerisms – his failure to rise for the Bangor brethren is, by most accounts, not intended as a slight – and, worse, they refuse to minister to the Northumbrians near their monastery.[35] The monks' passive refusal constitutes hostility, an active deliverance of those same Northumbrians to the frightening eternity the monks are themselves made to confront. Implicitly, therefore, Bede's account intimates Northumbrian vengeance and asserts Northumbrian strength, even superiority, with and without the divine.

Geoffrey of Monmouth, writing of Chester, only selectively follows Bede's account in his pro-Welsh *Historia Regum Brittaniae*. Geoffrey adds that the Bangor abbot Dinoot "proved to [Augustine] on a whole series of grounds that they owed him no allegiance at all," and that the English to whom Augustine compelled them to preach the gospel had "persisted in depriving them of their own fatherland" (*qui augustino petenti ab episcopis britonum subiectionem. & suadenti ut secum genti anglorum communem euangelizandi laborem susciperent. diversis monstrauit argumentationibus ipsos ei nullam ei mullam subiectionem debere. nec suam predicationem inimicis suis impendere ... &gens saxonum patriam propriam eisdem auferre perstarent*).[36] Portraying the English as aggressors against victimized Britons, Geoffrey claims that the monks' refusal to evangelise compels Ethelbert, King of Kent, to stir up the other "petty kings," including Æthelfrith, against the Britons. Only after defeating the Britons' army does Æthelfrith discover the Bangor monks within the city. Hearing that they came there to pray for his army's destruction "he immediately let his soldiery loose against them" and, thus, "twelve hundred monks won the crown of martyrdom and assured themselves of a seat in heaven" (*At ethelfridus civitate capta. cum intellexisset causam adventus predictorum monachorum. iussit in eos primum arma verti. & sic mille ducenti eorum in ipsa die martirio decorati. regni celstis adepti sunt sedem*).[37] As we might expect, Geoffrey's reworking of Bede disparages the English and particularly the Northumbrians. They are mere mercenaries performing the dirty work of the Kentish king. Geoffrey portrays the Welsh nation against that of Bede's English state.

Surprisingly, in his disparagement of Æthelfrith's army, Geoffrey's account of the Battle of Chester echoes William of Malmesbury's own rendering. William and Geoffrey shared the same patron in Robert Earl of Gloucester, the illegitimate son of Henry I and half-brother to Matilda. But Geoffrey's and William's aims are quite different in their histories and this is evident in their use of Bede as a source. Geoffrey of Monmouth does not rely solely on Bede's account, but, rather, uses other sources in his description of the battle. We might also note here that Henry of Huntingdon, in his *Historia Anglorum*, simply repeats Bede's account of Chester in full, with little visible change, and Geffrei Gaimar follows the account in the *Anglo-Saxon Chronicle* for his *L'Estoire des Engleis*.[38] If Geoffrey of Monmouth's account diminishes Bede's nationalism in either the English victory or in the divine sanction that Bede claims this victory holds, then William labors to counteract Bede's regionalism.[39] Though William lacks affection for the Britons himself, he radically curtails Bede's account, explaining the battle in one nearly bloodless sentence: "The king ambushed [the Britons] and put them to flight, venting his frustration first of all on the monks, who had gathered in crowds to pray for the success of the army" (*GR*, I, 64–65) (*quos ille insidiis exceptos fudit fugavitque, prius in monachos debachatus qui pro salute exercitus suplicaturi frequentes convenerant*). William's radical truncation of Bede's detailed account includes emptying the Northumbrian cause of any martial or religious justification. In Bede's telling, Æthelfrith meets Welsh soldiers (*militis*), yet, in William's version, the Northumbrian King "ambushes" (*insidiis*) the "townsmen ... rushing out to battle in disorder" (*GR*, I, 64–65) (*oppidani ... effuse in bellum runt*) for the purpose of rebuffing an inevitable siege of their city. William admits empathy for these "townsmen" who die at the hands of the cruel Northumbrians because they would "endure anything rather than a siege" (*GR*, I, 64–65) (*qui omnia perpeti*

The Father of English History? 47

quam obsidionem mallent). He lends further compassion to the Bangor monks themselves. No mention is made of their meeting with Augustine, which mutes Bede's implication that the monks' slaughter is divine punishment or even Northumbrian vengeance. William only suggests that the pagan King massacres the monks for their Christian prayers against his army.

William supplements his lone sentence on the battle with a second observation on the doomed brethren of Bangor: "Their numbers would seem incredible in our own day, as is evident from the ruined walls of churches in the monastery nearby, the complex arcading, and all that great pile of ruins, such as you would hardly find elsewhere" (*GR*, I, 64–65) (*Quorum incredibilem nostra aetate numerum fuisse inditio sunt in vicino cenobio tot semiruti parietes aecclesiarum, to anfractus porticum, tanta turba ruderum quantum vix alibi cernas...*). The passage correlates with Bede's earlier commentary on the size of Bangor Is-Coed. Bede claims of the monastery, "when it was divided into seven parts ... no division had less than 300 men" (*HE* 141) (*ut cum in septem portioned esset cum praepositis sibi rectoribus monasterium diuisium, nulla harum portio minus quam trecentos homines haberet*). For Bede, the monastery's vastness merely complements the number of monks who die at Chester. By contrast, for William, the description of the monastery allows him to look past the corpses in the foreground of Bede's account. Rather than muse on the number of slaughtered monks, William instead gazes on the symbolic ruins of the monastery they once inhabited. William's narrative is likely shaped by his own visit to the site of Bangor Is-Coed, but his brief illustration of the abbey's contemporary rubble does greater ideological work.

Bede's account of the battle proves one of the darkest moments in his *Historia*. It contributes, further, to a generally macabre undercurrent in his text as a whole. Gransden tellingly finds in Bede's history a "touch of morbidity ... Bede likes to write of prophecies of death, visions of the afterworld, death-bed scenes, coffins and corpses."[40] This death-effect accents some of the notable northern moments in Bede's history, moments that William of Malmesbury finds, arguably, disturbing. This northernness is, thus, intertwined with a traumatic focus on death at work in Bede's text. Geoffrey of Monmouth explains that the monks achieve "a seat in Heaven," but while Bede frames their deaths as retribution for religious obstinacy and a failure of their monastic office to minister to Northumbrians, he is content to stay silent on their souls following the slaughter. Bede's regionalism, perpetrated through violence, and Bede's silence regarding the monks' final damnation leaves Christian bodies symbolically un-interred on the fields of Chester and in his own pages. William moves quickly past the battle and the monks' subsequent slaughter, fleeing to the now-ruinous monastery at Bangor Is-Coed. In his revulsion, William overwrites Bede's Chester narrative in just two sentences. The absence of the monks' vehemence towards Augustine redeems the fatal sin through which Bede readily condemns them, and William points to the monks' remarkable numbers, not in slaughter but as testified to by the remarkable size of their abbey's ruins. Through his account, William inters the monks symbolically within the very stone walls they once inhabited, and this textual burial closes the bloody space of a spectral North.

Ruinous Preoccupations: The North and Beyond

In his account of the Battle of Chester, William of Malmesbury deploys the ruin of Bangor Is-Coed to dilute the regionalism of Bede's *Historia*, wherein the Northumbrian army of Æthelfrith acts as divine instrument, punishing the Britons for their rejection of the Roman church and for their refusal to aid the pagan English. And this attraction to ruins in Book I of the *Gesta Regum Anglorum* gestures toward William's larger understanding that the dilapidated structures of England's history signify the failures of its cultural and political community. As I will discuss below, William's attention to ruins explains his confrontation with the uncanny North inherent in Bede's *Historia* and in England's more recent past. If we return, briefly, to William's description of Bede's birthplace, then we find he intentionally connects the North (that "most distant region" in England (*in remotissima*)) with ruin. In this way, the region "once fragrant with religious houses ... and brilliant with many cities of the Romans' building" becomes the wrecked landscape of the early twelfth century "made wretched by the Danes of old or Normans in our own day" (*GR*, I, pp. 82–3) (*Plaga, olim et suave halantibus monasterirorum floribus dulcis et urbium a Romanis edificatarum frequentia renidens, nunc vel antiquo Danorum vel recenti Normannorum populatu lugubris, nihil quod animos multum alliciat pretendit*). This passage entangles the North's glorious past with the wasteland that William perhaps saw first-hand in his own travels. Consequently, it reminds us of the North's integral role in shaping English identity while, at the same time, it recalls the region's chronic enmity for any authority but its own. As his history moves beyond the purview of Bede's text, Williams' illustration of this convoluted dynamic of regionalism and nationalism – of the North's sanctity and its damnation – grows more complex. In William's second recounting of the Harried North in the *Gesta Regum Anglorum* – as well as the repetition of this passage in his *Gesta Pontificum Anglorum* – William, again, explicitly juxtaposes Northumbria's Roman past with the North's present wastes. These subsequent accounts in the later books of the *Gesta Regum Anglorum*, specifically, inform his meditation on Rome itself as a once-great civilization now in decline. Rome is profoundly important as a cultural and political concept for the learned monk, and, yet, William acknowledges its long regression when he ponders Hildebert of Lavardin's elegy "*Par tibi Roma nihil.*" As I argue here, William's juxtaposition of this ruinous poem within his account in Book IV of the promising but ultimately failed kingship of William II helps us to understand the historian's derision of Northumbria and the North as microcosm of England's larger decline.

The event that seems to drive much of William's anti-northern sentiment is the "Harrying of the North" by King William I in the winter of 1069–70. Higham calls the Conqueror's brutal crusade "perhaps the most destructive single campaign in England's history."[41] Through his assault on the region, William I responded to apparent plots for his overthrow between the people of the North, the English claimant to the throne, Edgar Ætheling, and the Danish King Swein II. In his *Historia Ecclesiastica Anglorum*, Orderic Vitalis records William I's remarkable deathbed confession, in which the penitent King himself recalls the devastation he brought upon the people of northern England:

> In mad fury I descended on the English of the north like a raging lion, and ordered that their homes and crops with all their equipment and furnishings should be burnt at once and their great flocks and herds of sheep and cattle slaughtered everywhere. So I chastised a great multitude of men and women with the lash of starvation and, alas! was the cruel murderer of many thousands, both young and old.
>
> (*Vnde immoderato furore commotus in boreales Anglos ut uesanus leo properaui domos eorum iussi segetesque et omnem apparatum atque supellectilem confestim incendi, et copiosos armentorum pecudumque greges passim mactari. Multitudinem itaque utriusque sexus tam diræ famis mucrone multaui. et sic multa milia pulcherrimæ gentis senum iuuenumque proh dolor funestus trucidaui.*)[42]

The sheer horror of the campaign – the Conqueror admittedly moved to animal-rage, the murder of men, women, and children, the burning of all arable land in northeast England, the slaughter of all livestock – suggests that it was an effort not merely to subdue a sense of northern autonomy but to destroy it completely.

William of Malmesbury does not appear sympathetic to the North of England in his account of the "Harrying," but the wasteland left in the Conqueror's wake continues to inform William's representation of the North and northern-ness throughout his histories. William details the incursion of the Scots into this territory as impetus for the Conqueror's campaign as well as King William I's concern to leave no resources in the North that "a raiding pirate could find and carry off if he had to make a rapid return home, or use for food if he thought he could stay longer" (*GR*, I, pp. 464–65) (*Ea precepti ratio, ut nichil circa oram maritimam predo piraticus inveniret, secum asportaturus si citius remeandum, vel fami consulturus si diutius manendum putaret*). Of the destruction wrought in the King's assault, William witnesses how

> a province once fertile and a nurse of tyrants was hamstrung by fire, rapine, and bloodshed; the ground for sixty miles and more left entirely uncultivated, the soil quite bare even down to this day. As for the cities once so famous, the towers whose tops threatened the sky, the fields rich in pasture and watered by rivers, if any one sees them now, he sighs if he is a stranger, and if he is a native surviving from the past, he does not recognise them. (*GR*, I, pp. 464–65)

> (... *provintiae quondam fertilis et tirannorum nutriculae incendio, preda, sanguine nervi succisi; humus per sexaginta et eo ampilius miliaria omnifariam inculta; nudum omnium solum usque ad hoc etiam tempus. Urbes olim preclaras, turres proceritate sua in caelum minantes, agros laetos pascuis irriguos fluuiis, si quis modo videt peregrinus, ingemit; si quis superest vetus incola, non agnoscit*).

In lines that are repeated, in effect, in Book III of the *Gesta Pontificum Anglorum*, William again places Northumbria's glorious past – its "towers whose tops threatened the sky" – alongside its hellish present. The sight of the North's destruction compels the visitor to sigh, but worse, the native will not even know his own homeland. And this is perhaps the point. The Conqueror desired that no invading army might sustain itself through the region's resources, so he burned the province to the ground and, then, the ground itself. Besides the immediate plot for his overthrow, William I can be said to react to the North's whole history of violence and rebellion, a history that William of Malmesbury is keen to recall. William's commentary on the unrecognizable North seems almost hopeful that northerners will divorce themselves from past insurrection and conform to the sovereign rule of a Norman king. The "Harrying" set the

North back nearly a century and left the region quite literally devoid of life.⁴³ For William the devastation brought on by the Conqueror seems only to enhance the spectral nature of the North. Twelfth-century historiographers, like William, come to view the region through the guise of this wasteland and to understand the destruction as the product of a fatalistic vision of regional autonomy in the face of centralized rule. As William plainly states of the Northumbrians: "Freedom or death was their tradition" (*GR*, I, pp. 364–65) (*a maioribus didicisse aut libertatem aut mortem*). At the same time, however, the North's history of rebellion only provokes questions, for William, about a whether a national collective would ever be possible in England.⁴⁴

William's imagery of the Harried North clarifies the region's plight in the wake of the Conqueror's campaign, but comparisons to other historiographer's accounts of the devastated region suggest that William's approach is more repressive than he lets on. Orderic Vitalis laments of the Harried North, "so terrible a famine fell upon the humble and defenseless populace that more than 100,000 Christian folk of both sexes, young and old alike, perished with hunger" (*Vnde sequenti tempore tam gravis in Anglia late seuit penuria, et inermem ac simplicem populum tanta famis inuoluit miseria, ut christianæ gentis utriusque sexus et omnis ætatis homines perirent plus quam centum milia*).⁴⁵ Symeon of Durham, offers his own gripping description in the *Historia Regum*:

> so great a famine prevailed that men compelled to hunger, devoured human flesh, that of horses, dogs, and cats, and whatever custom abhors; others sold themselves to perpetual slavery ... others, while about to go into exile from the country, fell down in the middle of their journey and gave up the ghost. It was horrific to behold human corpses decaying in the houses, the streets, and the roads, swarming with worms.
>
> (... *adeo fames prævaluit, ut homines humanas, quines, caninas, et catinas carnes ... alii vero in servitutem perpetuam sese venderent ... alii extra patriam profecturi in exilium, medio itinere deficientes animas emiserunt. Erat horror ad intuendum per domos, plateas, et itinera cadavera humana dissolvi, et tabescentia putredine cum fœtore horrendo scaturire vermibus*).⁴⁶

Both Orderic's and Symeon's accounts differ notably from William's in their attention to the human costs of the Harrying of the North.⁴⁷ Orderic notes the sheer number of lives "young and old" starved to death, and Symeon's physiological testimony – bodily hunger, exhaustion, and human decay – distinctly contrasts William's interest in the crumbling "cities of the Romans' building." Orderic's and Symeon's accounts portray the North as one ghostly topography, a scene of uncannily unburied bodies physically starved, burned, bashed, stabbed, and trampled to death, yet they are symbolically un-interred and left to haunt the physical and historical landscapes where they perished. Much like the slaughtered monks at Chester, William seems figuratively to bury them in the landscapes and structure he chooses to foreground over their bodies. We might imagine that William of Malmesbury, so quick to deride the North of England in his works, might revel in the rebellious region's punishment much as Bede is seen to revel in the destruction of the Bangor monks. Yet, if Bede "likes to write of prophecies of death, visions of the afterworld, death-bed scenes, coffins and corpses"[48] and if Orderic or Symeon are willing to show the human toll of war, then William, by contrast, ignores mortality by displacing death into the ruinous monuments and crumbling edifices dotting the English landscape.

These monuments that William of Malmesbury seeks – the wreckage of the "Romans' building" in Northumbria, the North's once-great cities, the ruins of Bangor Is-Coed – allow him to repress the horror of death linked with England's internal strife and, specifically, the northern-ness that persists in its history. In William's texts, Northumbrians are brutal, barbarous of speech, and unwilling to be ruled, the results of which amount to a bloody and fractious past that cannot be easily written into the seamless history of the English people he labors to construct. John Gillingham famously concludes that William of Malmesbury's concept of history was grounded in a general movement from barbarism to civilization.[49] It is the countermovement of the North in William's historical model that seems to infuriate the monk. Making William sound much like the orientalist, Gillingham asserts three elements that the historian thought necessary for a civilized state: widespread education, humane government, and the development of markets and towns.[50] As his repetitious derision of the North shows, William finds the North lacking in precisely these categories. In his description of Bede's Northumbria, the contemporary North is "wretched," while in his retelling of Gregory and the slave-boys William points to the petty nature of northerners still willing – "even in our own day" – to sell off their own for "trifling" profit. Further, in illustrating the devastation of the "Harrying of the North," William is clear that its former cities are destroyed, the agricultural infrastructure wrecked. The North of England in the early twelfth century is neither educated, civically humane, or economically developed. Indeed, its language is "uncouth" – another way of playing on the very meaning of "barbarous" – its people rebellious, and its markets and towns razed to the ground. William Kynan-Wilson makes clear, "[o]ne of the recurring motifs of the *Gesta Pontificum* at large, and of the third book in particular, is the desolate and isolated state of northern England."[51] And while William has other topics of concern in both the *Gesta Regum Anglorum* and the *Gesta Pontificum Anglorum*, his coupling of Roman ruins with the North suggest that he is reminded of the rebellious region even when he speaks otherwise.

In the prologue to Book III of the *Gesta Pontificum Anglorum*, which focuses on Northumbria and where he repeats his account of the "Harrying," William inserts within this narrative a note on the Roman ruins at Carlisle:

> In some ruined buildings, though, whose walls were not completely destroyed, you may see remarkable Roman work: for example, at Carlisle a *triclinium* [dining room] vaulted in stone that no violence of the elements, or even the intentional setting alight of timbers piled up against it, has succeeded in destroying. (*GP*, I, p. 324–25)
>
> (*In aliquibus tamen perietum ruinis, qui semiruti remansere, uideas mira Romanorum artifitia: u test in Lugubalia ciuitate triclinium lapideis fornicibus concameratum, quod nulla umquam tempestatum contumelia, quin etiam nec appositis ex industrial ignis et succensis, ualuit labefactari.*)

The passage subtly juxtaposes the splendor of classical Roman architecture with its destruction, even its being set on fire, in a larger narrative of the North's destruction at the hands of William I. The descriptive detail and other evidence in the *Gesta Pontificum Anglorum* suggest that William visited the North as part of what Thomson calls a "grand tour of England" that included Carlisle, Durham, and York, as well as Bangor.[52] Similar to his introduction of Bede in Book I of the *Gesta Regum Anglorum* and in his depiction of the "Harrying" in Book III of that work, William cannot help but entangle the North's former glory, signified in its Roman ruins, with its present destruction due to chronic rebellion. As he continues describing the *triclinuium*, William's comparative structure grows more pronounced:

> The district is called Cumberland, and its inhabitants Cumbrians. On the front of the structure one can read the inscription "To the victory of Marius." I am doubtful what this means; it may be that some of the *Cimbri* settled of old in these parts after being driven from Italy by Marius. Of course, the whole language of the Northumbrians, particularly in York, is so inharmonious and uncouth that we southerners can make nothing of it. This is the result of the barbarians beings so near, and the kings, once English, now Norman, so far away; for they, as is well known, spend more time in the south than in the north. (*GP*, I, pp. 324–27)[53]

(*Cumberland vocatur regio, et Cumbri vocantur homines, scripturaque legitur in fronte triclinii "Marii victorie." Quod quid sit hesito, nisi forte pars Cimbrorum olim his locis insederit cum fuissent a Mario Italia pulsi. Sane tota lingua Nordanhimbrorum, et maxime in Eboraco, ita inconditum stride tut nichil nos australes intelligere possimus. Quod propter viciniam barbararum gentium et propter remotionem regum quondam Anglorum modo Normannorum contigit, qui magis ad austrum quam aquilonem diversati noscuntur.*)

Much as the previous passage, William finds an intriguing bit of evidence inscribed on the Roman wall, but the elaborate history implied by these ruins becomes bound up with the inhospitable landscapes of the North. Indeed, the account of the Carlisle ruins is surrounded in his narrative by the North's physical destruction and its cultural barbarism. William switches quickly from musing on the Carlisle *triclinium* to levelling critique at northerners, not simply Cumbrians but the rest of the North as well. The degenerative northern tongue is merely the symptom of a more general uncouthness attributed, in part, to their "being so near" to the Scots and "so far away" from the Norman kings in the South. In his complaint, we hear William's "imperialist mentality," as Gillingham would have it. Yet, William's comments nevertheless frame the North *within* England. As Fenton explains, "Malmesbury sometimes recognises division within a people whom he calls the English and sometimes he flags almost separate peoples or nations but which are included within a geographical sense of England."[54]

William is critical of rebellion throughout his histories, but, for him, Northumbria's repeated resistance to the rule of Saxon and Norman kings sets the region apart. In the North, the historian finds a degenerative Englishness that must be corrected because it threatens the political unity he hopes to illustrate – or manufacture – in his own histories. The North's problem is, in part, that "barbarians" are "so near." And William plays upon the infiltration of northern England by other non-English parties in the *Gesta Regum Anglorum*. In his reckoning of the Harried North, William describes York as,

> the only remaining refuge for rebels ... [where] so many of the citizens perished by famine or sword; for that was where Malcolm, King of Scots with his forces, where Edgar and Morcar and Waltheof with English and Danish troops often made a snug nest for tyranny and often cut to pieces William's [the Conqueror's] generals. (*GR*, I, p. 463)

> (*Eboracum, unicum rebellionum suffugium, civibus pene delevit fame et ferro necatis. Ibi enim rex Scottorum Malcolmus cum suis, ibi Edgarus et Marcherius et Waldefus cum Anglis et Danis nidum tirannidis sepe fovebant, sepe duces illius trucidabant.*)

But William is also admittedly a "southerner" and his bias for southern urban centers like London or Canterbury occasionally curb a balanced history. As Daniel Gerrard points out, William is quick to praise Londoners in their defense of the city against the assaults of Swein and the Danes in 1013, but he fails to point out London's resistance to William I following the battle of Hastings. Similarly, Gerrard argues that William exaggerates Canterbury's historic sanctity in order to clarify the city's place as the center of ecclesiastic authority in England.[55] Thus, William asserts that Canterbury's citizens are "more than other Englishmen still proudly aware of their long-established nobility, and this makes them the readier to pay honour to others and welcome them as guests, but also the fiercer in driving off those who might do them injury" (*GP*, I, pp. 1–2) (*...plusquam ceteri Angli conscientiam adhuc antiquae nobilitatis spirans, et ad honoricentiam et hospitium cuiuslibet pronior, ad propulsandas iniurias acrior*). Fenton notes here how "the people of Canterbury are presented as a *gens* within the *Anglii*" whereas, in William's remark on the Northumbrian slave-boys, the Northumbrians "are seemingly presented as more separate, underlined by Malmesbury's use of the term *natio* (*Huius tempore uenales ex Nothanimbria pueri – familiari scilicet et pene ingenita illi nationi consuetudine*)."[56] Gerrard explains, similarly, "Where the men of Canterbury are characterised by refinement and virtue exceeding that of all other Englishmen, the men of York are almost barbarians, barely English at all."[57] And while we might place the implied comparison of York and Canterbury within ecclesiastical debates over the primacy, extant in William's period, he intimates anxiety over national identity as well. As Gerrard wryly observes, "For William . . . some men were more English than others,"[58] and the question of Englishness is paramount in his work.

It is ironic that the most prominent dismissal of northern speech in the literary history of England – as discussed above, William's mocking of northern English in Book III of the *Gesta Pontificum Anglorum* – is uttered in procession from his description of a Roman ruin. The ruins at Carlisle, like the "cities of the Romans' building" in William's depiction of Bede's Northumbria, testify to earlier civilizations in the North – of Roman occupation and ecclesiastical high learning – that are all the more lamentably lost given the state of the North of England in the early twelfth century. Here, William of Malmesbury unwittingly explains his anxieties about the North. His preoccupations with Rome are both nostalgic for classical culture and learning and, at the same time, reminiscent of what he viewed as a profound political unity. William's repeated assertions of his own *romanitas* or Romanness, his investment in classical literature and history, is personal and professional. In the *Gesta Regum Anglorum*, both Cicero's *De Offiicis* and Suetonius' *Vitae Caesarum* afford William models for his presentation of Norman kings.[59] His own Latin prose was profoundly indebted to classical writing, as his quotations of the *Aeneid* throughout the *Gesta Regum Anglorum* testify.[60] Classical Roman authors largely shaped his prose style as well. William explains, for example, in the prologue to Book I of the *Gesta Regum Anglorum* that he aims to "give a Roman polish to the rough annals of our native speech" (*GR*, I, pp. 14–15) (*exarata barbarice Romano sale condire*). But, beyond the personal or professional, William's interests in Rome throughout his histories is also, implicitly national. The Roman polish he hopes to apply is also political. The roughness of England's native history, its inelegance in the face of Rome's political and cultural glories, informs his fixation on ruins. Thus, William Kynan-Wilson finds of the historian, "in considering the language of the Northumbrians to be other than English, he perceived these people to be barbarians while concurrently aligning himself with ancient Rome via the Latin inscription." Kynan-Wilson continues, "In this light, William's own erudition . . . is emphasised, but so too is the way in which the material remains of Rome allowed him to comment upon what he perceived to be the decline of northern England."[61] Yet, we might ask here, if Roman ruins in the North signify that region's degeneration from a once-great territory of Roman settlement and ecclesiastical learning, then how are we to understand William's attention to the ruins of Rome itself?

Nowhere is William of Malmesbury's attention to Roman ruins more pronounced than in his citation of Hildebert of Lavardin's (*c.*1055–1133) poem "*Par tibi Roma nihil*," a thirty-six-line elegy on Rome's classical past as witnessed in its medieval wreckage. Thomson observes, "This poem is a noble lament on Rome's fall and present ruinous and anarchic state contrasted with its former grandeur."[62] The ruins are a lesson "in Rome's past greatness," but there is now "no possibility of restoration."[63] The decline of Rome is a great blow to William personally. Thomson sees in the poem a "key" to "William's psychology," an explanation as to why William devoted such time and space to the classical readings that made him "exceptional in his time."[64] But, as I've already shown, William's ruinous preoccupations connect England with Rome, and I suggest here that these previous moments in his histories, where he recalls England's own Roman ruins, inform his attention to Hildebert's poem beyond the monk's pronounced classicism.

William places the poem within Book IV of the *Gesta Regum Anglorum*, which is devoted largely to rendering the life of King William II (hereafter,

Rufus). The first fourteen lines establish Julius Caesar's important presence in Rufus' turbulent life:

> In ruins all, yet still beyond compare,
> How great thy prime, though provest overthrown.
> Age hath undone thy pride: see, weltering there,
> Heaven"s temples, Caesar's palace quite, quite down.
> Down is the masterpiece (Araxes dire
> Feared while it stood, yet grieved to see it fall),
> Which sworded kings and senate's wise empire
> And Heaven did stablish sovereign of us all.
> Caesar to have her for his private ends
> All loyalties, all kindred set at naught.
> By threefold arts she grew: foes, crimes, and friends
> By arms, laws, gold she vanquished, tamed, and bought.
> Raised with unsleeping toil by men of old,
> By generous strangers helped and neighbouring wave.
> (GR, I, pp. 612–16)

> (*Par tibi, Roma, nichil, cum sis prope tota ruina;*
> *quam magni fueris integra, fracta doces.*
> *Longa tuos fastus aetas destruxit : et arces*
> *Cesaris et superum templa palude iacent.*
> *Ille labor, labor ille ruit quem dirus Araxes*
> *et stantem tremuit et cecidisse dolet ;*
> *Quem gladii regum, quem provida iura senatus,*
> *quem superi rerum constituere caput;*
> *quem magis optauit cum crimine solus habere*
> *Cesar quam sotius et pius esse socer ;*
> *qui crescens studiis tribus hostes, crimen, amicos*
> *ui domuit, secuit legibus, emit ope ;*
> *in quem, dum fieret, uigilauit cura priorum,*
> *iuuit opus pietas hospitis, unda locum.*)

Caesar is the pivotal figure here, signifying at once world domination and Rome's internal implosion. Though Rome does not fall in the wake of his own failed powerplay, Caesar's presence gestures unwittingly toward Rome's demise. The palace of the Caesars is thrown under "Heaven"s temples," its ruin foreseen in Julius' undoing of "all loyalties, all kindred" for "his private ends" and power lust. Caesar plants a seed that sprouts "friends" but also "foes [and] crimes." The poem wrestles with the remnants of man's near-Faustian aspirations, lamenting the state of a great city "in ruins yet still beyond compare." At the same time, the poem reasserts this sinful vanity, venerating man's capacity to "make of Rome a city higher / Than toiling gods could wholly overthrow." In its illustration of man's ability to supersede the creative capacities of the gods – "These sculpted gods the gods themselves amaze" – C. Stephen Jaeger claims that the poem "posits the victory of representation over nature," that it is about "overcoming and going beyond mimesis."[65] As though challenging Nature (and by implication God), the poet claims that "man creative doth deify," that "art" or man's "toil" "makes these gods and not divinity."

William's own lamenting language in introducing the poem, however, suggests a very different register. Rome, "once mistress of the world and now ... more like a small town" serves as the dwelling for "the most inactive of mankind, who put justice on the scales against gold and set a price on canon law" (*GR*, I, pp. 612–13) (*quae quondam domina orbis terrarum, nunc... videtur oppidum exiguum, et de Romanis... nunc dicuntur hominum inertissimi, auro trutinantes iustitiam, pretio venditantes canonum regulum*). William proceeds from the poem to narrate Rufus' rule, as it dissolves into vanity, thievery, and ultimate tragedy. Yet he prefaces that long decline with a particularly vigorous scene in Rufus' life, a scene that actually precedes Hildebert's elegy in the *Gesta Regum Anglorum*, that, indeed, seems to set up our understanding of Rufus' relationship to Caesar and, thus in William's work, England to Rome. William claims that "the soul of Julius Caesar pass[ed] into King William [Rufus]" (*GR*, I, pp. 566–67) (*anima Julii Cesaris transierit in regem Willelmum*).[66] His claim is informed by an event in Rufus' life said to emulate Caesar's own. In responding to the siege at Le Mans in 1098, which he had recently added to his holdings when his brother Robert Curthose fled Normandy to crusade, Rufus defied a sea storm and sped across the Channel to aid the town. Rufus relieved the town and captured Helias of La Fleche, who defiantly derides Rufus: "You have captured me by chance ... if only I could get away, I know what I should do." To demonstrate his own courage, Rufus releases his prisoner, claiming, "I give you free leave to do your worst ... If you beat me, I shall ask for no quarter in exchange for letting you go like this." William points out that Lucan's *Pharsalia* recounts just such an action by Julius Caesar, but William quickly clarifies that Rufus "never had either the interest or the leisure to pay any attention to literature," so he could not have known the precedent for his own action. Rufus' carelessness might be used as evidence, negatively, of his rash behavior. But William equates it to Rufus' "innate fire of mind, and conscious valor" (*GR*, I, pp. 566–67) (*Veruntamen sunt quaedam de rege preclarae magnanimitatis exempla... "Fortuitu" in quit "me cepisti; sed si possem euadere, noui quid facerem"... Concedo tibi ut fatias quicquid poteris, et ... si me uiceris, pro hav uenia tecum paciscar.*)

Gillingham has recently pointed out that critics tend to misunderstand William of Malmesbury's life of Rufus as strictly negative, that William follows upon Eadmer of Canterbury in presenting Rufus as a debauched ruler whose death was, as Eadmer asserts, "the righteous judgment of God" (*usto judico Dei*).[67] And the manuscript history of both the *Gesta Regum Anglorum* and *Gesta Pontificum Anglorum* reveal that William revised his works at times to lessen his criticisms of Rufus' reign. As William himself admits, "truth is often disastrous and falsehood profitable, for in writing of contemporaries it is dangerous to criticize" (*GR*, I, pp. 540–41) (*naufragatur veritas et suffragatur falsitas; quippe presentium mala periculose*). He even claims to shrink from the task altogether, only finally re-engaging with his work after the goading of several of his friends: "Quickened therefore by the encouragement of those whom I love ... I set to work" (*GR*, I, pp. 540–41) (*Illorum itaque quos penitus" reposito amore diligo hortatibus animatus assurgo...*). But, as Gillingham contends, William's account of Rufus' life is "far more balanced" than is often claimed.[68] Bjorn Weiler aptly notes the dynamic of William's narrative, wherein Rufus is "praised as much for his courage and generosity as he [is] condemned for his greed and unwillingness to rein in his court and household."[69] Sønnesyn clarifies that William relies expressly on Suetonius' *Vitae Caesarum* in constructing his life of Rufus, as well as that of his brother Henry I, and this model follows a topical – rather than chronologic – order. Sønnesyn is clear that this model is not, for William, merely a frame within which to present historical matter; rather; the form itself fittingly works to explain "how the king, having reached a point where the main rivals to his royal office were either beaten or supported his tenure, started to lose his grip on his throne and turned from a promising young man into a mature tyrant."[70] Early in his portrait of Rufus, William is effusive:

> Brought up as he was by his parents with greatest care, and naturally gifted with a spirit prolific of great ideas, he reached the highest point of supreme power – a prince unquestionably without peer in our own time, had he not been overshadowed by his father's greatness, and had fate not overtaken him at an early age, and thus prevented the faults developed by unlimited power and youthful spirits from being corrected by mature years. (*GR*, I, p. 543)

> (*Ingenti cura parentum altus, cum et illi naturaliter inesset ingentia parturiens animus, ad culmen supremae Dignitatis evasit: incomparabilis procul dubio nostro tempore princeps, si non eum magnitude patris obrueret, nec eius iventutem fata precipitassent, ne per aetatem maturiorem aboleret errores licentia potestatis et impetus iuenili contractos.*)

Rufus' decline is attributed, in part, to the death of Lanfranc, Archbishop of Canterbury:

> At the beginning of his reign, while Archbishop Lanfranc was still living, he refrained from all wrongdoing ... On Lanfranc's death, for some time he showed himself changeable, virtue and vice equally balanced; but now in his later years all his love of virtue grew cold, while the heat of viciousness boiled up within him. (*GR*, I, pp. 554–55)
>
> (*Inter initia, uiuente Lanfranco archiepiscopop, ab omni crimine abhoreebat, ut unicum fore regum speculum speraretur; quo defuncto, aliquandiu uarium se pretitit aequali lance uitiorum atque uirtutum; iam uero postremis annis omni gelante studio uirtutum, uitiorum in eo calor efferbuit.*)

These passages support Gillingham's suggestion that William offers a balanced account of Rufus' life. More than this, however, they illustrate that Rufus was, for William, a figure of profound promise and tragic decline.

Ambiguously both a complement and a curse, Caesar's *animus* within the English king is retroactively reinterpreted by Hildebert's poem. Here, Julius Caesar is, like Rufus, a figure of both immense virtue and unwitting self-destruction. We begin to understand, now, the entanglement of Hildebert's poem with Norman kings and the relationship of northern England's Roman ruins with historical authorities of centuries past. Placing the "*Par tibi Roma nihil*" within his portrait of the Icarus-like Rufus, William makes clear his correlation of Rome with England. Rome's decline, as evidenced in the poem, from a global empire to a "small town" prophesies England's own regression from an emergent nation-state to a collection of disparate provinces not unlike the heptarchy of kingdoms in Bede's own time. As we have seen, William's interests in ruins are bound up both with his innate *romanitas* and, at the same time, with real political devastation that often surrounds his ruinous accounts in the first place. More than simply informing William's inclinations to classical literature, the monk's use of the Roman elegy in Book IV of the *Gesta Regum Anglorum* crystallizes his correlation of ruins and death brought on by internal strife within the *res publica*. In this way the poem becomes not merely an elegy on the end of the classical age but a connection to the remnants of Roman Northumbria, the wastelands of the North of England, and to the potential ruin of England itself through a North–South divide.

Repression and Reckoning

We might explain William's own obsession with ruins through two very different understandings of the Middle Ages' attraction to Rome's material remains. In an inconspicuous footnote, nineteenth-century historian Jacob Burkhardt mentions William's quotation of *"Par tibi Roma nihil,"* a poem Burkhardt calls "one of the most singular examples of humanistic enthusiasm in the first half of the twelfth century."[71] This reference comes as a surprise given Burkhardt's centrality to the characterization of the Middle Ages as "diachronically innocent" or historically naïve to the classical past. Burckhardt's famous study, *The Civilization of the Renaissance in Italy* (1860), illustrated for generations of scholars the ways in which the ruins of ancient Rome aroused the passions of numerous intellectuals and artists who instigated a new cultural epoch, the Renaissance. As Jennifer Summit carefully points out, Burckhardt portrays the Middle Ages as a "period of suspended historicity," an age "[w]hose response to the classical past was at best ignorant and forgetful, and at worst iconoclastically repressive."[72] In opposing this medieval-early/modern divide, Summit engages specifically with medieval readings of the ruins at Rome, including Petrarch's "Letter to Colonna," the *Mirabilia Urbis Romae*, and Chaucer's *Second Nun's Tale*. She argues that rather than confirming medieval ignorance towards, and repression of, the classical past, these texts "represent historical change as a form of conversion that did not so much destroy or supplant the past as conserve its outward forms while assigning them new meanings."[73] In turning "the visible signs of pagan Rome into vital evidence for a material history of Christianity,"[74] Summit argues, these texts situate the Middle Ages as a period every bit as capable as the Renaissance of contemplating historical change and Christian futurity. William of Malmsebury lands somewhere in between.

In Burkhardtian fashion, William looks through the rubble he foregrounds as sublime object to the past beauty of a monastic community at Bangor, a religiously fervent and neo-Roman Northumbria, and to Rome itself as the epitome of civilization. At the same time, he has already redefined these ruins, though not in the positive terms of Summit's equation. Instead, they function as symptoms of his anxiety about the self-destructive drives inherent in the English national community and epitomized by the North of England. If the ruins in William's text serve as a repressive device through which he maintains the illusion of Englishness and national unity, then the ruins at Rome uncannily turn into the signifier of that community's implosion and, ultimately, its impossibility. Northumbria's haunting violence and perfidiousness, of which Bede's history reminds William, manifests in the ruinous landscapes and degenerative speech of the Harried North. And much like the ruins of Bangor-Is-Coed or those at Rome, the North in William's period constitutes both an empty space and a reminder of the devastating and crippling effects of internal discord. If William aims to repress this frightening realization by reflecting on the ruins at Rome, his anxieties are realised nonetheless in the years following the completion of his towering histories, when Henry I died and England plunged into the Anarchy, a civil war fought for the crown between Henry's daughter Matilda and his nephew Stephen of Blois.

The Anarchy will resolve in the rule of the Angevins under Henry II, though discord will continue to gnaw at England's emergent sense of self. The self-destructive discord that William feared within the realm was recreated on a much smaller stage within the medieval universities in the centuries following William's death. Born out of the twelfth and early-thirteenth centuries, the institutions of Oxford and Cambridge came to symbolize, in their own way, an emergent English realm, but it is their own peculiar conflicts among groups of scholars, fittingly termed "nations" but arrayed in a North–South divide, that once more threatens England the nation as it reasserts itself on the European stage.

CHAPTER 3

The North–South Divide in the Medieval English Universities

In the previous chapter, I examined the ways in which the North of England as a cultural pariah and a spectral political presence undermines the work of William of Malmesbury as he labored to write a new history of the English people in the early twelfth century. In William's northern consciousness we read the naissance of a cultural and political North–South divide in the literature of medieval England. By the early fourteenth century, this divide is institutionalized in the organization of scholars at England's universities, Oxford and Cambridge. In this chapter, I will examine the phenomenon of the so-called university "nations" as it played out in physical and ideological conflicts over institutional discrimination, educational jurisdiction, and, in the end, royal and papal authority.

In the context of the medieval universities, we encounter the confused state of the term "nation." Latin *natio*, in its relationship to "natus," refers implicitly to one's birth: birthplace, language, customs. As I discussed in the previous chapter, the terms *gens*, *natio*, and *populus* were used interchangeably in the Middle Ages, yet even in their somewhat haphazard deployment of these terms, historiographers like William of Malmesbury did not render the concept *gens* or *natio* static. As William's histories intimate, one *gens* might meld with another. Sigbjorn Sønnesyn points out, for example, that William, like his predecessor Bede, "distinguishes between *Angli*, *Saxones*, and *Jutae*" while, at the same time, he can be seen to "refer to these peoples collectively as *Angli*."[1] Over a century later, the uses of *gens* and *natio* are remarkably similar. In her parsing of the rhetoric of nationhood in the political and constitutional contexts of late thirteenth- and fourteenth-century England, Andrea Ruddick explains, "Given the widespread knowledge of the English people's historically hybrid origins ... as set out in many late thirteenth- and fourteenth-century chronicles ... it seems likely that uses of *gens /gent* by the same chroniclers to describe the English people allowed for this notion of multi-ethnic accretions to a people."[2] With the rise of vernacular literature in a trilingual England, the potential for confusion mounts. Thorlac Turville-Petre suggests that the Middle English "*nacioun*" carried ethnic or racial overtones in the early fourteenth century: "division and conflict were likely to have racial origins, whether the cause was aliens interfering in the life of the nation as at the time of the Barons' War, or, more deep-seated, the mixed ancestry of the so-called 'English' nobility which underlay the civil war during Edward II's reign."[3] Such examples inevitably reach back, once more, to concepts of birth, such as the mixed Norman/English parentage that historians William of Malmesbury and Orderic Vitalis are quick to point out in their own biography.[4] This notion of "descent" nevertheless also reverts back to geography and to the particular customs, languages, and laws subject to scrutiny by those whose origins lie elsewhere. William of Malmesbury, for example, comments on the "uncouth" speech of Northumbrians, as well as the barbarism of their practice of slavery. It is arguably this regionally-inflected definition of "nation" that informs the organization of scholars in the medieval universities of Europe in the thirteenth and fourteenth centuries. We might, for example, speak of nations at the University of Paris, which included Normans, Poitevins, Burgundians, Lombards, Bretons, Sicilians, and Flemish.

The division of scholars within the medieval universities of England was radically reduced to the northern and southern nations. While violence among these corporations at universities in Europe was common, the duality of nations at Oxford and Cambridge seems, arguably, to pressurize the tensions between these distinct groups and to provoke numerous confrontations born of a heightened sense of regional identity, even as many of these students were far-flung from their own *patrias*. In his exhaustive history of the University of Oxford, seventeenth-century antiquarian Anthony Wood offers several examples of violent encounters among Oxford's students in the Middle Ages. In 1319, Wood illustrates:

> In the vigils of S. Kenelm, King and Martyr, fell out in the evening a most grievous Conflict between the Northern and Southern Clerks: the former of which being in pursuit of the other in Catstreet, it hapned that one Luke de Horton came then out of his door to make it and the gutter clean, but Elias de Hubberthorp supposing him to be one that belonged to the Southern party, gave him a cut on the head with his Sword, which being deep to the brain he died soon after. There were several that had that night received wounds, but darkness coming on they were forced to part.[5]

Elias de Hubberthorp is not some brigand ambushing his personal rival in Luke de Horton. Neither is their disagreement one of scholarly debate, competition for fellowship monies or university position, or even contest over the romance of a local girl. As Wood explains it, this violence is perpetrated by a "Northern" student against his "Southern" counterpart. If, as the passage suggests, Luke de Horton is simply in the wrong place at the wrong time, choosing to clean his gutter as Elias de Hubberthorp moves past, then Wood notes that Elias' attack is because the clerk assumes his victim belongs "to the Southern party." The murder of Luke de Horton is but one example of the volatile relations between the organizations of students called "nations." Central to much of the conflict in the medieval English universities is the national rift, the North–South divide, between the many students who flocked to colleges at Oxford and Cambridge throughout the late thirteenth and fourteenth centuries.

Whether in England or on the continent, political authorities such as the English king understood that the universities bespoke the sophistication and political unity of their respective realms. It is no wonder, then, that King Edward III intervened decisively in the most notorious of these many conflicts – the Stamford Schism – in order to settle matters of argument and violence among the nations at Oxford just prior to the outset of the Hundred Years War. The phenomenon of the English North–South divide finds its greatest expression, and its bloodiest repercussions in the narrow confines of Oxford and Cambridge. The colleges, halls, and streets of these university spaces subsumed into larger towns, consequently, come to resemble contestable borderlands within which conflict proliferates for centuries. When Chaucer tells us in his *Reeve's Tale* that the Cambridge students John and Alleyn are from "fer in the north" (I, 4015), he not only invokes the national conflict of the North–South divide, and the linguistic humor provoked by his clerks' northern tooth, he also intimates the highly contained yet extremely volatile conflict between nations at the English universities. As I will show in this chapter, the tension of the North–South divide within the segregated spaced of medieval Oxford erupts in the 1330s in a secession of northern scholars to an alternative university in Stamford. The so-called Stamford Schism and the political response it generates confirm the profound importance of the medieval universities to the national imagination in the early fourteenth century while they also illustrate the impact of the North–South divide on England's national identity at a precarious stage of its development.

Violence Among the University Nations

Nations as distinct university entities appear in the very early thirteenth century at Bologna as subdivisions of colleges within the university formed among the non-Bolognese law students. Pearl Kibre suggests that, in this early stage at Bologna, "nation" referred to a student's place of birth and, later, to his native tongue.[6] The mindset of the university nations, which aimed to sustain a body of common interests and kinship, derived in part from the guild system of medieval towns and cities.[7] These varied and small organizations of scholars periodically came together in two larger bodies: the *universitas ultramontanorum*, which consisted of students from outside of Italy; and the *universitas citramontanorum*, comprised of students from Italy and its surrounding islands.[8] Fourteen nations existed in 1265 within the *ultramontani* at Bologna: the French, Spanish, Provencal, English, Picard, Burgundian, Poitevin, Tourainian, Norman, Catalonian, Hungarian, Polish, German, and Gascon. The *citramontani* consisted of three large nations: the Lombard, Tuscan and Roman and, given that this was the largest contingent of students because of sheer proximity of their homelands to the city, these groups were further subdivided into partitions known as *Consiliariae*.[9] Eventually every non-Bolognese student who entered the university took membership in one of the nations.[10]

At Paris, students and masters of common regions congregated together in university houses, but sometime in the early or mid-twelfth century these bodies became corporate entities (termed "nations") with seals, treasuries, oaths of membership, and direct and indirect influence on university governance.[11] All students belonged to nations by requirement, but the business of these corporate bodies was conducted by the masters themselves.[12] The assembled nations at Paris comprised one of the four faculties of arts in the *universitas* (the guild of masters), the others being theology, law, and medicine. The nations of Paris divided into four main bodies of association: French, Picard, Norman, and English. Scholars from underrepresented regions were placed within one of these larger bodies. The French nation, for example, comprised of scholars from Paris and southern France, but students from Spain and Italy, as well as other eastern Mediterranean territories including Greece, were also placed within the larger group.[13] The Norman nation consisted of students from the regions of Rouen and Brittany, while the Picards consisted of students from the Low Countries and from northern France. Finally, the English nation was made up of students from several northern European territories, including Britain, Holland, Flanders, Germany, Sweden, Denmark, Norway, and Finland. The organization of scholars within these four larger bodies may have been at the expense of any coherence of ethnic and regional groupings. The composition of the Paris nations appears less derived from the strict geographies of its members' origins rather than by what Kibre describes as "convenient, administrative grouping," and there were often sub-groups within a single nation, such as the division of the French nation at Paris into five smaller entities that included Paris, as well as Sens, Reims, Tours, and Bourges, the last of which hosted Spanish, Italian, and Greek students, among other non-natives.[14]

These divisions within the larger body do not detract from students' rampant adherence to their designated nation or to the violence that stemmed from this peculiar form of "nationalism." William Courtenay explains, "Belonging to a nation not only coincided with their years of study and teaching in the faculty of arts, but continued while studying and being promoted in a higher faculty."[15] Within the organizations of nations, scholars spent much of their time together, including the attendance of mass, as well as numerous liturgical ceremonies and feast days throughout the year. Furthermore, as Courtenay points out, each nation had its own specific church at which to worship. The English nation at Paris, for example, worshiped at the parish church of Saint-Come.[16] In the case of Bologna, and perhaps of Paris later, these communities mime the larger university's desire for autonomy from the civic authority of the cities and towns in which they resided. Kibre notes that students desired these unions of nation for "mutual protection and collective security against local authorities,"[17] but the universities as a whole aimed to protect their broader interests from these same authorities by governing themselves. The university's desire for legal autonomy played out in sometimes strange stipulations. At the University of Bologna, local Bolognese students could not be part of any organization of nations because university officials felt that their citizenship in the city and, consequently, their subjectivity to the laws of the commune compromised the university's ability to govern in both their studies and their general conduct. Indeed, the first professors at Bologna were excluded from the nations as well because they were made up almost entirely of Bolognese residents. Students, then, had to choose their officers from the student body.[18] Other medieval universities, including the English universities at Oxford and Cambridge, sought similar independence from local secular authority. Certainly, this legal autonomy was welcomed by the scholars of these various institutions. As Steven Overman wryly notes, "medieval students exploited their protection from civil law conveyed by clerical status in order to engage in boisterous and rowdy exploits in the university towns and then beat hasty retreats to the sanctuary of the university."[19] The legal autonomy from civic rule that many universities enjoyed, however, may have enhanced the internal tensions among the nations at these *studia*. If the tight-knit communities of university nations were formed initially to defend students against secular authorities, then the sense of solidarity in these groups is quickly redirected to the defense of their own against the other nations within their respective institutions.

The problem of conflict among the nations becomes acute as their individual sizes increase. Courtenay notes of Paris that numbers within a single nation might be 500 students or more, with up to 40 masters, and even the smaller nations – such as the English at Paris – numbered 150.[20] In his *Historia Occidentalis*, the thirteenth-century chronicler Jacques de Vitry complains of the Paris students, "They wrangled and disputed not merely about the various sects or about some discussions; but the differences between the countries also caused dissensions, hatreds and virulent animosities among them and they impudently uttered all kinds of affronts and insults against one another."[21] Accordingly, the Parisian clerks

> affirmed that the English were drunkards and had tails; the sons of France proud, effeminate and carefully adorned like women. They said that the Germans were furious and obscene at their feasts; the Normans, vain and boastful; the Poitevins, traitors and always adventurers. The Burgundians they considered vulgar and stupid. The Bretons were reputed to be fickle and changeable, and were often reproached for the death of Arthur. The Lombards were called avaricious, vicious and cowardly; the Romans, seditious, turbulent and slanderous; the Sicilians, tyrannical and cruel; the inhabitants of Brabant, men of blood, incendiaries, brigands and ravishers; the Flemish, fickle, prodigal, gluttonous, yielding as butter, and slothful. After such insults from words they often came to blows.

Jacques' complaints are rife with regional and national stereotypes – the Bretons' Arthuriana, the Sicilians' cruelty, the French's effeminate demeanor. What is more, they suggest these many students partake of a number of pastimes that are violent (ravishment), slothful (obscenity and gluttony) and even bestial (the English have tails!). A short poem found in Paris, Bibliotheque Nationale, MS. F. FR. 837, known as *Le Chasthement Des Clers*, attacks the university's students, claiming that their internal dissensions and their violence against one another within the university now threaten the very institution itself. According to the poem, the clerks are blinded with pride; they seek confrontation with one another, and they even kill their fellow students (*"Quant l'une nascions muet pot l'autre tuer"* (10)). *Le Chasthement Des Clers* plays on the prominent metaphor of the University of Paris as a "fountain of knowledge" (*Qu'il sordoit a Paris de toz sens la fontaine* (14)), a designation that the University actively promoted in the thirteenth century.[22] As Daron Burrows notes, in a letter dated

February 4, 1254, university authorities illustrate this fountain of knowledge flowing into the four faculties (*unde sapientie fons scendit, qui in quatuor facultates*) much as the four rivers flow out of Paradise into the four quarters of the world (*in iiij paradysi flumina distributes per quator mundi climate derivatus universam terram irrigate et infundit*).²³ Consequently, Burrows argues that the poem satirises Paris' presumed glory by reinscribing the "fountain of knowledge" as a diabolic watering hole full of anguish (... *mais, quar deable l'amaine / Fontaine de dolor* (15–16)). Whereas the fountain of knowledge flowed out into the four faculties, now the devilish water nurses the murderous intent of the four nations (*De la fontaine est droiz qu'encore vous dions / Ses ruissiaus espandi en iiij. nacions / plus gleteus xiij. tans qu'escume de lyons / Quant il est enragiez n'es pas droiz qu'en rions* (21–24)). F.M. Powicke explains that the university at Paris was "intensely self-conscious and self-important" but he goes on to suggest that this arrogance "had been fostered by flattery and protection and was kept lively by constant disputes over the judicial immunities of the Parisian scholars."²⁴ Like the universities themselves, these students were nearly immune from civic law. A poem such as *Le Chastement Des Clers* might scold the students for their mayhem, but their misdeeds often went unpunished by either civic authorities or their universities. No doubt, then, that the violence between the nations at Paris, as well as Bologna, Oxford, and Cambridge – institutions that sought similar independence – elicited both mockery and resentment from civic officials and townspeople. If the universities reveled in their legal autonomy, then it must have been humorous – or morbidly ironic – to figures of law and governance that these institutions could not contain the brutality of their clerks toward one another.

Quite often, hostilities between the nations at Bologna and Paris arose over disagreements concerning the position of rector at the university. The rectorship was seen as a seat of immense power. At Paris, the rector was chosen in rotation from among the individual nations, yet, when elected, he presided over them collectively. Other confrontations among the nations concerned questions over the geographic border between territories that determined whether a scholar would enroll in one nation or another. At Paris, for example, in 1266 a certain scholar named Jean de Ulliaco, resident of a Picard territory, desired to incept instead into the French nation. The Picard nation, however, refused to give him up. The ensuing conflict between the French students and the Picards resulted in Jean's own kidnapping. The dispute, further, lead to the French nation's brief resignation from the university faculties, and the matter was only later settled through the mediations of the papal legate Simon de Brie. Loyalties generated by one's nation in the university – loyalty to a particular group of masters and scholars rather than the university as a whole – frequently, if surprisingly, devolved into deadly confrontation. Such an incident occurred in either 1278 or 1281, when a dispute between the English and Picard nations at Paris resulted in several deaths and substantial property damage to the Picard houses of the university. Several members of the Picard nation subsequently fled from Paris for fear of their lives.[25]

What seems to antagonize the situation between nations is the very fact that these early medieval universities desired autonomy as places of learning, free from the influence of city or territorial laws. In these unaffiliated spaces, then, power was at play for any number of candidates in elections for such positions as proctor or, again, rector. Infusing a population of young men into such an environment wherein their criminal activities often went unchecked and where they were arrayed into distinct corporate groups based on regional identity merely begs such violence. By contrast to other associative groups, such as the faculty in medicine or law at Paris, the nations played upon identity for the sake of fostering protective communities among the universities' many young clerks, but these universities' freedom from secular rule augmented positions of power within their governing bodies and, consequently, exacerbated already competitive academic spaces between the nations until they became arenas of physical violence. Such clashes are amplified in the smaller confines of the English universities at Oxford and Cambridge.

Australes et Boreales

In the medieval English universities, nations were not tied directly to university infrastructure and politics. If at Bologna the nations controlled academic policy, then at Oxford and Cambridge they had no intended effect on the governance of university life. In other words, as Kibre argues, "They never appear to have had any importance in academic matters."[26] But Emden is quick to point out a statutory requirement "very probably deriving from the original institution of the office that one of the two proctors of the University [Oxford] should be a Northerner (Borealis) and the other a Southerner (Australis)."[27] While agreeing with Kibre that the nations were not intended to play a role in university affairs, Emden claims of this statute, "In this way the nascent University, while setting its face against the existence of organized 'nations' in its midst, made allowance for the strong regional antipathies which so frequently and so dangerously disturbed its peace."[28] Despite the intentions of the founders of the various halls and colleges at Oxford and Cambridge, as well as the efforts of university administrators over the course of the Middle Ages, the nations had a profound impact on university life and reputation broadly in England until the early sixteenth century.

Evidence suggests that Oxford attempted to produce a form of the four nations such as what we find at Paris in the late twelfth and early thirteenth centuries. Documents concerning a dispute between townsmen and the university scholars in 1228 allude to four masters who headed groups of students, and historians have taken this number to suggest that it alludes to four nations at Oxford.[29] But England's universities did not draw students from such a large geographical area as did Bologna and Paris, and it seems that any notion of a Paris-like structure was quickly abandoned for two distinct nations, northern and southern. Scots were placed, typically, among the northern nation while Welsh and Irish students enrolled in the southern nation.[30] Historians of the University of Oxford long believed that the recognized geographic border for the North and South – by which it classified its northern and southern students – was the River Trent,[31] though both Rashdall and Emden, among others, proposed the River Nene much further south and running through Northampton and Peterborough before heading North to the Wash.[32] Cambridge clearly had organizations of nation as well, though, as Allan Cobban points out, very little testimony appears as to the sanctioning and practice of nations there due to the loss of thirteenth-century records by fire.[33]

Most of the colleges and halls at Oxford demonstrated a reasonably strict adherence to regional preference (whether they preferred northern or southern students). This was determined in most cases by the regional ties of these colleges' and halls' respective founders, who often had specific desires regarding the places from which their *studia* drew its clerks. As Emden points out, upon founding Exeter College in 1314, the Bishop of Exeter, Walter Stapeldon, required eight of twelve foundation fellowships be distributed to men of Devon and Cornwall.[34] Exeter College, thus, remained a largely southern-oriented college in the Middle Ages. Merton College (f. 1264) was also largely comprised of southern scholars, but rumor had it that Walter de Merton intended some admissions to be directed toward students from Durham – and the prior of Durham wrote letters urging the college to uphold this intention in the early fourteenth century. The fellows of the college, however, seem to have ignored his request. New College, founded by William of Wykeham around 1379, garnered most of its students from Winchester because the college held property there. All Souls, founded in 1437, and Magdalen, founded in 1458, housed predominantly southern students as well.[35] University College (f. 1249) and Balliol College (f. 1263), founded by John Balliol and his wife, the Lady Dervoguilla,[36] were comprised almost exclusively of northern scholars, as was Queen's College (f. 1341) and Lincoln College (f. 1427), while Oriel College (f. 1326) had both northern and southern students. Though northerners appear to have been more prominent at Oriel, fellowships reserved for students from Somerset, Dorset, Wiltshire, and Devon testify that the college housed southern students as well.[37]

Boys as young as twelve or thirteen entered Oxford as freshman students, a far cry from the minimum age of twenty at the University of Paris.[38] Here, they moved between the city streets and the various buildings that comprised the colleges, halls, and other residences that ranged throughout the city and beyond. Charles Mallet paints an interesting if romantic picture of the crowded scene:

> Hundreds of students thronged the narrow lanes – little fellows still learning Latin in the grammar schools, older boys of fifteen and sixteen already started on their University careers, youths in the first flush of manhood, eager for mysteries to solve, for worlds to conquer, and ripe for any mischief that hot blood could suggest.[39]

Though these scholars were poised to learn theology and law among other pursuits, they seemed often to pursue with equal vigor the temptations of youth and, specifically, the distractions offered by the town. Overman explains that university students throughout Europe engaged in numerous sports, including at Paris *au crocet* with a curved stick similar to that used in modern hockey. At Cambridge, students practiced archery, while football was so popular that Oxford banned its students from playing in the city streets, and James I of Scotland would ban its play throughout the country in 1424, though students seem to have continued football well after.[40] Mallet, however, suggests that innocent athletic contest was less frequent than mischief and even mayhem:

> Sport was certainly not unknown. Hawking and cock-fighting were common enough ... Poaching in the woods and streams round Oxford was perhaps more popular still. The roads near the University were sometimes infested by outcast scholars on the look-out for prey, who added the joys of the highwayman to the delights of sport. ... The chief amusement of the age was fighting. ... Gambling may have needed sharp discouragement. Rowdyism and practical joking required it even more.[41]

"Hot-blooded" youths and scholars-turned-outlaws doubtless contributed to quarrels at Oxford. So-called town-and-gown rivalries arose frequently between local citizens and clerks. This common discord lies at the heart of John the carpenter's derogatory anecdote towards Nicholas in Chaucer's *Miller's Tale* – "As ferde another clerke with astromye" (I, 3457) – and Symkyn's pleasure at stealing from the university in the *Reeve's Tale* – "He craketh boost and swore it was nat so" (I, 4001). But just as conflicts between townspeople and clerks were common, symptomatic of the university's legal autonomy, so too were clashes between the scholars themselves.

Besides normal hostilities that arose naturally between young men and boys who were absent of parents and guardians, numerous disturbances great and small abounded between the bodies of northern and southern scholars at Oxford in the thirteenth and fourteenth centuries. As we find in the European universities, reasons for conflict between the nations at Oxford often revolve around the election of officials, particularly the office of proctor. Oxford had two proctors whose duties were numerous. Proctors were, in a sense, the chief internal lawmen of the university, attending to crimes committed by students, collecting fines, doling out punishments, and enforcing statutes and other disciplinary decisions made by the university and its head, the chancellor. Proctors, further, supervised elections, administered oaths, and managed the university's finances. University regulation stated that the two proctorships should be divided among northern and southern candidates, which implies that even though Oxford did not incorporate the nations into its system of operations, as at Paris, it could not ignore them. Oxford, further, regulated the election of many other offices, so that at any point wherein two offices of equal stature were open for election, those elected had to comprise of one northerner and one southerner. This was the case for collators of university sermons (one northern, one southern), for determiners for undergraduate admission (two northern, two southern), for the keepers of the university's various administrative and loan chests (one northern, one southern for each chest), and even for the *scrutators* (officials) of the elections for grammar masters (one northern, one southern). As many as thirty-four offices were subject to these regulations, excepting only the offices of chancellor, chaplain, beadle, and registrar.[42] Despite the lengths to which equality among the nations was sought – though perhaps because of it – animosity persisted between the two larger bodies of students and masters.

The history of the university at Oxford teems with bloody conflict between the two nations. A coroner's inquest dated May 4, 1314 for David de Kirkby describes an altercation between several northern and southern students armed with "bows, arrows, swords, and bucklers, and other diverse arms" (*cum arcabus, sagittis, gladiis, bokelariis et aliis armis diversis*).[43] Apparently, following their defeat in this clash of arms, five northerners fled to their hall, which overlooked the battlefield. Seeing the unfortunate southerner David de Kirkby standing nearby, one northern offender shot and killed him with an arrow. Anthony Wood describes another remarkable example of conflict in the history of the Oxford nations from 1258, when northern students, in this case allied with the Welsh (who were typically grouped with the southern nation) and flying their own division flags, engaged in a pitched battle near town with their southern counterparts. Wood intimates this engagement's connection with, perhaps its instigation by, the Baron's Wars ongoing between Simon de Montfort's faction and King Henry III. Wood reasons that the northern students and the Welsh aligned themselves with Simon de Montfort's nobles, who included "Leoline, Prince of Wales," while the southerners tied themselves to the King and Prince Edward because they included among their number several Frenchmen and other Europeans – in Woods' words, "Strangers and Aliens that were in England" – who were living at the university at the King's behest.[44] The engagement resulted in multiple deaths on both sides and drew the ire of Henry III, who refused the victor's (the northerners' and the Welsh) offer of financial compensation. These students were saved only by Henry III's own distractions with the Baron's Wars.[45] We should not be surprised, then, when Chaucer veers from analogues of the *Reeve's Tale* by arming his students with "sword and bokeler" (1, 4019).[46] After many years of violence, a 1274 agreement briefly united the nations at Oxford into a single body sworn to support the chancellor in putting down any further disturbances that might arise. This treaty, interestingly, promises to cease the use of the term "nation" itself.[47] Rashdall muses that the unification of the Oxford nations in the 1274 statute is "a symbol of that complete national unity which England was the first of European kingdoms to retain."[48] And while this accord lasts only briefly before similar and escalated confrontations proliferate again in the early fourteenth century, Rashdall's nineteenth-century nationalism might nevertheless inform our understanding of the gravity of the most jarring conflict between the nations at Oxford: the Stamford Schism.

Fleeing the *Studia*

If violence in the universities frustrated everyone from administrators to the King of England, then the gravest threat to these institutions, and the signifying power they held for their respective realms, was student flight. Often, as a result of disputes between local officials, local citizenry, or with their fellow scholars, Oxford and Cambridge students fled their universities for other *studia*. Cambridge itself began, in 1209, as an alternative place of study following several scholars' migration from Oxford. John Fletcher explains that these students migrated initially to avoid capital punishment at the hands of civic authorities in Oxford. At that time, Oxford was also suffering through a lack of royal favor from King John as he fought with Rome. Only in 1213, were the hostilities between the university and the town resolved, but the ability of Cambridge masters and students to carry on uninhibited for some years afforded Cambridge the opportunity to firmly establish itself as a university in its own right.[49] England did not, however, desire so significant a rift to occur again.

Students might flee from civic oppression as well as from internal strife, and they might take a learned body of masters and fellows with them. Student migration of this sort imperiled the stability of the university financially, but it also undermined local economies that depended on revenue from the students and their masters. Courtenay, for example, notes how the Proctor's Book of the English nation at Paris included expenses for "providing food and drink for the masters on a regular bases at numerous taverns on the Left Bank in Paris, after vespers on Friday, after mass on Saturday, and after saints' feasts commemorated by the nation, which were many."[50] Student spending in local towns provided a boon to local business. The leaders of the Bolognese commune passed statutes aimed to prevent student secession, which conveyed banishment on any student conspiring to, or encouraging, migration from Bologna. While these laws are harsh, they testify to Bologna's fear of losing the university altogether because of the lucrative economic benefits it afforded and because of the esteem these institutions endowed on their respective cities and towns. When the civic authorities in Bologna aimed to curb infighting among the nations by seizing the universities' right to choose its rector, Pope Honorius III stepped in to encourage the students' secession, upon which they acted between 1217 and 1220.[51] After reconciliation, further civic impositions on the office of rector – that this official swear an oath never to remove students from Bologna – and the doctors – that they swear never to teach elsewhere – provoked more migrations in 1222. Only afterward did the civic authorities of Bologna concede students' rights to elect and swear an oath to their rector. Going further to maintain good relations with students, the commune exempted students from military service, from communal taxes, and from customs on their books; in addition, students were allowed to buy their own grain.[52] As this reconciliation and conciliatory action suggests, the importance of the university as a "fountain" of knowledge and, as we find in England, the embodiment of national intellectual power, was too precious to chance.

Rashdall claims that as many as half of the European universities were founded through the secession of students from other *studia*, but Fletcher is quick to point out that "Very few of these movements resulted in the immediate establishment of new *studia*,"[53] and this testifies to the civic authorities' willingness to negotiate in order to protect the universities as commodities. We find several instances of scholars fleeing their universities within the histories of England's institutions. At Cambridge in 1261, a "sanguinary and brutal" struggle erupted between the northern and southern scholars, this time joined by townspeople on both sides. In the melee, several properties sustained damage; most notably, the records of the university were consumed in a fire.[54] Several scholars fled the turmoil to Northampton, where they were followed by many of their Oxford counterparts a short time later.[55] Henry III even acknowledged the settlement of the Northampton university that year, although it was short-lived. Eighteenth-century antiquarian Francis Peck suggests that the Oxford group's migration to Northampton in 1264 occurred after several disputes with local townsmen. These Oxford men, then, by chance or poor luck, resided in Northampton during the Baron's Wars, and they, in fact, aided a futile defense of the town against King Henry's men. Although the King pardoned them, later – it is thought only to appease any youth who might identify with the young scholars – he dissolved the university at Northampton and forced its students to return to Oxford and Cambridge. Though the loss of records prevents us from knowing the whole story at Cambridge for several decades following the 1261 migration, Oxford continued to witness numerous conflicts between its nations. No secession was more dramatic than the Stamford Schism of the 1330s.

Causes of the Stamford Schism range from internal discord surrounding discrimination toward northern scholars regarding admission practices and the distribution of scholarships to the belief that both the town and the university had grown physically threatening to northern clerks residing there.[56] Wood discusses discontent among the members of Merton College, in particular, that "the Members of Merton College refused at this time and before to elect North Scholars into their Society."[57] But this seems to be a complaint of exclusion from, rather discrimination within, a college and there appear to be other charges of actions against northerners leveled by the church of Durham.[58] Brasenose College historian Falconer

Madan suggests, further, that the "stress of internal faction" rather than any quarrels with the town, or otherwise, led to the removal of the scholars to Stamford.[59] In a petition dated January 1334, the scholars make known their complaints to King Edward III, as well as their desire to remain at Stamford with the blessing of the crown.[60] In it, they claim that they migrated to Stamford because of "many debates, counsels, & differences which long time have been, & still are in the university of Oxenforde, whereby great damages, perils, deaths, murders, maims, & robberies oftentimes have happened" (*par resound de plusours debatz, concels, et melles qels long temp on teste et uncont son ten la universite de Oxenford, donc grantz damages, perils, morts, mordres, maihemes et robberies sovent fois sont avenuz*).[61] There appear to have been thirty-six scholars in all who fled east to a new college. Emden claims that the leader was the Master (*magistri*) William de Barneby, a Yorkshireman.[62] With Barneby were fifteen other masters, the majority of whom also came from Yorkshire.[63]

One must ask why these scholars went to Stamford of all places. Anthony Wood, perhaps with tongue-in-cheek, alludes to the prophecies of Merlin:

> *Doctrinae stadium quod nunc viget ad vada buom*
> *Tempore venturo celebrabitur ad vada fixi.*
>
> (The studious throng which Oxenford doth cherish,
> In time to come the Stonyford shall nourish.)[64]

Certainly, their destination was influenced by the monks at Durham, who offered their Stamford property, St Leonard's Priory, as a building in which the exiled scholars might house their studies. But Stamford had been a successful university town in its own right for many years prior to the Schism.[65] Carmelites settled here in the mid-thirteenth century, establishing several schools around which the structure of a formal university gradually gathered over the next several decades, even if it was never named or officially recognized. Henry III's dispersal of the Northampton school following the resistances of 1265 further strengthened the Stamford *studium*. According to Wood, in 1291 Robert Lutterel conferred to the Gilbertine convent of Sempingham a manor in Stamford for the sustainment of students studying there.[66] Afterwards, the town's university community witnessed a significant outgrowth of colleges, halls, inns, and monastic schools.[67] So, the Oxford scholars immersed in the Stamford Schism were not fleeing to the wilds of Lincolnshire; rather they moved to a thriving university community, which at the time may have been asserting itself against the two established universities, Oxford and Cambridge.[68]

But these migrations from Oxford in the 1330s precipitate the demise of Stamford as a place of learning, "for the energies of Oxford and Cambridge were called into action."[69]

What the Schism becomes is another drama, albeit a unique one, in the long history of North–South relations. As we witnessed in Chapter 2 of this study, the North as a region was subject to both physical and ideological attacks by those from elsewhere in England. Some of these assaults were justified, while others resembled the disparaging rhetoric that is so often directed toward the region from a southern hegemony of law, culture, and commerce. Throughout the Middle Ages, the North's history of rebellion and its defiant autonomy consistently threaten the broader communitarian desires of the ruling powers of England, and these were acute in 1333, as a young Edward III, labored to suppress the Scottish threat and to assert himself against the French. While the conflict at Oxford between northern and southern students might not hinder the king's military goals, it nevertheless imperiled England's aspirations to become a European center of learning and law. If the conflict of nations in the universities were so often contained within the small confines of the colleges, halls, and towns of Oxford and Cambridge, then the Stamford Schism illustrates just how the North–South divide inevitably works its way out of, and beyond, the local to once again jeopardize national interests.

The emotional pitch of the Schism is best exemplified by two obscure poems that appear to be authored by northern clerks who participated in the events of the Stamford migration. The poems are found in British Library Royal MS. 12. D. xi, described by H.E. Salter as a formulary written at Oxford, which contains most of the correspondences pertaining to the Schism, as well as other university correspondence between 1330 and 1339.[70] Salter describes one of these poems as a "paean by the northern party over the death of a southern champion named Fulk."[71] Though the poem does not itself offer any explicit commentary on the situation of the Stamford Schism, it can be linked to the events surrounding the migration through the name of its antagonist, Fulk. Emden claims that in worse-than-usual violence between northerners and southerners that preceded the migration of scholars, one southern master, Fulk de Lacy, died of wounds received in the fighting.[72] Though we do not know whether Fulk de Lacy's death inspired the poem, these verses' occurrence in the manuscript with another more distinct poem about the secession to Stamford suggests that the works are related. The first poem begins:

Fulk, hero of the southerners, whose nation fostered brotherhood,
O, has the northern dog not bitten you Fulk?
O Fulk, Fulk, Jesus did not exist to you;
You lie in a foul ditch, eaten by worms.
Perhaps you learned what bears on the exaltation of the mind
In Christ's service you sowed rage,
Since you were an effuser of blood, a mutilator,
An avenger and mocker. Master, why were you not afraid?
You begot crimes when you could,
Warlike fool, but you struck with arrogance.
Now having deserved death – your corpse lies unburied.
In you are they signified. Worthy God gives all things according to their desert.
O ashes of your demise, which are to you the body of honor,
You rashly conducted so many devastating and bloody campaigns.
Tell us where is Roger now, where is Satan your accomplice,
in savage murder; he willed what you willed.
Hereford the flag bearer, leader of that sinister band,
And Sporman, leader of the campaign and an agent of death.
Speak of the true conflict, which was always hidden;
They fled from truthful speech, they ascribed the reverse.
Wyk, say where you are, or say where is Wymbury;
When death appeared, neither's sword was discerned.
Vengeance of the divine over time is efficient;
Finally, the fault of the worthless culprit buries your corpse.
Whether you are southern or northern
Such is fitting punishment for evil-doers.[73]

(*Fulco vir australis, quem gens laicana colebat,*
O non mordebat te, Fulco, canis borealis?
O Fulco, Fulco, spes non fuerat tibi Iesus;
In tetro sulco latitas, quia vermibus esus.
Forsan novisti quid fert elatio mentis;
In famulos Christi sevisti more furentis.
Sanguinis effusor, mutilator quando fuisti,
Ultor et illusor. Dominum cur non metuisti?
Criminis ortator fueras quando potuisti,
Stultus bellator, set cum fastu cecidisti.
Mortis condigna – funus pro funere restat –
In te sunt signa; digno deus omnia prestat.
O cinis ex cinere, quo sint tibi carnis honores,
Egisti temere tot devastando cruores.
Dic ubi Rogerus, Sathane tuus ille satelles,
In ferienda ferus; vellet quod dicere velles.
Herford vexilli lator, dux ille sinister,
Et Sporman belli ductor mortisque minister.

Dic in conflictu finali, quo latuerunt;
Veraci dictu fugerunt, terga dederunt.
Wyk dic quo fuerat, vel dic ubi Wymbyriensis;
Cum mors affuerat, nuetrius cernitur ensis.
Ulcio digna dei per tempora longa pepercit;
Demum culpa rei vili te funere mersit.
Seu sis australis, seu tu sis vir borealis,
Talibus est talis congrua pena malis.)

The poet's emotions are evident. Driven to animal rage – signified by the metaphoric northern canine (*canis borealis*) – northerners strike at this southern champion, Fulk, with deadly results. The northern protagonists, however, are not aggressors actively seeking a fight or declaring war on their southern counterparts. Instead, they are victims of attack who defend themselves aptly. This Fulk "sows rage" with bloody contempt, striking "arrogantly" against northerners and backed by a demon band, including Hereford, Wyk, Wymbury, and – by implication – Satan himself abetting the murder of northern men.[74] Despite the apparent regionalist stakes involved, the poet intimates that the issue is one of morality rather than nation. Acknowledging the heart of the matter, the poet posits, "Whether you are northern or southern, Fulk's death is fitting for such an evil doer." This final line, however, does not overwrite the rest of the poem's regionally conscious imagery, particularly the poet's revelry at the rotting body of Fulk, lying in a "foul ditch."

If the "Fulk" poem sounds like an emotional outburst by one or more youths following yet another violent and bloody confrontation between northern and southern students, the second poem is more clearly attendant to the Schism itself. Explicitly addressed to Richard Fitzralph, the chancellor of Oxford at the time of the Schism, the poem both derides the young administrator for his reaction to the Stamford migration and subtly threatens his person as well.[75] Fitzralph was, in the late 1320s, a fellow at Balliol, where he took his MA, before proceeding to University College for his doctorate, which he completed in 1331. He was already famed for his lectures on Peter Lombard's *Sentences* when he rose to the chancellorship of Oxford on May 30, 1332.[76] Fitzralph would go on to even greater notoriety as a theologian following his time at Oxford, influencing Wyclif, among others, with his attention to questions of poverty within the church and his anti-fraternal literature directed specifically at the Franciscans. Given that this poem's content suggests that the parties await a decision from the King, we may tentatively date its composition prior to August 2,

1334, when King Edward called for the dispersal of the Stamford school by the sheriff of Lincoln.[77]

Fitzralph is believed to have made a brash speech, after the initial migration had transpired, in which he wagered his head that the episode would be over in six months.[78] His statement apparently inspires a whole rhetoric of decapitation in the poet:

Fertile Fitzralph, you who live with abundant provisions,
While pouring forth other provisions, let your vows be from somewhere else.
You appear to spare a capital crime with your promise,
Yet, since evil motivates your words, you only convict yourself with your pledge.
While your language seems strong towards the so-called guilty, who have already
    been seized, as though your oaths were realized in actuality,
It is not necessary for you to offer your head expressly.
In Stamford, now, is a place of study,
One hated by its enemies. According to a certain proctor,
We ought to be suppressed, lest the ship be without oarsmen.
You promised yourself that a head would be cut off within a year.
But what if we persist, and the king and the law willingly allow our *studia*?
The virtues of peace have been commanded, so our exodus is not a crime,
It remains that you suffer what was agreed upon, and you will pay with your
    own head as the pledge.
Such is the fate of the wretched; then, you will throw back your old words.
It is clear to all; things will come and things will go
But the severed head will never return
You prophesied by the stars
You watched the stars while you sought to cut us off
You trampled us; only the snare is broken by the foot of he who set it,
You made this multitude of ours, propagated from what was severed from your
    university; your words are not prophetic.
I reject the bloody ford of the horned ox.
I choose, instead, suitable pasture; I welcome this fertile place.
Beneath the shield of Stamford I will live safely,
Where I think it good; thus, I exchange oppression for a nobler life.[79]

(*Fy-Rauf fecunde, qui rebus vivis habunde,*
Res alias funde, tua pignora sint aliunde,
Parcere letali prodest pene capitali,
Et, quia causa mali, convinci pignora tali.
Dum rea possesse valeant quasi pignus in esse,
Set caput expresse non est offere necesse.
In Vada Saxosa, que nunc loca sunt studiosa,
Ilustibus exosa, profers quedam capitaosa,
Nos debere premi, nisi sint sine remige remi,
Anno sub demi capud hinc spondes tibi demi.

Quid si perstemus, velit et rex lege volente?
Cum non sit facinus, pacis virtute iubente.
Restat pacta pati, capud et pro pignore solves.
Heu miseri fati; tunc dicta priora revolves.
Omnibus est visum; veniet res resque peribit,
Sed capud abcisum per tempora nulla redibit.
Cum divniasti cursus sectando planete,
Sidera servasti, dum nos vis iungere mete;
Nos conculcasti; modo frangitur a pede rete;
Plurima plantasti; non sunt tua verba prophete
Cum bove cornuto vada sanguinolenta refuto;
Pascua permuto; loca fertiliora saluto.
Sub saxi scuto magis est michi vivere tuto,
Quo meliora puto; sic tempus nobile muto.)

While the poet and his peers clearly await the King's decision – thus, neutralizing the King himself as any embodiment of centralized authority in the poem – they portray Fitzralph as an oppressive power striking at their new college and their northern nation. The contested crime, here, is admittedly a capital one ("*capitali*"), the punishment of which is death. The poet's use of "*capud*" and "*caput*" (heads) suggests the violent stakes of the poem as a responsive utterance to Fitzralph's own promise of "heads." It seems that both proverbial and literal "heads" will roll. The poem employs a disturbing play on dissection and, specifically, decapitation or headlessness ("*Capud abisiscum*"). Wryly jabbing at Fitzralph for the chancellor's arrogant profession that the Schism would end so quickly, the poet asserts that Fitzralph should not offer his own head through misguided vows of retribution against the Stamford scholars. In other words, Fitzralph condemns himself through his apathetic and, at times, aggressive response to the exiled students' concerns. Continuing the play on headlessness, the poet argues that although Fitzralph wants heads – the symbolic head of the Stamford group, perhaps William Barneby, and the literal heads of all those involved – the chancellor will pay for the scholars' wrongful oppression with his own, in the end. And while we may easily envision this retort to Fitzralph's brash statement and his handling of the Schism as mere vindictive word play, the poet confuses the matter by implying ambiguously that the "severed head will never return." The image works both for the Oxford head, Fitzralph, whom the poet seems to argue should be removed from his powerful position – and, of course, Fitzralph's tenure was ending in 1334 as the Schism persisted – and for the exiled students who hope to remain at Stamford. The poet endows these scholars, perhaps his colleagues, with a certain ethos that marks them as an essential part of the Oxford corpus, a head that will never return to its abusive body.

Still, this rhetoric of decapitation intimates a national problem. The act of beheading historically signifies a ritual of nationhood, a moment of emergent community identity, from the very moment David claimed the head of the Philistine giant Goliath and Israel was affirmed. Margaret Owens suggests that the display of the head "serves as a striking, unmistakable icon signifying not only the defeat and demise of the victim but, more crucially, the transfer of political power that is often consolidated through this act of violence."[80] The fragmentation of the enemy's body inversely denotes the wholeness of the victor. But, as Owens clarifies, representations of decapitation also serve as "symbolic markers of national, ethnic, and religious difference."[81] Owens' equation holds for the Stamford poet who sees not one head but two in this poem of decapitation. For the Stamford poet, the severed head figures as a symbol of the separation and autonomy of the alternative *studia* at Stamford. He further views Oxford, signified through Fitzralph, as a different body altogether. It is, then, a case of two different heads and two different bodies, Oxford and Stamford, northern and southern. This duality illustrates the inherent antagonism that problematizes North–South relations, not merely in the university but broadly in the realm of England.

The University Nations and the English Nation

Clearly, the Stamford Schism caught the attention of more than just the body of Oxford scholars and their chancellor who witnessed the break first-hand. Not only does King Edward III involve himself significantly in the dispute, but we can also see the people of Stamford and larger Lincolnshire – as well as the Durham monks responsible for St Leonard's Priory where the exiled scholars resided – as stakeholders in the ensuing debate as to whether the Stamford university should remain. Indeed, interest stretches across the North and East of England beyond Oxford, making clear the national implications of the conflict. If some Stamford *studia* that existed prior to the events of late 1333 was already perceived as a threat to Oxford or Cambridge prior to 1334, then, with the advent of the Stamford Schism, "[t]he danger becomes acute."[82] To make matters worse for the schismatics, King Edward III and Queen Philippa appear to have had significant connections to both Oxford and Cambridge. One of Oxford's first documented responses to the secession was to write a letter to Queen Philippa in which she is praised as "a careful nurse to students all at Oxford."[83] Such praise implies that the Queen was already a noted supporter, financially or otherwise, of the university and its clerks. What is more, just a few years later, in 1341, her own clerk Robert Eglesfield founded *Aulum Regine de Oxoni* (later Queen's College) in her honor and under her patronage.[84] Edward I himself endowed Oriel College, as well as further supporting the King's College at Cambridge, founded by his father Edward II.[85]

In their letter to the Queen, dated February 14, 1334, Oxford officials clarify their immanent concerns that "every day many others" are drawn to Stamford's "false assembly" (*et toutz les jourz treount aultres par leur fauses covines*).[86] They further appeal to the Queen as benefactor, asserting that the schism will be the "destruction" of "our university" (*en destruction quant en eus est de nostre Universite seu sont treez a Estanford*). A letter written in June 1334 by the chancellor (it is unclear whether this is still Fitzralph but seems too early to have been Robert de Stratford (commenced in 1337)) pleads for the aid of Henry, Bishop of Lincoln, within whose diocese both Oxford and Stamford lie. Like the regents' letter to Queen Philippa, the chancellor's plea points to the seduction of his students by the Stamford school (*...passim quos possunt dampnabiliter alliciunt et inducunt*), with its degenerate sons (*filii degeneres*). Also evident in the chancellor's letter are the broader political concerns of the Schism and its relevance to a national divide. As he urges the King to write to Pope Benedict XII for mediation, the Oxford chancellor also begs Edward to "prohibit the hurtful and pestiferous and so new concourse of their scholars to Stanford under pretence of holding schools there, the same being both a hinderance to our university in particular, as well as a general nursery to the divisions of the whole kingdom" (*reliquum siquidem malum quod per omnem modum nocivum et pestiferum arbitramur, novum scilicet concursum scolarium ad oppidum Stanfordie pretext scolastice discipline, quod fortassis quia tam in dispendium studii nostril, quam in tocius Regni discordiarum seminiarium generale redundare*).[87] The chancellor's appeal to "divisions of the whole kingdom" should not be surprising, given that the Schism is prompted by disputes between northern and southern students and, also, that the migration occurred at a politically precarious moment for England. Doubtless, the timing of the Schism inhibited the cause of the Stamford masters and students, as the King was engaged with Scotland in this period leading up to the Hundred Years War and wanted a quick resolution. Fletcher points out, "From 1332–37 the administrative capital of the kingdom was to all intents and purposes York."[88] The development of the Auld Alliance between King David II and the

French threatened England to the North and the South of its borders. We might imagine that Edward cared little to entertain the sort of internal conflict at his universities that the Stamford Schism signified and that pointed to what was in the country, even by this point, a chronic North–South divide.

King Edward does not, at first, appear to take a one-sided approach, having understood the complaints of the Stamford students against Oxford in their letter to him from the previous January of 1334. He ordered both the university's chancellor and Oxford's mayor to Westminster on September 2, so that they might "inform the King of certain matters and to do further what shall be ordained by them."[89] In a writ from August 2, 1334, the King orders cessation of all studies at Stamford, but he also explains his desire for "speedy justice to be shown to those who wish to complain of violence or injuries suffered at Oxford, before justices there, specially deputed for this purpose," and he alludes here to the letter from the "several masters and scholars" who imparted this to him. A panel of distinguished bishops (from Durham, Coventry, Lichfield, and Norwich) were appointed to hear the scholars' complaints.[90] Later correspondences between the King and the University illustrate his further investigation into Oxford's violent setting, on which the schismatics comment in their initial correspondence. It appears, however, that many masters and scholars in Stamford were not compelled by the King's writ to abandon their new university. For the town of Stamford, which was in economic decline in the early fourteenth century, the influx of students was a boon. As John Fletcher explains, "It could be that the readiness of the townsfolk of Stamford to assist the migrating scholars by providing suitable accommodation is one explanation of their reluctance to leave the town and return to Oxford."[91] Indeed, there seems also to have been significant violence in Oxford at this time, though it is unclear whether this was prompted by the return of some schismatics from Stamford. Wood claims evidence that "divers persons armed, gathered in unlawful meetings, committed several outrages both by day and night, killed some, wounded others, and took away divers goods ... but whether these Malefactors were Scholars or Townsmen, or Northern or Southern Clerks, I find it nowhere expressed."[92] So, we should not wonder why the scholars are not easily dispersed back to Oxford.[93] On November 1, 1334, repeating his demands from the October decree, Edward again directs the sheriff of Lincoln to Stamford in order to proclaim that "none shall presume to hold study or exercise scholastic acts elsewhere than in the King's universities, under pain of forfeiture," and the King further asks for "the names of these whom he shall find doing the contrary after this proclamation."[94] By March 1335, many of the students were dispersed, but half of the original thirty-six scholars in question came back and began their studies again. By July 1335, well after his initial prohibition, King Edward was expectedly out of patience and, thus, disbanded the *studia*, taking the names of the remaining scholars and confiscating all their goods. A list of schismatics was produced by either the Lincolnshire sheriff or escheator William Trussell, who was also sent to Stamford. The list included nearly forty names in all, with seventeen masters, one bachelor, six parish priests, and fourteen students, besides "many scholars of a lower order and servants."[95] New Oxford chancellor Robert de Stratford would write a letter to his counterparts at Cambridge in April 1337 encouraging the university to have nothing to do with William de Barneby, one of the chief Stamford schismatics.[96] That these scholars would remain at the Stamford school in the face of royal decree testifies to the power of the town's draw and to the persistent threats that might await the scholars back at Oxford. But their defiant stasis also illustrates exactly the threat posed to Oxford and Cambridge by the Schism.

The contest of nations in the medieval English universities is remarkable in that it performs in miniature the ideological and psychological antagonisms of the larger medieval North–South divide. Neither ranged across broad geographies (above and below the Humber) nor feuding across historical borders (as I noted in William of Malmesbury's relationship to Bede), these northern and southern scholars faced off in the tiny confines of their colleges and towns. Despite the intensely local nature of the conflict, the university nations threatened the stability of England's two great "fountains of knowledge," Oxford and Cambridge, which were fast becoming intellectual symbols of the English realm. In this symbolism lies the significance of the Stamford Schism, which, more clearly than any other episode between the nations at the medieval universities, illustrates the connectivity of these institutions to the national fabric. The Stamford Schism imperiled the university as signifier of England's growing cultural and political strength and its emboldened nationalism on the European stage at a time when the nation began to reassert itself internationally under King Edward III.

Despite the seeming finality of the Schism, violent struggles between the nations at Oxford and Cambridge continued well after 1335. Kibre notes that in 1389 another pitched battle took place between the Welsh and southern students against the northern students. The northerners were victorious and they pressed their victory by sacking the inns of the losers, stealing their goods and driving the Welsh out of town altogether, "while shooting arrows at them and subjecting them to gross insults."[97] John Trevisa, the translator of Ranulph Higden's popular *Polychronicon*, was expelled himself from Queen's College in 1378 for his part (perhaps as instigator) in a severe quarrel between northern and southern scholars.[98] It is ironic, then, that Trevisa will translate several of William of Malmesbury's anti-northern diatribes in his vernacular edition of Ranulph Higden's *Polychronicon*: "*Al þe longage of þe Norþhumbres, and specialliche at ȝork, is so scharp, slitting, and frotynge and vnschape, þat we souþerne men may þat longage vnneþe vnderstonde.*"[99] Trevisa's patron, Sir Thomas Berkeley, brought Trevisa's text to London around 1387 for further distribution.[100] It is perhaps merely coincidental that Geoffrey Chaucer, around this time, penned his *Reeve's Tale* about two scholars from the "solar halle" at Cambridge who speak in a funny northern tooth.

CHAPTER 4

Chaucer's Northern Consciousness in the *Reeve's Tale*

London poet Geoffrey Chaucer must have known something of the nations in England's universities, for he famously plays upon the regional identity of two Cambridge students in the *Canterbury Tales*, in the story told by the pilgrim Oswald the Reeve. In concert with his contemporary, John Trevisa, who repeats William of Malmesbury's seminal complaint about "þe longage of þe Norþhumbres" in a translation of Higden's *Polychronicon*, Chaucer mimics northern English dialect in the speech of his two clerks, John and Alleyn. Considered one of the most striking instances of regionalism in medieval English literature, Chaucer's use of northern tongue in the *Reeve's Tale* has monopolized critical reception of the story and provoked many readers to hear Chaucer's wit ringing in the clerks' odd northern dialect set against Chaucer's London English. We are meant to laugh at John's proverb – "Man sal taa of twa thynges: / Slyk as he fyndes, or taa slyk as he bryngges" (I, 4129–30) – just as we are supposed to snicker at the muddied students chasing their manciple's horse through the fens of Cambridgeshire, northern bumpkins duped by the crafty miller Symkyn. Yet, there is nothing funny about the violence perpetrated by John and Alleyn later in the tale – the rape of Symkyn's daughter Malyne or the beating of the Miller himself. The darkness of the tale's finale befits the choleric Reeve, who aims to *quit* the pilgrim Miller with his tale, and it arguably unnerves most of the pilgrims who are the Reeve's immediate audience. *The Reeve's Tale*, then, intimates a far more complex northern consciousness in the "Father of English Poetry" than we might have first guessed.

Recent regionally inflected readings of Middle English texts have posited the notion of a provincialism that participates in the larger conversation of nation. Thorlac Turville-Petre claims of the early fourteenth-century poem *Havelok the Dane*, "The integration of divided loyalties is the driving force behind *Havelok*, as it constructs a revised national story in which the Lincolnshire community plays a central part."[1] By examining the Lincolnshire from which *Havelok* emerges, then, Turville-Petre "stud [ies] the ways in which local communities expressed their sense of regional distinctiveness but at the same time demanded to be included in the image the nation had constructed of itself."[2] In contrast, Robert Barrett studies a substantial corpus of Cheshire texts that "attends to the intranational tensions between Cheshire and the larger English community," tensions that decry centralization over regional autonomy.[3] Such an investigation reveals "the strategies whereby local writers, texts, and performances maintain regional continuity in response to the administrative pressures of academic and political centers."[4] *The Canterbury Tales* emerges amidst the social and political turmoil of the 1380s and early 1390s. And like *Havelok* or the Cheshire texts of Barrett's study, Chaucer's text demonstrates an assured interest in negotiations of the local and the national with its diverse group of pilgrims from "every shires ende" (I, 15) who are forced to confront internal difference in order to achieve communal salvation at the shrine of Thomas Beckett.

Chaucer's position in London distinguishes his regionalism from that of the *Havelok* author or Cestrian writers. He does not pen his text from the margins of the realm, hoping to overwrite cultural difference and sheer distance in order to infuse his local place into the national imagination; rather, Chaucer writes from what is, in the late fourteenth century, the emerging center of English politics, law, and culture. London's centrality is not unproblematic. Noting the scant literary production of England's chief city during the early and mid-fourteenth century, Ralph Hanna finds that "before Chaucer, London may truly have been 'provincial,' among England's vernacular literary backwaters, just another locality."[5] Hanna's words and the terminus of his study (1380), however, localize Chaucer himself as a transitional figure, while Chaucer consciously places his own southeastern vernacular literature in the foreground of a national framework with London as the focal point. This telescoping is evident in the *Reeve's Tale*. In his sociolinguistic study of the tale's dialectology, Robert Epstein claims that the northern speech ultimately "serves to demonstrate that only the London dialect is the proper form of artistic expression; all other dialects become variations from the norm."[6] More than linguistic hierarchies, however, Chaucer's regionalism in the *Reeve's Tale* (and over the course of the *Canterbury Tales*) argues that London is the center around which the rest of England turns, whose gravity draws in provincials and foreigners alike. While the city is, as David Wallace has shown, "absent" from much of Chaucer's *oeuvre*, "it nevertheless haunts the works of the poet for whom it is a backdrop in his daily life."[7] By the end of the fourteenth century, London becomes the icon for a clear English hegemony in the Southeast – comprised of Westminster, London, and Canterbury as seats of law, commerce, and church – a designation cemented by the intense government consolidation in the later fifteenth century that I will discuss in the next chapter.

If we find Chaucer writing from London as the center of English government, commerce, and culture, then it proves easy to reduce his northern consciousness in the *Reeve's Tale* to a novelty. Literary historians famously have designated the *Reeve's Tale*'s linguistic northernisms the first use of dialect for comedy in English literature. J.R.R. Tolkien establishes what becomes a frequent refrain in the critical canon, calling the tale's northern dialect "primarily a linguistic joke" while also claiming it as "dramatic realism" and the product of "philological curiosity."[8] Critics in his wake consequently viewed the tale's dialect as shallow regionalism born of a few instances of the northern /a/ among other northernisms that largely serve what A.C. Spearing – echoing Tolkien – takes to be the tale's "consistent realism" or what Derek Pearsall finds to be its inherent comedy: a thieving miller bested by two "rustic buffoons."[9] Explicitly, Epstein argues that Chaucer's role in depicting northern speech in the *Reeve's Tale* "resembles [Edward] Said's description of an Orientalist," whose representation of the *other* seems "objective, accurate, for the purpose of 'useful knowledge,' but the knowledge is useful to groups already in socially superior positions, whose authority is further legitimated by their access to philological knowledge."[10] In this sense, the *Reeve's Tale*'s funny northern speech is meant to quell anxieties about a dangerous northern *other*, so that Chaucer's southeast might feel more assured of the North's place within the realm. John Bowers has called this communitarian impulse an "'inside job' undertaken by members of the ruling elite, Chaucer included, [whose] goal was the extension of a sense of collective belonging from the *polis* to the *patria*, from the face-to-face society of the city to the abstract community of the nation."[11] The North becomes an object of study whose representation in the literature of London and the southeast bears witness to a presumed inferiority.

The North of England, however, maintains a significant and sustained presence within the narrative landscape of the *Canterbury Tales*, which implies that the region has far greater implications for Chaucer than the linguistic humor and realism that has occupied attention for much of the *Reeve's Tale*'s critical history. Including the Reeve's own story, four of the eight tales set on English soil refer to the North of England at some point in their narrative.[12] In the *Man of Law's Tale*, Constance finds herself washed ashore "Fer in Northumberlond" (II, 508) where her own "Latyn corrupt" (II, 519) is hardly understood. The devil-yeoman of the *Friar's Tale* hails from "fer in the north contree" (III, 1413), and the Summoner sets his own tale in Yorkshire in "A mersshy countree called Holdernesse" (III, 1710). *The Canterbury Tales* draws to a close with the Parson's vehement rejection of the northern alliterative verse form: "I am a Southren man; / I kan nat geeste 'rum, ram, ruf,' by lettre" (X, 42–43). Katie Wales argues that the northern dialect draws on more than a "simple opposition between southern superiority and northern inferiority," and her history of northern English speech offers various historical circumstances that might undergird Chaucer's use of dialect, including the Anglo-Scottish Wars and Richard II's proclivity for Cheshire during his tumultuous reign.[13] Wales finds in the tale that "the mythology of the 'North–South divide' is intensified and complicated by new images of the political and ethnic, as the border conflicts and defence of the 'frontier' began to heighten the sense of an 'English' nation."[14] Given the focus of her study, which aims at a diachronic social history of northern English from the Saxon period to the present day, Wales does not further elaborate on her provocative comments about the *Reeve's Tale*. But her observations adumbrate the literary effect of a northern consciousness on England's emerging national literature. Such a comment suggests that we might profitably re-examine the North's role in the *Reeve's Tale*, and the *Canterbury Tales* broadly, as participating in a dialectic of region and nation.

There is clearly something more to be said about the North in the *Reeve's Tale*. Rather than focus solely on the narrative's use of dialect, in this chapter, I will suggest that dialect is symptomatic of Chaucer's larger northern consciousness, a complex integration of the English North and the historical phenomenon of the North–South divide. In reading Chaucer's regionalism in the text – from the simple dialect of the students to their violent turn that, nevertheless, undermines Symkyn's socially subversive aspirations – I will argue that the tale constitutes an attempt by the poet to measure the North's uncanny presence in England. Chaucer's Englishness has been a point of contention among scholars concerned with whether to see the "father-figure" as truly an English poet or a European writer, yet the grounds of this conversation most often consist of Chaucer's vernacularity.[15] I want to analyze Chaucer's brief but significant attention to England's physical, cultural, and political geographies, namely the North–South divide. In the *Reeve's Tale*, I suggest that we discover Chaucer's own emergent national consciousness and the ways that regional identity complicate and contest the social project of the *Canterbury Tales* and the emergent English nation.

Far in the North

Little should we doubt that Chaucer uses northern speech for comedic ends in the *Reeve's Tale*, but this is not the sum of Chaucer's northern consciousness. The North of England was not a mysterious otherworld for Chaucer, nor was it simply the proverbial butt of Chaucer's regionalist jokes. Various circumstances brought the North to the forefront of late-fourteenth century political machinations at the very same time that the country wrestled with the destabilization of the monarchy under Richard II and chronic war with France and Scotland. Indeed, Chaucer knew very well the region's major centers of political power – Alnwick Castle, Durham, and Bamburgh, to name but a few – and he understood the power of marcher lords such as the Percys and Nevilles, as well as the means King Richard II took to afford them power. What is more, Chaucer could not have missed the efforts the King made, later, to dilute that same power through the appointment of John of Gaunt, Chaucer's patron, as King's Lieutenant in the North from 1379 to 1384. Tensions between Henry Percy, the Earl of Northumberland and Gaunt, the Duke of Lancaster, led to Percy's locking Gaunt out of Bamburgh Castle in 1381, when the Duke fled the Peasant's Revolt.[16] In her recent and expansive biography of Chaucer, Marion Turner reminds us that the poet maintained many northern connections beyond Gaunt. As his feud with the Earl of Northumberland continued, John of Gaunt began cultivating a local lord, John Neville of Raby, to counter Percy's power in the region, and, to that end, Gaunt intended his daughter – and Chaucer's niece – Joan Beaufort to marry Neville. Furthermore, Chaucer's friend Sir Peter de Bukton was from Holderness, wherein lay the port city of Hull, as well as Bridlington Priory. As Turner reasons, then, the North, with its extensive network of castles and trade, "was not, for Chaucer, an alien marginal place defined by brutality and otherness."[17] Yet, as I contend in this chapter, Chaucer appears nevertheless aware of stereotypes of the North as culturally backward and brutal, and he deploys these conventions in the *Canterbury Tales*. And if King Richard II struggled to curb the power of his northern magnates, he also seemed well aware of traditional tensions between the North and South, playing upon the social phenomenon of the divide when he moved the Bench and Chancery to York in 1392, as Helen Jewell notes, to "spite London."[18] Bowers suggests, further, that such a move was practical, "an early experiment at distancing the offices of government as well as the king's *familia* from the antagonistic southeastern counties."[19] Richard also brought several northerners into his intimate circle, including the soon-to-be-deposed English Chancellor Michael de la Pole from Hull, whose brother Edmund (perhaps ironically) owned a water mill at Trumpington.[20] Thus, Chaucer would have known the push and pull of the North in English politics.

In addition to understanding the North as a zone of contested loyalties, both productive for, and dangerous to, English national identity, Chaucer seems specifically aware of the long history of literary and cultural representations of the region – representations that reduced the many localities and populations in northern England simply to "the North," with its funny speech and its backwater "bumpkins." As I discussed in this study's introduction, Chaucer's contemporary, William Langland, deploys biblical typology in the C-text of *Piers Plowman* to make a joke at the expense of the North of England, a joke that intimates old northern stereotypes while nodding to the North's problematic politics. In *Passus 1*, Langland cites the biblical North alluded to in *Isaiah 14:13*, wherein Lucifer sits in hopes of rebellion against God. Lady Holy Church hedges on any explanation of Lucifer's geography with a clear jibe at English northerners: "Ne were it for northerne men a-non ich wolde telle" (115). And, yet, in this passage Langland includes a Latin quotation that implicitly references Augustine's exegesis of *Isaiah 14:13*. Here, Augustine finds the biblical North both damning and salvific. He explains that "the devil had held dominion over the ungodly, . . . and all whatsoever there was of humankind anywhere throughout the world by cleaving to him [the devil], had become North." But, Augustine reminds us, in the end, that the North becomes the seat of Christ's return, for, as Augustine claims (in reference to *Job 37:22*), "Out of the North come clouds of golden colour: great is the glory and honour of the Almighty."[21] We find, then, that Langland's "typological joke" does similar work to Chaucer's dialectology in the *Reeve's Tale*; beyond the surface of its regional humor, the biblical North of Augustine's exegesis embodies the perplexing duality of the North of England: damning as the seat of rebellious and overmighty subjects (like Lucifer); and, at the same time, salvific as the frontline of England's defense against the Scots and their French allies (a "wall" of the new Zion, as Augustine explains).[22] Not to be outdone, Chaucer offers his own allusion to *Isaiah 14:13* in the *Friar's Tale*.

The Friar means to attack his rival, the pilgrim-Summoner, through the corrupt machinations of the fictional summoner in his tale. But the narrative's unlikely hero, a devil in disguise, calls to mind the desired and derided North of Langland's joke and, subsequently, Augustine's scriptural interpretation. At the outset of the tale, we are introduced to this thief:

> Withouten mandement a lewed man
> He koude somne, on peyne of Cristes curs,
> And they were glade for to fille his purs
> And make hym grete feestes atte nale.
> And right as Judas hadde purses smale,
> And was a theef, right swich a theef was he;
>   (III, 1346–51)

This Judas-figure extorts, "Withouten mandement," money from innocents through his position as a servant to the archdeacon's court. If this summoner seems nasty, then he quickly meets "A gay yeman, under a forest syde" (III, 1380) with whom he shares baleful affinity. The stranger admits, "by extorcions I lyve. / For sothe, I take al that men wol me yive. / Algate, by sleyghte or by violence" (III, 1429–31). When the summoner asks from where he hails, the yeoman responds, "fer in the north contree, / Whereas I hope som tyme I shal thee see" (III, 1413–14). Before we learn the true nature of this yeoman-stranger, we are made to recall, already, the same lines from the *Reeve's Tale* that place the two Cambridge clerks in a similarly-amorphous – but northern – geography. Chaucer completes his own typological reference a few lines later. When the summoner presses his newfound brother for a name, the yeoman smiles with admission: "I am a feend; my dwellyng is in helle" (III, 1448). As the tale unfolds, the yeoman-devil's identity remains, much like his professed geography, devoid of stasis. He explains that he takes many shapes, that he is "Somtyme lyk a man, or lyke an ape, / Or lyke an angel" (III, 1464–65). In these contingent forms, he works for hell while deriving power from God – "For somtyme we been Goddes instrumentz / And meenes to doon his comandementz" (III, 1483–84) – and he even occasionally achieves the salvation of men, though, like the Pardoner, that is not his task or care.[23] The duality of the yeoman-devil, his hellish origins and heavenly work, plays out in the tale's last scene, as he rids the region of the criminous summoner who he drags to hell on a widow's curse. Chaucer's typological reference to the North, then, remains true to Augustine's exegesis. The yeoman-devil in the *Friar's Tale* from "fer in the north contree," much like the biblical North of *Isaiah* and *Job*, proves both damning and salvific at the same time. The Friar's strange conclusion to his tale plays upon this ambiguity. He warns his audience, "Beth war, as in this cas: / 'The leoun sit in his awayt alway / To sle the innocent, if that he may'" (III, 1656–58). His caveat does not necessarily add up. We might assume the "leoun," here, is the sly pilgrim-Summoner preying upon innocents in the jurisdiction of the archdeacon's court, but it is the yeoman-devil in the tale who lurks "under a forest syde," waiting for the summoner, who proves "innocent" only in his knowledge of Hell (but not for long). The Friar's warning might be directed at his fellow pilgrims, a perfectly biblical message for sinners: no one knows when judgment will arrive. But in this very confusion, the Friar's caveat reminds us that the yeoman-devil from "fer in the north" has rid the region of the corrupt summoner. The devil is the hero, here, and doesn't this befit the perplexing figure of the North of England?

The biblical duality of the North informs the *Man of Law's Tale* as well, with its narrative of Constance's conversion of pagan Northumbria to Christianity and its implicit ties to Bede's story of the Northumbrian slave-children – from Ælla's kingdom – who inspired Gregory the Great to send missionaries to Britain in 597 CE. Chaucer might have known the latter tale from Bede's *Historia Ecclesiastica Gentis Anglorum*, but also he would have found Bede's account in the Dominican friar Nicholas Trevet's Anglo-Norman *Chroniques*.[24] Indeed, Trevet's recounting of Gregory's encounter with the angels of Northumbria immedieatly precedes his narrative on Constance that serves as the primary source for the *Man of Law's Tale*.[25] Both Chaucer's and John Gower's versions of the Constance story derive from Trevet, but Gower follows his source in detail by placing the heroine "Under a Castel with the flod, / Which upon Humber banke stod" (*Confessio Amantis*, II, 719–20).[26] Chaucer rejects the definitive Yorkshire landscape "upon Humber banke," within what would have been the Angle kingdom of Deira. Instead, his Constance washes up "Under a hold that *nempnen I ne kan*, / Fer in Northhumberlond" (my emphasis; II, 506–7).[27] As with the *Reeve's Tale* ("I kan nat telle where"), it is enough for Chaucer that we understand Constance to be, simply, in "the North."[28] The vague "Northhumberlond" (Northumbria) of the *Man of Law's Tale*, with its king, Ælla, nevertheless, grounds England's historical re-conversion to Christianity and, consequently, recalls the biblical North of Augustine's scriptural reading. For the tale's readers, the duality of the North is evident as a pagan land from which, through Constance (much as the historic slave-boys), Christianity will emerge once more into England. Suzanne Conklin Akbari argues that the juxtaposition of pagan Syria with pagan Northumbria in Constance's travels "highlight the variable nature of strangeness," but Northumbria "goes on to become not only a Christian country but part of England itself. It is both strange (then) and familiar (now)."[29] And while Trevet's own juxtaposition of the narrative of the Northumbrian slave-children with Constance's tale might work to subsume England into the larger European Christian community, Kathy Lavezzo suggests that the earliest readers of the *Man of Law's Tale* would have seen, instead, a story centered within a English national framework. The *Man of Law's Tale*, for Lavezzo, "signified not in a universal Roman but in a specifically English register" because Constance's very presence in Northumbria is divined: "the divine pilot of Custance's ship to England makes the English less Rome's holy subjects than God's chosen people."[30] But this "English register" also provokes specific thinking about the North of England given the conversion enacted by Constance of these pagans, with the biblical North – both damning and salvific, the place of the devil now remade into the seat of Christ's return.

While the spiritual component of the *Man of Law's Tale* proves compelling, so too is the story's subtle understanding of the North of England's liminal position between the hegemonic South and the enemy, Scotland. As James Goldstein points out, Chaucer veers from either Trevet or Gower by introducing King Ælla, first and foremost, as "worthy of his hond / Agayn the Scottes" (II, 579–80), and only when Ælla is in Scotland, "his fooman for to seke" (II, 718), does Donegild work to the destruction of the King's wife and newborn son. As Goldstein observes, Ælla's motivation for war with the Scots is never clear, but by the time of Donegild's treachery, "Alla has earned the reader's sympathy and respect"; thus, "[t]he tale apparently invites us to consider any enemy of Alla's our enemy."[31] Whether he veers from Trevet or follows him closely, Chaucer would have found in Trevet's *Chroniques* a jingoistic text that champions English claims against Scotland. Trevet had significant ties to the court of Edward I and his son. He may have written his earlier *Annales* on the Angevin kings for Edward II, and he dedicates *Les Chroniques* to Edward's sister, the nun Mary of Woodstock, composing the work in the period between the Treaty of Edinburgh in 1328 and her likely death in 1332, even though he might have continued it into the following years, motivated by Edward III's recapitulation of the Anglo-Scottish War in 1333.[32] Trevet's propagandist's vigor on the Anglo-Scottish Wars – *Les Chroniques* concludes with the year 1320 – proved relevant for Chaucer in the late fourteenth century, whether because of Richard II's Scottish campaigns, the embarrassing loss of English forces at the Battle of Otterburn in 1388, or, near the end of Chaucer's life, Henry IV's vigorous claims of Scottish overlordship based on historical precedent. Trevet appears quite aware of the North of England's strange geographic and political position when, in Constance's story, a messenger stops at Knaresborough in North Yorkshire on the way to Scotland to deliver

King Ælla letters on the birth of his son Maurice. Trevet explains, "*A cel temps estoit Downild, la mere le roi, a Knaresbourgh entre Engleterre et Escoz, auxi com en lieu mene*" (At that time, Domild, the King's mother, was at Knaresborough, between England and Scotland, thus as in a middle place).[33] Here, the Yorkshire setting is "entre Engleterre et Escoz," and we should not be surprised by Trevet's representation of this northern locale as somewhere between "true" England in the South and the enemy Scots. Given his support of Edward II, Trevet would have watched the King both fumble his war with Scotland and face revolt by northern barons such as Thomas of Lancaster, who attempted Edward's overthrow in 1322. And just a few months later, the Earl of Carlisle Andrew Harcla worked – without Edward's leave – on a treaty with King Robert I of Scotland. Lancaster's supporters had seized Knaresborough Castle in 1317, and the town suffered mightily during a Scots raid in 1318.[34] Chaucer does not mention Knaresborough in the *Man of Law's Tale*, but even this omission from what he saw in his source intimates Chaucer's political awareness. John of Gaunt held the honor of Knaresborough from 1372, but his hold was contentious, in particular between 1387 and 1390, when locals led by William Beckwith attacked, and attempted assassination of, Gaunt's officials while the Duke was away in Castile.[35] What is more, as Goldstein reminds us, Chaucer's son Thomas, became constable of Knaresborough Castle in 1399.[36]

Chaucer's northern consciousness is fully developed in the *Canterbury Tales*, and his depiction of the North and northerners proves a compelling blend of cultural stereotype and regional humor that, nevertheless, belies a more serious engagement with the politics of the North–South divide in late medieval England. Even in the *Summoner's Tale*, we find northern solidarity set against a roving friar hoping to exploit a foolish village. As Turner concludes, "At the end of the tale, the community as a whole joins together across class lines to mock the unscrupulous, itinerant friar ... [and] prove more than able to beat the friar at his own games – at wordplay, sophistry, and the language of education."[37] If Chaucer's engagement with the North of England seems, at first glance, humorous – the funny speech of the *Reeve's Tale* or the northern village's jocular equation for splitting the "soun or savour of a fart" (III, 2226) in the *Summoner's Tale* – then that humor is complicated by the strange desire and derision we are made to feel for his northerners. They are heroic in outwitting socially subversive millers and extortive summoners and friars. They pledge themselves with resurrecting Christianity in pagan Britain, and yet they are diabolic and, at times, utterly violent in their heroic turns.

Chaucer's tales suggest he knew something of the typical stereotypes of northerners held by those whose identities lay further south, but we also know that Chaucer's dealings with King Richard II and with John of Gaunt, among many other friends and acquaintances, made him well aware of the North's complex character on the English political stage. It is, then, not linguistic snobbery, or cultural stereotype or even political reality that informs Chaucer's northern consciousness; rather, it is all of them together. Consequently, when we revisit Chaucer's most famous regionalist mimicry, in the *Reeve's Tale*, we must appreciate the complex nature of his northern consciousness in our interpretation.

Unsettling Geographies

Even before the clerks' northern idiom, Chaucer subtly imbues the tale's narrator, the Reeve, with a particular cultural geography. If Turner perceives in the village of the *Summoner's Tale* Chaucer's "ability to delineate a regional community and its social and economic networks," then the Reeve's own description attests to the poet's anxiety over the influx of regional personas into London.[38] Like the northern students in his tale, Oswald the Reeve is an ambivalent persona, far more unsettling than comical. The Reeve's own Norfolk dialect associates him with the great number of East Midlanders who poured into London in the fourteenth century. Tim William Machan finds the Reeve's speech "unmistakably regional,"[39] and Thomas Garbáty points to the Reeve's Norfolk idiom as something "all Londoners knew," that the Reeve is a "stock figure in London."[40] Derek Pearsall further exclaims of Oswald, "That one of the nastiest people in the *Canterbury Tales* should come from Norfolk seems a gratuitous slur, and one suspects that Chaucer is playing on Londoners' contempt for parvenu immigrants from that area, especially given that they came into London in such numbers."[41] Oswald, then, occupies the uncanny space of a "common" London stranger.[42]

Oswald's East Anglia origins also make him one of what John Trevisa calls the "men of myddel Engelond" who "understonde better þe side langages, norþerne and souþerne, þan norþerne and soþerne understonde eiþer oþer" (II, 163). It is not surprising, then, that the Reeve can mimic northern dialect in his tale and also speak to southerners such as those on the pilgrimage with him. He is truly a "myddel man." This intertwining of the familiar and the strange in the Reeve's immigrant status and linguistic acumen carries over into his presence in the *Canterbury Tales*. His emergence from the "hyndreste of oure route" (I, 622) to the center of the contest in order to quit the Miller, his self-description of his "hoor heed and ... grene tayl" (I, 3878) and his "olde lemes" (I, 3886) and "coltes tooth" (I, 3888), his likeness to the "open-ers" (I, 3871) or medlar's fruit that is rotten yet ripe at the same time, all frame the context of an ambiguous North in his tale. The paradox of the Reeve outlines the ensuing contemplation of the North as "intimate stranger," which subtly underlies his narrative.[43]

Chaucer's apparent simple evocation of northern-ness through dialect in the *Reeve's Tale* affords a threshold into the poet's expanded confrontation with the North's equivocal identity and a glimpse into his national consciousness. Epstein's suggestion that Chaucer is an orientalist remains, for the purpose of his study, at the philological level. But whether the North is an exotic "other" or, to a lesser extent, a signifier for what troubles England's communitarian impulse, attention to the tale's action, specifically its violent end, and what I will show is an enlightened close reading by the Cook suggest that the *Reeve's Tale*'s representation of northerners – a kind of doubling of the northern other – works against its implied nationalist aims. The North of England was not, for Chaucer, an exotic land in the same way that we might imagine the "land of Tartarye" (V, 9) and the court of Cambyuskan in the *Squire's Tale*. But Chaucer certainly plays upon the North–South divide in the *Canterbury Tales* and he subtly deploys northern stereotypes and other cultural tropes that had depicted the North as an "intimate stranger" within England for centuries. Again, his representation of the North in the *Canterbury Tales* suggests that he understood the uncanny political and cultural character of the North. Patricia Clare Ingham explains that the very term "uncanny," a Freudian one, resonates with the submission required by national communities,[44] that nations fantasize their unity through acts of doubling wherein the problematic other is domesticated into the larger community. But such doubling or mimicry, as Homi Bhabha has taught us, "must continually produce [the other's] slippage, its excess, its difference,"[45] and in Chaucer's second *fabliau* the representation of the two clerks brings with it the full and frightening weight of northern strangeness, a grave threat to Chaucer's national imagination. If in mimicking northerners the *Reeve's Tale* aims at a literary surmounting of northern otherness to the benefit of the English nation, then that doubling produces instead a menacing North that undoes Chaucer's project altogether.

Elements of this entanglement of the familiar with the unfamiliar overwhelm the *Reeve's Tale* and its context. Ignoring Cambridge as the *locus amoenus* of his story, the obvious rebuttal to the Miller's Oxford setting, the Reeve instead takes us to Trumpington. The quitting game between the Miller and Reeve obscures the fact that this quarrel is not specifically Cambridge set against Oxford. Oswald provides some mundane details of the place – a "brooke," "brigge," and "mille" (I, 3922–23) – and we are assured that Trumpington is "nat fer fro Cantebrigge" (I, 3921). Yet the tiny crossroads is *not* Cambridge and we are denied the surer footing of a town setting similar to that of the *Miller's Tale*'s "at Oxenford" (I, 3187). If we consider the pilgrim's place at this moment in the *Canterbury Tales*, then we realize that the Reeve's audience is between Southwark and Greenwich ("Lo Grenewhych, ther many a shrewe is inne!" [I, 3907]), listening to a stranger from "Biside ... Baldeswelle" (I, 620) tell a tale that takes place "nat fer from Canterbrigge." The pilgrim route to Canterbury is well known and Trumpington is not unknown, but the geography in and around the *Reeve's Tale* remains unsettling. This always-liminal status is illustrated further in the sequence of descriptors that inform John's and Aleyn's origins "fer in the North" (I, 4015). The clerks are "from a town heighte Strother" (I, 4014), but if we find any surety of place here, it dissolves in the Reeve's "I kan nat telle where" (I, 4015).[46]

The clerks' vague origins should not obscure the fact that, like their narrator, they intimate London connections. This stems from the role served frequently by their college in service of the crown's administrative works in London. John and Aleyn arrive at Symkyn's mill from the "greet collegge ... / Men clepen the Soler Halle" (I, 3989–90), a likely reference to the King's Hall at Cambridge. As Alan Cobban has shown, the King's Hall garnered a substantial portion of its scholars from Yorkshire.[47] Founded by Edward II as the Society of King's Scholars and endowed by Edward III, the college "seems always to have been intended to provide a supply of graduates in both ecclesiastical and secular spheres particularly for the king's service."[48] The clerks, then, may have been common to London, employed in the Chancery or any number of other services. Cobban posits, "Even if Chaucer did not actually visit the college (although he may very well have done), his close court connections and career as a royal servant make it more than likely that some of the King's Scholars would have been numbered among his acquaintance."[49] Walking about London speaking in a regional tongue, the northern "soler halle" scholar like John or Aleyn might be seen paradoxically as both familiar and strange, not unlike the Norfolk Reeve.

Given the allusions to immigrants in London embedded in the figure of the Reeve and his narrative, the *Cook's Prologue* and *Tale* is an appropriate response. The Cook, it must be pointed out, is the only one who laughs at the *Reeve's Tale*'s violent finale, wherein the northern clerks "beete [Symkyn] well and lete hym lye" (I, 4308). The pilgrims, who "for the moore part ... loughe and pleyde" (I, 3858) at the *Miller's Tale*'s end, sit silently at the Reeve's conclusion, yet the Cook of London chuckles: "Ha! ha!" (I, 4327). The Cook's laughter is explained, arguably, in his affinity for Flemish proverbs – "sooth pley, quaad pley" (I, 4357). Perhaps the Cook is the only one who would be comfortable with Flemings and other immigrants, including Norfolk men and northerners, in London. "Hogge of Ware" was himself once an immigrant, who has now seemingly settled permanently in the city. Twice called the "Cook of London," Roger, in his own words, hails from Ware, a town north of London in Hertfordshire. Wallace notes Ware's reputation as a site of significant resistance to the Statute of Laborers in the 1350s and whose citizens played a prominent role in the events of 1381 (notably sacking John of Gaunt's Savoy Palace). As Wallace suggests, "The name of Ware comes freighted with suggestions of unruliness or violence imported to the city from the provinces."[50] What might the *Cook's Tale* have offered on the topic of strangers not merely lurking in Trumpington or in the Scottish marches but within London? The centrality of Roger of Ware and his penchant for alien proverbs foreground the reality of, and the ideological concerns for, the foreigner, the stranger, or the alien within Chaucer's city.

If Symkyn operates far from the city in the *Reeve's Tale*, then the London associations of the Reeve, the two clerks, and the Cook intimate the threat of newcomers and upstarts that supplement the depiction of the ambitious miller from Trumpington. Each of these strangers provokes anxiety for the multiple geographies that inhere in them and for the uncanny way their "real" and textual personas are conflated – the manner in which details of their descriptions allude to the "strange" in London. They come to embody marginalized communities enfolded over the English center.

The Local and the National: *Fabliau* and Romance

In pitting northerners against "deynous Symkyn" (I, 3941), the *Reeve's Tale* aims to achieve the containment of both. Symkyn's character offends in numerous ways. The Reeve overwhelms us with Symkyn's description, nearly eighty of the tale's 404 lines. We are told, of the miller, "As any pecok he was proud and gay" (I, 3926), we know that "Pipen he koude and fisshe, and nettes beete" (I, 3927), but more significant, "He was a market-betere ate fulle" (I, 3936). This local bully does not much hide the fact that "A theef he was for sothe of corn and mele" (I, 3939) and his wife is the illegitimate daughter of a parson. Both he and his wife consciously produce a spectacle in their processing to the church on a feast day, she in her "gyte of reed" (I, 3954) and he in "hosen of the same" (I, 3955). This is both poor choice and poor taste on their parts as the red clothes declare their ill-gotten wealth and their own social airs. If Symkyn's thieving is well known – certainly to the Cambridge students – then, as Craig Bertolet contends, "Symkyn's fellow villagers could have identified his wife not as the spouse of a wealthy yeoman but as a conventional medieval symbol for excess, licentiousness, and pride."[51] In parading thus on a holy day when all will be present at church, Symkyn and his wife "intend to show how much better they are because of what they can purchase."[52] Symkyn, further, partners with his parson father-in-law in order to marry his daughter "into som worthy blood of auncetrye" (I, 3982), which will certainly benefit him as well, and they will use "hooly chirches good" (I, 3983) as her dowry.[53] The tale foregrounds Symkyn's villainy at the outset, setting up the two clerks, John and Aleyn as protagonists intended to stymie Symkyn's social disruption, much as the Reeve aims to "Stynt [the] clappe!" (I, 3144) of the pilgrim Miller when he interrupts the storytelling contest. In this way, the tale signifies its northern clerks as unlikely heroes put in service to the greater good, symbolically quelling the social unrest of Symkyn's local quasi-rebellion and putting Symkyn in his proper place quietly grinding corn.[54]

The national implications underlying gestures to the English North in the *Reeve's Tale* seem beyond the realism, moral subversion, and atmosphere of *game* that we find typically in the *fabliau*.[55] But the *Reeve's Tale* does not lend itself to such a strict interpretation of the genre as does its counterpart, the *Miller's Tale*. V.A. Kolve has said, "Although Chaucer's program calls for us to hear two fabliaux in a row, he avoids the mere repetition of mood and material by altering almost totally the context in which we hear the second."[56] Speaking specifically of Arthurian romance, Ingham argues that "medieval community is imagined not through homogeneous stories of a singular 'people,' but through narratives of sovereignty as a negotiation of differences, of ethnicity, region, language, class, and gender."[57] Her comment is applicable to romance more broadly, and it complements Geraldine Heng's explanation of romance as a genre whose "objects of attention are crises of collective and communal identity – the identity of the emerging medieval nation of England."[58] But the *Reeve's Tale* also demonstrates an attention to such crises.[59] In a moment revealing of its national consciousness, the *Reeve's Tale* subtly gestures towards romance through an overlooked correlation with the *Knight's Tale*.

Symkyn patronizes the clerks, who come to the miller's house to solicit lodging after a long day chasing their loosed horse through the fens. Symkyn challenges them in their own clerkly terms – to "make a place / A myle brood of twenty foot of space" (I, 4123–24). Numerous critics follow the logic that Symkyn's mocking equation stems explicitly from the town-and-gown rivalry we witness in the *Miller's Tale*, in, for example, the carpenter John's dismissal of the clerk Nicholas' learning: "Men sholde nat know of Goddes pryvetee" (I, 3454). But Symkyn's metaphoric "myle brood" house finds its precursor in Theseus's "noble theatre" (I, 1885) in the *Knight's Tale*, whose "circuit a myle was aboute" (I, 1887). Theseus' arena signifies the Duke's power over his subjects in the act of its construction, in its sheer physical presence, and its function as an arena for a contest of strangers. Theseus' arena literally surrounds not just Athenian citizens, but prisoners and foreign armies. It becomes a site of naturalization, of gentrifying those who are unfamiliar, strange, and offensive. Theseus, according to William Woods, embodies "a world of chivalry where princes' wills preserve the order of things inherited from old times."[60] But if Theseus "tempers the chivalric with the domestic,"[61] then he also, specifically, domesticates the foreign, an ethic that informs Chaucer's own interests in London's strangers, including those surrounding the *Reeve's Prologue* and *Tale*: the Reeve, the two clerks, and the Cook. Though he tears down the walls of Thebes, Theseus encloses the leftover Thebans, Palamoun and Arcite, in the Athenian walls of his prison house. His marriage to Hypolita, his inquisition of the crying Theban widows – "why that ye been clothed thus in black" (I, 911) – his conquest of Creon for the Theban king's strange treatment of dead Argive bodies, and, again, his war theater, all serve to render knowable, and consequently safe, the alien other. In their mock-war for the hand of Emily, the two Theban princes Palamoun and Arcite are supported by whole armies of "straunge" men – under the "kyng of Trace" (I, 2129) and the "kyng of Inde" (I, 2156), men carrying a "Pruce sheeld" (I, 2122) or the "clooth of Tars" (I, 2160). Theseus masterfully surrounds these foreign forces with his theater where his own Athenian citizens, his true subjects, observe and, thus, come to know these exotics in the context of *safe* entertainment.[62]

The narrator Knight performs his own naturalizing act in the description of the two armies, linking the foreign, mercenary knights of Palamoun's and Arcite's forces with domestic, English knights:

> For if ther felle tomorwe swich a cas,
> Ye knowen wel that every lusty knyght
> That loveth paramours and hath his might,
> Were it in Engelond or elleswhere,
> They wolde, hir thankes, wilnen to be there
> (I, 2110–14)

A hypothetical "Were it in Engelond" modifies the "cas" of fighting for Emelye's hand, yet it also informs "every lusty knyght." Chaucer's English Knight speaks for fellow "lusty" English compatriots who, because of their devotion to "paramours," would take up this competition whether it was conveniently at home in England or elsewhere. His interjection makes the foreign armies more English.

We expect such explicit colonial discourse from a romance like the *Knight's Tale*. Yet this attention to crises and the resultant domesticating impulse witnessed in the *Knight's Tale* is at work in the *Reeve's Tale* as well. The everyday concerns of the *fabliau* become, as Bhabha might describe them, "[t]he scraps, patches, and rags of daily life [that] must be repeatedly turned into the signs of a national culture, while the very act of the narrative performance interpellates[sic] a growing circle of national subjects."[63] Symkyn's equation links his house to the elaborate theater of Theseus, which parallels the miller's own noble aspirations; all the while, we are reminded that his house is not merely small but poor. With stones jutting from Symkyn's floor – he is "sporned at a stoon" (I, 4280) when he fights Alleyn – and a hole in the wall of his chamber, we realize that the miller's own house is not so well built.[64] More than this, however, Symkyn means his house to become, like Theseus' arena, a sign of his own triumphs over the clerks, but his dwelling becomes instead a theater in which a contest between strangers plays out. John responds to Symkyn's mocking provocation to "make rowm of speche" with another of the tale's northernisms:

> by Seint Cutberd,
> Ay is thou myrie, and this is faire answerd.
> I have herd seyd, "Man sal taa of twa thynges:
> Slyk as he fyndes, or taa slyk as he brynges."
> (I, 4127–30)

If we have forgotten their northern-ness by this point in the tale, John's evocation of the northern St Cuthbert and his curious maxim spoken in northern inflections remind us that the miller brings clerks more strange than usual into his home. Chaucer is clever enough not only to mimic northern dialect but also to include the subtle detail of John's exclamation to the definitive northern saint. Again, the North is not so strange to him, but, at the same time, in the *Reeve's Tale*, Chaucer plays upon reductive cultural stereotypes he knew, which paint the picture of a singular entity, THE North. Symkyn's tiny house, his mock-war arena, will aim to naturalize the strange northern clerks. Contrary to John's dictum, however, these northerners take both what they find and what they bring.

Northern Doppelgängers

In the Miller's house, Symkyn and the northern clerks – "Right in the same chambre by and by" (I, 4143) – confront each other blindly, "for it was derk" (I, 4225), and the day ends badly for the miller. Darkness necessitates the tale's bedroom melee and seems almost to activate the frightening turn in the clumsy northerners, who then prey on the wife and daughter. In his own investigation of the term "uncanny," Nicholas Royle admits, "Darkness is a factor that stares us in the face ... when it comes to considering the various dictionary definitions of *heimlich* and *unheimlich*."[65] But darkness here, as a literal lack of sight or blindness, equates further to a figurative sightlessness. The Reeve's narrative is consumed with deception. The clerks first head to Symkyn's mill for a contest against an outrageous thief (I, 3998), determined that Symkyn "sholde not stele hem half a pekke / Of corn by sleighte, ne by force hem reve" (I, 4010–11). Susan Yager shows that the *Reeve's Tale* "contains numerous references to visual perception, especially examples of hindered or restricted sight," and Helen Cooper witnesses in the tale "linked ideas of illusion, understanding, and blindness."[66] Elizabeth Scala, further, explains that "[u]nlike the Miller's tale of erotically motivated trickery by 'sleigh' Nicholas, the Reeve offers one of nearly gratuitous deception that seeks power for its own sake, turning 'pleye' into 'force.'"[67] The tale's violent shift in the bedroom seems brought on by the lack of light. Woods tellingly notes at this moment in the narrative a "freedom" that unleashes the clerks' "natural" aggression, their violent tendencies.[68]

In the climactic scene of the *Reeve's Tale*, the clerks are not merely opponents to the thieving Symkyn but his unwieldy doubles. Symkyn has spent part of the tale miming clerical speech – his ironic proverb, for example, "The gretteste clerkes been noght wisest men" (I, 4054)– while the clerks have pursued milling – John will "se howgates corn gas in" (I, 4037) and Aleyn notes "how that the mele falles doun" (I, 4042). But

John and Aleyn do not come to double upon Symkyn until they inhabit the tiny confines of the dark bedroom. This doubling action most explicitly begins when Aleyn couples with the miller's daughter, Malyne. Aleyn claims the daughter's virginity as repayment for losses he has accrued, and in taking possession of her maidenhood, the very thing that Symkyn wields towards the refashioning of his own peasanthood, Aleyn comes to double on Symkyn himself. Malyne has been an instrument through which her father and grandfather, the village parson, play out their socially-distorted designs. Now, however, she profits Aleyn by leading him to the clerks' baked grain. Blinded by pride, much as Symkyn throughout the story, Aleyn climbs back into what he thinks is his own bed and proceeds to recount his sexual exploits unwittingly to the miller himself. Their ensuing fight sets off the tale's final chaotic moments. Before his own undoing, however, Symkyn quite literally reshapes Aleyn into his own image:

> And on the nose he smoot hym with his fest.
> Doun ran the blody streem upon his brest;
> And in the floor, with nose and mouth tobroke,
> They walwe as doon two pigges in a poke.
> (I, 4275–78)

Symkyn gives Aleyn the same "kamus nose" (I, 3974) he and his daughter notably wear, and the miller and clerk then fall into a pile indistinguishable as "two pigges in a poke."

Remaking the room by moving the cradle, John takes up the place of Symkyn, even the place of the miller's bed. John, further, doubles on Symkyn quite literally taking his place atop the miller's wife in copulation. Like the diminutive hero of Chaucer's mock romance, *Sir Thopas*, who "pryked as he were wood" (VII, 774), John "priketh harde and depe as he were mad" (I, 4231), performing, as Woods notes, a sexual grinding that parallels Symkyn's milling.[69] John's sporting with the wife seems both funny and frightening. Daniel Pigg, however, reads the description of John's lovemaking unambiguously as "[transforming] the sexual coupling into an act of violence."[70] Such a reading reflects back on Aleyn's own lovemaking.

The analogues to the *Reeve's Tale* all involve some sort of complicity on the part of the miller's daughter, whether this be her clear acceptance of the clerk into her bed or, in the case of *De Gombert et des II clers* and *Le Meunier et les deux clers*, a faux ring taken from a cooking pan meant to express the clerk's earnestness.[71] Diverging from these earlier tales, Chaucer's version suggests a darker crime:

> And up he rist, and by the wenche he crepte.
> This wenche lay uprighte and faste slepte,
> Til he so ny was, er she myghte espie,
> That it had been to late for to crie,
> And shortly for to seyn, they were aton.
>
> (I, 4193–97)

Aleyn does not proposition Malyne with words or ring, but rather simply attacks her so fast that she cannot even cry out. The question of rape here may never be answered, and Malyne's near weeping at Aleyn's dawn departure challenges the argument altogether.[72] Yet Pigg sees her crying as "recognition that she could not possibly prove it now," and other readings of the scene by Elaine Tuttle Hansen and Tamarah Kohanski, without hesitation, speak of "the Reeve's description of the rape of Malyne."[73] Nicole Nolan Sidhu clarifies that, though rape is not uncommon to the *fabliau*, "[t]he violence suggested in Chaucer's description of the episode diverges from fabliau representations of rape, which tend to soft-pedal sexual assault as a comical matter, devoid of sorrow or pain."[74] Indeed, the entire conclusion of the tale is, as Scala claims, "a spectacle of violence and aggression."[75] The clerks' assaults on Symkyn and his family complicate the tale's aim to domesticate the northern other and illustrate the slippages that are always the product of doubling.

For Symkyn, bringing the clerks into his home was to conclude his humor of both making the clerks more peasant-like, as himself, and at the same time making himself more clerical. Subsumed into his domestic space, the clerks are initially what Symkyn would have them be: doubles of himself that are ambivalently the same as him, yet inferior. In this way, they symbolically affirm the continuation of his thievery and his livelihood. But the excess violence adhering in Aleyn's rape and the excess pleasure the wife derives from John's unSymkyn-like lovemaking forebode the miller's demise. We realize, in the little bit of light that permeates the miller's bedroom, the moment when the double, in its slippages and difference, becomes, as Freud himself might term it, "the uncanny harbinger of death."[76]

In the final scene of the tale, the "litel shymeryng of a light" (I, 4297) from the moon effects a process of unfortunate enlightenment for Symkyn and his wife. In the newfound clarity of the bedroom, the full weight of the clerk's violent turn comes to fruition, and this is contributed to by one last derivative of *fabliau* comedy. Symkyn's wife commits an act of misrecognition:

> And whan she gan the white thyng espye,
> She wende the clerk hadde wered a volupeer,
> And with the staf she drow ay neer and neer,
> And wende han hit this Aleyn at the fulle,
> And smoot the millere on the pyled skulle.
>
> (I, 4302–6)

Like a "crack of doom," this figurative deathblow signals the end of Symkyn as we know him – he cries, "Harrow! I dye!" (I, 4307) – his larger-than-peasant body, his own strangeness, reduced to mere normalcy. Ironically, the promise of light in an otherwise dark room provokes the wife's misguided blow, a point that only further illustrates the fragility of sight intrinsic in one's confrontation with the intimate stranger and rehearsed throughout the *Reeve's Tale*. In the "white thyng," the bald head mistaken for a clerk's voluper, she cannot recognize the familiar from the strange.[77]

Stunned by her blow, Symkyn is helpless as the clerks "beete hym weel and lete hym lye" (I, 4308), but by their own final and brutal act, the tale's investment in the North has soured. *The Reeve's Tale* aims to surmount northern otherness through the comedy of regional speech and through the quitting of the economic other, Symkyn, but the violence perpetrated by the clerks implies a decidedly unfunny remainder of the North that redoubles not only on the miller but on the tale's nationalist impulse. The North becomes what Bhabha would describe as the "double vision that is the result of ... the partial representation/recognition of the colonial object."[78] The clerks' assault on the miller and his family does not merely fail to naturalize their northern-ness; it infects the miller's family with strangeness. As in numerous anxieties about the sexual prowess of the ethnic or cultural stranger that proliferate throughout western history, Aleyn fuses his strange northern body to Symkyn's daughter; and her anguish at his departure suggests that she takes pleasure in it. The wife's confusion at the gratification she derives from John – she too finds it pleasurable – further underlines the dangerous possibilities inherent in the stranger's presence. John's act defuses Symkyn's overt masculinity, making him strange to his wife: "So myrie a fit ne hadde she nat ful yoore" (I, 4230). At the same time, wife and daughter are figuratively converted in what Gila Aloni calls a "series of optical errors and confusions that ... reveal that those whom Symkyn believes to be the most intimate to him – his private property, his wife and daughter – are the most foreign to him."[79] Herein lies the significance of the Cook's laughter.

Knife, North, and Nation

The Cook, in a fit, exclaims, "'For Cristes passion, / This millere hadde a sharp conclusion / Upon his argument of herbergage!'" (I, 4327–29). These lines are frequently glossed in reference to Symkyn's patronizing acceptance of the two clerks as his houseguests and to his own anticlericism in the moment, when he mocks the two Cambridge clerks for their "lerned art" (I, 4122) and challenges them of his house to "make it rowm of speche" (I, 4126). It seems, thus, that Symkyn the "gylour" is "hymself bigyled" (I, 4321). Yet the Miller's bad experience with lodgers, his "sharp conclusion," is not merely mock-philosophic. If we consider Symkyn's description in the *Reeve's Tale*'s opening lines, then we realize that the Cook's close reading might mean something quite different, that he alludes, rather, to Symkyn's own knife with his modifying "sharpness." The arsenal of blades is so prominent in the Reeve's sketch of the miller:

> Ay by his belt he baar a long panade,
> And of a swerd ful trenchant was the blade.
> A joly poppere baar he in his pouche;
> A Sheffeld thwitel baar he in his hose.
>
> (I, 3929–31, I, 3933)

What lies subtly among these weapons is actually the tale's first evocation of the English North: the "Sheffeld thwitel," a detail of Chaucer's knowledge of the North that signifies much like the clerks' own dialect. The Cook's facetious remark tellingly links that northern blade with the northern clerks. Ironically, like the men within the *Knight's Tale*'s amphitheater who wear Tarsian cloths and Prussian shields, Symkyn bears a weapon exotic in its own insular way. Lingering "in his hose," the northern knife prefigures the miller's demise. Indeed, Symkyn carries the North in his pants, and the irony should not be lost. The Sheffield steel, familiar as a weapon on which Symkyn depends for protection and, more, for intimidation, figuratively redounds upon him in the northern students' violent attack on the miller and his family.

The knife, however, gestures beyond the tale itself, offering what can be seen as a fitting caveat about the North of England. In his own prologue, the Cook responds to Symkyn's fate with a biblical admonition: "'Ne bryng nat every man into thyn hous,' / For herberwynge by nyghte is perilous. / Wel oghte a man avysed for to be" (I, 4331). The imperative is explicit: one shouldn't be flippant about the persons he allows into his home. But the Cook's careful attention to the Reeve's story, more careful than we would expect, highlights characterization of the uncanny North lurking in the tale, and his point about the miller's "sharp conclusioun" suggests a more complex exegesis of Solomon's proverb on "herbergage." The Cook's "by nyghte" implies both the literal and figurative darkness that facilitates the violent assaults in Symkyn's bedroom. This is the effect of darkness, one's "being in the dark," unaware of who or what stands in front of them or who sleeps beside them ("Right in the same chambre by and by" (I, 4143)). Such darkness might not allow "a man avysed for to be," just as Symkyn's arrogance blinds him towards the dangerous potential of the two bumbling Cambridge students, just as he carries a northern blade on him each day.

The Cook's close reading reminds the tale's audience that the North is already within the borders of England, in "thyn hous," as are the northern clerks in Symkyn's dwelling and the northern blade in his pants. Symkyn inadvertently replaces his northern blade with two northern pricks that ravish both his wife and daughter and leave him in a bloody heap. Symkyn's knife, figuratively, comes back on him. In juxtaposing the North with the more immediate social threat in Symkyn, Chaucer's tale plays on regional stereotypes of the North of England, but the story also betrays a desire to measure the region's place, in the broadest sense – in an expanding English community, a desire complicated by the push and pull of northern England in the English political theater. If Symkyn has threatened the local Cambridge economy, then the North, signified in the two clerks, threatens England's economy of nation.

A question, then, emerges, that reflects on the ambivalence of the medieval North and, indeed, it is a question Chaucer himself might have pondered as he surveyed the political realities of overmighty marcher lords, war with Scotland, and rebellious subjects in his patron's northern holdings: what can one do about the "man" already in one's house, the man whose motives are shadowed and to whose potentialities one is blind? Perhaps he might respond as Lady Holy Church in the C-text of *Piers Plowman*: "Ne were it for northerne men a-non ich wolde telle" (115). In William Langland's typological joke, the North is both damning and salvific. In his own depiction of the familiarly unfamiliar North in the *Reeve's Tale*, we find Chaucer's astute politics coming to the fore. Much as the *Man of Law's Tale* intimates the North of England's liminal position between England and Scotland, even as it explicitly narrates the second coming of Christianity to England in the late sixth century, so does the *Reeve's Tale* puzzle over the North's liminal identity as either damning or salvific to the processes of both social change and nation-formation in the late fourteenth century.

In the figures of the Reeve, his clerks, and the Cook, we witness Chaucer's regionalism, his writing from the center, in service of its apparent opposite, nationalism. But by depicting such troubling yet common strangers, Chaucer illustrates, perhaps unwittingly, the pressures under which his own ideological narrative succumbs. His nationalist text is riven by difference at the very moment it evokes the North, the intimate stranger within England. Of course, Chaucer knew men from the North and had likely travelled to its key political centers during his life, but just as his knowledge of good friars and monks does not stop him from investing in the broad satire of anti-fraternal and anti-monastic literature, so too does Chaucer engage base regional stereotypes as a threshold into a sophisticated regionalism invested in thinking through an English national community. And perhaps what he realizes in this invested thinking is the impossibility of such a cohesive community altogether, a point of view we might expect, in the end, from a poet celebrated for his "Europeanness." Chaucer's regionalism, in fact, reverses the figurative centeredness of the pilgrims as a whole. Rather than bringing England together "from every shires ende," the uncanny North in the *Reeve's Tale* aids the redistribution of regional identity to the gathered pilgrims. No longer are they signifiers of a multi-polar England subsumed into a single body and marching toward salvation in Canterbury; instead, they reflect the still-disembodied state of the English nation, with its pieces colluding, crashing into, and repulsing one another, wilting along the road of a never-ending journey towards redemption. If Chaucer hopes to understand his own region in the southeast as a center whose unity will reflect out towards the margins of the realm, his preoccupation with the North suggests that what he saw reflected back was instead impracticable wholeness; rather than a city wiped clean of difference, London is, for Chaucer, populated by a mesh of Norfolk men, Ware men, northern scholars, Flemings, and others who call into question a singular English nation.

National narratives must work to deny and hide these ruptures, and we might view such intentions in the *Reeve's Tale*'s contemplation of the North and the ensuing repetitions of the North in the *Canterbury Tales*, but they are already undone the moment Symkyn's northern blade is named. This is why all of the anxiety and fear provoked by the Reeve and his clerks does not add up for the "hilarious nonsense" so often read into the tale's "brilliant connotative linguistic joke," a joke Chaucer's audience according to critics is supposed to have found "excruciatingly funny."⁸⁰ We might suppose that Chaucer desires to imagine an English nation in the *Canterbury Tales*, and in those tales where he considers the North, his fantasies are most promising and yet problematic at the same time. In its familiarity, the North intimates the productive possibilities of national fantasy, but in its horror, it only threatens to render sterile such desires – an imagined community snuffed out by the "Sheffeld Thwitel."

CHAPTER 5

Centralization, Resistance, and the North of England in *A Gest of Robyn Hode*

Chaucer's Cook wonderfully close-reads the *Reeve's Tale*, but Roger of Ware's own initial story sputters to a halt in a manner that proves quite productive for scribes within the history of *Canterbury Tales* manuscripts. Twenty-five extant manuscripts include the spurious outlaw tale *Gamelyn*, with most of these manuscripts situating the narrative after the *Cook's Tale*. As A.S.G. Edwards illustrates, for example, in BL Landsdowne 851, the Cook grows so frustrated with his tale of Perkyn revelour that he finally throws up his hands: "Fye þerone it is so foule I wil nowe tell no forþere." The Cook now plans to tell a story "of a knyhte and his sounes," that is the *Gamelyn* poem.[1] If we believe that Chaucer might have intended the narrative of *Gamelyn* as a potential second *Cook's Tale* and if we also recall how the *Friar's Tale*'s devil first appears, Robin Hood-like, in the greenwood – "A gay yeman, under a forest syde / A bowe he bar, and arwes brighte and kene; / He hadde upon a courtepy of grene" (III, 1380–82) – then we might recognize Chaucer's own penchant for outlaw narratives such as we find in the Robin Hood ballads. Unlike the well-developed narrative of *Gamelyn*, many of the extant Robin Hood ballads are short and narrowly focused poems. But *A Gest of Robyn Hode*, likely written in the century following Chaucer's death, affords us a sustained and episodic text that engages the North–South divide from a perspective quite different from Chaucer's southerly-orientated view.

Critics have long regarded the fifteenth-century *Gest* as a distinctly northern text. The extant prints of the *Gest*, as Masa Ikagami has shown, clearly demonstrate dialect characteristics common to the general area of southern Yorkshire where the ballad's events are said to take place.[2] The narrative, further, references various northern locales. At the outset of the poem, Robin instructs Little John, Much the Miller's Son, and Will Scarlet to "walke up to the Saylis, / And so to Watlinge Strete / And wayte after some unkuth gest" (69–71).[3] Later, disguised as an agreeable archer named Reynold Greenleaf, Little John tells the Sheriff of

Nottingham that he comes from "Holdernes" (593) in East Yorkshire. We learn at one point that Robin Hood has relieved Plumpton Park within "the compasse of Lancasshyre" (1425) of its deer, and in the ballad's conclusion Robin Hood goes to his death at "Kyrkely" (1815) in West Yorkshire. Speaking specifically of the early Robin Hood poems, R.B. Dobson and John Taylor concede, "the association of Robin and his band of outlaws with a comparatively confined area of northern England is one of the most distinctive features of the greenwood ballads, a feature shared by few of the other items in the repertory of so-called traditional ballads."[4] Yet, despite this near consensus, critics have rarely read the ballad in a regional context.

The *Gest*'s northern-ness is significant given the period in which it was probably composed, the late fifteenth century – one of the more turbulent ages in England's history.[5] Amidst the Wars of the Roses, the decline of the Lancastrian monarchy, the rise and fall of the Yorkists, and the coming of the Tudors, England's government underwent substantial and lasting centralization.[6] Consolidation of power to a southern-based government and monarch seemed to spell an end to the independence of the North of England, the autonomy of which was bound up in its long history of rebellion and, more recently, in the provincial rule of its great magnates, of whom the Percys and Nevilles are exemplars.[7] These men maintained great private armies and held vast estates, and their loyalty to the crown was tenuous. Throughout the Middle Ages, northern sentiments for independence never waned.

Beyond regional jurisdiction, however, centralization provoked a crisis of sovereignty, playing out debates on the sovereign's status: particularly, whether a monarch's authority was ceded to him conditionally by the people or whether it was unconditional. I suggest here that this question should inform our understanding of Robin Hood's paradoxical status in the *Gest* as an outlaw and, at the same time, a northerner who "love[s] no man ... / so well as I do my kynge" (1541–42). No episode is more striking in this lengthy ballad than when, in the eighth fit, the famous outlaw and his "seven score of wyght yonge men" (1555) ride out from the forest of Barnsdale with the King of England, himself all dressed in "Lyncolne grene" (1685). This remarkable band of outlaws and their king emerge from the greenwood occupied in friendly competition, "Shotynge all in fere, / Towarde the towne of Notyngham" (1690–91). The citizens of Nottingham, however, do not find it all in good fun. Unable to recognize their monarch, dressed in Robin's characteristic livery, the townspeople cry, "I drede our kynge be slone; / Come Robyn Hode to the towne, iwys / On lyve he lefte never one" (1710–12). Chaos ensues as "Fuly hastly they began to fle" (1713) until they finally perceive King Edward unharmed and laughing at their misguided terror. Riding down from the North with his liveried and feed army, side by side with the King, and striking fear in southerly Nottingham, Robin Hood does not resemble a base outlaw so much as he signifies a great northern magnate. Reading the ballad in this context reveals a distinct regionalism in the text, positioned against government and monarchical centralization and romanticizing a period wherein the northern magnate both served his king by protecting the borders of the realm and served the interests of his family and region. Robin Hood can be seen to embody an older form of lordship waning in the face of centralized sovereign absolutism. Robin Hood's and King Edward's ride from the forest becomes the last gasp of sovereignty based in mutuality between the King and his subject.

The North and Centralization

Resistance to centralization can be seen in various fifteenth-century northern texts. Patricia Clare Ingham has noted an example in the *Awntyrs off Arthure*, a poem probably composed in the Cumberland region, the extant manuscripts of which date from the middle to the later fifteenth century. In the *Awntyrs*, the Scotsman Galleroun and Arthur's champion Gawain duel over land originally inherited by Galleroun. Correlating the scene of their encounter with the political upheaval of the Wars of the Roses, Ingham calls Galleroun's and Gawain's combat a "useful metaphor for [outlying regions's] struggles with a London-based aristocracy deploying regional alliances and identities ('Yorkists' and 'Lancastrians' in its battles over centralized power."[8] Noting the regional determinism of this poem, she views Scotland as "a metaphor for regional concerns ... [that] offers a means at once to resist English moves toward centralization and at the same time to deny that English centralization complicates northern loyalties at all."[9] In other words, the far-northwest community of England could safely channel its frustrations at government consolidation through the figure of the Scottish knight Galleroun fighting for what is rightfully his against the English monarch's imperial reach. Comparing the *Awntyrs* and *The Knightly Tale of Golagros and Gawane*, Randy P. Schiff similarly finds that these texts "register regional reactions to processes of nation formation sweeping away the borderlands society that had fed off the almost continuous armed conflict of the fourteenth and early-fifteenth centuries."[10] Conflict meant money and power for provincial families like the Percys, Cliffords, Greystokes, and Nevilles; they used their private armies to dictate the politics of the region. But war with Scotland, ongoing from 1296 to the end of the Middle Ages, also secured their significance in England's nationalist and imperialist interests. As England's kings well knew, these powerful locals were the only ones who could draw enough support from the surrounding population to mount a proper defense. Thus, the Anglo-Scottish wars provided balance to the magnates's contradictory position within England as both servants of the crown (protectors of the realm) and "Kings in the North."

The onset of the Scottish threat coincided with the rise of Parliament in the early fourteenth century. As this body's authority increased, so too did checks on the king's power and on his capability to govern as an uncontested authority. Because of this lack of coercive power, it was, as A.J. Pollard explains, "both necessary and desirable for a king to rule with and through his greater subjects who effectively controlled the localities"; thus, Pollard continues, "political harmony and civil order depended on the maintenance of a delicate balance between king and greater subject."[11] Edward III's government took the opposite track of his grandfather Edward I by endowing great power and prestige on provincial appointments.[12] Richard Lomas explains the irony of this power granted to the magnates: "The consequence of this development was to give this small group of magnates an enhanced authority which enabled them to dominate lesser landowners." He continues, "they frequently intermarried to form a related clique, and they had no opposition in the form of magnates whose major interest lay outside the region but who had estates within it. Thus, an agency whose purpose was to enforce the crown's authority was tending to become the means of self-aggrandisment and independence."[13]

The size of their estates, among others, and the armies they could muster from these vast holdings made these regional lords significant military threats if and when they chose to oppose the government and king, which, of course, they did on more than a few occasions in the later Middle Ages.

The sway of these northern lords' authority may have reached its height collectively under Henry VI's tumultuous rule (1422–1461, 1470). But centralization, which had fleeting moments of success under Edward I (1274–1307) and Henry V (1413–1422), recommenced with full vigor during the reign of Edward IV (1461–1470, 1471–1483). The result was not only a significant loss of power by the northern magnates; a strong central government curtailed the regional autonomy of the North as a whole.[14] If any formal end to the North as an unruly region might be cited, it is in Henry VIII's re-establishment of the Council of the North in 1537, though there would be one more significant revolt in 1569. Though the Council began under Richard III, whose power and support was concentrated in the region, Henry reconfigured it as a body to control northern upheaval. For Henry VIII, the Council, in R.R. Reid's words, "solves the problem of the North at last,"[15] and marks the culmination of consolidated rule more broadly by the English monarch. As I will discuss in the next chapter, it was in 1537 – in the wake of the Act of Supremacy (1534), the dissolution of the monasteries (begun in 1536), and the largely-northern rebellion known as the Pilgrimage of Grace (1536–37), all of which greatly impacted the staunchly Catholic North – that Henry VIII took the lands of the Percys, and subsequent northern franchises, including Beverly, into his direct control once and for all. The culmination of centralized monarchy and absolutist power in Henry VIII's reign has led James Simpson, among other scholars, to view this moment as the definitive shift from the Middle Ages to the early modern period. Simpson argues, "only new concentrations of political power enable such powerful redrawings of the periodic map."[16] Centralization did not simply shift jurisdictional maps, replace provincial elites with friends of the King, and establish London and Westminster as the nucleus of English law; consolidation made possible the emergence of modern sovereignty in England – the absolutist king of Jean Bodín and Thomas Hobbes – and the modern English nation-state. The realization of the modern sovereign in England was feasible only after provincial power and regional autonomy had been seized from the North and its lords.[17]

Dating from a period only slightly later than the *Awntyrs off Arthure*, and before *Golagros and Gawane*,[18] *A Gest of Robyn Hode* can be read similarly as a text of resistance for the disillusioned northern aristocracy. Though the broad social appeal of medieval Robin Hood stories is undeniable – fitting matter for taverns and town halls – the ballads were as likely the subject of aristocratic performance.[19] Critics frequently have perceived the Robin Hood stories as a product of "yeomen minstrelsy," but J.C. Holt argues that entertainers "surely sought larger audiences and better pay" than could be provided in a yeoman's household. The only audience capable of such support, for Holt, was "the crown, the aristocracy and the landed gentry ... their retainers and dependents."[20] David Fowler's history of the ballad stresses the provincial tendencies of these minstrels. Seeing the late fourteenth-century London court as an "international cultural center demanding the sophistication of a Chaucer while perhaps deriding the provincial talents of the minstrel," Fowler claims that the fate of these now-cast-off performers, consequently, "became entwined with that of the great barons of the north and west, who were at that time engaged in a power struggle with the king."[21] Thus, while Robin Hood was likely a figure for royal and noble entertainment in London, he could also be a figure of protest for the provincial aristocracy and for the entertainers who found refuge in their courts. When the *Gest* or some version of it was recited for a northern audience, they may have found in the chivalrous and cunning outlaw a symbol of resistance to southern encroachment on their territory, authority, and identity.

Resentment of centralization is most clearly signified in *A Gest of Robyn Hode* in the role played by England's distant capital. In a text dominated by northern locales, London functions as a hub for transactions of injustice rather than a site for appeal to good law. For workers of treachery in the ballad, London is a place to which they must travel in order to advance their interests – particularly, to deprive the ballad's protagonists of land, life, and wealth. In the opening fit, Robin encounters the good knight, Sir Richard at Lee, in Barnsdale wood. To pay off the family of a man whom his son had killed, Sir Richard took a loan from the treacherous Abbot of St Mary's, York, for which the knight put up his ancestral lands as collateral. When Robin's men find him, Sir Richard is heading to the abbey to announce his inability to cover the debt. Robin loans the knight the money to pay back the Abbot. Already planning his seizure of the knight's property, the Abbot is incensed at the repayment of the loan, and he dispatches his cellarer to "London-ward, / There to holde grete mote, / The knyght that rode so hye on hors, / To brynge hym under fote" (1009–12).[22] Having failed to take the knight's lands through forfeiture, the Abbot aims to capture the knight's holdings through treachery via a shadily negotiated legal writ in London. Later in the *Gest*, the Sheriff of Nottingham speeds to "London towne" (1287) to render what we expect will be a biased account of Robin Hood's and Sir Richard's actions in Nottingham, Barnsdale, and Lancashire; in fact, the Sheriff warns the King that Robin Hood "wyll be lorde, and set you at nought, / In all the northe londe" (1295–96). Christine Chism suggests:

> the localization of law enforcement that accompanied the centralization of monarchical authority over law ... gave local officials the power legally to represent the monarch and gave the gentry and locally prominent citizens more influence within the evolving system of courts ... [with the] result [that] the already sinewy local networks that bound together the provincial elite could exercise more leverage than before.[23]

The North and Centralization 119

The Abbot and the Sheriff form a Yorkish clique in pursuit of Sir Richard's lands. As Chism implies, both men are figures participating in or working directly for a centralized administration in London, and they depend on that distant city as much or more than on their "local network" to work treachery. In the shire courts of the late fourteenth and fifteenth centuries, sheriffs represented the crown directly by, among other duties, propagating royal proclamations. Beyond court, they acted as lawmen on the King's behalf – declaring outlaws, seizing their property, and issuing court summonses, as well as raising the local *posse comitatus* to defend the interests of the crown against rebellion or insurrection.[24] Alluding to the potential for corruption in such figures as the Abbot and Sheriff, Gerald Harriss asserts that the centralizing authority of the later Middle Ages "was exposed to strain and failures, either through the attempt by central government to override local power or by the temptation for a local power to turn royal authority to its own advantage."[25] Yet if centralization empowered such lesser men and local powers as a greedy abbot or a corrupt sheriff, it did not necessarily do the same for the magnates. Indeed, consolidation of power to London siphoned authority from these ruling families and into the hands of the crown.

The narrative movements to London by the Abbot and Sheriff signal a subversion of provincial power rather than that power's complicity in London's authoritative reach. While the immense authority of the magnates afforded them opportunities to exploit lesser landholders – and they certainly did in some cases – we should temper such a negative view with the fact that these lords understood their precarious situation at the Anglo-Scottish border. In order to protect their own holdings, the Percys and other ruling families needed a loyal following of local men to aid their cause. As Norman McCord and Richard Thompson point out, "most magnates recognised that this entailed caution in exploitation of estates, for income was often subordinated to 'good lordship' to obtain a loyal following in dangerous times."[26] In the later fifteenth century, for example, peasant farmers and other prospectors illegally encroached upon and ate away at forest lands with new farm settlements. Rather than punishing the offenders or extorting them, the Percys frequently legitimated the practice by granting tenancies at will which "at least brought income, and could multiply [their] dependents and [their] supply of fighting men in dangerous times."[27] For the men of northern England, the border magnates were protectors of the realm, but, more importantly, they were protectors of the North. Exploitation of the local population would seem only to weaken their claim to the people's loyalty. A network between a corrupt local sheriff and London would, thus, undermine, rather than enhance, the authority of the provincial elite.

The Sovereign and the Outlaw

Unlike its contemporaries, the *Awntyrs off Arthure* or *Golagros and Gawane*, *A Gest of Robyn Hode* figures animosity towards monarchical centralization directly. Rather than channeling hostility through the figure of a Scottish "other" (Galleroun) the *Gest* depicts a northern Englishman, Robin Hood, attacking figures of local administration – representatives of the king's law – directly. Stephen Knight seems to be correct to say of the Robin Hood stories that "the concept central to the whole myth ... appears to be resistance to authority."[28] Peter Stallybrass, likewise, sees Robin Hood "legitimat[ing] popular justice against the official ideological and legal apparatus which claims to have a monopoly of justice."[29] What better way indeed for northerners to protest the loss of legal authority and rule of their own territory than by attacking new figures of royal jurisdiction through a chivalrous, cunning, pious, and revered outlaw such as Robin Hood. But Robin's anti-authoritarian dynamic is more complex than such arguments suggest, for he always reveres the sovereign. Though he rejects the King's court towards the *Gest*'s end, he will always "love no man in all the worlde / So well as I do my kynge" (1541–42). As Douglas Gray comments, "The ideal 'image' is an outlaw regarded as an agent of justice or a restorer of morality, opposed to the corruption of local officials (subordinate figures) rather than to the king himself."[30] Through the northern outlaw who is like a king and has a special relationship with England's king, *A Gest of Robyn Hode* evokes mutuality between the sovereign and his subjects and, at the same time, anticipates its deterioration amidst government consolidation and claims to absolutism in the late fifteenth century.

Robin Hood's peculiar duality in the *Gest* – outlaw king and legal outcast – corresponds to his perplexing relationship with King Edward, his seeming affinity for and antagonism towards the sovereign. As an outlaw Robin Hood is literally banned from society; he takes on the "wolf's head," a designation coming down from the laws of Edward the Confessor. For example, in the late fourteenth-century *Gamelyn*, with which this chapter began, the protagonist and newly crowned "king of outlawes" (691) is told that his brother the sheriff "hath endited the and wolfesheed doth the crye" (706). As Maurice Keen explains of the outlaw given this peculiar designation, "he had no more rights than a hunted beast ... the price on his head was originally that upon a wolf."[31] The outlaw could be killed with impunity; and his death would not be considered a crime, a homicide. The Italian philosopher Giorgio Agamben compares the medieval outlaw with the ancient Roman legal figure *homo sacer* (sacred man), also a social outcast, who, in his bare existence – excluded from legal or civil rights – could not be sacrificed but whose murder did not constitute a legal homicide. Examining Marie de France's *Bisclavret*, with its werewolf-baron, Agamben contends, "The life of the bandit, like that of the sacred man, is not a piece of animal nature without any relation to law and the city. It is, rather, a threshold of indistinction and of passage and inclusion: the life of the bandit is the life of the *loup garou*, the werewolf, who is precisely neither man nor beast, and who dwells paradoxically within both while belonging to neither."[32] In this way, the outlaw's confounded identity intimates his unique connection to the king. The sovereign absolute who "speaks law" may also declare the so-called state of exception, the place wherein law is suspended. Sovereignty, thus, occurs at that point where law and exception intersect, at that threshold between the juridical and the non-juridical. The outlaw's banishment from the legal realm – ironically through procedures of law – limits him to the very same space. Indeed, Robin Hood's and King Edward's relationship in *A Gest of Robyn Hode* is not determined by their adherence to, or violation of, law; rather, their affinity rests in their being bound up in the paradox of law's creation and abeyance.

The protagonists of the *Gest* believe that good law emerges not from London but only from the body of the King. Sir Richard requests that the Sheriff of Nottingham terminate the siege of his castle "Tyll ye wyt oure kynges wille, / What he wyll say to the" (1283–84). Later, when he frees Sir Richard from Nottingham jail, Robin declares, "Thou shalt with me to grene wode, / Without ony leasynge, / Tyll that I have gete us grace / Of Edwarde, our comly kynge" (1409–12). Robin and Richard are content to wait for this "grace" to come from the King. What follows over the course of the "fourteenyght" before the King's journey to Nottingham is a brief period of unusual and eerie calm. Everyone returns to his normal station: The sheriff "went hym on his way, / And Robyn Hode to grene wode, / And Lytel John ... / dyd hym streyght to Robyn Hode" (1306–11); Sir Richard goes "hauking by the ryver-syde" (1323). Though it is short-lived, this peace testifies to these subjects's intense belief in the power and justice of the sovereign. But if Robin Hood and Sir Richard expect the King's justice for the Sheriff's treachery, then Edward disappoints. The King, instead, declares Sir Richard's lands forfeit to any man who will kill him.

His act is justified – Sir Richard has indeed harbored an outlaw by taking Robin Hood into his castle – but it is also self-interested, much like the suits by the Abbot and the Sheriff. Like the Arthur of the *Awntyrs*, King Edward's actions suggest imperialist intention. The King seizes the lands of a chivalrous knight – who, like Galleroun, inherited his land from ancestors "An hundred wynter here before" (187) – in order to give them to a "new man" who will perform the work of imperialism, a minion whom the King can more readily call upon from his seat in London and Westminster.

Edward's pronouncement against Sir Richard relegates the knight to the bare life of outlawry and, consequently, marks the knight's murder as a licit act. Together with the seizure of Sir Richard's lands, the King's centralizing machinations morph overmighty subjects into the living dead, a population of legally dead men who the sovereign can dispose of with impunity. This is the result of centralization broadly, as the *Gest* figures it. Agamben ponders the way that sovereign exceptional action slowly and subtly becomes the norm: "together with the process by which the exception everywhere becomes the rule, the realm of bare life – which is originally situated at the margins of the political order – gradually begins to coincide with the political realm, and exclusion and inclusion ... enter into a zone of irreducible indistinction."[33] For the author of the *Gest*, centralization is the great equalizer of men and regions in England, through which all coalesce into the same poor life that lies prone to the King's divine will, and it is this will that becomes the central focus of the poem.

Nearly the final third of the ballad focuses on King Edward. There is no reference to the "king" or the "kynges'" possessions, enemies, or "wille" until line 1275, but from there variations of "king" appear sixty-one times in the ballads final 549 lines. This sudden interest in the sovereign does not stem simply from the ballad's use, in fits 7 and 8, of the "King and Subject" motif – a story in which a king-in-disguise encounters one of his lesser subjects who frequently treats the sovereign and his laws with contempt before the monarch reveals himself. It is clear that the *Gest* alludes to this popular storyline, yet the *Gest* turns the humorous trope of "King and Subject" into an encounter of high seriousness. The King is figuratively and literally confronted not with a crass laborer or a craftsman but a second "king." When confronted by Robin Hood's army of foresters in the seventh fit of the *Gest*, Edward remarks, "His men are more at his byddynge / Then my men be at myn" (1563–64). These later episodes of the *Gest* resonate with debates on the peculiarities of sovereignty that occupied legists, clerics, philosophers, and politicians for much of the Middle Ages.

It was the parallel between the earthly monarch and the divine – rather than the outlaw – that exacerbated theoretical discussions of sovereignty in the Middle Ages and into the early modern period. If the king could be seen as the all-powerful and single originator of law, he was, at the same time, merely the chief authority within law, ever beholden to his people who first granted him this power. The laws of ancient Rome that allowed for and excluded the figure of *homo sacer*, the precursor to the English outlaw, offered an exploitable source for both rulers and ruled in the Middle Ages. Holy Roman Emperor Frederick II had appealed to ancient Roman law to bolster his absolutist rule at the end of the twelfth century, but it was largely resistance to increasing sovereign power within Europe's many kingdoms during this period that led to renewed interest in a Roman precedent. The incomplete *De legibus et consuetudinibus Angliae* (*ca.* 1220–1260), attributed to the English jurist Henry Bracton, recalls the Roman *lex regia*.[34] This ancient legal precedent ceded absolute power to the ruler both to endow the king with legal superiority and at the same time to keep him under the law with the understanding that his power originates in the people. Ernst Kantorowicz illustrates how Bracton

> inserted a qualification of the maxim "Quod principi placuit" by qualifying the very word placuit, "please." Unlike Frederick II, Bracton ... deduced from the word *placuit* not an uncontrolled and God-inspired rule of the Prince, but a Council-controlled and Council-inspired, almost impersonal or supra-personal, rule of the king. What "pleased the Prince" was Law; but what pleased him had, first of all, to please the council.[35]

Bracton's concept of the Council-pleasing monarch was indicative of a widening philosophical gap between thinkers on sovereignty. F.H. Hinsley points out that the assertion of absolute power by rulers and the corresponding resistance to this absolutism by legists, political philosophers, and regional magnates "[initiated] in the more developed societies a rapid development of constitutional procedures and ideas ... organization of Parliaments and Estates in the interest of the magnates who were in fact increasing their powers."[36] The sovereign of the *De Legibus* was still powerful, still in most cases above the law, but he was bound by divine or natural law, the principles of morality implicit in rational thought and action and, for many legists, handed down from God. These thinkers saw natural law as the basis for positive law, which was conceived and instituted by the political body of the state or the sovereign but that was ultimately dependent on natural law.[37] As Kantorowicz states, the sovereign "was bound to the Natural Law not merely in its transcendental and metalegal abstraction, but also in its concrete temporal manifestations, which included the rights of clergy, magnates, and people – a very important point in an England which relied predominantly on unwritten laws and customs."[38] The idea of the king as both within and without the law is carried over into the Thomist movement of the later thirteenth century and to the Ockhamist/nominalist debates of the fourteenth century.

For Thomas Aquinas, God had created law and, in so doing, committed himself to its integrity. Thus, we may understand God and the law through reason and, further, we might act on this understanding. Aquinas notably denied the need for pope or emperor because natural law was, as Jean Elshtain explains, "unalterably fixed by God, the Bible was to be preferred to the pope as the authority even in religion, and the kingdom was a natural human community set up by God for the maintenance of order."[39] But contradictions in the Thomist doctrine of sovereignty precipitated the absolutist views that followed. As Elshtain asks, "if God is so accessible to us, what happens to God's omnipotence, his awesome power that stuns us into worshipful silence?"[40] The eleventh-century monk Peter Damian, in his *De divina omnipotentia*, had argued, notably, for God's absolute power and arbitrary will, and his argument re-emerges in the early fourteenth-century thought of William of Ockham. Like Dante and Marsilius of Padua, the Oxford theologian Ockham was an anti-papalist, holding that Christendom was not a political community to be ruled (by the Pope). But this was merely part of his stripping away the sense that God acted for any reasons other than his arbitrary will. According to Ockham, God's will was not always humanly comprehensible, as the Thomists had claimed. The result is a more distant God, a view that "diminished the intelligibility of the world and threw medieval thought and practice into a whirlwind of controversy from which it never recovered."[41] Nevertheless, in all these debates, the thirteenth-century legists's sense of the Roman *lex regia* – the choice of the people to endow the ruler with absolute power – remained, and controversy concerning who possessed the right to rule on earth oscillated between the sovereign and his subjects.

These debates haunt the later episodes of *A Gest of Robyn Hode*. In the seventh fit, King Edward's aforementioned charter, which offers Sir Richard's lands to any man who might kill the knight, does not have the effect the King intends. A "fayre olde knyght, / That was treue in his fay" (1445–46) informs the King that "There is no man in this countre / May have the knyghtes londes, / Whyle Robyn Hode may ryde or gone" (1449–51), and he warns Edward that any man brave enough to pursue the King's warrant "shall lese his hede" (1453) at Robin's hands. Subverting the King's own decree, the outlaw redraws the King's charter into a death warrant for the man who carries it out. The effect of Robin Hood's presence in the North here suggests that he has already accomplished what the Sheriff prophesied to the King: "He wyll be lorde, and set you at nought, / in all the northe londe" (1295–96). And the King's consternation is with Robin Hood rather than Sir Richard anyway. Though Edward asks the local men "After Robyn Hode, / And after that gentyll knyght" (1418), he tellingly swears only "wolde I had Robyn Hode" (1435). Ironically, it is Robin's status as outlaw that enhances his elusiveness for King Edward. Edward can only legally pursue Sir Richard. The King does not offer money for the head of Robin Hood, nor can he earnestly draw up any charter declaring some property of the outlaw fair game, because Robin Hood has no possessions, no quantifiable fiscal presence in records, charters, or roll books. He has, of course, accumulated great wealth in the greenwood, but no one knows (perhaps not even Robin) how much, and, most importantly, it is not his own. As an outlaw and, consequently, without legal property or rights, Robin is, as Keen says, "civilly dead (*civiliter mortus*)," and poor King Edward cannot legally assault a dead man.[42]

The complexity of Robin's character is exemplified in his assassination of the Sheriff of Nottingham in the sixth fit. In his aggression towards the Sheriff, Robin might be seen to act as an outlaw (one who attacks legal authority from the outside), but he seems to act as a harbinger of natural law, ridding the town of a corrupt official and, in this way, righting the legal domain. Robin's connection to the law is evident when he confronts the Sheriff in the streets of Nottingham. In this pivotal moment, he declares his eagerness to hear "some tidinges of oure kinge" (1379). To know the King is to know both the law and the exception. Robin, here, acts as though he is the King's own agent, acting on the Sheriff in retribution for this official's numerous offenses to the law and its office. Robin subsequently buries an arrow in the constable's chest and "smote of the sheriffs hede" (1391). Throughout the ballad, the Sheriff has committed acts that warrant justice. He is present, for example, when Sir Richard confronts the Abbot of St Mary's in the second fit. The scene makes clear that a local justice is "holde with the abbot / Both with cloth and fee" (425–26). In other words, the Abbot has bought off this representative of the King's law; he has put the official at his call and in his pocket, as Chism points out, "usurp[ing] a power reserved to the king alone."⁴³ The Sheriff is complicit in the crime. Further, ignoring what the King declared – that he would take Robin Hood and Sir Richard himself – and ignoring his own oath to Sir Richard that he would cease his pursuit "Tyll ye wyt oure kynges wille" (1283), the Sheriff ambushes the knight and takes him to Nottingham jail. This is the second oath broken by the Sheriff. In the third fit, Little John's trickery lures the Sheriff to Robin Hood in the greenwood, where the constable is outmatched and outmanned. The Sheriff, then, promises to uphold Robin's request that he "never awayte me scathe, / By water ne by lande" (807–8). Yet, just a few lines later, following the shooting contest at Nottingham (won by Robin), the Sheriff orders his men to seize the outlaw. In pursuing Robin and seizing Sir Richard, the Sheriff ignores the oath he swore to each man, as well the King's own declaration to bring justice to these outlaws himself. The irony of his murder by Robin Hood is palpable: while the Sheriff is executed for what the outlaw perceives as his legal failings, the image of the head of Nottingham law lying headless in the city streets betokens the absence of justice in the region altogether. Legal authority will only re-emerge when the King himself arrives.

The Sheriff evokes failed positive law; worse, in speeding to the King to condemn Sir Richard and Robin Hood, the Sheriff violates a foundational premise of natural law: *audi et alterum partum* (the right of both sides to make their case), the principle of fair hearing that descends from the Roman law that so significantly informs the English legal code from the twelfth century onward.⁴⁴ Robin emerges from the forest, dressed in green, as an embodied and corrective natural law, to destroy the Sheriff. One might ask how an outlaw can signify any form of law at all, but in medieval legal theory, natural law always precedes and supersedes positive law, from which the outlaw is cast. Natural law, then, stands outside of positive law just as the outlaw does.

Robin Hood's liminal status as outlaw, both within and without the law, informs his relationship to the King. Though it is the foundation on which positive law stands, natural law also dictates the King's ability to go beyond the law. The early twentieth-century German jurist Carl Schmitt famously argues that the sovereign is "he who decides upon the exception,"⁴⁵ but the notion of the sovereign exception comes from the sixth-century Justinian Code, which medieval legists, in their zeal for Roman law, appropriated for debates on sovereignty in the early Middle Ages. Michael Wilks explains the place of the exception for these medieval thinkers; he notes that there will always remain cases which the existing law does not cover, or cases of emergency or special circumstances in which it would be detrimental to the common good, to the *status republicae*, to enforce the law as it stands. In these cases equity (which may be equated with *justitia* or natural law) demands that the law should be ignored: it has temporarily ceased to conform to the standards of ultimate rightness which give it validity and force. A "case of necessity" thus becomes seen as an occasion when natural-divine law, which transcends positive law, is directly involved. Consequently, it is a sacred duty for the ruler as animate divine natural law to override the provisions of the common law of the community.[46]

Wilks' account alludes to the interconnectedness of natural law and the sovereign exception. It is in the cause of natural or divine law, the rightness of which can never be questioned, that the King declares himself beyond positive law, a kind of constitutional dictatorship.[47] We can see, then, how the idea of natural law and the figures of the sovereign and the outlaw correspond. The King's ability to declare someone outside of the law affirms his position as originator of positive law while also calling to mind his capacity to declare himself beyond the law, a declaration allowed for by natural law. The King's authority to declare the state of exception, the state wherein he acts beyond the law, testifies to his boundless authority, and it is this power that legists labor to counteract in the Middle Ages when they contend that even the king must adhere to natural law. The outlaw is, then, implicated in the defining actions of sovereign power. Both the King and the outlaw prove exceptions to positive law. Robin Hood, as an outlaw existing outside of the law and, at the same time, embodying natural law, parallels the figure of the King.

Robin's confrontation with figures of positive law (the Sheriff) or with the *polis* itself (Nottingham, London) foregrounds the dichotomy between nature and politics, between natural law and positive law, in the *Gest*.[48] Robin Hood offers a kind of retributive justice and economic redistribution based on what he judges to be inherently right and good no matter what the prescribed law of the Sheriff and the town claims, just as he asks his men to pick out a guest on the road by Barnsdale Forrest that "wol be a good felawe" (56). Even in the time of Bracton, such questions of the King's power – where and how the sovereign corresponded to natural law – were already under debate. Hinsley explains,

> Already before the end of the thirteenth century men who maintained, like Bracton, that the king had no equal or superior in some respects ... also insisted that the king could not make or modify laws without the agreement of his barons ... It was not long before some men began to urge that the

meaning of the Roman "lex regia" was that supremacy resided rather in the community in the sense that the original right of the People had been transferred to the monarch only as the temporary concession of an office which the People could at any time revoke.[49]

But, in this complex argument of one-upmanship, the crown's own legists countered. If the kingdom's subjects

> sought security against the [c]rown by grounding their rights – and especially those in property and from the contract of government – in natural law, which placed them above the reach of positive law, of statute, of the state [then] [t]he [c]rown supplemented its growing insistence that the rights and the powers acquired by parliaments were privileges arising from positive law, conceded by the state and freely revocable by the ruler, with an equally marked insistence that kings were God's agents who could not alienate their powers.[50]

Centralization in late medieval England aided the ever-strengthening crown's argument because it sought to capture provincial estates, offices and titles and, consequently, to head off future resistance (including that of the provincial elite). This is not merely an assertion of sovereign power but a redefinition of natural law. No longer the ultimate check on the King's power, natural law becomes the will of the divinely sanctioned sovereign. This is symptomatic of a shift in terms of sovereignty in western Europe.

In all their emphasis on rational law and the sovereign's relationship to his subjects, the Thomists actually allowed for the sovereign exception. Wilks explains that, for Aquinas, an "exceptional event in which human [or positive] law fails to conform to natural law becomes a period of emergency, a state of necessity in which all law ceases … [which] provides the justification for the ruler to act absolutely in certain cases."[51] Natural law, as the foundation on which positive law is built, provides a failsafe when positive law proves inadequate. For the nominalists, however, "natural law" corresponds to the King's absolute authority. Elshtain notes, "When Ockham appeals to nature and natural law, he means a law imposed on human beings and the universe by divine fiat – an outside coercive and impositional command: the primacy of will over reason."[52] This redefinition of natural law will later bear on new assertions of sovereign rule in the following centuries, in Bodin and Hobbes. But the change is evident already in the later fits of the *Gest*.

In the aftermath of Robin Hood's encounter with the King in the forest, a shift takes place in which the outlaw ceases to be a figurative check against corrupt law and even sovereign authority and becomes fully immersed within the sovereign political machine. Agamben explicates what he calls the "Hobbesian mythologeme of the state of nature," in which "the foundation of sovereign power is to be sought not in the subjects's free renunciation of their natural right but in the sovereign's preservation of his natural right to do anything to anyone, which now appears as the right to punish."[53] Agamben's view of the sovereign exercise of natural right testifies to that redefinition of natural law against which the *Gest* struggles. Government centralization – and with it the consolidation of power and autonomy from the northern provinces to the crown – replaces the sovereign who is governed by natural law with the absolute sovereign whose will is law.

What is at stake, then, in the final episodes of the *Gest* is the regional effect of this redefinition of natural law as the sovereign's will, wherein the outlaw is no longer an entity beyond the reach of the law but one merely awaiting the retributive hand of the sovereign. The ballad ultimately juxtaposes Robin Hood, as a figure of Thomistic natural law, against a centralized and centralizing monarch who is tied to London and who fears that the outlaw will, as the sheriff once claimed, "set his power at nought in the north londe." The King's coming from London reminds us of the center/periphery model under which a centralized monarchy operated. But in the scenes that follow, the King comes face to face with Robin Hood the outlaw, and the remarkable intimacy of their meeting intentionally closes the geographical and ideological distance between Barnsdale and London.

The Greenwood as a "Zone of Indistinction"

In the *Gest*, the greenwood serves the outlaw as both a place of operations and a sanctuary. Unsuspecting knights, monks, and abbots wander into the forest where they encounter either a playful or violent outlaw, and Robin and his men retreat back to the dense woods to escape the pursuits of the Sheriff. The fact that Barnsdale, historically, was never a royal forest, and that the Sheriff of Nottingham had no business trying to enforce law there, only make its inclusion in the story more interesting.[54] Gray argues that a "distinctive feature of the Robin Hood poems is the mysterious separateness of the outlaw realm."[55] He refers here to several aspects of the medieval forest: its distance from town, its mythic qualities – the stuff of medieval folklore, the Green Man or Robin Goodfellow – and the way it juxtaposes wild nature and civilized man. Speaking of the sovereign ban, the act by which one becomes "outlaw," Steve DeCaroli claims, "A necessary condition for the possibility of banishment is boundary – real or virtual, terrestrial or divine – outside of which one may be abandoned."[56] The greenwood of the *Gest* is just such a terrestrial boundary. Rather than representing the domain of the outlaw as a space of resistance and illegality set against the politicized spaces of Nottingham and London, the *Gest* figures Barnsdale Wood as an imaginative threshold wherein nature and politics intersect, where wildness and civility come together, and where natural law and positive law harmonize.

Robin Hood and his men are outlaws (and Edward is king) only outside of the forest. Within it, their identities muddy – both are sovereigns; both outlaws – while unspoken threats, acknowledged clemency, and playful reciprocity conflate in the moment of their encounter in fits 7 and 8. The forest becomes a liminal space wherein the King, briefly without absolute power, is entertained not simply by an outlaw but a great northern lord (the king of the outlaws) and his retainers, who – though they might resist the monarch because of their own great power – nevertheless defer to their sovereign in worshipful respect and service. The King has been spiteful and vengeful toward Robin Hood and his men to this point in the narrative, but, when he enters the greenwood, Edward calls to mind older ideas of kingship: the sovereign governed by natural law, the King of the *lex regia* who depends for his power on his subjects' will. The King and Robin, in this brief scene, do not stand in opposition to one another but rather in accord. Though this encounter ultimately anticipates the end of Robin's power in the North, it first recalls the balance born of northern power within national interests and sovereign authority within natural law.

King Edward's meeting with Robin has analogues in the "King and Subject" stories, also known as "King in Disguise," circulating in the same period. In these tales the King, usually incognito in some sort of plain garb, encounters a low-ranking subject.[57] Not knowing that he speaks with his monarch, this low type typically offends with his rude manners, his quick temper, or his breaking of the King's law. He is later reconciled to the King, after some embarrassment, and often rewarded for his pains. "King and Subject" texts have direct material connections to the earliest Robin Hood ballads. For example, the lone copy of the *King Edward and the Shepherd* poem is included with the only text of *Robin Hood and the Monk* in MS Cambridge University Library MS Ff. 5.48 (*ca.*1450). *Robin Hood and the Potter* exists solely in MS Cambridge University Library MS Ee 4.35 (*ca.*1500), another miscellany which contains a second "King and Subject" text, *The King and the Barker*. Thomas Ohlgren notes the significance of the Robin Hood ballads included in these compilations, where the other contents "may have offered source-texts for the *Geste*-poet to adapt."[58] Yet, despite the parallels that critics have pointed out, the encounter between King Edward and Robin Hood in the *Gest* does not proceed in the same manner as meetings between the King and commoners in these humorous stories.

In *King Edward and the Shepherd*, Edward III, in disguise as a merchant fittingly named "Joly Robyn," happens upon a shepherd called Adam. The shepherd complains that "I hade catell; now I have I non; / They take my bestis and don þaim slone, / And payen but a stik of tre" (34–36).[59] He brags about his great skill with a sling, and, as they walk through the woods, the King encourages Adam to shoot at some rabbits he has spotted along their path. Fearing that the "Wode has erys" (268) and worried about the "зong men thre" (271) who serve the chief forester by patrolling the woods, Adam staunchly refuses the illegal act with much protest: "Hit is all þe Kyngus waren; / Ther is nouþer knyзt ne sqayne / Þat dar do sich a ded" (229–31). But when they arrive at Adam's modest dwelling, the dutiful shepherd produces a feast literally fit for a king, a meal that includes illegally poached rabbits and venison that the shepherd proudly claims to have killed with his "slyng for the nones / Þat is made for gret stonys" (425–26). The two men and Adam's wife dine and play a drinking game, after which Adam displays further riches and skill with his sling. Upon leaving, Edward tells Adam to come to court, where the King claims to reside as a "marchande of gret powere" (575), and to bring his tally-stick, a device that lists the government's debts to Adam for his livestock. Yet, if Adam comes in earnest wearing his "russet clothyng ... / In kyrtil and in curtebye" (588–89), the King, in game, brings all his men at court in on the joke. The matter is "þaire gammen" (609) and the King swears, "зe shall have gode bourd, in certayne" (612). The King even wagers on the shepherd's poor manners: "Þer is no lorder þat is so gode, / Þouз he avayle to hym his hode, / Þat he wil do of his" (626–28). Adam is forced to dine with the nobles who, given his rude manners and shabby clothing, "alle þat hym aboute stode" (875) and think him "wode, / And lowз to hethyng" (876–7). They "lowgen alle / When any cuppe зede amys" (999–1000) until the King finally informs Adam of his true identity, upon which Adam "On knees he fel downe lawe" (1084) and begs for mercy. The poem ends here, incomplete, but we might imagine, as in other "King and Subject" texts, that Edward rewards Adam with some financial prize or some position at court.

Parallels between *King Edward and the Shepherd* and the *Gest*'s seventh fit are apparent. Much as the King plays a successful merchant for the shepherd Adam, Edward comes to Barnsdale in disguise "Ryght as he were abbot-lyke" (1487), and the King is met quickly by Robin and his men. Of the lavish feast Robin offers the faux-abbot, we are told that Robin Hood and his men "served our kynge with al theyr myght" (1567):

> Anone before our kynge was set
> The fatte venyson,
> The good whyte brede, the good rede wyne,
> And therto the fyne ale and browne.
>
> (1569–72)

As in *King Edward and the Shepherd*, Robin Hood and his guest dine on the King's deer illegally taken from the forest. In both texts, the dinner scene is a wonderfully liminal moment, wherein the law bound in the King and the non-law signified in Adam or Robin Hood blur into indistinction. The King is a sort of quasi-outlaw here, enjoying the spoils of poaching, but we might just as easily see Adam and Robin as the King's lawful servants. The very fact that the King eats his own deer makes their poaching suddenly complicit.

Similarities grow scarce from this point, however. In contrast to the circumstances of the feast in the *Gest*, the context under which the shepherd and Edward dine in the wood is one of defiance. Adam's first utterance to Edward upon their meeting is a complaint: "I am so pylled with þe Kyng / Þat I most fle fro my wonyng" (31–32). In the *Gest*, the faux-abbot elicits Robin's dinner invitation by displaying the King's seal, the "brode targe" (1537), at which sight Robin quickly "set hym on his kne" (1540) and proclaims, "I love no man in all the worlde / So well as I do my kynge" (1541–42). If Adam's motives for feeding King Edward are less honorable – Edward claims he can help Adam receive what is owed him by the government, and Adam relishes the opportunity to brag about the ways he profits against the King's will – Robin in contrast invites the disguised Edward to dinner "For the love of my kynge" (1547).

Robin's overt reverence for the sovereign insignia actually heightens the tension of the following lines. Robin declares to Edward, "Now shalte thou se what lyfe we lede, / Or thou hens wende; / Than thou may enfourme our kynge" (1577–79). He of course refers to the fun and games of the greenwood, but when his men all jump up and draw their bows, the King "wende to have be shente" (1584). Edward's fear for his own life in this moment marks the *Gest*'s most significant departure from the "King and Subject" motif. In those comedies of peasant fallacies, the King never fears for his safety, never lowers himself to implied victimhood. In the threshold space of the *Gest*'s greenwood, however, both the King and Robin are at risk; one imperils the other by his very presence. Despite his protestation that he always loves the King, Robin's outlawry undercuts the Edward's authority. At the same time, Robin craves pardon from the King because only the King may absolve him. Similarly, Edward, far from his armies and his castles, solicits mercy from Robin because he is exposed as a "mere" man in the greenwood. Yet these many tensions evoke a balance of power that proves profitable in due course for everyone.

In the contest of pluck and buffet that follows between Robin, his men, and the King, we glimpse the fairness and humility inherent in the natural state of the forest. According to this game, the loser loses his "takyll," his weapon and, figuratively, his power. Even more, the loser must then stand for a blow at the hands of the victor. This passage evokes a scene of similar contest in *Robin Hood and the Monk*. Here, Robin and Little John engage in a shooting contest, but Robin is beaten badly and he refuses to acknowledge John's victory or his prize (five schillings). He even goes so far as to strike John for his perceived insubordination ("smote hym with his hande" (56)). Robin's tyranny as outlaw king in this awkward moment is nevertheless repaid with dutiful service as Little John, ignoring Robin's offense, rescues the outlaw from the Sheriff later in the ballad. In contrast, the game of the *Gest* exhibits no such antagonism. The king of the forest, Robin Hood, loses this game of skill and humbly submits to the confiscation of his weapon, which he cedes to the disguised King Edward – "I delyver the myn arowe" (1619) – who Robin then asks to strike him. The King delivers a forceful blow, knocking Robin to the ground, the sheer force of which gives the King away. We are told, "Thus our kynge and Robyn Hod / Togeder gan they mete" (1635–36). Robin's reaction to the King's presence suggests a significant if mysterious connection between the two. "Robyn behelde our comly kynge / Wystly in the face" (1637–38), but we wonder when or where Robin has seen the King before? Robin's men do not respond to the face of the King but rather kneel because Robin does – "Whan they see them knele" (1642) – as feudal retainers should. The King asks mercy of Robin for himself and his men, but, continuing this moment of humble reciprocity, Robin returns the King's request with one of his own: "I aske mercy, my lorde the kynge, / And for my men I-crave" (1651–52). When all is revealed (that this monk is indeed King) Robin does not pounce, nor does the King seize Robin as the Sheriff had done Sir Richard. Instead, they partake of further revelry and celebration.

The end of the greenwood scene, however, foretells a less blissful conclusion – that this revelry will not be a lasting end for Robin Hood, for the law, or for the North. Granting Robin's pardon, the King has a proviso: that Robin Hood and his men come with him to court in London. Having already established London as a place of corruption, the *Gest* foreshadows Robin's own demise. As though aware of this, Robin counters the King's proviso with his own – "But me lyke well your servyse, / I come agayne full soone, / And shote at the donne dere, / As I am wonte to done" (1665–68). Tellingly, the King does not respond and the seventh fit ends. The eight fit begins as the King asks, "Haste thou ony grene cloth ... / That thou wylte sell nowe to me?" (1669–70), but Edward's appropriation of Robin's livery does not imply his adherence to the life of the greenwood. Again, the ballad has already clarified the meaning of London and, while conditioning our reading of Robin's journey to the capital, it also conditions our understanding of Edward's appropriation of Lincoln green. He will invert the hierarchy designated by the outlaw's livery, buying Robin Hood's autonomy both figuratively and literally, and bringing it back to London as his own.[60]

"To London Towne"

If the end of the seventh fit forbodes Robin's ruin, the *Gest* provides one more brilliant scene of mutuality between the King and Robin Hood. Indistinguishably arrayed in Lincoln green, Robin and Edward ride out of the forest toward Nottingham. The King has pardoned Robin and his foresters, yet the King and his own men ride out "as if" they were outlaws – "Outlawes as they were" (1692). As explained above, the people of Nottingham are so confused that they scurry around the city in terror, fearing the worst from the outlaw band: "Than every man to other gan say, / "I drede our kynge be slone: / Come Robyn Hode to the towne, iwys / On lyve he lefte never one" (1709–12). Their confusion is not mere humor. Edward will later laugh at them, but the moment of their terror highlights the remarkable nature of the King's and the outlaw's previous coupling. The townsmen cannot discern who is king and who is outlaw or whether their sovereign lives at all. The King who fears for his life in the greenwood when seven score of yeoman leap up with weapons drawn, the monarch who can be killed by the outlaw (in the eyes of the townsmen), is not a figure of absolute authority – but the moment is fleeting. We briefly forget here, in Edward's donning of the outlaw's livery to ride on Nottingham, what the ballad has already forewarned. The lightness of the moment only accentuates the radical shift about to take place when Robin arrives in London, a distinct metaphor for centralization. If Edward's and Robin's pairing recalls the mutuality of the King and his subject, at the same time it laments the inevitable dissolution of that relationship. Robin returns to London as a subject of Edward and, thus, as one exposed to the whims of sovereign power.

In London, under the close watch of the King, Robin's men fall away – "By than the yere was all agone / He had no man but twayne" (1737–38). Robin cannot keep up with the lavish spending of the court, complaining after a year in the King's company that "My welthe is went away" (1744). If his riches are gone, so is Robin's skill: "Somtyme I was an archere good / A styffe and eke a stronge" (1745–46). The intimacy between the King and the outlaw, between the King and his great subject from the North, dissolves:

> "Alas!" then sayd good Robyn,
> "Alas and well a woo!
> Yf I dwele lenger with the kynge,
> Sorowe wyll me sloo."
> (1749–52)

Robin "longeth sore to Bernysdale" (1765), but he does not suffer merely from homesickness. Robin's return to the North, distancing himself from the London court, constitutes one last act of resistance, one last assertion of apparent power, which he ritualizes when he "slewe a full grete harte" (1785) upon arriving in his familiar wood. But Robin's defiance here significantly contrasts with his murder of the Sheriff of Nottingham. Centralized, used-up, and rendered to a bare existence in the greenwood, Robin's rebelliousness now takes only a passive form. Once a figure of retributive natural law, Robin now quietly slays nature's beasts. Though he blows his horn and all "seven score of wyght yonge men / Came redy on a rowe" (1791–92), things are not as they were. Robin knows his forest rule is empty, his freedom doomed. He dwells in the wood "Twenty yere and two" but "For all drede of Edwarde our kynge" (1798–99).

Robin's death comes, in fact, at the hands of a woman "That nye was of hys kynne" (1804). The prioress of Kirklee's treacherous murder of Robin, in collusion with the knight Sir Roger of Donkester, testifies to the new North to which Robin has returned. Divorced of its autonomy, of the familial networks within which that autonomy and power were bound, the North comprises a series of corrupt networks that all link back to London. The scene of Robin Hood's death resonates with the murder of Henry Percy, fourth Earl of Northumberland. On April 28, 1489, at Cocklodge near Thirsk in north-central Yorkshire, an angry throng of northerners confronted Percy as he sought to collect the King's taxes – taxes the Earl himself only reluctantly endorsed. The mob pulled Percy off his horse and slew him. Accounts suggest that Percy's retainers simply watched the killing and offered no aid to their lord. M.E. James long ago suggested the involvement of Henry VII's court in the Earl's unfortunate end. Though the King had restored Percy to his seat as Earl of Northumberland in 1486, he did not grant Percy back the Wardenship of the Marches, from which the Percys had garnered so much power previously. As James suggests, the monarch "may well have feared that sooner or later the ingrained violence of the north would once more be unleashed."[61] And, given that the Earl's heir was a minor, Percy's death meant that his far-reaching estates in the North would fall to the King during the Earl claimant's minority.[62] The King's attitude toward northern opposition to these new taxes was, according to James, "forthright and provocative," and the King's response "made inevitable a direct confrontation between the Earl ... and the resistance movement ... [which] set the scene, as it were, in which his [Percy's] death was to be encompassed."[63] In a long poem on the Earl's murder, John Skelton rails against the northerners responsible for the death of "your chyfteyne, your shelde, your chef defence" (57), and he recalls how "Barons, knightis, squyers, one and alle, / Togeder with servaunts of his famuly / Turnd ther backis and let ther master fall" (92–94).[64] The King's alleged provocation of the incident and the complicity of Percy's retainers in the Earl's murder calls to mind the legality of homicide in the outlaw's death. If the Percys, like Robin Hood, had opposed the English sovereign as "Kings in the North," then each figure ultimately becomes a mere outlaw – able to be killed with impunity – whose power fails under the weight of centralization and the redistribution of authority fully into the hands of an absolute monarch.

CHAPTER 6

The Towneley Plays, the Pilgrimage of Grace, and Northern Messianism

In an undated letter, King Henry VIII complains to a justice of the peace in York concerning the "late evil and seditious rising ... at the acting of a religious interlude of St Thomas the Apostle, made in said city on the 23rd of August now last past." For the King, this rising was "owing to the seditious conduct of certain papists who took part in the preparing for the said interlude."[1] No year is mentioned in the letter, but Richard Steele, in the second of his edited volumes of Tudor royal correspondences, pins its date to 1536 without explanation.[2] While we may never know the year within which Henry grouses over the discontent sewed through this York drama, Steele's suggestion seems fitting. It would not be surprising, certainly, to find dissent in the North of England in 1536 expressed through a religious play.

As the Reformation took hold, much of England was uneasy, but resistance was most pronounced in the staunchly Catholic and conservative North. Henry had declared the Royal Supremacy in 1534, placing himself as head of the realm and its church. He, further, passed a series of measures that targeted the institution, its doctrines, and its income, all of which affected the North arguably more than other parts of the country. Thomas Cromwell, now the King's principal secretary and minister, had been meticulously examining the wealth of the monasteries throughout 1535, setting up the Court of Augmentations, headed by Richard Riche, to handle the monies and property that would come to the crown with the dissolution of these religious houses. The *Valor Ecclesiasticus*, compiled in the first part of that year, and the visitations that followed into 1536, forecast the seizure of church wealth and the destruction of the great monasteries of England, all for the benefit of the crown and its coffers. The Act of Suppression of the Lesser Monasteries, passed in March 1536, ordered the dissolution of monasteries with incomes of less than £200 per year. While the Act offended many in England, both in the North and South, sheer numbers suggest that the North suffered more than other regions of England. In the four border counties, twenty houses out of twenty-four were subject to dissolution. If Yorkshire was less impacted than the border regions, then it nevertheless forfeited nearly 20 percent of monastic revenues, while southwestern counties, for example, forfeited only about 7 percent.[3] Another issuance, the Ten Articles, in June 1536 diluted the importance of the Sacraments, culling the seven to three – baptism, penance, and communion. The Ten Articles, further, challenged the very notion of purgatory and, consequently, the need to pray for souls therein, a practice that had proved financially lucrative to clergy for centuries.[4] These measures, passed by the so-called Reformation Parliament over the course of Spring 1536, fomented rebellion in various parts of England, but this was most fully realized in the North in a rising known as the Pilgrimage of Grace.

The *Thomas* play witnessed in August 1536 likely fit the turmoil of the time, a subversive performance that anticipated the rebellions which would consume the fall and winter months into the new year. The story of Thomas explicitly and centrally concerns the body and real presence of Christ, a core tenet of a Catholic faith that was now under attack. In *John 20:25*, Thomas declares, "Except I shall see in his [Christ's] hands the print of the nails and put my finger into the place of the nails and put my hand into his side, I will not believe" (*autem dixit eis nisi videro in manibus eius figuram clavorum et mittam digitum meum in locum clavorum et mittam manum meam in latus eius non credam*). When Christ appears two verses later, he urges Thomas to "Put in thy finger hither and see my hand. And bring hither the hand and put it into my side. And be not faithless, but believing" (*infer digitum tuum huc et vide manus meas et adfer manum tuam et mitte in latus meum et noli esse incredulus sed fidelis* (20:27)). The popular narrative of "Doubting Thomas" becomes a profound comment on faith and, like many narratives of the Christian New Testament, a remarkable illustration of the connection between the spirit and the flesh, between the broken and bloody body of Christ and the worship of his followers. The original letter sent by King Henry regarding the *Thomas* play is now lost, but its transcriber and translator (the original was in Latin), James Orchard Halliwell notes, when publishing the letter in 1848, that "an early play on the subject of St Thomas is still preserved."[5] Halliwell might refer to the text found in the York Register (*ca.*1463–77), though this manuscript would only come to rest in the British Library in 1899 (BL Add MS 35290). Patricia Badir suggests that Halliwell, instead, refers to the Scriveners' pageant of *St Thomas the Apostle* found in the Sykes manuscript, which is dated between 1525 and 1550. Like its counterpart in the

York Register, the Sykes *Thomas* play illustrates Jesus' appearance to his disciples, a scene in which the risen Christ directs attention to his material body: "Behold and se my handis, my feett, / And grathely grapis my wondis weytt, / All that here ys" (47–50).[6] Jesus asks for sustenance – "Bryng now forth vnto me here / Some of your meyt" (61–2) –in part, to prove his physical presence. Eating with his disciples for the first time since the Last Supper, however, Jesus' words playfully recall the previous meal. In lines that are close to those in the York Register version, he declares:

> Now haue I doon, ye haue seen how,
> Bodeley here etyne wyth yow.
> Now stedfastly luke þat ye trow
> Yett in me efte,
> And takis þe remland vnto you
> þat here his lefte.
>
> (77–82)

In proclaiming that he has physically or "Bodeley" eaten with his followers, he reminds them, at the same time, of the "body" they ate when he offered them bread and wine, and he accentuates this reference by asking them to "takis þe remland" or remainder.[7] If the play focuses initially on the body, then its conclusion, the moment of Thomas' confrontation with Christ's wounds, reminds its audience of the blood. Echoing the titular skeptic in the York Register version, Thomas rejoices, "A, blod of pryse, blyst myght thou be! / Mankynd in erth, behold and see / This blissed blod" (180–82). Badir points out, "It is in no way surprising that at the dawn of the Reformation – as the doctrine of Transubstantiation came under the scrutiny of Protestant reformers – York inhabitants performing an interlude bearing some relation to a play dedicated to figuring the real presence of Christ would arouse the suspicion of Henry's councillors."[8]

While the *Thomas* play of the Sykes manuscript proves a good candidate for the subversive performance about which Henry complains, I suggest an alternative: the *Thomas* play found in the Towneley manuscript (Huntingdon MS HM 1). Towneley's version, titled in the manuscript *Thomas Indie*, is over three times longer than the Sykes or York Register versions and, arguably, more substantive for singular performance. More important, the Towneley *Thomas* play amplifies Eucharistic allusions made by Christ and his disciples and attends, further and in more detail, to Christ's physical presence. In the play, Jesus appears briefly to the apostles, who, then, converse on the physicality of his appearance. Octauus Apostolus remembers, "We se the woundys in hym was wrought, / All blody yit were they" (255–56), while Novenus Apostolus muses, "He cam and stode vs by, / And let vs se ilkon / The woundys of his body" (263–64). Thomas is not with his colleagues at this time, but he appears afterwards alone and contemplating the scene of crucifixion: "To se the stremes of blood ryn, / Well more then doyll it was, / Such great payn for mans syn, / Sich doyllfull ded he has" (289–92). When his friends recount Christ's appearance to them, Thomas mocks them with questions: "When Crist cam you to vysyte, / As ye tell me with saw, / A whyk man from a spryryte, / Wherby couth ye hym knaw?" (373–76). Sounding much like the reformists cursing Catholic superstition in 1536, Thomas suggests, "That God, I trow full wele, / Goostly to you light, / Bot bodely neuer a dele" (451).[9] Indeed, the debate with his fellow disciples goes on for over 260 lines, more than the full length of the two York versions in the Sykes manuscript and the York Register. A.C. Cawley finds this discussion "unduly" or "tediously prolonged" and the Towneley additions to the Thomas story generally "unsuccessful," but this expansion sustains the context for debate over the body and the blood, over real presence.[10] Thomas is, for example, rebuked by Peter, who recalls the Last Supper explicitly: "Iesu, Goddys son of heuen, / At soper satt betweyn, / Ther bred he brake as euen / As it cutt had beyn" (465–68). Jesus reappears and halts the debate. He begs of Thomas, "Putt thi hande in my syde" (565). In the two York versions previously discussed, Christ commands Thomas' touch but we are never sure that this touch happens. In both the Sykes and York Register versions, Thomas merely offers a six-line stanza celebrating the blood and begging God's mercy. By contrast, Towneley's Thomas, having clearly probed Christ's wounds, rambles for forty-seven lines, proclaiming the gore on his hands: "My hande is blody of thi blode!" (570). The Towneley *Thomas* play, then, more explicitly than its York counterparts, foregrounds the body and blood of Christ, and if this is the sort of *Thomas* play that the King found dangerous, then it is not difficult to see why. Attacks on the sacraments and transubstantiation were swelling in a reformist tide that challenged Catholic ritual and belief broadly, so it is possible to imagine York, an ecclesiastical center of the old church in the staunchly Catholic North, staging a religious drama that both celebrates Catholic belief and, at the same time, works as a collective show of discontent. The Towneley *Thomas* play uses the Blessed Sacrament as the "*medium congruentissimum*," the instrument of harmony, or what Eamon Duffey terms "the source of human community."[11] Pamela King has argued, similarly, that the host as ritual site for community and collective experience is a central tenet of the York cycle.[12] Whether King

Henry refers in his letter to the *Thomas* play in the Towneley manuscript or not, it is nonetheless fitting that a biblical drama anticipates by mere weeks one of the most pronounced rebellions in England's history, a northern rebellion whose banner bore the five wounds of Christ.

To what extent was religious drama of this sort provocative of rebellion in 1536 in the North of England, and to what extent does the turmoil of Reformation in England and the subsequent rebellions of 1536–37 resonate in the northern religious dramas of the mid-sixteenth century? To answer these questions, I will take up the plays found in the Towneley manuscript, arguably the most popular collection of religious drama in English literary history, within the context of the Pilgrimage of Grace. I argue, here, that the Towneley manuscript as a compilation can be read as protest literature emerging from this northern Catholic rebellion. Over the course of this chapter, I will examine the Towneley plays alongside other protest literature born of the Pilgrimage of Grace. Shared concerns and parallel themes between these many texts suggest that we consider the Towneley compilation in light of this rebellion that shook Tudor England to its core. The northern rebels of 1536–37 opposed religious and government reform that threatened the North of England's culture, and, as I hope to flesh out, the eclectic collection of plays within the Towneley manuscript takes up a similar regionalist ethos that extends the rebellion's economic and political concerns, its Catholic dissent, further into the sixteenth century.

The Towneley plays are rarely, if ever, analyzed in light of the mid-sixteenth century dating of the manuscript in which they appear. But I aim to take Paul Whitfield White's advice that "we need to stop periodizing [Towneley] as 'medieval plays' and think of their interpretive fields within the space of individual decades, not one-hundred- or two-hundred-year segments."[13] Scholarship on the Towneley dramas has betrayed a commonplace desire to maintain these plays' medieval credibility and, for many decades, to witness definitively a Corpus Christi cycle performed at Wakefield, the Yorkshire manor-town whose name appears on the manuscript's very first page, at the outset of the *Creation* pageant, as well as on the first page of the *Noah* play. Many of the dramas in Towneley, of course, are borrowed in full or in part from the late medieval York cycle, but Towneley lacks several plays we might expect per the York model – plays of the *Nativity*, the *Temptation*, Christ's ministry, and his trial at the hands of Herod – while further lacuna in the manuscript, specifically twenty-eight missing leaves, suggest more absent plays, such as those concerning the life of the Virgin. It seems that Wakefield had Corpus

Christi plays, and perhaps an entire cycle, as Wakefield burgess records from 1556 and 1559 mention Corpus Christ pageants either in the context of performance dates or, in the case of two 1559 records, censorship under Elizabeth I's Protestant regime.[14] The Towneley manuscript has grown younger over the years, but its origins remain murky. Once dated to the mid- or late fifteenth century, and then to the first quarter of the sixteenth century, the most recent claims, based on Malcolm Parkes' analysis of scribal hands and the manuscript's elaborate strapwork, suggest a date between 1553 and 1558. Ownership is also a vexing issue. The name "Thomas Hargreaves" appears twice (ff. 73v and 90r) and this might be the same Thomas listed in the Register of the Burnley Parish Church as having been buried in 1566.[15] The first page of the manuscript, however, bears the press mark of the antiquarian Christopher Towneley (b. 1604) of Lancashire. Robert Harding Evans' enthusiastic description of the manuscript for the 1814 auction of materials from the Towneley Hall Library argued that the manuscript originated at "the abbey of Widkirk," though he likely meant one of the parish churches or the priory, as there is no abbey in Woodkirk. But the antiquarian Francis Douce, who supplied much of the information in Evan's description, later suggested that the plays were performed by monks at Whalley Abbey in Lancashire and, by implication, that the Towneley family, who lived in nearby Burnley, took the manuscript from Whalley when the monastery was dissolved in 1537 for its role in the Pilgrimage of Grace.[16] As Meg Twycross' recent study of Douce's correspondences show, however, Douce revised his view yet again, reasoning finally that Whalley was not a candidate either, though he never explains why.[17]

It is not, I think, out of the question to discuss the Towneley manuscript, or its individual plays, within the context of the religious and political turmoil of the 1530s and, specifically, the Pilgrimage of Grace. Both Barbara Palmer and Garrett Epp have debunked the notion that Towneley represents a performance text for a Corpus Christi cycle located exclusively in Wakefield. Instead, Palmer sees the manuscript as a "Lancashire–Yorkshire compilatio" comprised of "disparate and uneven materials ... compiled to form an artificial cycle."[18] Perhaps a poet adapted the York *Thomas* play into *Thomas Indie* for the seditious performance in 1536, and maybe this was just one of many religious plays this author/editor altered and which found their way into the compilation we now know as the Towneley manuscript. Palmer, late co-editor of the *West Riding Records of Early English Drama,* points to a flourishing dramatic scene in the North that includes Pontefract, Doncaster, York, Fountains

Abbey, Beverly, and Ripon, and, while she assures us that these are "all Yorkshire sites with rich cultural and entertainment activity,"[19] they are also all key sites in the Pilgrimage of Grace. Palmer, herself, points out that the Pilgrimage of Grace links all of these places, including Whalley Abbey, together in a network of drama and rebellion. Corpus Christi performance activity by local guilds is also noted in Preston, Kendal, and Westmorland, all of which played some part in the rebellion. Parkes' dating of the manuscript between 1553 and 1558 stems from Towneley's coupling of legal script with elaborate strapwork evident on many of its pages. But this same strapwork is known to have existed as early as 1500. And the narrow window into which Parkes fits Towneley – the reign of the Catholic queen, Mary I, wedged between Protestant monarchs – is uncomfortably neat. One wonders whether it is too convenient that a manuscript of apparent Catholic plays, some of which likely date in their original form to the mid-fifteenth century, could only have emerged in a Catholic revival under Mary. As White, among others, has shown, both Catholics and Protestants found appeal in religious drama in the sixteenth century and, more emphatic, Protestant governments – with the exception of Elizabeth in the wake of the Northern Rising of 1569 – did not consistently suppress religious drama.[20] It is, then, possible to reconsider the plays found in the Towneley manuscript as linked to, or inspired by, the Pilgrimage of Grace. Palmer believes that the manuscript was, in her words, "always" in Lancashire,[21] and she reasons, further, that the plays probably came from Doncaster, Pontefract, and the Wakefield area.[22] Gayle McMurray Gibson and Theresa Colletti offered, recently, the possibility that the Towneley manuscript was a wedding gift marking the 1556 marriage of John and Mary Towneley. This John Towneley, often known as John Towneley of Gray's Inn because he was a lawyer, would become one of the more notorious and defiant Catholics of Elizabethan England, living out his life under the scrutiny of the government until his death in 1607. Could his family have collected plays known to be subversive? Or, perhaps, this collection was previously owned by Sir John Towneley (d. 1540), grandfather to the later John Towneley and an ardent Catholic during the troubles of 1536–37. It is possible that the so-called Wakefield Author or Wakefield Master intended – but failed – to unify the various plays to the degree that we find in the Chester cycle.[23] If the Towneley manuscript was indeed in the Towneley family in the mid- and later sixteenth century and, given the adamant Catholicism and recusant practices of the Towneleys under their patriarch, John of Gray's Inn, then it is not far-fetched to view the manuscript's Catholic plays as a literature of protest.

Whatever its place of origin, the Towneley manuscript derives from dramatic activity in Yorkshire, and possibly Lancashire, in towns and cities that were moved to rebellion only about sixteen years prior to Parkes' earliest dating for the Towneley manuscript.

The plays of the Towneley manuscript are, first and foremost, celebrations of Catholic doctrine. Of the manuscript's famous and anonymous presence, the Wakefield Author, Peter Happe concludes, "his orthodoxy is not in question and his contributions support the emphasis upon Catholic doctrine spread through the cycle."[24] The Creation to Doomsday model is distinctively a northern affair in the late medieval and early modern period. As P.J.P. Goldberg contends, "This regional identity is also reflected in the evidence for borrowings between cycles, notably of York material within the Towneley cycle, and evidence, at least in terms of the pageants recorded, of similarities between the Beverly and York cycles."[25] Yet, while the Towneley plays on the whole bear orthodoxy, they also speak to political and economic concerns of Tudor England, specifically, I will argue, concerns voiced during the Pilgrimage of Grace. Although religion was a main point of contention for both the Lincolnshire and northern rebels in 1536, economic fear also contributed to the discontent. Tax subsidies had been passed by parliament in 1534 and levied in the following two years, and these coincided with general agricultural decline. In addition, the Statute of Uses moved through parliament the following spring and took aim at complex practices of landholders who, for many decades, enfeoffed others with legal title to their land in a sort of passive trust. This allowed them to hide property from creditors, among other benefits; but, most important, inheritors could avoid fees to the crown for their inherited lands.[26] While all of England felt the pangs of these economic measures, the combination of economic hardship and shocking religious change, moved by a centralized government at London and Westminster, fomented rebellion in the North of England.

Protest and Pilgrimage in the North

The initial disturbances began not in the North, in Lancaster or Yorkshire, but in Lincolnshire. Fear over the seizure of church wealth led the men of Louth to lock themselves inside St James' Church on the night of October 1, 1536 in order to protect its goods. For five days, these fears escalated and, ultimately, provoked a much larger force of rebels from around Lincolnshire – nearly 10,000 strong – to march into the town of Lincoln. There, they drew up articles that were sent to King Henry.

With the assembly of the Duke of Suffolk's forces and an angry rebuke from the Earl of Shrewsbury, however, the rebels quickly and anticlimactically dispersed. The rebels' concerns were made apparent in the so-called Lincolnshire Articles, which opposed "the suppression of so many religious houses" and the appointment of "divers bishops ... that hath subverted the faith of Christ."[27] Their concerns were also temporal. The rebels complained of the King's councillors, namely Cromwell and Riche, who they claimed were "of low birth and small reputation" and who "procured the premises most especially for their own advantage."[28] They, further, viewed the clerical tax, first fruits and tenths, recently issued by the government, as inhibitive not only to God's work but towards the care of the poor and impoverished who often received assistance from local churches and monastic houses. R.W. Hoyle argues confidently that "Monasteries may well have been a familiar and valued part of the fabric of early-sixteenth century northern society, but the risings of 1536 were not primarily about their defense,"[29] yet it is difficult to view the dissolution of the lesser houses coupled with the broader movement against churches and church goods as anything other than a pronounced assault by the King and government on the very livelihood of the faith.

All of this was more acute for the North of England than anywhere else. In May 1536, Sawley Abbey (West Riding) was suppressed and in August numerous priories were dissolved, including Ellerton (East Riding), Armathwaite (Cumberland), and Easby (North Riding). By the time the Lincolnshire rebels had sent their petition forward to the King, the rising in Yorkshire was underway and, in short space, the rebellions north of the Humber would come to dwarf the initial events in Lincolnshire. Within four days of the Louth rising, the Archbishop of York, Edward Lee, warned his liberties about the disturbances, as well as the crown's impending military response. In the midst of these events, a Yorkshire lawyer named Robert Aske had accidentally happened upon the Lincolnshire rebels while on business there and had been sworn to their cause. When, after two days, he made his way back across the Humber, he found the countryside ready for revolt. Over the course of the next week, much of the North and East Ridings rose up, sparked by events at Beverly, where the Lincolnshire Articles arrived on October 8. Aske would quickly become the Yorkshire rebels' captain, leading a growing army of northern men in what he termed a "pilgrimage of grace," the connotations of which rang with both piety and military force, because the rebels adopted the crusading banner of the five wounds of Christ.[30] As Hoyle explains, Aske's use of "pilgrimage" served two purposes: "it stole the spiritual high ground and declared the pilgrims to be the arbiters of the true church" and, further, "[i]t combined the familiar act of Pilgrimage…with the political act of making a supplication."[31] Hugh Latimer, the Bishop of Worcester and a chief proponent of reform in England's early transition to Protestantism, preached a fiery Latin sermon on June 9, 1536 at Convocation denouncing the practice of pilgrimage. Indeed, pilgrimage seems to bring together all that Latimer thought wrong with Catholicism: worship of image, superstition, devotion to the object be it a relic or picture, and, of course, the cult of saints.[32] Latimer's speech received the King's endorsement, so it is fitting that the northern rebels took on the guise of pilgrims in order to oppose the governments' temporal and religious policies. If the Lincolnshire rebellion had fizzled out, then Aske's rebellion would find a clearer identity and an aggressive path forward. On 16 October, the city of York submitted peacefully to Aske and his force of 4,000 to 5,000 men; he processed ceremoniously through the town to the minster, and, then, to the high altar inside.[33]

The various factions of the rebel movement in the North coalesced almost completely into a massive force that descended on Pontefract Castle, in the keeping of Lord Darcy. On October 19, Darcy opened the castle to Aske and his men and was quickly sworn to their cause. One week later, a rebel army of 20,000 confronted the Duke of Norfolk at Doncaster and the King's military commander had no choice but to negotiate terms. Over the next month, more rebels would gather, and further insurrection continued in the northwest in Lancashire, Westmorland, and Cumberland. On October 27, at Doncaster, the rebel leaders issued five articles of complaint aimed at generating a dialogue with the government that would allow them to articulate, further, details of their grievances. The King's initial response to their petition was tepid and he denied the rebels' request for a general pardon. But they responded with twenty-four articles, more detailed, that were agreed upon by the leaders at Pontefract on December 3 and given to Norfolk the following day.

These new and revised articles, as we might expect, addressed religious objections that drove the original rebellions in Lincolnshire and elsewhere, but, unlike the Lincolnshire Articles, they were also regional in nature. The northern rebels asked, for example, to "have the parliament in a convenient place at Nottingham or York" and that "no man upon subpoena is from [River] Trent north to appear but at York."[34] These demands were born of the frustration that parliament and courts of equality took place only in London and Westminster to the disadvantage of those far flung from the capital. Even the seemingly overt religious concerns of the so-called

Pontefract Articles, which echoed those of the Lincolnshire movement, took on a decidedly regional valence. In testimony following the rebellion's demise in early 1537, Aske explains the articles and how they attended specifically to the loss of monastic estates:

> many ther tenauntes wer ther feed servaundes to them, & servuyng men, wel socored by abbeys; & now not only theis tenauntes & servauntes wantes refresshing ther, both of meat, cloth & wages, & knowith not now wher to have any liffing, but also strangers & baggers of corne as betweix Yorkshir, Lancashir, Kendall, Westmoreland & the bischopreke, was nither cariage of corne & merchandisse, greatly socored both horsse & man by the said abbeys, wher now they have no such sucour; & wherfor the said statut of subpression was greatly to the decay of the comyn welth of that contrei, & al thos partes of al degreys greatly groged ayenst the same, & yet doth ther dewtie of allegieance alwais sauyd.[35]

While the loss of monastic estates signals a deprivation of spiritual health and wealth, Aske's concerns here are also the employment and basic sustenance of northern peoples. His attention is directed to the "comyn welth of that contrei," that is the North of England. Aske makes clear, as well, that the impoverishment of the North directly affected the northern defenses, a point the pilgrims were quick to make and the crown was reluctant to challenge:

> And that now the profites of abbeys suppressed, tentes awnd furst frutes went out of thos partes. By occasion wherof, within short space or (sic) yeres, ther should be no money nor tresor in those partes, nether the tenant to have to pay his rentes to the lord, nor the lord to have money to do the king service with all, for so much as in thos partes was nether the presence of his grace, execucion of his lawes nor yet but little recours of merchaundisse, so that of necessite the said contrey should eyther "patyssh" [ally] with the Skotes or for very povertie, enforced to make comocions or rebellions.[36]

The implication is clear: the dissolution of the monasteries broadly constricts the northern economy, but also specifically inhibits the "king's service," that is the defense of the borders, a significant concern given the recent war with Scotland in 1532–33. Further, there would be no means of defense should the Scots, with the aid of the French, decide on formal invasion. Otherwise, Englishmen in the border counties, and perhaps Yorkshire and Lancashire, must rather work with the Scots to sustain local commerce and trade and to head off the raiding and plundering of goods and livestock that constituted life at the Anglo-Scottish border.

Regionalist ethos abounds in the most popular protest song of the rebellion, a song said to be "in every man's mouth about Bridlington and Pomfret [Pontefract]" during the winter of 1536. John Pickering's polemical poem, "O Faithful People," begins forcefully:[37]

> O Faithfull pepull of the boryall Region,
> Cheiff bellicous champions, by dyvyn providens
> of god hie electe, to maike Reformatione
> off gret mysch[e]ves and horrible offence,
> goo ye forwarde valyently in your peregrinacyon!
> It is chryste pleasure, and to your salvacion.
>
> (1–6)[38]

The opening line perfectly melds the fused interests of religious tradition and regional identity that characterize much of the Pilgrimage. The people of the North, the "boryall Region," are "Faithful" to their northern homeland and, at the same time, to their Catholic faith. Continuing a religious play on words, Pickering's poem deploys "Reformatione" as a generic noun rather than as a term for the advent of Protestantism. Hence, the warlike or "bellicous" people of the North are destined to counter the "gret mysch[e]ves and horrible offence" set in motion by the King and his new religion. This pilgrimage, then, will save the North and work for "chryste pleasure." While the poem focuses on the religious turmoil of its present, it nevertheless reminds its audience that "The northorne pepull in tyme longe paste / haith lytyll beyn Regardyde of the awstrall nacione" (7–8). The present confrontation, however, affords the North renown for the "holle congregacyon" against "these Sothorne herytykes, devode of all virtu" (10–11). The use of "holle" here, of course, does double work, clarifying the unity of the "whole North" while, at the same time, intimating that the North is the "holier" of the two regions.

"O Faithful People," sometimes known as "An Exhortation to the Nobles and Commons of the North," was intended as a marching song for the Yorkshire part of the Pilgrimage of Grace. Pickering was a prior of Blackfriars in York in the 1530s who apparently authored correspondences during the first and second phases of the rebellion. Cromwell himself writes that Pickering was "busy in both insurrections" and that he "wrote seditious letters."[39] It was the prior's literary ability that led John Hallom, later captain of the short-lived third phase of the rebellion, to encourage him to write the poem. Pickering was at Pontefract in December 1536 and was one of the men gathered in the Priory of St John of the Cluniac monks, there to debate concerns of the Pilgrimage specific to religion, such as the reformist attack on purgatory, the clerical taxes of first fruits and tenths, and the worship of saints, all of which were bound up with opposition to the suppression of the monasteries and the royal supremacy. William Wood, a prior of Bridlington who briefly housed Pickering and lent him a horse in order to ride to Pontefract, explains that Pickering "used to say the insurrection was well done for the wealth of the church, and made a rhyme, to encourage the commons."[40] Pickering testified that he penned the 150-line work as he and other pilgrims awaited word of the King's reaction to the initial five articles posed by the rebels at Doncaster on October 27. As Susan James suggests, "the poem seems to be aimed more at the nobility and clergy who were literate than at the peasant soldier who was not."[41]

Stanza three of the poem brings the political force of the Pilgrimage of Grace into the foreground. The Pilgrimage intends "These heretykes to suppresse, and tyranny Restrayne" (16), and, here, the poem is pointed in its rhetoric, quoting *1 Maccabees 3:58*: "*Accingemini et estote filii*" (Gird yourselves, and be valiant men) (18). This command comes from Judas, himself, as his army prepares to face the Seleucid force at Emmaus in what will be the definitive Jewish victory in the Maccabees' war against Seleucid rule. But the allusion to the Maccabees does darker work as well, hearkening to a biblical moment that fused religious protest with bloody resistance. Pickering's quotation from the *Vulgate Bible* reminds northern Catholics, fighting their own religious war, of the rousing victory of orthodox religions past over the heresy of an encroaching empire. Most startling, however, is the scene in *1 Maccabees 1* that leads up to Judas' imperative. Here, Mathathias murders a Jew, at the altar no less, who was willing to compromise his faith practice, sacrificing in the Jewish temple at the command of the Seleucids. No doubt if an audience were ready to grasp Pickering's explicit reference to Judas' command in the third chapter, then they would have known Mathathias' bloodily defiant action from *1 Maccabees 1* in which a religious reformist is brutally put down.

Pickering's bellicose imagery rings throughout the poem. Again, he recalls the Maccabees, who "being few in the comparison / Of their enemies that in number were many more, / But trusting in God, they had corroboration, / And many of them they did overthrow" (41–44). Pickering imagines "warriors most bold" (36), who see it "better in battle for to die" (13) at war with "these southern Turks perverting our law" (38). The crusader rhetoric is impossible to overlook and befits the 1536 rebels, who not only bore a flag but also wore badges bearing the five wounds of Christ, which were left over from Lord Darcy's 1511 crusade to North

Africa to fight the Moors. As Ethan Shagan claims, "Along with their badges and crosses, many participants in the revolt believed that they would receive the 'crusade indulgence': remission of sins and the offer of paradise as reward for their participation."[42] James argues, further, that "there is a deeply felt personal anger evident in Pickering's language, which exhorts with the moral suasion of a crusade against the infidel rather than with the responsive humility of a loyal pilgrimage made in the name of a benevolent, if deluded, monarch."[43] Pickering's poem illustrates the religious fervor, regional fears, and economic discontent of the rebellion and informs the full list of grievances that emerged from rebel meetings of which Pickering was a part in December 1536.

A host of rebels met with Norfolk at Doncaster on 6 December, and, two days later, Lancaster Herald alerted the pilgrims to a final confirmation of general pardon for all, a promise that a parliament would be held at York, and assurance that the religious houses recently restored by the pilgrims during the revolt would be allowed to stand for the moment. Following the peaceful resolution of December, Henry VIII hosted Aske for the Christmas holiday. But, if all seemed won, then victory was fleeting. Discontent remained among the northern commons who distrusted their gentry commanders, many of whom were unwillingly sworn into the rebel hosts during the early stages of the rising. These commanders, who ultimately helped to conceive the Pontefract Articles, maintained landholding interests that ran counter to the grievances of the commons. What is more, the commons remained suspicious of the King's sincerity in response to the articles or to the pardon he promised. When Lancaster Herald rode into Durham at the end of December to cry the pardon, he was attacked and survived only through a daring escape on horseback. Another phase of the rebellion quickly followed.[44] While the proceeding movements in this third and last phase of the Pilgrimage of Grace did not yield the massive armies witnessed under Aske, substantial numbers of rebels still confronted the King's forces, including a contingent of 6,000 that besieged Carlisle in February 1537. In the east, Sir Francis Bigod and John Hallom, fearing the garrisoning of Scarborough and Hull by the King for the purposes of suppressing unrest, assaulted these towns in late January. They were quickly defeated, however: Hallom by local alderman and Bigod by the force of Sir Ralph Ellerker, the elder. The third phase of the Pilgrimage failed because, as Michael Bush explains, leaders could not mobilize their collectives in the quick and efficient manner of their predecessors the previous fall. This was a product of disinterest on the part of many northerners, who were content with the King's response to the Pontefract Articles and who were unwilling to risk royal pardons already offered to them. But these last risings in January and February, in Henry's mind, voided his previous terms. Conspirators from the entirety of the Pilgrimage of Grace, consequently, were rounded up for testimony and punishment. Aske, Darcy, Bigod, Hallom, Pickering, and hundreds more faced execution in the proceeding months, ending what was arguably the largest revolt in English history.

Scholars shirk at historian Rachel Reid's old argument that a northern rebellion was "inevitable" by 1536, or the view that regionalism informs the Pilgrimage of Grace at all.[45] Indeed, the rebellion began in Lincolnshire rather than north of the Humber, the Lincolnshire Articles are subsumed into the northerners' petitions, and only five of the twenty-four Pontefract Articles agreed upon by the northern host concern expressly northern issues. Bush claims, "the Pilgrims were principally aggrieved by national issues" and he points out, rightly, that "any sense of the north was complicated by regional divisions of interest ... that essentially distinguish the counties taking the brunt of Scottish attacks and of border raiding ... from the rest of the north."[46] The Kendal rebels, for example, did not even bother to meet the main body of men, led by Aske, at Doncaster in October 1536 where they confronted Norfolk. Yet, Bush concedes that "a north/south distinction featured frequently, both in the Pilgrim's declarations of complaint and in the government's responses to them" and a sense of "northern-ness" bring these rebels together over the course of the fall and winter of 1536.[47] The pilgrim commons, their gentry leadership, and the government opposing them, provoked and responded to a sense of northern-ness and a distinction between the North and South of England in the Pilgrimage of Grace.

The Towneley Manuscript, "The Sawley Ballad," and *Isaiah 14*

Though their roles are obscure at best, both Sir John Towneley and his debased brother, also named John, participated at some level in the Pilgrimage of Grace. An apparent rebel correspondence dated October 20 is addressed to "Cousin Towneley" from "Mr. Captain," presumably either the "Captain Poverty" figure from the Richmondshire risings or Aske himself. The letter asks that the commons of Lancashire be raised and, in the process, it seems to distinguish Sir John from his brother, the author claiming to be "displeased with your brother for not being sworn." The message concludes with the request that Towneley appear with his company "Theweseday next ... in all your best array."[48] Whether or not

"Cousin Towneley" is Sir John or his brother is not clear. One would assume that Sir John, a prominent landowner and, as recently as 1532, Sheriff of Lancashire, would be more apt at raising the duchy. In a note dated November 24, a list of potential attendees from the rebel host for the coming Pontefract meeting with the Duke of Norfolk mentions "John Towneley, brother to Sir John Towneley," but a correspondence on December 5 from the Earl of Derby to the King, "Touching Sir John Townley and Sir James Layburn," asserts a rumor that Sir John is "much with the commons and . . . sworn to them."[49] By January 1537, however, Sir John Towneley is being directed by the government to distribute the King's peace following the negotiations with the rebels. A brief discussion appears in the State Papers that explains how the King might "obteigne the hertes of his suiectes in the north partes." The list of directives anticipates the King's response to rebel demands initially made in late October, the most important of which is the King's willingness to "confirm his gracius and liberall pardon."[50] The item suggests that letters be issued and presented across the North announcing the King's response to the rebels' demands and the general pardon he was, at first, reluctant to grant. Sir John Towneley is named as one recipient – and, therefore, a distributor – of such a letter. With his paradoxical appearances in these correspondences, we cannot discern whether Sir John would have supported fully the rebel cause or not. The Pilgrimage of Grace did not find as much enthusiasm in Lancashire as in the North and West Ridings of Yorkshire, or even in Westmorland and Cumberland, but unrest nevertheless occurred in these places during the rebellion.

Whether he was a rebel or not, Sir John Towneley likely remembered March 11, 1537, when a Whalley monk named William Haydock was executed beside the abbey for his part in the Pilgrimage of Grace. Haydock's death came just two days after the Abbot of Whalley, John Paslew, met the executioner in Lancaster. These deaths might have had a profound effect on Towneley. Sir John descended directly from Geoffrey, the early thirteenth-century Dean of Whalley, he probably took his education at Whalley, and his home, Towneley Hall, was nearby in Burnley. Whalley Abbey's fate was sealed at the height of the 1536 risings. On October 25, 1536, the Earl of Derby, himself a steward of Whalley, sent a letter to Paslew alerting the monks that he intended to muster forces there. News spread instead that Derby was coming to destroy Whalley. The local commons rose to meet him at the abbey but found that Nicholas Tempest and a rebel contingent of 400 men were already there and that, by force, they had sworn the monks to their cause. Whalley Abbey's demise, in the wake of the Pilgrimage of Grace, was significant, for although the monastery had not yet been dissolved prior to the rebellion, the King moved quickly to possess the building, its goods, and its lands, following suppression of the rebel factions.[51] The Earl of Sussex wrote to the King on March 24, 1537 detailing the Abbey s inventory, and it is possible that the wealth of Whalley was either confiscated or sold off soon after.[52] Sir John Towneley, an ardent Catholic, may have acquired Whalley Abbey's vestments as well as various papers at this time. These vestments, a chusable, two dalmatics, and a maniple – with their remarkable scenes of the Virgin's life and Christ;s infancy – remain in Towneley Hall today.[53]

The initial reason that the Earl of Derby went to Whalley was to stage an attack on nearby Sawley Abbey, where monks had returned to their dissolved house. The Sawley monks' defiant act enraged the King, who called for their destruction. In a gathering of State Papers related to Sawley Abbey, a rhyme once ascribed to the monks at St Mary's Abbey, York, is mentioned by its first and last stanzas.[54] The Dodds sisters, early historians of the Pilgrimage of Grace, place authorship of the poem on the monks of Sawley during the rebellion, and the poem, more recently, has been labelled the "Sawley Balled."[55] As we might expect, the poem argues the case for monastic houses, echoing the claims made by Aske and other pilgrims. For the poor, the religious houses had "Both ale and breyde / At tyme of nede, / And succer grete / In all distress."[56] But the poem's main argument is more forceful and political. The ballad opens, fittingly, with a vocative on the five wounds of Christ, which adorned the banner of the rebel hosts throughout the northern revolt of 1536 – "Crist crvcifyd! / For thy woundes wide / Vs commens guyde!" (1–3) – and this reference quickly shades into the imagery of political upheaval. Imagining the fall of covetous kings, the poem evokes *Isaiah 14*:

> Bot on thing, Kynges,
> Esayas [Isaiah"s] saynges
> Like rayn down brynges
> Godes woful yre,
> Harrying the subiect
> There dewtis to forgett
> And pryncex let
> Of such disyre.

Here, oracles relating the Babylonian context of the Israelite captivity become an analogy for the plight of northern monastic houses in an imaginative opposition to an overbearing tyrant. As I have discussed in both Chapter 1 and Chapter 4 of this study, "Esayas saynges" [Isaiah's sayings] in chapter 14 allude to the stunning prophecy of the reversal of Israel's plight at the hands of Babylonians. *The Vulgate* reads, "Thou shalt take up this parable against the king of Babylon, and shalt say: How is the oppressor come to nothing, the tribute hath ceased?" (*Sume parabolam istam contra regem Bablylonis et dices quomodo cessavit exactor quievit tributum*). It is easy to understand the appeal of *Isaiah*'s visions to the 1536–37 rebellions: an oppressive ruler who harries his subjects will be cast down.

Isaiah 14 connects the Babylonian kings to Lucifer himself, the angel who boldly attempts to usurp the throne of God, but, again, it is the place of Lucifer's brief glory in these passages that comes to inform the North–South divide in England, as well as a crucial connection between the "Sawley Ballad" and the Towneley manuscript. In *Isaiah 14:12*, the narrator asks, mockingly, "How art thou fallen from heaven, O Lucifer, who didst rise in the morning?" (*quomodo cecidisti de caelo lucifer qui mane*). He continues in verses 13–14, "And thou saidst in thy heart: I will ascend into heaven, I will exalt my throne above the stars of God, I will sit in the mountain of the covenant, in the sides of the north" (*Qui dicebas in corde tup in caelum conscendam super astra Dei exaltabo solium meum sedebo in monte testamenti in lateribus aquilonis*). In his lectures on *Isaiah*, delivered in 1527, Martin Luther attempts to clarify that "This is not said of the angel who once was thrown out of heaven but of the King of Babylon, and it is figurative language,"[57] but, in doing so, Luther reminds us of the verse's intentional confusion between the Babylonian ruler and the bold usurper of God's throne, Lucifer, who aspired to the highest peak of sovereignty in Heaven. The "Sawley Ballad" follows a similar logic of intentioned confusion. The tyrant Henry VIII, in his supremacy over church and state, aspires, Lucifer-like, to the sovereignty of Heaven, and this poem imagines his overthrow.

The "Sawley Ballad's" use of *Isaiah* 14 also links it interestingly to the Towneley manuscript, where the political geography of England intimated in "Sawley" becomes more pronounced. In the Towneley *Creation* play, following the fifth day of God's work and his command for his creatures to "Multiplye in erth and [s]e" (58), the Cherubim praises God's making of the angels and, most significant, his creation of "Lucifer so bright" (68). There is no figuration in the play; Lucifer is clearly present. The Cherubim ascribes the name "Lucifer" to this glowing angel because "none of vs ys so bright as he... / For lufly light that he doth bere; / He is so lufly and so bright / It is grete ioy to se that sight" (70–74). Lucifer, then, continues to praise himself, reminding us – if we had forgotten – that he is "thowsanfold / Brighter then is the son" (89), the play on the word "son," as the morning star and the "son" of God, augmenting his conceit. Yet, as he proudly attempts to "sit in trone / As kyng of blis" (100–1), Lucifer's brazen usurpation of divine power is quickly repaid with his being cast into Hell. The latent messianism of this scene – the defeat of the Devil – is unexceptional in religious dramatic cycles that move from Creation to Judgment, within which the oppression born by man at the hands of Lucifer is thrown off by the victory of Christ through his crucifixion and the harrying of Hell. But in the York and Chester cycles, and in the N-town collection, Lucifer's appearance occurs in a "Fall of the Angels" episode that precedes a *Creation* play. In contrast, the Towneley *Creation* play has already begun when the Lucifer episode intrudes. God has made the Earth and its animal inhabitants when Lucifer appears sitting in the North. In this way, the play ignores the metaphysical or cosmic "*aquilonis*" of the other versions for a material world already manufactured by God, a geographical North whose landscape is fraught with political significance in early sixteenth-century England. In the Towneley *Creation*, then, when Lucifer "sits in the North," we might well see him sitting in the North of England. If we take the Wakefield Author's well-known allusions to northern locations and topography mentioned elsewhere in Towneley's plays – Goodybower, Horbury shrugs, and the crooked thorn[58] – and the oft-quoted shepherd's attack on Mak the sheep-stealer's southern tongue in the *Second Shepherds' Play*, then the *Creation*'s use of *Isaiah 14* calls forth an English cultural and political geography within which resonates a longstanding typological joke.

As I suggested in this study's introduction and, further, in Chapter 4, this joke is made prominently by William Langland in the late fourteenth century in the C-text of his religious allegory *Piers Plowman*. In *Passus I*, Langland employs *Isaiah 14* to render a regionalist jibe at the North of England: the Devil sits in the North (of England)! As Alfred Kellog has shown, the Latin passage Langland inserts into this section – *Ponam pedem meum in aquilone, et similus ero altissimo* – quotes Augustine's own paraphrase of *Isaiah 14* rather than the *Vulgate Bible* and, consequently, calls forth Augustine's own complex exegesis of this scriptural passage.[59] According to Augustine, God eventually will remake Lucifer's seat into the city of God upon Christ's return: "*Out of the North come clouds*, and not black clouds, not dark clouds, not lowering clouds, but of golden colour. Whence but by grace illumined through Christ?"[60] If the biblical

North provokes disdain for Lucifer's presence, then it also intimates messianic hope in the promise of Christ's luminous and salvific return. Augustine's exegesis of *Isaiah 14* perfectly encapsulates the liminal position of the North of England in the early sixteenth century, the very same position spelled out by the rebels of 1536 in their complaints to royal councilors: it is both defender of the nation's borders and, at the same time, a Catholic territory set in rebellion against its heretical government. The provocative coupling of biblical and political geography in the context of the northern rebellion connotes a tyrant in the North who will be overthrown by the power of the one, true God. The messianic reversal of Lucifer's arrogant and sedentary presence through the coming of Christ resonates in the later plays of the Towneley manuscript, through the Nativity in the shepherds' plays, in Christ's return in the *Judgment* play, and, as I will argue later, in the peculiar placement of the *Lazarus* play following the *Judgment*.

Agrarian Politics in Towneley and the Pilgrimage of Grace

The typology of Lucifer in the North resonates in the regionalist protest of the Pilgrimage of Grace and the rebellion's complaints about a king who usurped the throne of the church and whose temporal policies seemed more tyrannical each day. If the Towneley *Creation* shifts Lucifer's celestial arrogance into an imagined political geography, then the manuscript's two shepherds' plays afford a derisive commentary on political overreach, burdensome land policies, and religious indifference in which resonates the rebel complaints of fall 1536. In the *First Shepherds' Play*, Gyb consoles himself in his poverty:

> For he that most may
> When he syttys in pryde,
> When it comys on assay
> Is kesten downe wyde.
> (18-21)

Gyb's lines remind us, again, of *Isaiah 14*, of Lucifer sitting in his pride in the heights of the North. But in place of the Devil, Gyb imagines the "Horsman Iak Cope," a figure of wealth, whose "fall" is his being made to walk rather than ride on his rich steed. Gyb seems to find solace in the humiliation of such a rich man, which eases his own suffering. As Norma Kroll claims of the shepherds' plays in both Towneley and Chester, they "do not simply repeat or reinforce theological points of view … rather, they subordinate such perspectives' emphasis on divine might in the universe to human potency on earth by representing the rustics' deeds as vital contributions to God's plan."[61] In other words, the shepherds' plays foreground the commons' ability to effect God's will over and against the cruelty and cunning of tyrannous regimes.

While the complaints of the three shepherds in the *First Shepherd's Play* sound conventional, further examination suggests that they befit, specifically, the context of discontent among the commons in the fall of 1536. Gyb bewails "mekyll vnceyll" as fortune sways to and fro: "Now in hart, now in heyll, / Now in weytt, now in blast" (7–8). His poor luck stems from the loss of his sheep. Gyb explains "The rott has theym slone" (36–38). His worry, here, over livestock plague is shared in the Chester *Shepherds' Play* as well, which begins with the first shepherd looking for herbs with which to "heale them [sheep] from the rott" (34). And it is certainly a trope in the shepherds' plays of Towneley, Chester, and York that the herdsmen are, in the words of a York pastor "ovir poore" (110). But Gyb's worries extend beyond commonplace hardships. In lines unique to the Towneley play, Gyb worries, "Fermes [rents] thyk ar comyng, / My purs is bot wake" (44–45). Concerns over raised rents and the chronic reduction of arable land to enclosed pasture pervade both shepherds' plays, and while complaints about enclosure are longstanding in late medieval and early modern England, they are foregrounded by the rebels of 1536–37. In his own deposition on the events of the rising, William Stapleton explained that one of the chief concerns of the East Riding rebels, whom he and Aske led, were the "Raysing of ffarmes, sore taking of gressomes or Incomes pullin downe of Townes and husbandries, encloasers, Intaykes of the comon, wourshipfull men taking of ffarmes and yomens offices."[62] The context for these complaints goes back to the early years of Henry VIII's rule, when a system of tenancy was developed to address, simply, a dearth of tenants, and lords had to agree to fixed rents in order to attract them. But this policy was done away with due to population growth – and thus more tenants – in the 1530s. As Bush explains, "With a growing abundance of would-be tenants, lords now had the chance to raise landed revenues."[63] What is more, the Pilgrimage of Grace came on the heels of two years of agricultural disaster, followed by further raising of rents. Gyb's worry over raised "fermes," then, might speak directly to agrarian anxieties that were at the heart of the commons' rising.

In the play, the shepherd John Horne clarifies the plight of commoners in the North of England and augments Gyb's complaints about exploitation at the hands of more powerful men. He decries "robers and thefys" (76) as well as "bosters and bragers" (80). In a northern context, "robers and thefys" might allude to the marauding bands of Scots who regularly attacked the northern commons throughout the fourteenth, fifteenth, and sixteenth centuries. Reiving was always a threat to those persons livings at the borders, and, given the most recent outbreak of Anglo-Scottish hostilities in 1532–33, this practice might have become pronounced in the years leading up to the Pilgrimage of Grace. Beyond the Scots, Englishmen labeled by the government as *Homo silvestris* attacked farms in the northern counties and further into Yorkshire. In the 1520s, the east and middle marches suffered from the weak presence of the aging magnate Lord Dacre (d. 1425). The King had intently denied the fifth Earl of Northumberland the wardenship and a general "decay of the borders" ensued.[64] Indeed, Aske's fear that the commons at the Anglo-Scottish border might "Patyssh with the Skotes" because there was "nether the presence of his grace" nor the "execucion of his lawes" echoes a proclamation delivered by the Cumberland rising on October 20. They claim that they revolt because "the rulers of this country do not come among us and defend us from robbing of the thieves and Scots."[65]

Jak Horne's fear of "bosters and bragers" (79) suggests a much closer antagonist. In their edition, Cawley and Stevens gloss this line as a reference to the retainers maintained by lords such as Dacre, who were often accused of exploiting their tenants. The latter is, again, pertinent to the complaints of the pilgrims in 1536–37, who voiced frustrations against the Earl of Northumberland, the Cliffords, and the Bishop of Durham for altering, to their advantage, rents on lands far enough from the border so that tenancy was not payable through military service. The rebels complained, further, that these lords created new tenancies by converting waste and redrafting customary tenancies into life warrants that afforded them the chance to collect more fees. The poor shepherds overcome their poverty, briefly, in an imaginative banquet. Gyb declares "Oure mete now begyns" (308) and each shepherd voices his menu: "leg of a goys, / With chekyns endorde, / Pork, partryk to roys, / A tart for a lorde" (336–39). Their immaterial meal calls to mind the "King and Subject" poems I discussed in Chapter 5, wherein a commoner of the forest puts on a sumptuous meal for the disguised sovereign. Indeed, Nisse finds that the shepherds' feast of words performs "an imaginative 'poaching' ... of aristocratic culture," but one that imbibes "the theatricality of the events of Corpus Christi during the 1381 Peasants' Revolt."[66] And while we find the shepherds, as Kroll says, "play-acting to make life seem more bearable,"⁶⁷ Gyb has been clear from the beginning that the play will end and the harsh realities of life will confront the audience once more: "For after oure play / Com sorrows vnryde" (16–17).

Gyb begins the *First Shepherds' Play* calling to mind the image of prideful Lucifer sitting in the North in *Isaiah 14*, a figure that projects the fall of tyrant kings, but both he and Slowpase complete the prophetic intent of *Isaiah* towards the end of the pageant.⁶⁸ Here, an inverted quotation of Virgil's messianic fourth eclogue appears – "*Iam nova progenies celo demittitur alto; / Iam rediet Virgo, redeunt Saturnia regna*" (558–559) (now a new generation descends from Heaven on high / Now the Virgin returns, the reign of Saturn returns).⁶⁹ For medieval and early modern Christians, Virgil's words were seen to predict the coming of Christ, and they precede Gyb's own near translation that "from heven / A new kynde is send / Whom a vyrgyn to neuen, / Our mys to amend" (569–72).⁷⁰ Slowpase reponds that "ther shuld be, / When that kyng commys new, / Peasse by land and se" (583–85). At this moment, Slowpase is startled by the angels' song: "Now, brethere, adew!" (586). The new king has arrived in the *First Shepherd's Play*, and the shepherds go to the child to offer their humble gifts. These passages appear on one of the more worn pages of the Towneley manuscript (f. 37r), and the words have been touched up by a later hand.⁷¹ We might not be surprised to find that the moment announcing Christ's nativity was of interest to the manuscript's reader, but we might also hear, in Gyb's and Slowpase's dialogue, a hope for new rule and peace in the political context with which the play begins. As Nisse concludes of the *First Shepherd's Play*, "those in power might well catch the warning encoded in the peasants' learned and lewd spiritual discourses."⁷²

While it is difficult to understand a compiler's motivation for the inclusion of two shepherds' plays – the *incipit* to the second play follows on the same page as the *explicit* of the first and the plays are labeled *Una pagina pastorum* and *Alia eorundem* – the *Second Shepherds' Play* comically amplifies the first shepherds' hardships while importantly playing out the Nativity within the cultural geography of the North of England. The shepherds of the *Second Shepherds' Play* begin with their own complaints on numerous difficulties, not the least of which is their lot in life as husbandmen-turned-pastors. In some of the most worn pages of the Towneley manuscript, Coll loathes "these weders cold!" (1) within which he "walkys on the moore" (15). In a play on words, he reasons, "No wonder, as it standys, / If we be poore, / For the tylthe of oure landys / Lyys falow as the floore" (18–21). Their lands are dormant because these former husbandmen are dormant, that is, because the land has been converted to pasture, Coll merely "standys" and watches his sheep. This sedentary existence – sitting "on a stone" (73) – only cultivates his poverty and his loneliness. Lisa Kiser claims, "these shepherds feel the effects of the newly-experienced loneliness and isolation ... meant, here, to pointedly contrast with the more humanly comforting communal labors of village agriculture that the shepherds have been forced to abandon" (343). Kiser points to the "prevalence of enclosure sweeping away an agricultural economy in the fifteenth century"[73] but enclosure was also a point of contention among the rebels of 1536–37. During negotiations with the Duke of Norfolk in the November 1536 truce, rebel leaders issued orders that "no man rob or spoil ... or to enter upon lands, cast down enclosures or assemble unless commanded by our captain."[74] Their order implies that this was a common form of protest. More specific, Item 13 in the Pontefract Articles demands the revocation of the statute for enclosures and, further, "all intakes and enclosures since 4 Henry VII to be pulled down except mountains, forest and parks."[75] Just one year prior to the rebellion, in the summer of 1535, 300–400 rioters had torn down enclosures in Giggleswick, about twelve miles north of Sawley Abbey.[76] Like the northern commons in the 1530s, the former husbandmen of the *Second Shepherds' Play* are frustrated by the loss of their livelihoods to sheep-farming.

The play affords regional context to the shepherds' complaints when the sheep-stealer Mak approaches them in the poorly played guise of a king's man. Mak, "*in clamide se super togam vestitus*" (dressed in a cloak that covers his garments), bounds into the very doleful scene wherein the shepherds lament their poor state. When Gyb asks him, simply, "where has thou gone?" (288), Mak protests:

> What! ich be a yoman,
> I tell you, of the kyng,
> The self and the some,
> Sond from a greatt lordyng,
> And sich.
> Fy on you! Goyth hence
> Out of my presence!
> I must have reuerence.
> Why, who be ich?
>
> (291-99)

Mak seems to believe that his professed association with the southerly king will curry "reverence" (205) from his potential victims. But, put off by his performed southern dialect and his threat to "make complaynt, / And make you all to thwang / At a word" (306–8), Coll rebuts Mak's commands: "Now take outt that Sothren tothe, / And sett in a torde!" (311–12). His scolding is quick and to the point. Reversing the humor that we frequently find directed toward northern English from William of Malmesbury to Chaucer, Coll's jibe equates southern speech – and arguably those who use it – with shit. Beyond such linguistic humor, however, Coll's derision of both Mak's southern tooth and his desire to play the part of the King's yeoman afford a northern ethos to the shepherd's earlier complaints about the husbandry he might no longer practice. These are northern shepherds beset by poverty brought on by land policies proffered by the King and his ministers.

Critics have often viewed Mak, with his necromantic spell circle, as an antichrist or a devil set against the virtuous shepherds who aim to sniff out his plots.[77] Mak's complaining, then, draws a fitting proverb from Daw: "Seldom lyys the dewyll / Dede by the gate" (332–33). With his own southerly identity, poor as it is, devilish Mak calls forth, once more, the usurping Lucifer boldly asserting his position in the North. But Mak suffers as well. Mak first appears in the play walking the moors, alone in prayer: "Thi will, Lord, of me tharnys. / I am all uneven" (277–78). He wishes, "Now wold God I were in heven, / For the[r] wepe no barnes / So styll" (279–82). Mak admits that confusion about God's intent and his poor state "moves oft my harnes" (279) (wracks my brains). Within this frame, Mak's bumbling schemes are comic, but also desperate. Indeed, Mak will do whatever it takes to feed his "barnes" who weep. His words recall Coll's own stasis: "If I stande stone-styll, / I ete not an nedyll / Thys moneth and more" (336–38). Mak missteps, however, when he aligns himself with the King and, consequently, the law. Certainly, as Robert Sturges explains, "the *Second Shepherds' Play* attributes the financial misery of the peasants . . . directly to the gentry and their henchmen."[78] Yet, while this connection is clear, Mak's "Sothren tothe" and his claim to be a yeoman of the King remind us that the source of such misery remains the centralized government of the southerly sovereign and his ministers. Perhaps, for this reason, the shepherds refuse to follow the prescriptions of that law when they catch Mak stealing their sheep. Both Gyll and Mak remind the reader that he has committed a capital crime. Gyll envisions him "in a bande" (407) (noose) while Mak, caught in compounding lies, swears to his honesty lest they "gird off my heed" (622). Rather than capital punishment, however, the shepherds toss Mak in a blanket and are rewarded for their own grace with news of the Christ-child, whose hopeful coming might restore peace to mankind.[79]

Given all the devilish references to Mak in the text, if he proves a poor man's Lucifer, then his star is replaced in the northern sky by a new light, one that does not restore these former husbandmen to their lands; rather, it leads them away into the imaginative spaces between Horbury and Bethlehem. Mak once played a yeoman of the King of England, but that king is forgotten with the coming of the "sufferan savyoure" (1037). The intensification of northern space in the *Second Shepherds' Play* only heightens the conversion of this politicized landscape to a Messianic geography, a seeming precursor to the extended journey that Christ prescribes in the *Ascension* play when he commands: "Therefor ye shall go tech / In all this warld so wyde" (149–50). This teaching will emanate from the North in the shepherds' own song, which they have been trying to sing from the beginning of the play and which is, now, translated into a new frame. We are reminded, through Mak's dubious dialect, of the law coming from a southern king, a law that oppresses these shepherds. Their benevolent acts, however, announce the coming of a Messiah in the North who will put down all tyrants in the end.

The biblical typology in *Isaiah 14* informs both northern resistance in the Pilgrimage of Grace and the inherent regionalism of the Towneley plays. Lucifer's arrogant leap into the North contextualizes for the rebels what they viewed as a southern assault on the provincial wealth, religion, and culture of the North, and their complaints echo in the Towneley shepherds' plays. William Langland's precedence in using *Isaiah 14* within the context of the English North in the late fourteenth century, thus, goes further than playful jesting at the expense of fringe communities. As Nisse claims, the Wakefield Author "borrows from the literary culture of *Piers Plowman* in order to reimagine the terms of labor, poverty, and prophecy in an alliterative biblical theatre," and in this re-imagination we hear "an undertone of revolt."[80] While we expect the prophecy of a savior to right the world's wrongs, including political strife and oppression, Towneley's use of *Isaiah 14* affords the manuscript a particularly pointed northernness, even as such regionalist ethos was eroding in the face of Tudor centralization and provincial oppression.

The Messianic and the Profane, or *Lazarus* after *the Judgment*

The Towneley *Judgment* play neatly bookends the regionalism inherent in the *Creation* play's use of *Isaiah 14*. The Second Demon urges his colleagues to get moving toward the scene of the Last Judgment so they might affirm the souls they have won through sin: "Let vs go to this dome, / up Watlin Strete" (185–86). This thoroughfare could refer to the Milky Way. Chaucer uses "Watling Street" to this end in *House of Fame* (939).[81] But a road called by this name also ran through the West Riding, entering at Bawtry, moving through Doncaster towards Pontefract and, then, northward to York and Durham.[82] Given other references in the Towneley manuscript to place names in the area of Wakefield, it is reasonable to think that the Watling Street mentioned here in the *Judgment Play* refers to the Yorkshire highway that ran North to Durham. If the North of England is the site of Lucifer's imaginative kingship in the *Creation* play, then it becomes the site wherein the Son will return in the *Judgment*, just as Augustine explains in his exegesis of *Isaiah 14*. Redemption will rain down from the North of England much as the rebels of 1536–37 had hoped.

The Second Demon's desire to head North toward the place of Judgment might have had specific meaning to an audience in the years following the Pilgrimage of Grace. In March 1541, a conspiracy known as the "Wakefield Plot," which aimed to overthrow King Henry VIII, was exposed and crushed. Fifteen men were executed for their participation in the plan. Just a few months later, Henry made his way to York to receive a lavish spectacle of performed supplications made by numerous northern populations for their part in the Pilgrimage of Grace. On September 15, some 120 persons, including the mayor of York, met the King at Fulford Cross. William Cankerd, master recorder for the city, delivered an address:

> Most myghty and victoryous prynce vnder almyghty god supreme heyd of the Churche of Englond our naturall souereign beyng all tymes by the inspiracion of the holy gose repleyt with mercy and pety as evidently haith been shewyd by your grace to your Subjectes layte offendours in thies North partes.[83]

Cankerd continues a long and penitent plea to the King *in apologia* for the rebellion of five years past. In part, to mark this occasion and to celebrate the royal supremacy, the city of York staged the Mercer's play of *Doomsday*. As Patricia Badir claims, "The pageant was chosen ... to show that York itself was not above the judgment of higher powers."[84] The playing of a *Judgment Play* at York illustrates, again, religious drama's important role in matters of sovereignty and law. Specifically, the 1541 pageant affords context for the playful additions that the Wakefield Author makes to the Towneley *Judgment* play. Is there an inside joke, then, that muses on real judgment lying just up Watling Street from Wakefield, where King Henry once lorded over his (quite literally) prostrated and penitent subjects?

The Towneley *Judgment* play, however, reverses the 1541 York supplication. The demons are not northern penitents sheepishly prostrating themselves to a *Deus* who "lokys full grisly" (195) as the First Demon muses. Rather, they are Lucifer's agents, potentially southern ones at that, if they must head "up" Watling Street. If Lucifer had been usurper in the North, then the demons now head north with their tally books of men's sins in preparation for a reckoning. The Second Demon frames his future in legal terms:

> It sittys you to tente
> In this mater to mell
> As a pere in a parlamente,
> What case so befell.
> It is nedefull
> That ye tente to your awne,
> What draght so be drawne;
> If the courte be knawen,
> The iuge is right dredfull.
> (174–82)

Certainly, the description of a dreadful judge befits an angry king such as we might imagine Henry VIII in 1541, but the demon envisions his colleague as a "pere in parlamente," making what he hopes is a forceful case, whatever the counter-argument. The First Demon, further, urges his fellows to "take oure rentals" (196) so as to "Examyn oure bokys" (206). These demons take on the guise of lawmaker and landowner, and their damned rent rolls (rentals or "bokys") account for the vast array of sins they have witnessed in men over time. While the Mercer's pageant of 1541 marked a dramatic end to the Pilgrimage of Grace, performing judgment on the North for its sinful revolt against the King, the Towneley *Judgment Play* revels in a northern messianism. The Second Demon muses, "The poore pepyll must pay, / If oght be in hande; / The drede of God is away / And lawe out of lande" (276–79), but he and his colleagues remain apprehensive about the trumpets sounding to the North. The First Demon ironically imagines himself a pilgrim, in the conventional sense: "I had lever go to Rome / Yet thryse on my fete / Then for to grefe yonde grome" (187–89). Tutivillus' gleeful admissions, further, tie tax collection, legal corruption, and religious reform together. He claims, "I was your chefe tollare / And sithen court-rollar; / Now I am master Lollar" (309–11). While many readers of the Towneley *Judgment* see Tutivillus' self-proclaimed Lollardy as a fifteenth-century phenomenon, it makes more sense in the context of Henry's religious reform. During the Pilgrimage of Grace, rebels complained of the Wycliffite heresies perpetuated by the King and his evil councillors. The Pilgrim articles sent to Henry VIII in December 1536 decry at their very outset "the heresies of Luther, Wycliffe" and others.[85] In this way, Cawley's and Stevens' note holds, if not in the sense that it was originally intended: "In identifying Tutivillus as a Lollard, the playwright is thus consigning his worst enemy to hell."[86]

Tutivillus and the demons ponder the profligacy of society evident in their ledger, and their attention rests consistently on sartorial excess. Tutivillus muses on the "Gay gere" (343) of a haughty father, with his "hode set on koket, / As prowde as pennyles" (344–45) but "his barnes bredeles" (351). Notable, here, is his description of a "las in lande" (376) who is "hornyd like a kowe" (391). Tutivillus remembers a woman wearing a horned-headdress, a peculiar adornment dated, roughly, to the first third of the fifteenth century. Though scholars have previously used this allusion to date the play or the Wakefield Author to this period, such attire might have remained symbolic for sartorial excess for decades after its being in fashion. Juanita Wood explains that the church saw the horned-headdress as a form of fashion that encouraged "unhealthy interest in vanity at the expense of concern for the soul."[87] In her argument, Wood refers to the so-called "dishonest alewife" carved into a mid-fifteenth-century misericord at St Laurence Church, Ludlow. The woman, dressed in this gear, is carried by two devils to the gates of Hell. This art, thus, suggests that the sin of haughty excess through clothing was a recognizable scene of forthcoming judgment. Martin Stevens points out, "The two most basic sins against which the energies of Tutivillus and the demons seem to be directed are excessive adornment (especially in apparel) and the frauds practiced by men of the law."[88] But such complaints are contemporary to the Pilgrimage of Grace as well. The drama *The Godley Queen Hester*, dated to around 1529, presents the story of Esther and her struggle with the evil councillor Haman, whose lavish wardrobe signifies his many sins. In the play, the allegorical figure Pryde complains that "Aman that newe lord, / Hath bought up all good clothe, / And hath as many gownes as would serve ten townes" (372–74). *The Godley Queen Hester* is seen by critics to attack, specifically, Lord Chancellor Thomas Wolsey through its depiction of Haman. James argues that the play's date might be moved forward just a few years to the mid-1530s and that the play instead attacks

Cromwell. The plurality of positions Haman holds in the play befits Cromwell instead, who over the course of the early 1530s was also Chancellor of the Exchequer, King's Secretary and Master of the Rolls, and Vicar-General. The gifts offered in the play to Haman – bulls, ring and seal – befit Cromwell's position as Lord of the Privy Seal.[89] Alongside the play, Cromwell was indelibly linked to the Esther story when, on April 2, 1536, Anne Boleyn's chaplain John Skip preached a fiery sermon depicting King Henry as Ahasuerus and Cromwell as Haman, whose goal was the destruction of Esther (not so subtly implied as Anne).[90] So, it is not surprising that the play *The Godley Queen Hester* is the chief source for John Pickering's own attacks on Cromwell, just a few months later, in his poem "O Faithful People." For Pickering, Cromwell is the cruel councillor who "In the north doth pursue the faithful commonty, / By his great expenses intending utterly / Us to destroy and bring in captivity" (99–102). Thus, in the literary depictions of Henry's evil councillors that emerge in the 1530s, we have the sins of both sartorial excess and legal fraud.

The *Judgment* play's finale affords a distinct ending – "Make we all myrth and louyng / With *Te Deum laudamus*" (829–30) – yet the Towneley manuscript is not done. In a peculiar sequence, the Towneley compiler appended the *Lazarus* play and a *Judas* fragment to the end of the manuscript, after the *Judgment* play. While the *Lazarus* play appears in the hand of the main scribe, the *Judas* fragment does not.[91] If the *Judas* text is, clearly, a later addition to the manuscript, then the *Lazarus* play's emplacement remains a mystery. The Towneley *Lazarus* likely found inspiration from the *Shepeards Kalendar*, an English version of the French *Kalendrier des bergiers* (ca.1493) printed by Richard Pynson in 1506.[92] The *Kalendar* incorporates the *Visio Lazari*, an account of Lazarus' sufferings in Hell that was previously deployed in *The Prick of Conscience*.[93] Excluding *Lazarus*, the Towneley collection contains no ministry plays, unlike its counterparts Chester and York. Critics have suggested scribal error or, perhaps, that the scribe came upon the play after his completion of the manuscript's Creation to Judgment sequence. Murray MacGilvray, for example, contends, "The presence of the *Lazarus* play anachronistically at the end of the manuscript after the *Last Judgment* play is another instance where the scribe's uncertain access to materials is *prima facie* a more plausible explanation than any presumed theological intent."[94] Garrett Epp reasons that the play is "best considered and performed on its own, as a sort of biblically based morality play."[95] Yet, the Towneley compiler's peculiar placement of the *Lazarus* play might not be a mistake at all. J.W. Earl, among others, has argued that the placement of *Lazarus* at the end of Towneley proves fitting because of the titular character's final speech on the pains of Hell; the speech itself is an addition unique to Towneley.[96] And, perhaps, the play does more ideological work than mere Hellish didacticism. Theresa Coletti and Gail McMurray Gibson consider the placement of the *Lazarus* play in relation to the manuscript's possible ownership by the ardently Catholic and recusant family of John Towneley. In this context, the play signifies the "lost body of the faithful Catholic community" reconstituted "after human history is played out in the *Last Judgment*."[97] Coletti's and Gibson's intriguing metaphor proves even more compelling if we shift its context back just two decades to the Pilgrimage of Grace. In the wake of the rebellion's repression and the many martyrdoms that ensued, the *Lazarus* play becomes a remarkable supplement to Christ's own resurrection and to the messianic force of his return, a profane remnant to a faith now imposed by the government, to a religion rendered sacred only within the purview of Henry's sovereignty.

Lazarus is not absent from the Towneley plays' dramatization of Christ's life; rather, the pageants preceding *Lazarus* consistently prepare the audience for his emergence at the end. In the *Conspiracy*, a soldier mentions to Pilate the miracle that Jesus performed: "the loth Lazare of Betany / That lay stynkand in a sted, / Vp he rasyd bodely / The fourt day after he was ded" (150–53). And Pilate will note the act himself when he interrogates Jesus later in the play. In the *Buffeting*, a torturer testifies to the perceived witchcraft of the accused: "Lazare can he rase– / That men may persave– / When he had lyne iiii dayes" (144–46). In the *Crucifixion*, a torturer mocks Christ, reminding him of the raising of Lazarus, while in the *Harrowing of Hell*, Satan fumes at the "gawdys and g[i]lory" (168) Christ seeks by raising Lazarus. Ribald continues the metaphor of contest, seeing the event as when Jesus "wan the Lazare away" (179). Finally, in the *Thomas of India* play, Thomas begs to Jesus "Mercy, for the teres thou grett / When thou rasid Lazare" (599–600). With the reader's attention being directed to this dead man by everyone from Pilate to Satan himself, we might be surprised that the event has not, at any point, already occurred. These references do not mark a past event; instead, the appearance of the Lazarus miracle at the end of the manuscript renders these allusions prophetic. Rather than anticipating the second coming and the Judgment, the Towneley plays anticipate the resurrection of Lazarus, while calling into question the very restraints of time that govern the traditional biblical cycle.

In the *Lazarus* play, Jesus quickly shatters our notions of eschatological time. In the text's opening lines, Jesus assures Martha that her brother will rise again, but Martha assigns his confidence to "the dredfull day of dome" (47) to which all men are subject and in which Lazarus will, in her words, "come before the good justice" (46). In the Towneley manuscript, however, the *Judgment* has already come. We read it with our own eyes. As if anticipating our confusion, Jesus responds to Martha's sense of biblical teleology by cancelling it altogether. He declares, "I am rising and I am life / And whoso truly trowys in me, / That I was ever and ay shall be, / Oone thyng I shall hymn gif: / Though he be ded, yit shall he lif" (52–56). In Jesus' assertion of his own atemporality – his "ever and shall be" over the "ded" and "lif" – he unsettles the progress of men from birth to death, from Creation to Doomsday.

Lazarus' resurrection is not redemption. Emerging back into the earthly world, he is neither in Hell – where, at the end of the *Judgment* play, the demons lead bad souls – nor is he in Heaven, where the good soul claims to be "On oure way os we trust" (828). What is more, Christ's miracle of resurrecting his friend is quickly overshadowed by Lazarus' own speech. Barbara Gusick calls it "a gallingly ungrateful monologue characterised by haughty self-display and unrighteous condemnation."[98] Lazarus' sermon is bound up in an ethos derived from his having witnessed Hell; as he admits: "to hell I soght" (107). A French cult of Lazarus grew out of the belief that his relics were brought to Autun and this Burgundian precedent affords Lazarus, in Pamela King's words, "a peculiar status beyond his position in the chronological gospel accounts."[99] In this tradition, Lazarus is "a figure of penance . . . . [who has] been to Hell and seen what awaits those who do not take prudent prophylactic measures."[100] In the Towneley manuscript, then, Lazarus emerges literally at the end of the Creation to Judgment sequence to warn the audience of the dangers of Hell, not with the spectacle of Revelation, but with the simple words of the dead man now living again in the world. In this way, his figure becomes pregnant with the entirety of the cast of biblical characters who precede him, characters most critics find incredibly human in their sin and their compassion, in their potential to be both damned and saved. Lazarus has sinned and suffered and, yet, been reborn. Lazarus reminds us all that "with Dede thay shall be dight / wheder he be king or knight" (125–26) and that our seeming possessions are merely "Goddys goodys all" (193). Lazarus' message, thus, deconstructs the material and vocational concerns expressed in previous plays, including those of the shepherds, rendering inoperative the very

The Messianic and the Profane 169

binaries of means and ends, of labor and yield, of payment and goods that prove so divisive in the temporal world of politics and religion.

Most important, here, Lazarus has followed Christ in his resurrection rather than preceded him. He is, as he says, "youre boke: / Your sampill" (121–22). It is crucial to realize, in his self-declaration, that Lazarus is singular, an example ("sampill").[101] Lazarus is, then, neither mundanely human or divine, neither sinner or saint. Indeed, he has been to Hell and back. His unique experience renders him as a third term in this biblical cycle, and his tertiary status befits the strange placement of the play after the *Judgment* in the Towneley manuscript. G.R. Owst long ago observed that Lazarus' speech is closely based on John Bromyard's (d. 1353) sermon about the fate of the dead.[102] But we must consider how the compiler of Towneley reconfigures Lazarus in the context of the manuscript and its subtle northern consciousness, all within the purview of the Pilgrimage of Grace. The raising of the dead man overturns the eschatological finality of the *Judgment*; in the wake of the Pilgrimage of Grace, the play sends the reader into an imaginative future of a Catholicism divorced of sovereignty and politics, beyond contests between two religions, and beyond the bloody executions of, and performed supplications to, Henry VIII.

The sudden appearance of the *Lazarus play* following the *Judgment* works powerfully as a political declaration. In Lazarus' grotesque and nearly mummified and decaying body we find connection with Christ's body, so vividly depicted in its gore throughout the Towneley manuscript. Epp sees a problem in Towneley with the fact that the Eucharist is never presented clearly, but Christ's sacrificial body is everywhere leading up to the *Judgment*, including the *Thomas* play with which this chapter began.[103] And while we might find, in the connection between the bloody and broken bodies of Lazarus and Christ, a potent reminder of Catholic doctrine in a reformed England, it is Lazarus' post-apocalyptic resurrection that does specific political work here. As signifier of the lost church, Lazarus, according to Coletti and Gibson, "offers the last word, remembering doctrine and the broken body of the Catholic faithful from dissolution and ruin and exhorting to steadfastness even in the face of danger and death."[104] In the prophetic poems that circulated among rebels throughout the Pilgrimage of Grace, and that are recalled by several participants in their testimonies to the state in the rebellion's aftermath, a common theme occurs: that of a dead man who shall appear once more.

In the most explicit example of this theme, from a poem entitled "The Cock of the North," a "dede man shall com" (59) and make the Saxon encroachers accord.[105] This man "that was dede and buryed in sight / Shall ryse aheyne and leve here in londe" (61–62). "The Cock in the North" likely originated in the early fifteenth century and concerned, in its original conception, the 1402 rebellion of Henry Percy (Hotspur) and Owen Glendower against King Henry IV. The allegory imagines a rising in the north, "Whan the cok in the north hath buylded his nest / And gadered his byrdes and busked hym to flee." The cock was initially Hotspur, but the second stanza begins with more specific Percy imagery: "Than shall the mone aryse in the northwest / In a clowde so blak as they byll of a crow." The crescent moon, a heraldic device of the Percys, is unmistakable here, as are a "dredefull dragon" connoting Glendower and a bull signifying the Nevilles.[106] The birds and beasts battle for the sovereign claim of the lion, "The boldest and best / That was in Brytayne syth Arthure dyed." The lion, probably the Scottish king, and his band move on their enemies, "The molle and the marmayde." R.H. Robbins points out that the poem was taken up again in the Wars of the Roses. And this same poem is transformed a third time for the purposes of the northern rebels during the Pilgrimage of Grace.

In the context of the Lancastrian and Yorkist conflicts of the fifteenth century, the mole is Westmorland and the mermaid Queen Margaret, but by 1536, the mole is King Henry, who "Cryst that is our creatour hath cursed." Richard Bushop of Bungay, for example, testified to Cromwell on May 16, 1537 about a prophecy wherein "The king was spoken of as a mole who should be subdued and put down."[107] But if the villainous mole is beaten, the poem envisions, further, a dead man, who brings peace: "When they here hym speke yt shalbe greate [won]nder." This man will be the bride of Fortune:

> The whele shalbe turned to hym full ryght
> Whom Fortune hath chosen to be her fere,
> In surrey shalbe shewed a wonderfull syght
> Which Babylon shall bryng many a won in bere.

Like the oracles of *Isaiah 14*, the poem imagines the biblical overthrow of Babylonian oppressors and, further, a crusade wherein "the Holy Cross wonne shalbe / And the same barne shall bere the beme." At this point, the dead man, who was "buryed in sight," rises to lead this group in triumph not only in battle against their tormentors but on pilgrimage, bearing the rood in front of a community marching to salvation. As Sharon Jansen explains, "If we look at such a prediction in terms of the hopes and fears of the 1530s, this seems once again to be a strong piece of anti-government propaganda, looking forward to a rebellion in the north and the arrival of . . . a deliverer, of some sort."[108] To what extent, then, does the oddly-placed *Lazarus* afford the Towneley manuscript such a man "that was dede and buryed in sight" but who will "ryse aheyne and leve here in londe"? As the culmination of a series of plays that perform biblical drama in a contemporary English political context, the *Lazarus* play unmoors geography and time, profaning the North against the sacred and legal power of the reformed church and its sovereign head. The Towneley *Lazarus* imagines a post-apocalyptic and profane resurrection.

A political theological distinction between the sacred and profane comes into view here. As Catholic protest literature, the Towneley manuscript subverts Henry's supremacy over church and state, over the sacred and the legal, with its own profane Catholicism. As a conclusion, the *Lazarus* play imagines a space wherein the sovereignty of the King has played itself out. The protest literature of the Pilgrimage of Grace muses on Judas Maccabees striking at dynastic encroachers and it longs for messianic figures to come. The peculiar placement of *Lazarus* at the end of the biblical cycle extends this imaginative literature with an abstracted landscape, a third space, emerging after the Final Judgment and liberated from the oppressive geography of a North–South religious divide or the political teleology of nationhood.

The Towneley manuscript has perplexed scholars since the early-nineteenth century catalogue of Towneley Hall materials that bore Francis Douce's description: "A volume, very fairly written . . . in the reign of Henry VI. or Edw. IV . . . formerly belonging to the Abbey of Widkirk."[109] Given our uncertainty as to Towneley plays' relationships to one another within the larger manuscript or to their performance histories, emphasis more recently has been placed on reading the plays individually. But many of the Towneley plays exhibit a distinct northern consciousness and, given both Parkes and Palmer's work in dating the manuscript in a more precise manner, it is important to consider the Towneley manuscript itself as a product of the early to mid-sixteenth century and, as Palmer suggested long ago, as a compilation of scripts from both Lancaster and the West Riding. This chapter has argued that the Towneley plays might be read within the context of the northern rebellion known as the Pilgrimage of Grace and that this manuscript constitutes resistance literature born in the wake of that conflict and government assaults on northern Catholicism that continue throughout the century. Alexandra Johnston contends that drama in the North repeatedly "acted as the flash point between the Protestant ecclesiastical and civil authorities and the lingering conservative Catholicism of two cities whose civic pride was bound up in their lavish plays."[110] And MacGilvray admits, the Towneley manuscript "seems designed to be impressive as a document, perhaps acting as a sign, in its very aesthetic, of Catholic triumphalism."[111] Perhaps, it was the Towneley family, harboring recusants throughout the reign of Elizabeth I, who used the manuscript for private performances, and this is why, as Wann's analysis long ago showed, the manuscript experienced significant use.[112] In the wake of the northern rebellion of 1569, in which John Towneley of Grays Inn was himself implicated, Elizabeth worked to suppress the civic dramas of York and Chester. Reading the Towneley plays in any specific context remains, admittedly, problematic given the numerous lacunae that continue to perplex scholars. But the plays resonate with the specific interests of the 1536–37 rebellion and in the context of a Catholic pilgrimage-turned-crusade. From the figuration of a usurping tyrant in the north in the *Creation* play to the atemporal *Lazarus* play, Towneley imagines the throwing off of sovereign power for what that theorist of the German mourning play, Walter Benjamin, might have called the "real state of exception."[113] Barbara Palmer once suggested, ironically in Benjamin's terms, that we read Towneley as a "mosaic rather than an oil painting."[114] The emergent pattern of Towneley's dramatic shards and pieces, then, reveals a northern commentary on the religious and political upheaval of 1536–37, radically informing one of the most significant events in history of the English North–South divide.

CHAPTER 7

Conclusion: A Medieval and Modern North–South Divide

In 1815, William Wordsworth published "The White Doe of Rylstone," a poem that memorializes the Northern Rising of 1569.[1] The poem muses on Rylstone Hall, the seat of the Norton family who were at the center of this last great revolt in the Tudor era. Through young Emily Norton, the poem witnesses the family's trials and tribulations within a Catholic countryside moved to war with the southerly government's Protestant forces. Over the course of the poem, Emily befriends a white doe that will continue to appear to her as she laments the loss of her family and faith, and eventually the creature will keep vigil at her grave at Bolton Priory after she dies. Rylstone is a significant setting for the poem, but Bolton is *locus amoenus* of the poem's lament over England's Catholic past. Wordsworth's choice of Bolton Priory was compelling for the hybrid nature of the building as the poet might have known it. Following the dissolution of the priory in 1539, the western end of the nave was allowed to remain in use while the eastern half fell into ruin. Canto I of Wordsworth's poem begins by witnessing a call to Protestant worship, and as we watch "What sprinklings of blythe company / Of lasses and of shepherd grooms, / That down the steep hills force their way" that call emerges "From Bolton's old monastic tower" whose "bells ring loud with gladsome power" (1–2). In the ruins of the old priory and the extant church, Wordsworth finds the North of England a now-Protestant domain sitting astride a Catholic wasteland.

It is fitting that the 1569 rebellion in the North, with its brutal quelling by England's first Protestant queen, should take place exactly five hundred years after the "Harrying of the North" by the first Norman king, William I (the Conqueror). But like the Pilgrimage of Grace a few decades prior, the Rising of the North in 1569 was no simple holy war; rather, it was a coming to a head after years of Tudor centralization that targeted northern autonomy, playing upon the North's financial decline. The 1555 Tillage Act, among other laws, strained the northern pastoral economy, even as

173

local lords were being challenged and replaced by new men firmly in the hand of the crown. The ascension of the Protestant monarch Elizabeth I with her act of religious settlement was too much to bear. As we already saw in the last chapter, when the sovereign's centralized government engages the economic with the religious – attacking the Catholicism that was central to northern spirituality even after the dissolution of the monasteries – the North will not abide. The Northern Rising of 1569 draws together various strands from this study and proves a fitting endpoint for the discussions it has offered.

On November 14, 1569, Thomas Percy, seventh Earl of Northumberland, and Charles Neville, sixth Earl of Westmorland, marched to Durham with sixty or more horsemen. The earls made their way to Durham Cathedral, where they proceeded to destroy Protestant bibles, service books, and the communion table before going out to Palace Green to announce the forbiddance of Protestant worship in the Cathedral or surrounding churches. No doubt, the rebellion was a religious one. The earls sought "the restoration of the old faith, of all ancient customs and liberties to God's church and this noble realm." Their goal was not far-fetched, as Catholicism remained in practice in much of England and particularly in the North, despite the Elizabethan settlement. If the twelfth-century chronicler Richard Devizes held that the North of England was "full of filthy, treacherous, subhuman Scots," then in 1569 the North was full of eager, willing, Catholic Scots priests who, in fleeing Scotland's own recently realized Protestantism, found quick employment in the service of English recusants.[2] Driven by a desire to restore the faith, the earls' army moved quickly from Durham to Richmond and other parts of Yorkshire to call in support for their cause. In the days that followed, reports came to Elizabeth I's officers noting the religious fervor of the earls' followers. Sir Francis Leek writes to the Council of the North on December 3 that the rebels army, "both horse and foot, wear red crosses, as well as the priests as others."[3] Under zealots like Richard Norton, the former sheriff of York memorliazied by Wordsworth, the earls' armies marched with the banner of the five wounds of Christ, so prevalent just thirty years before during the Pilgrimage of Grace, and the banner of St Cuthbert that had, by that time, been born into battle by men of the North for nearly five centuries. The rebellion also marked the resurrection of Catholic objects. Emerging like Lazarus from shallow graves in quarries and other disguised locales, altar stones and holy water stoups reappeared suddenly in churches due to the diligence of local residents.

Much like the Pilgrimage of Grace, however, the Northern Rising subsumed into its Catholic–Protestant rivalry a political theater informed by the North–South divide. As Rachel Reid noted long ago, the great uplands with their steep landscapes, that comprise much of the North of England, were in the sixteenth century "a natural refuge for lost causes."[4] By the reign of Elizabeth I, the negative effect of Tudor government centralization in the North reached its gravest levels. If Mary I's reign offered a brief reprise, then it also arguably made the shift to Elizabeth's rule and, thus, a return to her father's policies, all the more jarring. Again, Henry VIII had worked to dilute the power of northern lords either native to, or with significant ties in, the region by replacing them with men whose status was directly dependent on his patronage. Even as Henry prepared to host Pilgrimage of Grace leader Robert Aske in December 1536, the King was reconfiguring the Council of the North to better suit the aims and needs of his government. The sickly Henry Percy, sixth Earl of Northumberland, granted his lands to the crown and would pass of ill health later in 1537 while his brother Thomas had been implicated already in the Pilgrimage revolt and was executed. The acquisition of Percy lands, to go with the old Neville lands already attained by his father, Henry VII, rendered the King's administrative body into a new order of power. As Rachel Reid explains, the Council "no longer connected with a Household nor burdened with the cares of estate management, had become a purely administrative and judicial body" with "supreme executive authority north of the Trent" and served as the "supreme court of justice, exercising the whole of the crown's criminal and equitable jurisdiction," and its reach now encompassed the five northern counties.[5] In the following decades, northern lands were ceded to southern gentry who remained absentee landlords or local men of lesser rank were elevated to positions of power in the face of the long-standing northern magnates. To take but one significant example, the Forster family of Adderstone, just southwest of Bamburgh, were Percy squires, but the fall of the Percies after 1537 afforded opportunities for these local gentry to gain significant power in the region.[6] John Forster grew up in the turbulent environment of the Scottish borders with his father, Thomas, marshal of Berwick, and young John rose quickly to prominence through land acquisition and dutiful service in border warfare. He was further advanced by the patronage of Thomas, Lord Wharton, who was a new favorite of Henry VIII in the North. Given the absence of Percy power and position, Forster found himself deputy Warden of the Middle March by 1556. While Mary I's Catholic government returned the position to Thomas Percy, the new seventh Earl of Northumberland, on January 18, 1558 – in this case both the East and Middle Marches – Percy understood that, with the regime change brought by Elizabeth's ascension, he would lose his position, so he resigned the wardenships in November 1559 and Elizabeth appointed Lord Grey of Wilton as his replacement.[7] As we might imagine, in his brief return to the wardenship, Percy labored to remove the various Forster kinsmen from power, position, and land,[8] but the upstart John Forster survived with the help of the Queen's privy councilor, Sir Ralph Sadler, no Percy partisan himself. By November 1560, Forster took the wardenship of the Middle March, the first gentry person to achieve such a position, and he did so with the help of both Sadler and Thomas Howard, fourth Duke of Norfolk, acting in his own new role as Queen's Lieutenant in the North. Percy remained on the Council of the North and Elizabeth even afforded him the position of High Steward of her lands in Richmondshire. But when the Queen ordered Percy to enforce a new tax there, the Earl sided with his tenants. He certainly did not want to wind up like his great-grandfather, murdered in 1489 by his own northern subjects as a perceived agent of the crown when he likely sympathized with their opposition.[9] His reluctance drew Elizabeth's ire and led to her subsequent humiliation of him. And while even these embarrassments did not drive Percy to rebellion, the conflation of government centralization with Protestantism provoked the Earl to act.

Upon the death of Cuthbert Tunstall in 1559, Elizabeth installed James Pilkington as Bishop of Durham. As Eamon Duffy points out, Pilkington was a "vehement Protestant activist," who had spent the Marian years on the Continent, where he was essential to the translation of the *Geneva Bible*. A few years later, Pilkington was joined by the radical Puritan William Whittingham, who had married John Calvin's sister (or sister-in-law) and whose appointment as Dean of Durham Cathedral – through the patronage of the Queen's favorite, Robert Dudley, the Earl of Leicester – was welcomed by Pilkington. As Duffy explains, the two men installed "a rigorous Protestant regime" at Durham, and one that "made preaching circuits to other parishes, where their abrasive reforming zeal frequently antagonized."[10] Whittingham himself is said to have attacked a statue of Durham's principal saint, causing "the image of St. Cuthbert ... [t]o be defaced, and broken all to pieces, to the intent that there should be no memory of that holy man," while Whittingham's French-born wife, Katherine, is rumoured to have burned Cuthbert's banner.[11] The Queen must have recognized as an omen the Earl of Northumberland's official reconciliation with the Catholic Church in

1567.[12] Pilkington might have been provoking revolt with his assaults on Catholic ritual and imagery, but, as K. J. Kesselring points out, "Pilkington combined his efforts at religious reform with a program to reendow the church with lands alienated by his predecessors and long in the hands of others, thus earning further enmity."[13] The combination of centralizing politics and religion came together best in the figure of Mary Stewart, Queen of Scotland, who had abdicated her throne in 1567 and fled to England a year later in order to escape the persecution of her young son's handlers. Elizabeth had quickly locked her cousin Mary up in Bolton Castle as a precaution, but Mary would remain the object of English Catholic affection and for many discontented northerners hoped that the Queen of Scots might be placed back on the Scottish throne, as a counter to Elizabeth, or on the English throne in order to rid England of Protestantism altogether. Prophecies stirred throughout 1569 about plots against Elizabeth, plots that aimed to wed Mary to the Duke of Norfolk, in spite of Norfolk's own Protestantism. Devout Catholics such as Northumberland only reluctantly agreed to such a match,[14] but the Earl of Westmorland was Norfolk's brother-in-law and he saw an opportunity to build a larger coalition against Elizabeth. Fervor for the proposed marriage was undeniable, as evidenced in one enthusiastic letter to interested parties in Rome, dated October 8, 1569: "it was rumoured ... that the Duke of Nortolf [Norfolk], a great personage and much beloved of the people, had taken to wife the Queen of Scotland against the Queen of England's will; and that the Queen of Scotland was a prisoner in a castle, which, if true, might occasion some disturbance in that kingdom."[15] Little did they know that the marriage plot had already failed just a few weeks prior to the letter's dating and that Norfolk was imprisoned in the Tower of London.

And the rebellion would also fail rather quickly. The rebels' hand-wringing over whether and how to revolt led to confused plans that were too much for them to overcome. Elizabeth moved Mary, Queen of Scots, from Tutbury to Coventry just a week after the Earls' march on Durham, ensuring that any act to free her on the rebels' part was now off the table. They simply sat in place, exercising their forces, only in agreement that they would *not* attack York. As Kesselring explains, "The Northern Rebellion grew from a complex blend of aristocratic intrigue, regional grievances against an aggressively centralizing state, and a widespread if inchoate dissatisfaction with ongoing Protestant reform," but "it did not in the end amount to much."[16] Duffy, similarly, characterizes the rebellion as "badly planned by an ill-matched consortium of northern nobles and gentry" and a "leaky conspiracy."[17] While they achieved brief success in taking Hartlepool – with hopes that a Spanish force might arrive via ship – and while they captured Barnard Castle in early December from Sir George Bowes – in part because some 225 of the garrison defected to the rebels' side – failure to secure definitive aid from the northern Lord Dacre and anxieties about the imminent arrival of the Elizabeth's southern force prevented the earls from further action. On December 13, both Northumberland and Westmorland were confronted by Forster, riding with the Earl's brother, Henry Percy no less, in a small skirmish that sent the rebels back to Durham. Little did they know that the southern army under the Earl of Warwick, with its 12,000 men, had reached Wetherby just west of York. Further news of Dacre's outright refusal of assistance, as well as a message that the Queen's navy was at Hartlepool, convinced Northumberland and Westmorland that their cause was lost. On December 20, they took a small contingent of horseman and crossed the border into Scotland.

The rebellion itself was not finished. We might recall William of Malmesbury's complaints that the North and its peoples were inferior in speech and learning because they were too close to Scotland. In the early months of 1570, a southern Protestant might make a similar observation as Westmorland and his men cavorted with the Scottish lords Ferniehurst and Hume, as well as the tortured Earl of Argyll, Archibald Campbell, still supportive of Mary and staunchly opposed to the Scottish regent, James Stewart, Earl of Moray. Moray was assassinated at Linlithgow on January 23, which only fueled a new hope for Mary's Scottish party, now joined with the English rebels in exile. And while Elizabeth sent an army into Scotland to capture the rebels and confront native support on that side of the border, she deftly managed the various threats around her, putting off the French – who threatened to aid the Scottish Marians – and appeasing the Protestant leadership of Scotland that she was not attacking their realm but rather bringing her own unruly subjects back to England for justice. Elizabeth entered into negotiations with her cousin Mary, still in English captivity, to ensure stability between Mary and the significant and powerful Marians in Scotland and, in this way, as Kesselring points out, they "destroyed the dangerous bond between the English rebels and Marian loyalists" and subtly set the stage for the future of the English crown.[18] A peace was signed between parties on September 3 and several of the Scots lords who had supported English rebels accorded with the young King James's faction. While the Scots parties of Mary and her son continued to fight among themselves, the English forces left Scotland following the peace.

Conclusion

In the immediate wake of the rebellion, Elizabeth's government exacted brutal justice on the population of the North. We might recognize a second "Harrying of the North" in the winter of 1569–1570. Evidence of participation in the revolt suggests that the earls' army amounted to as many as 6,000 men, but most rebels came from Durham and north Yorkshire, with further expectations of men from either Lancashire or Cheshire failing to materialize. And the crown would exact retribution on all communities who sent rebels into the field in service of the earls' cause. Marshall law was declared in Durham, North Yorkshire, and Northumberland. Sussex writes to William Cecil on December 28 1569 of his determination "to exequut specially, constables and other officers, that have seduced the people (under color of the Quenes Majesties service) to rebell; and suche others as have ben moste busye to further those matters." The summary nature of the Queen's justice was such that, in Sussex's words, "ther shal be no towne that hath sent men to the rebells, or otherwise ayded them, but some of the worst disposed shal be exequuted for example."[19] Pilkington himself laments that "The number off offendors is so grete, that few innocent are left to trie the giltie."[20] But the crown would have its way. Just a few days later, Sussex offered specific numbers of those to be executed: 314 persons in total, at Durham (80 persons), Darlington (42 persons), Barnard Castle (20 persons), and in towns and villages in the surrounding areas (172 persons).[21] Those numbers would double as marshal George Bowes moved his party further afield of those towns to cover every part of rebel territory. The cruelty of show is evident in Sussex's letter on January 19:

> I wowld have you makth examples grete in Rypon and Tadcaster; and, therefore, yf you find not suffycyent nombres within the townes that be in the doings of the late [rebellion], take of other townes that be in the doings of the late [rebellion], take of those other townes, and bring them to the execution to those places; for it is necessary that the execution be grete in appearance in those two places, though ether be the lesse, or none, in other places.[22]

Bowes will note a few days later that he has overseen the execution of "six hundreth and odd" men.[23]

While Elizabeth sought to stymie any further revolt in the North through the spectacle and expanse of these many executions, she further recognized the suppression of the rebellion as a financial opportunity. As Kesselring argues, for example, "Concerns for profit rather than straightforward vengeance shaped the resolution of the conflict; pardons and punishments became commodities to be bartered and exchanged" (214).

Indeed, Sussex directs Bowes to use his discretion in selecting a number of men from towns and villages to execute that "you may not execute any that hathe freeholds, or note welthye; for so is the Quene Majesties plesier, by her specyall commandment."²⁴ Much as her grandfather and father had done before, Elizabeth confiscated rebel lands and properties both to increase the royal coffers and further diminish the power and income of those northern lords who had defied the crown and its faith. Even the long-held autonomy of the Bishop of Durham over his see was challenged by the Crown – much to the shock of the Protestant zealot Pilkington – so that Elizabeth might subsume those most important lands of rebels that otherwise would have reverted to the bishopric.²⁵ Sussex writes to Cecil in December 1569,

> I find that all forfeitures that by this late rebellion should grow to Her Majesty in the bishopric, will by law fall to the bishop, which will be too great for any subject to receive; therefore, before I proceed against the offenders that have estates of inheritance or great wealth, Her Majesty should either compound with the Bishop for his royalties, and keep them still in her hands, or translate him to some other bishopric, whereby *sede vacante* all might grow to her.²⁶

Much as the "Harying of the North" had laid waste to the region five centuries before, retribution for the Northern Rising came to resemble a similar destruction. The forces under the command of Ambrose Dudley, the Earl of Warwick, took the opportunity of rebel defeat to wage a pillaging campaign. Even Warwick's colleagues, chiefly the Earl of Sussex, complained of his activities. For Sussex, the destruction Warwick wrought was to the detriment of the Queen both because "the pardons proclaimed by Her Majesty's command is no security" to the people at Warwick's hand and the property spoiled "should have been to her profit."²⁷ Ralph Sadler notes, further, that "there has been great disorder in spoil, as well of the innocent as the guilty, made by the Southern army by disordered and unruly soldiers," and the effect of this reiving is, as Sir Thomas Hargrave comments, "that the scarcity will be felt two or three years." We hear the resonance of William of Malmesbury's twelfth-century lament at the Conqueror's decimation of the North's great Roman buildings – its "towers whose tops threatened the sky" – in testimony that Warwick and his soldiers stripped churches of their beams and lead, among other structural elements. Some of Elizabeth's "new men" in the North also took part in this harrying. John Forster asserted his power over the structures that once signified Percy power in the North. Lord Hunsdon laments of Forster,

> ytt ys grete pytty too see how Alnwyke Castell and Warkworth are spoylded by hym and hys... And for the Abbey that stands yn Hull Parke, he hath neythar lefte lede, glase, ierne, nor so muche as the pypse of lede that convayd the water to the howse ... and, as I am credibly informed, he meanes utterly too deface bothe the uthar howsys, Warkwroth and Alnwyk, which wer grete pytty.

The Earl of Northumberland was in no position to stop the looting of his former residences. When he crossed the border in December 1569, Percy took sanctuary in Scotland with Hector Armstrong of Harlaw but he was eventually deceived and sold, in effect, to James Douglas, Earl of Morton. The winding down of the rebellion affords us an oft-repeated phrase first uttered by Lord Hunsdon in a December 31 letter to the Privy Council: "throughout Northumberland they know no other prince but a Percy."[28] And given this fitting ascription of Percy's power as a king in the North, it is, further, appropriate that the Northern Rebellion of 1569 concluded with the confluence of Percy and Douglas. Douglas delayed Percy's handover to the English for a year, and he even entertained a ransom from Percy's wife, Anne, the Countess of Northumberland. She informed her husband in a January 28, 1572 letter that "the ten thousand crowns required for his ransom have been obtained." Even the Pope and the King of Spain contributed to the Percy ransom.[29] But in duplicitous fashion, Douglas turned around and took that same amount from Sir John Forster on behalf of Elizabeth, and Percy was delivered into English hands. When he was handed over to Lord Hunsdon on May 29, 1572, Percy went to Berwick for several weeks. Hunsdon reports that Percy talked as much of "hawks and hounds than anything else," seemingly aware of his own doomed state as captured traitor to the crown (312). Percy spent several more months in captivity before he was executed on the pavement at York on August 22, 1572.

While Lancashire men remained distant from the 1569 rebellion, north and west Lancashire were ardently Catholic; as returns of 1564 demonstrate, eighteen of twenty-four JPs (Justices of the Peace) were of the old faith, including the lawyer John Towneley.[30] Narrowly avoiding involvement in the 1569 rebellion, the patriarch of the Towneley family remained always a dutiful Catholic. In his many run-ins with Elizabeth's government, Towneley was, not infrequently, aided by his half-brother, Alexander Nowell, the Protestant Dean of St Paul's. The 1601 painting *The Towneley Family at Prayer* hangs in Towneley Hall. The image depicts John and wife Mary, with their seven sons and seven daughters, engaged at a prayer desk with a prayer book, as well as a crucifix, dripping blood, before them. An inscription at the bottom of the artwork, which was once obscured by a board attached to the painting, illuminates John Towneley's legal sufferings as a devout Catholic and recusant in Protestant England. We are told that John:

> for professing ye apostolicall catholic Romaine ffaith was imprisoned first at Chester castell, then sent to marishalsea, then to yorke castell, then to ye blockhouses in hull, then to the gatehouse in Westminster, then to Manchester, then to broughton in Oxfordshire, then twice to Elie in Cambridgeshr, and so now of 73 yeares old and blinde, is bounde to appeare and to kepe within five myles of towneley his house, who has since ye statute of 23 [1584] paid in to ye Exchequer £xx ye mounthe & doth still, yt there is paid already above five iiith 1601.[31]

The inscription illustrates Towneley's much-travelled history as a heretic in Elizabeth's England. By 1601, the nearly blind lawyer is homebound by order and, having been imprisoned for much of his later life, has paid around £5,000 in recusancy fines.[32] Towneley would die in 1607, having outlived the Queen, if not her faith, yet he witnessed arguably the most significant event in North–South relations: the union of the English and Scottish crowns.

We might recognize in the Northern Rising of 1569 a desire between English and Scottish Catholics to forge a new British union, one that might have found Mary Queen of Scots as monarch of both realms. But the revolt had an equal and opposite effect, as negotiations between the Protestant regimes of England and Scotland illustrated increasingly common political ground between the two long-warring realms. As Kesselring claims, "This was made possible by the emergence of a newer 'British' identity, an identity premised on a shared Protestantism in the face of a pan-European Catholic foe, that began to compete with older national identities and hatreds."[33] No doubt, this new-found British identity made palatable the 1586 Treaty of Berwick and, then, the succession of James VI to the throne of England upon Elizabeth's death in 1603. As I have shown in this study, the North of England's proximity to Scotland was frequently the basis for its cultural, linguistic, and political derision in the literature of medieval England. The union of the crowns, however, suddenly made the Anglo-Scottish border an uncontested zone and, thus, rendered the North of England impotent as a frontline of defense against the auld enemy. Frank Musgrove is blunt in his historical survey of the North: "In 1603 the North became redundant . . . . The union of the English and Scottish Crowns . . . deprived northern England between Humber and Tweed of its great and heroic historic role."[34]

Conclusion 183

We must not overlook the identity forged in the wake of this last northern rebellion in Tudor England. As I have asserted in this book, the convoluted relationship of regionalism and nationalism in the North–South divide finds that the outlying North actually operates as a necessary, if not sufficient, condition for the processes of imagining a nation. Throughout the Middle Ages and into the early modern period, the North of England is not strictly a cultural or political "other" to the southern "one" in what amounts to an overly simple center–periphery model. The region, instead, proves quintessential to English nationalism, provoking questions of identity and desperation for unity through its rebellion but, also, assuring longevity to the imagined community of the English as a frontline of defense against the Scots and, by proxy, the French. The North gave birth to English history in the learned father Bede and it further nurtured a devotional culture that profoundly impacted English Catholicism for the whole of the Middle Ages. But this very same fervor melded with a history of rebellion to threaten Tudor power, consolidated in the South, as the country confronted and engaged the Reformation from 1534 through Elizabeth's tumultuous reign, and beyond. Nevertheless, we again recognize that the pronounced regionalism driving the Pilgrimage of Grace and the 1569 Rising of the North was necessary and constitutive of a new British identity that emerges in its wake. The damning region, with its heretical religion and its usurping angels – now fallen from their seats of power in the North – proves salvific to a new and necessary Britishness that will drive the realm into the age of global imperialism.

The North–South divide, however, does not vanish after 1603. In the wake of Britain's expanding empire in the eighteenth century, a new economy quickly emerged in the North of England and the Industrial Revolution was born. This explosion of industry created a new dynamic between North and South and the subsequent economic disparities between regions became the basis for analyzing England's modern rift. It is ironic, if expected of the divide's history, that industry would create new magnates of significant political and financial power in the formerly contested areas of the bishopric of Durham and the Percy lands in Northumberland. In the nineteenth century, barons of the coal industry began refurbishing and inhabiting old peel towers and other medieval residences. Sir William Armstrong took Bamburgh Castle, while James Joicey, W.D. Cruddas, and the coal-owning antiquarian Cadwallader Bates fought over the old Langley barony lands before Bates himself attained and restored Langley Castle in 1882. These preoccupations with medieval ruins correlate as well with a pronounced return of Catholicism to the North. As Bill Lancaster notes, "Whilst the elite created their pastiche Northumbria from derelict buildings, with the reestablishment of the Catholic hierarchy we see Northumbria being appropriated to form a religious landscape"; thus, several new Catholic churches were built and dedicated to the great Northumbrian saints: Aidan, Oswald, Wilifrid, and, of course, Cuthbert. The effect of northern industry – and its tycoons – on the landscape and economy of northern England was itself both salvific and damning to those arriving in its wake. Langland's old joke about *Isaiah 14*, about the devil in the North, resonates in Stephan Kohl's survey of twentieth-century travel writing, such as H.V. Morton's *In Search of England* (1927) and John Hillaby's *Journey Through Britain* (1968). Kohl concludes that "all writers discuss the landscapes of the 'North' as moral landscapes, and it depends only on their political affiliations whether that moral ugliness is ascribed to the inhabitants of the 'North' or whether the exploitation of the 'North' by the 'South' is held responsible for that 'hellish' condition of the 'North.'" The motion picture comedy *Brassed Off* (1996), for example, explores the lives of miners in the fictional Yorkshire town of Grimley, based on the real Grimethorpe, struggling with economic hardships born of the slow and agonizing demise of their local coal pit under the weight of Thatcherism and Tory economic reform in the 1980s. Facing further wage concessions and, ultimately, the pit's closure, the colliery's brass band carries on in hopes of making the national brass band finals in London, which they eventually win. The real Grimethorpe's closure was announced in October 1992, just weeks before the band headed to London for the competition. In the film's finale, the fictional bandleader Danny Ormondroyd (the real director was Frank Renton) gives an angry speech at the Royal Albert Hall about the national government's assault on the northern coal industry and, therefore, on their communities and their lives. As the credits role, the band sits atop a London tour bus moving through the city as they play, with irony, "Land of Hope and Glory." If we consider the medieval and modern North–South divide, it is quite fitting that artist Antony Gromley erected his massive steel sculpture on the former Team colliery pithead baths, south of Gateshead: the Angel of the North.

On February 16, 2009, a little more than a decade after the Angel of the North first rose beside the A1, the London charity and art organization Poetry in the City held an event for which local poets read original poems on the English North–South divide. In response to the BBC s coverage of the event, novice poets from the public at-large submitted their own

North–South musings, some of which were published on the BBC News site.[35] David Ashford of Kent finds the North of England defeated by politics, weather, and mere chance:

> Up North, rarely do I go there,
> At southerners, the folk do stare,
> Food nought but chips and pie,
> A southern softy, they call I,
> The colliery shut, Thatcher they blame,
> But who'd go back to that old game?
> Terraced houses are every street,
> Weather poor, Lord give me heat!
> Football is religion and more,
> About its tales the people bore,
> National anthem the Hovis song,
> Everything here has gone wrong,
> Not London but before Scotland,
> The North is a strange old land.[36]

Ashford depicts the region as a landscape of bizarre ritual, poor climate, and dull stories. Its industry, particularly coal ("the colliery"), is outdated ("who'd go back to that old game?"), its people cling to sports as salvation ("Football is religion and more"), and its cold streets are littered with indistinguishable houses that match the region's insipid character. Ashford's poem affords a telling line: "National anthem the Hovis song." Neither the commercials for which this song was used – a series of popular 1970s television ads for the British bread company, Hovis – nor the song itself – Antonín Dvorak's theme from the second movement of his *New World Symphony* – are as striking as Ashford's ascription of the tune as the North's "national anthem."[37] Here and throughout his poem, Ashford echoes the belief of such writers as Orwell or Bill Bryson, who claims in his *Notes from a Small Island* (1996) that the North "felt like another country."[38] What is more, Ashford's jibes at northern religion, northern work life, and northern food speak to a the strange confluence of region and nation in the North–South divide that this book has studied, a regionalism that, nevertheless, informs the English nation-state. The North is "Not London" but is "before Scotland," a strangely liminal space, and yet it remains distinctly English.

As I hope to have shown, the rift itself is undeniable even at the earliest stages of an emergent English identity, and these conflicting sentiments toward the North throughout this long history – from the medieval to the modern – muddle perceptions of the North–South divide. Another poet in the 2009 contest, Jan Church of Winchester, reflects on a very different North:

> Land of rocks, Of peaks and pikes,
> Fleetwith, Langdale, Scafell,
> Of edges: Alderley,
> Striding, Stanage, Robin Hoods, Froggatt.
> And wizards.
> The green knight with hair bristling,
> The wizard asleep by the Iron Gates,
> The wizard Earl of Northumberland
> And yet further
> The high hills of the Cheviot
> With curlews calling.

Church links northern geology to myth at Alderley Edge in Cheshire East, where one encounters the "wizard asleep at the Iron Gates." According to legend, the gates lead to a cavernous sanctuary in which sleeps a great army – in many versions of the myth this is Arthur's army – that will ride out one day to save Britain in battle.[39] Church evokes medieval narratives such as the Green Knight and others already discussed in the preceding chapters (the outlaw Robin Hood, the 1388 Battle of Otterburn in the Cheviot hills). For Church, the North's mysteries also fuse with its political history, specifically through "The Wizard Earl," Henry Percy, the ninth Earl of Northumberland (1564–1632), so-called for his pursuits in the study of natural philosophy and his patronage of scientists in the early seventeenth century.[40] Church's poem imagines a mythic North defined by its signature landscape of peaks, edges, and hills, intimately tied to its people and their folklore.

Amateur poets Church and Ashford capture the extant division in England between the North and South and, at the same time, the two poets' starkly different views intimate the uncanny nature of the North of England. Church's North is a place of wonder and mystery, and her words bespeak a fascination and restrained admiration for the region. Ashford's vision is derivative of the region as a hopeless place where "everything has gone wrong." Explaining such divergent views, historian Stuart Rawnsley argues that the North "evokes a greater sense of identity than any other 'region' of the country [while at] the same time it provokes the most derision and rejection from those whose identity has been constructed and shaped elsewhere."[41] And the location of that "elsewhere" remains a significant point of contention for the modern divide. Katie Wales explains

Conclusion

the phenomenon of shifting North–South borders over the course of the divide's cultural history:

> A great deal depends on the *origo* [her italics], the point of departure: southerners tend to place a "divide" much further south than northerners ... For Londoners and the metropolitan-oriented media, popular phrases like "North of Potters Bar" or "North of Watford", beyond the northern limits on the Metropolitan underground line respectively, suggest that these are cultural faultlines, the bounds of civilization.[42]

Indeed, for the modern North–South divide, the more distinct geographic boundaries of the Humber Estuary or the River Trent have melted away into cultural faultlines every bit as subjective as any other response to questions of culture. Poet Laureate and erstwhile Marsden native Simon Armitage is perhaps more on point in his partial memoir, *All Points North*. Unabashed, Armitage claims, the North is "where England tucks its shirt in its underpants." But Armitage also deftly plays on this long-held and convoluted question of locating the region in Great Britain: "The North can also be Lancashire, which is really the North-West, and it can also be Northumberland, which is the North-East, and sometimes it's Humberside, which is the Netherlands, and it can be Cumbria, which is the Lake District, and therefore Scotland."[43]

Cultural contests over boundaries aside, the geographic borders used repeatedly to set off the North from the rest of England in the Middle Ages, whether the Jurassic limestone that runs from the Tees to the Exe and that dictated early British settlement patterns or the Humber Estuary and the River Trent that emerges from it, continue to highlight economic, political, and social disparities between North and South. Following data gathered for the 2000 census, Sheffield University issued a report confirming that, as the new millennium began, the economic North–South divide was widening. The North of England grew poorer while the South grew richer. The study noted, for instance, that the financial base of London and the Home Counties created some 1.7 million new jobs between 1991 and 2001, while the northern provinces lost 500,000 jobs. Disparities between the North and South continued into the second decade of the 2000s reflected, further, in education, healthcare, and, specifically, death rates.[44] As we turn into the third decade of the twenty-first century, we find in the *Telegraph*, for example, political philosopher and conservative Phillip Blond offering "My five-point plan to fix the North–South divide."[45] Undoubtedly, the divide continues to pervade England's cultural and political identity. In a 1999 broadcast of

Radio 4's *In Our Time*, on the topic of the "nation-state," historian Norman Davies worried over the then-burgeoning regionalism of Great Britain and the campaigns of "Scotland in Europe" and "Cymru yn Ewrop" ("Wales in Europe"), noting that the North of England might also get in the game: "we'll have a Cumbria, and Lancashire and Yorkshire in Europe." Host Melvyn Bragg, himself a proud Cumbrian, agreed with Davies that "there is a strong feeling in the North that people are 'from the North.'"[46] In a speech delivered in Manchester in June 2014, then-Chancellor of the Exchequer George Osbourne called for a "northern powerhouse" aimed at cultivating the collective rebirth and sustained success of northern cities like Manchester and Liverpool that would lessen the economic weight on London. Today, the *Guardian* maintains a "North–South divide" page that captures all stories pertaining to what it explains as "perceived differences between southern England and the rest of Great Britain," but these stories most often focus on disparities specifically between the North and South of England. And at any given time, one can find some news piece that explains how, in some extant or additional category, the divide grows.[47] Even though the recent 2016 referendum on whether to remain within the European Union or not (the so-called "Brexit vote") revealed a somewhat expected scenario (rural and economically depressed areas voted in favor of exiting while metropolitan areas and those centered around substantial higher education centers voted to remain), the final vote that affirmed Britain's exit from the European Union was portrayed in terms of England's North–South divide. *The Independent* offered its own explanation for "Why the North of England will regret voting for Brexit"[48] – and referred to northeast England specifically as "Brexit Central."

In the eighth century, the monk Bede cultivated a new English history and he, further, intimated the possibility of English identity in spite of the various kingdoms that politically divided the island. Bede's abbot, Benedict Biscop, actively sought to Romanize Northumbria through Latin learning and Roman architecture and to establish that kingdom as a center for religion and learning in the West. And while contests between Britain's many realms and, later, Viking invasions rendered Biscop's vision a ruin, Bede's own historiography proved a keystone to the very concept of Englishness, particularly in the aftermath of the Norman Conquest. Yet, Bede's foundational history was always troubled by the very autonomy of Northumbria lingering within the *gentis Anglorum*. The North–South divide, thus, troubles English history from its outset, fostering a rift that spans the medieval to the modern era. The rhetoric of northern derision evident in the literature of medieval England – whether of dialect, religion, independence – establishes a cultural and political discourse that remains recognizable even in modern depictions of the divide. But the resonance of the medieval in the modern also betrays the still-profound desire for – the necessity of – the uncanny North in order to define English identity and the English nation. William of Malmesbury complained of the "uncouth" speech he heard at York. Over three centuries later, Ranulph Higden repeated William's claim, while a few decades later, still, John Trevisa translated those complaints into his own southern English. In the same period, Chaucer offered his own approximation of the northern dialect in the *Canterbury Tales* and a little over a century afterward, the Towneley *Second Shepherd's Play* took a jibe, similarly framed, at the "southern tooth." We might, then, speed forward to the present day, where a poet like Armitage muses on his own northern speech:

> These days a "regional accent" is usually thought of as a marker of authenticity and identity, but growing up we were told to speak properly and sometimes threatened with elocution lessons, because with the unsophisticated noises that came out of our mouths, we would never get anywhere.[49]

Armitage's comments frame a more recent desire for authentic regional speech as progression from an older, rigid point of view that professes a "proper" speech or received pronunciation, but we might also take the poet laureate's own experiences to demonstrate, once more, the desire and derision inherent in discourse on the North of England, a northern consciousness that values regionalism, or northern-ness, for its authenticity and a northern consciousness that derides it as an embarrassment or even a danger. Somewhere within these entanglements lies the story of Englishness.

Notes

1 Introduction

1 Charlotte Higgins, "Antony Gormley Drops 60-tonne load for monumental structure," *Guardian* 27 August 2010, www.theguardian.com/artanddesign/2010/aug/27/antony-gormley-exposure-sculpture (accessed November 23, 2021).
2 "The History of the Angel of the North," *Gateshead Council*, www.gateshead.gov.uk/article/5303/The-history-of-the-Angel-of-the-North (accessed November 23, 2021).
3 "The Angel Has Landed," *BBC News* online. 16 February 1998, news.bbc.co.uk/2/hi/uk_news/56000.stm (accessed November 23, 2021).
4 Martin Roberts, *The Buildings of England: County Durham* (Yale University Press, 2021), pp. 435–36.
5 Quotations of Langland are from *Piers Plowman: The C-Text*, ed. Derek Pearsall (Exeter: Exeter University Press, 1994). In this edition, Latin quotations not containing English words and/or not pertinent to the syntax of the surrounding English lines are unnumbered.
6 The linguistic ambiguity of "sonne" in the passage from *Piers Plowman* is twofold. The *Middle English Dictionary* shows the flexibility of the noun "sonne" as denoting the celestial object (sun) and, in some cases, *filius*, and this duality is at work in Augustine's own commentary on *Isaiah 14* below, which links a redeeming warmth with Christ's presence in the South.
7 See Alfred L. Kellogg, "Satan, Langland, and the North." *Speculum* 24 (1949): pp. 413–14.
8 "*Contrarius solet esse aquilo Sion: Sion quippe in meridie, aquilo contra meridiem*" – and then asks, "Quis est iste aquilo, nisi qui dixit, Ponam pedem meum in aquilone, et ero similis Altissimo" (qtd. In Kellog 413); Translation of Augustine taken from John Henry Parker, ed. *Expositions on the Book of Psalms by S. Augustine, Bishop of Hippo*, Translated with Notes and Indices in Six Volumes, vol. II, (Oxford and London: John Henry Parker; F. and J. Rivington, 1848), p. 289.
9 All quotations from Chaucer are taken from Larry D. Benson, ed. *The Riverside Chaucer*, gen. (Houghton-Mifflin, 1987) and cited by fragment (in

roman numerals) and line number in the text. It is appropriate, given the allusions to the North in *Isaiah*, that the yeoman-devil's declaration that he hails from the North appears in line 1413 of Fragment III of the *Canterbury Tales*.

10 Dave Russell, *Looking North: Northern England and the National Imagination* (Manchester University Press, 2004), p. 4.
11 J.C. Holt, *The Northerners: A Study in the Reign of King John* (Oxford University Press, 1961).
12 See Bruce M.S. Campbell, "North–South Dichotomies, 1066–1550," in *Geographies of England: The North–South Divide, Material and Imagined*. eds. Alan R. Baker and Mark Billinge (Cambridge University Press, 2004), p. 158. The South's prominence as the ruling center of England grew particularly in the late thirteenth and fourteenth centuries. Campbell notes that other than times of war, medieval kings spent much of their time in the South and Midlands, of which "London and Westminster ... were [the] nerve center," and which held the majority of their palaces and hunting grounds. Notably, by 1350, 85 percent of all councils and parliaments were held in London and Westminster.
13 D. J. Hall, *English Medieval Pilgrimage* (Routledge, 2019), 88. King Alfred and later kings Edward, Æthlestan, and Edmund issued royal injunctions to honor Cuthbert, and Æthlestan himself took the pilgrimage to Cuthbert's shrine, then at St Chester-le-strete in 934, and Edmund came ten years later.
14 Mathew Holford, "Durham: History, Culture and Identity," in *North-East England, c. 1200–c. 1400*, ed. M.L. Holford and K.J. Stronger (Edinburgh University Press, 2010), p. 33.
15 See Michael A. Penman, "The Scots at the Battle of Neville's Cross, 17 October 1346," *Scottish Historical Review* 80 (October 2001): 157–180.
16 George Orwell, *The Road to Wigan Pier* (London: Harcourt, 1958), p. 112.
17 See Dorothy W. Collin, "The Composition of Mrs. Gaskell's *North and South*." *Bulletin of the John Rylands Library* 54.1 (1971): pp. 67–98. Dickens suggests to Gaskell, in a letter dated July 26, 1854, "North and South appears to me to be a better name than Margaret Hale [Gaskell's own desired title]. It implies more, and is expressive of the opposite people brought face to face by the story" (qtd in Collin p. 75).
18 Rob Shields, *Places on the Margin: Alternative Geographies of Modernity* (Routledge, 1991), p. 207.
19 Neville Kirk, ed. *Northern Identities: Historical Interpretations of "The North" and 'Northernness'* (Ashgate, 2000).
20 Campbell, "North–South Dichotomies." p. 67.
21 Orwell, *The Road to Wigan Pier*, p. 110.
22 Patricia Yeager, "Introduction: Narrating Space," in *The Geography of Identity*, ed. Patricia Yeager (University of Michigan Press, 1996), p. 15
23 Yeager, "Introduction: Narrating Space," p. 20.
24 Andrea Ruddick, *English Identity and Political Culture in the Fourteenth Century* (Cambridge University Press, 2013), p. 11.

25 Ruddick, *English Identity*, p. 10.
26 Susan Reynolds, *Kingdoms and Communities in Western Europe, 900–1300* (Clarendon Press, 1984), p. 252.
27 R.R. Davies, "Nations and National Identities in the Medieval World: An Apologia," *Revue Belge D'Histoire Contemporaine* 34 (2004): p. 575. Davies points out, as a very early example, the common use of the term "Angelcyn" (*Angelkynne* in the Alfred quotation above) in the late ninth century to illustrate the "process of ethnogenesis, of creating people" that was taking place in the realm. In the entry for 886, the *Anglo-Saxon Chronicle* explains: "Ðy ilcan geare ge sette Ælfred cyning Lunden burh. 7 him eall Angel cyn to ge cyrde" (The same year King Alfred occupied London fort; and all the English race turned to him). This sense of a single people and their kingdom pervades extant rolls and legal documents, histories, and literary texts.
28 Ruddick, *English Identity*, p. 63.
29 See Michelle Warren's discussion of Benedict Anderson in *History on the Edge: Excalibur and the Borders of Britain, 1100–1300* (University of Minnesota Press, 2000), p. 10.
30 Geraldine Heng, *Empire of Magic: Medieval Romance and the Politics of Cultural Fantasy* (Columbia University Press, 2004), p. 99.
31 Kathy Lavezzo, *Angels on the Edge of the World* (Cornell University Press, 2006), pp. 7–8.
32 Lynn Staley, *The Island Garden: England's Language of Nation from Gildas to Marvell* (University of Notre Dame Press, 2012), p. 3.
33 Susan Nakely, *Living in the Future: Sovereignty and Internationalism in the Canterbury Tales* (University of Michigan Press, 2017), p. 4.
34 Ardis Butterfield, *The Familiar Enemy: Chaucer, Language and Nation in the Hundred Years War* (Oxford University Press, 2009), p. 21.
35 Davies, "Nations," p. 574.
36 Thorlac Turville-Petre, *England the Nation: Language, Literature, and National Identity, 1290–1340* (Oxford University Press, 1996), p. 4.
37 Patricia Clare Ingham, *Sovereign Fantasies: Arthurian Romance and the Making of Britain* (University of Pennsylvania Press, 2001), p. 9.
38 Ingham, *Sovereign Fantasies*, p. 9.
39 Emily Dolmans, *Writing Regional Identities in Medieval England: From the Gesta Herwardi to Richard Coer de Lyon* (D.S. Brewer, 2020), p. 3.
40 Robert W. Barrett, Jr., *Against All England: Regional Identity and Cheshire Writing, 1195–1656* (University of Notre Dame Press, 2008), p. 13.
41 Barrett, *Against All England*, pp. 14–15.
42 Daniel Birkholz, *The King's Two Maps: Cartography and Culture in Thirteenth Century England* (Routledge, 2004), p. 65.
43 Butterfield, *Familiar Enemy*, p. 14.
44 David Harvey, *Cosmopolitanism and the Geographies of Freedom* (Columbia University Press, 2009), p. 190.
45 See Campbell's summary of these divisions, "North–South Dichotomies," p. 150.

46 Helen Jewell, *The North–South Divide: The Origins of Northern Consciousness* (Manchester University Press, 1994), pp. 8–9.
47 Quotations of Alfred in Old English are taken from Henry Sweet, ed. *King Alfred's West Saxon Version of Gregory's Pastoral Care*, EETS, o.s. 45, 50 (Oxford University Press, 1871-72).
48 All quotations of William of Malmesbury's *Gesta Regum Anglorum* (hereafter cited as *GR*) are taken from *Gesta Regum Anglorum*, vol. I, ed. and trans. R. A. B. Mynors, R. M. Thomson, and M. Winterbottom (Oxford University Press, 1998).
49 Quotations of William of Malmesbury's *Gestum Pontificum Anglorum* are taken from William of Malmesbury, *Gestum Pontificum Anglorum*, vol. I, ed. M. Winterbottom, (Oxford University Press, 2007).
50 Quotations from John Trevisa are taken from Ranulph Higden, *Polychronicon Ranulphi Higden, Monachi Cestrensis; Together with the English Translations of John Trevisa and of an Unknown Writer of the Fifteenth Century*, 2 vols., ed. Churchill Babington (London: Longmans, Green, and Co., 1869) and cited by volume number (in roman numerals) and page numer in the specific volume.
51 All quotations of the Towneley plays are taken from A.C. Cawley and Martin Stevens, eds., *The Towneley Plays*, 2 vols (E.E.T.S. and Oxford University Press, 1994).
52 Katie Wales, *Northern English: A Social History* (Cambridge University Press, 2006), p. 4.
53 Ralph Hanna, "Yorkshire and York," in *Europe: A Literary History, Vol. I*, ed. David Wallace (Oxford University Press, 2016), p. 256.
54 Jewell, *North–South Divide*, p. 160.
55 Warren Hollister, *Henry I* (Yale University Press, 2003), pp. 241–44
56 For a discussion of the Canterbury forgeries, see R. W. Southern, "The Canterbury Forgeries," *English Historical Review* 73, no. 1 (1958): 193–226 and Robert F. Berkhofer III, "The Canterbury Forgeries Revisited" *Haskins Society Journal* 18 (2006): 36–50.
57 Sarah Rees Jones, *York: The Making of a City, 1086–1350* (Oxford University Press, 2013), p. 126.
58 Mark Ormrod, "Competing Capitals? York and London in the Fourteenth Century," in *Courts and Regions in Medieval Europe*, eds. Sarah Rees Jones, Richard Marks, and A. J. Minnis (Boydell and Brewer, 2000), p. 84.
59 William characterizes the Scottish tongue as "barbarous" when he discusses King Oswald's communications with the Scots. Further, when he looks to the future Scots King David I in his own period, William remarks that he was "A young man of more courtly disposition that the rest ... [who] had from boyhood been polished by familiar intercourse with the English, and rubbed off all the barbarian gaucherie of Scottish manners" (*GR* I, 727) (*iuuenis ceteris curialior et qui, nostrorum conuictu et familiaritate limatus a puero, omnem rubiginem Scotticae barbariei deterserat*).

60 Janet Burton, *The Monastic Order in Yorkshire, 1069–1215* (Cambridge University Press, 2009), p. 3.
61 A.L. Mayhew, ed., *Promptorium Parvulorum: the First English–Latin Dictionary* (Kegan, Paul, Trench, Trübner and Co., 1908), p. 282
62 Randy P. Schiff, *Revivalist Fantasy: Alliterative Verse and Nationalist Literary History* (Ohio State University Press, 2011), p. 102.
63 Mark P. Bruce and Katherine H. Terrell. "Introduction: Writing Across the Borders." *The Anglo-Scottish Border and the Shaping of Identity, 1300–1600*, ed. Mark P. Bruce and Katherine H. Terrell (Palgrave-MacMillan, 2012), pp. 1–14.
64 Richard Devizes, *The Chronicle of Richard Devizes of the Time of King Richard the First*, ed. John T. Appleby (Thomas Nelson, 1963), pp. 66–67.
65 Cynthia Neville, *Violence, Custom, and Law: The Anglo-Scottish Border Lands in the Later Middle Ages* (Edinburgh University Press, 1998), p. 195.
66 As Rachel Reid notes, clauses added from 1346 included the warden's commission to maintain truces and punish truce-breakers. "Office of Warden of the Marches: Its Origin and Early History," *English Historical Review* 32, no. 128 (1917): 482–83.
67 Henry Summerson, "Responses to War: Carlisle and the West March in the Later-Fourteenth Century," in *War and Border Societies in the Middle Ages*, edited by Anthony Goodman and Anthony Tuck (Routledge, 1992), p. 165.
68 Neville, *Violence, Custom, Law*, p. 75.
69 A.E. Stamp, ed, *Calendar of Inquisitions Miscellaneous (Chancery), Vol. III* (London, 1937), p. 1.
70 J.A. Tuck, "Northumbrian Society in the Fourteenth Century," *Northern History* 3 (1968): 36.
71 R.B. Dobson, *Church and Society in the Medieval North of England* (Hambledon Press, 1996), p. x.
72 Holford, "Durham: History, Culture and Identity," p. 22.
73 Holford, "Durham: History, Culture and Identity," p. 37.
74 See Holford, 'Durham: History, Culture and Identity," pp. 52–57.
75 Dobson, *Church and Society*, pp. 175–76.
76 Dobson, *Church and Society*, p. 88.
77 My emphasis. *Westminster Chronicle, 1381–1394*, eds. and trans. L.C. Hector and Barbara F. Harvey (Clarendon Press, 1982), p. 348-49
78 Quotations of "The Hunting of the Cheviot" are taken from Xavier Perret, "An Annotated Text of the 'Hunting of the Cheviot,' with a French Rendition," *English Studies* 86, no. 1 (2005): 1–39.
79 Warren, *History on the Edge*, p. 2.
80 Yeager, "Introduction: Narrating Space," p. 16.
81 Janet Burton, *Monastic Order in Yorkshire*, pp. 1–4.
82 Burton, *Monastic Order in Yorkshire*, p. 185.
83 Ibid.

Notes to pages 23–25

84 See Alison Hudson, "St Cuthbert and the South: A North of England Saint and South of England Reformers in the Late Tenth and Early-Eleventh Centuries," in *Saints of North-East England 600–1500*, eds Margaret Coombe, Anne Mouron, and Christiana Whitehead (Brepols, 2017), pp. 111–32.
85 Symeon of Durham, *Libellus de Exordio atque Procursu istius hoc est Dunhelmensis Ecclesie*, ed. and trans. David Rollason (Oxford University Press, 2000), pp. 197–201.
86 Dominic Marner, *St Cuthbert: His Life and Cult in Medieval Durham* (University of Toronto Press, 2000), p. 25. Marner points out a popular anecdote of the Cuthbert–Thomas rivalry. With the rise of Becket's status, Reginald of Durham contributed an additional story to his *Libellus* in which a Norwegian boy considers each of the saint's shrines at which to seek his cure. He chooses, ultimately, to go to Durham, where he is miraculously healed (33).
87 See Allan Doig, "Sacred Journeys/Sacred Spaces: The Cult of St Cuthbert," in *Saints of North-East England 600–1500*. Eds. Margaret Coombe, Anne Mouron, and Christiana Whitehead (Brepols, 2017 pp. 305–25.
88 Holford, "Durham: History, Culture and Identity," p. 34.
89 My translation; Latin from Thomas Walsingham, *Historia Anglicana*, edited by Henry T. Riley, 2 vols. (London, 1864), II, p. 189.
90 See Robert Bartlett, *Why Can the Dead Do Such Great Things? Saints and Worshipers from the Martyrs to the Reformation* (Princeton University Press, 2013), pp. 180–82.
91 Jonathan Hughes, *Pastors and Visionaries: Religion and Secular Life in Late Medieval Yorkshire* (Woodbridge, Suffolk: Boydell Press, 1988), esp. 299–311.
92 Hughes, *Pastors and Visionaries*, p. 306.
93 Burton, *Monastic Order in Yorkshire*, p. 285.
94 Denis Renevey, "Northern Spirituality Travels South: Rolle's Middle English Encomium Oleum Nomen Tuum in Lincoln College Library, MS 91, and Dublin, Trinity College, MS 155," in *Revisiting the Medieval North of England*, eds Anita Auer, Denis Renevey, Camille Marshall, and Tino Oudesluijs (University of Wales Press, 2019), pp. 13–24. Renevey notes a common practice of scribes to purge Rolle's works of Rolle's own northern English (p. 20).
95 See Claire Elizabeth McIlroy's introduction to *The English Prose Treatises of Richard Rolle* (D.S. Brewer 2004), pp. 1–20.
96 Ralph Hanna, 'The Transmission of Richard Rolle's Latin Works,' *Library* 14 (2013): 316.
97 Nicholas Watson, *Richard Rolle and the Invention of Authority* (Cambridge University Press, 1991), p. 261.
98 Elizabeth Freeman, "The Priory of Hampole and Its Literary Culture," *Parergon* 29 (2012): 15.

99 Ralph Hanna, "Lichfield," in *Europe: A Literary History, Vol. I*, Ed. David Wallace. Oxford University Press, 2016, p. 280.
100 Hanna, "Lichfield," pp. 269, 280.
101 Carol M. Meale, "'oft sipis with grete devotion I pought what I mi3t do pleysyng to go': The Early Ownership and Readership of Love's Mirror, with Special Reference to its Female Audience," in *Nicholas Love at Waseda*, ed. Shoichi Oguro, Richard Beadle, and Michael G. Sargent (D.S. Bewer, 1997), p. 20.
102 Hanna, 'Yorkshire and York,' pp. 272–73. Hanna notes here the possibility of clerks who moved with the royal offices from London to York in the early-fourteenth century and who may be responsible for the compilation.
103 Edward Casey, *Remembering: A Phenomenological Study* (University of Indiana Press, 1987), p. 229.
104 Martin Heidegger, *Being and Time*, trans. Joan Stambaugh (SUNY Press, 2010), p. 390.
105 Casey, *Remembering*, p. 229.
106 Marion Turner, *Chaucer: A European Life* (Princeton University Press, 2019), p. 428.
107 Barrett, Jr., *Against All England*, p. 18.
108 See Alexander Rose, *Kings in the North: The House of Percy in British History* (London: Weidenfeld and Nicolson, 2002). Rose sums up succinctly the situation of the Percys in the North: "In that tumultuous place, the Westminster-based, southern king's writ hardly ran. In Percy country, there was Percy law backed by a Percy army paid for by Percy money" (p. 1).
109 Barbara D. Palmer, "Recycling 'The Wakefield Cycle': The Records." *Research Opportunities in Renaissance Drama* 41 (2002): 108; Garrett P.J. Epp, "The Towneley Plays, or the Hazards of Cycling," *Research Opportunities in Renaissance Drama* 32 (1993): 121–50.
110 Eamon Duffey, *Stripping the Altars: Traditional Religion in England, c.1400–c.1580* (Yale University Press, 1992), p. 431.

2 William of Malmesbury, Bede, and the Problem of the North

1 Jeffrey Jerome Cohen, *Hybridity, Identity, and Mostrosity in Medieval Britain: On Difficult Middles* (Palgrave Macmillan, 2006), p. 47.
2 Dolmans, *Writing Regional Identities*, p. 6.
3 For a detailed analysis of the process of assimilation between the Normans and the English, see Hugh M. Thomas, *The English and the Normans: Ethnic Hostility, Assimilation and Identity* (Oxford University Press, 2003), p. 87.
4 Robert Stein, *Reality Fictions: Romance, History, and Governmental Authority, 1025–1180* (University of Notre Dame Press, 2006), pp. 89–90.
5 Richard Gameson, *The Manuscripts of Early-Norman England (1066–1130)*, (Oxford University Press, 1999), pp. 32–36.

6 Rodney Thomson, *William of Malmesbury*, revised ed. (Woodbridge, Suffolk: Boydell Press, 2003), p. 5. William described himself as "alumnus" of Glastonbury in the *Vita Dunstani* i. Prol. 1, ii. Prol. 1. He further had close connections with Eadmer of Canterbury, and displayed a keen interest in Anselm as well.
7 Thomson, *William of Malmesbury*, p. 12; see also Thomson, "John of Salisbury and William of Malmesbury: Currents in Twelfth Century Humanism," in *The World of John of Salisbury*, ed. Michael Wilks (Basil Blackwell, 1984), pp. 117–25.
8 Peter Damian-Grint, *The New Historians of the Twelfth-Century Renaissance: Inventing Vernacular Authority* (The Boydell Press, 1999), p. 91; N. J. Higham, *Re-Reading Bede: The Ecclesiastical History in Context* (London: Routledge 2006), p. 27; Antonia Gransden, *Historical Writing in England, Vol. I* (Routledge, 1996), p. 169.
9 Kirsten Fenton, *Gender, Nation and Conquest in the Works of William of Malmesbury* (Boydell and Brewer Press, 2008), p. 101.
10 Sarah Breckenridge Wright, "The Soil's Holy Bodies: The Art of Chorography in William of Malmesbury's *Gesta Ponitificum Anglorum*," *Studies in Philology* 111 (2014): 654–55.
11 Sigbjorn Olsen Sønnesyn, *William of Malmesbury and the Ethics of History* (Cambridge: Boydell and Brewer, 2012), pp. 123–24. As Sønnesyn points out, "In describing the origins of the Angles, Saxons, and Jutes in *Gesta Regum Anglorum* I, 5, these groups are both referred to as *populi Germaniae* and *gentes Anglorum*, showing both a synonymous usage of *populus* and *gens*, and the confusing status of the *Angli* as both a group of parallel status to Saxons and Jutes, and a collective term for all three groups" (p. 122).
12 In my discussion of William of Malmesbury's work, I will use the term *gens* to denote the "English people" as a political unit, as Sønnesyn suggests. I acknowledge, however, the profound ambiguity with which these terms signify, even as Sønnesyn explains further in his study (see pp.106–24); see also Robert Bartlett, Medieval and Modern Concepts of Race and Ethnicity," *Journal of Medieval and Early Modern Studies* 31 (2001): pp. 39–56. Bartlett examines R.B. Mynors own choices for translating William's Latin *gens* for the Oxford Medieval Texts editions. As Bartlett concludes this illustrative example, "in the space of one work by one author gens can be rendered 'race,' 'nation,' 'people,' 'tribe,' 'stock,' or 'family.'" (p. 44); Geraldine Heng's recent study, *The Invention of Race in the European Middle Ages* (Cambridge University Press, 2018), affords an in-depth examination of "race" as a structural concept in medieval Europe. Commenting on Gerald of Wales' *Topgraphia Hibernia*, with its animalization of Irish natives, Heng finds "Colonial racism of the medieval kind ... [that] found rich afterlives in the colonial racism of the postmedieval centuries, as subsequent English empires spread their umbra across the world" (p. 42). I would also note Cord Whitaker's discussion in *Black Metaphors: How Modern Racism Emerged From Medieval Race-Thinking* (Philadelphia, PA: University of Pennsylvania

Press, 2019), which clarifies how medieval texts actively meld the metaphoric blackness of "unrepentant sinfulness" (p. 2) with black persons, contributing to racial frameworks that inform racism in the present. As Whitaker contends, the Middle Ages "allow us to examine the social construct of race during its construction, to see the foundation and the frame without their obscuring facades of brick and siding" (p. 7).

13 Sønnesyn, *William of Malmesbury and the Ethics of History*, pp. 161–62.
14 Thomas, *The English and the Normans*, p. 271.
15 Gransden, *Historical Writing*, p. 24.
16 Higham, *Re-Reading Bede*, p. 77.
17 Ibid., p. 98.
18 R.R. (Reese) Davies, "Nations and National Identities," p. 574.
19 Henry Archdeacon of Huntingdon, *Historia Anglorum, The History of the English People*, ed. Diana Greenway (Oxford: Clarendon Press, 1996), p. 7.
20 Emily Joan Ward, "Verax Historicus Beda: William of Malmesbury, Bede and historia," in *Discovering William of Malmesbury*, ed. Rodney M. Thomson, Emily Dolmans, and Emily Winkler (Boydell and Brewer Press, 2017), p. 187.
21 Thomson, *William of Malmesbury*, p. 13.
22 Ibid., pp. 18–19.
23 All quotations of Bede's *Historia Ecclesiastica Gentis Anglorum* (hereafter *HE*) are taken from *Bede's Ecclesiastical History of the English People*, ed. Bertram Colgrave and R.A.B. Mynors (Clarendon Press, 1969). "'Bene' inquit; "nam et angelicam habent faciem" ... "Bene" in quit "Deiri, de ira eruti et ad misericordiam Christi vocati" ... "Alleluia, laudem Dei Creatoris illis in partibus oportet cantari."" *HE*, pp. 134–35.
24 Ælfric, *Catholic Homilies: Second Series*, ed. Malcolm Godden, EETS SS 5 (Oxford University Press, 1979).
25 Lavezzo, *Angels on the Edge of the World*, pp. 40–41.
26 Frank Musgrove, *The North of England: A History From Roman Times to the Present* (London, 1990), pp. 56–57.
27 Higham, *Re-Reading Bede*, pp. 88.
28 Dates for the battle range from 606 to 616, but most historians now date it between 613 and 616 AD.
29 Katherine Allen Smith, *Encountering War in the Scriptures and Liturgy* (Boydell and Brewer, 2012), pp. 28–29.
30 Augustine notes three points of dispute: "to keep Easter at the proper time; to perform the sacrament of baptism... and to preach the word of the Lord to the English people in fellowship with us" (*ut pascha suo tempore celebretis, ut ministerium baptizandi... ut genti Anglorum una nobiscum verbum Domoni praedicetis...*). *EH*, pp. 138–39.
31 Gransden, *Historical Writing in England*, p. 20.
32 The Synod, presided over by King Oswiu of Northumbria, comprised official arguments, largely on the dating of Easter, between representatives of the Celtic church and Roman church. Archbishop of Northumbria Colman

presented the Celtic argument and was opposed by Wilifrid. The Roman argument won the day, which meant that the Northumbrian church officially and universally adopted Roman rites and practices. Colman and the Celtic contingent retired to Iona in lasting disagreement, their positions in the Northumbrian church taken by new men including, eventually, Wilifrid himself. See *EH*, pp. 296–308.

33 Alfred Smyth, "The Emergence of English Identity, 700–1000," in *Studies in Ethnic Identity and National Perspectives in Medieval Europe*, ed. Alfred Smyth (MacMillan, 1998), p. 31.

34 Smyth, "The Emergence of English Identity," p. 31.

35 Bede's words describing the archbishop's failure to stand make explicit its randomness: "Now it happened that Augustine remained seated while they were coming in" (*factumque est ut venientibus illis sederet Augustinus in sella*). *HE*, pp. 138–39.

36 Acton Griscom, ed. *The Historia Regum Britanniae of Geoffrey of Monmouth* (Longmans, Green, and Co., 1929), p. 509.

37 *Historia Regum Brittaniae*, p. 510.

38 See *Lestorie des engles solum la translacion Maistre Geffrei Gaimar*, ed. Thomas Duffus Hardy and Charles Trice Martin (London, 1889), pp. 32–33 (lines 1081–1101). Geoffrey follows the entry for AD 606 in the *Anglo-Saxon Chronicle*: "Aethelfrith led his army to Chester and there killed a countless number of Welsh; and thus was fulfilled Augustine's prophecy which he spoke: "If the Welsh do not want peace with us, they shall perish at the hands of the Saxons." There was also killed 200 priests who had come there in order to pray for the Welsh raiding-army. Their chieftain was called Scrocmail, who escaped from there as one of fifty." *The Anglo-Saxon Chronicle*, trans. M.J. Swanton (J.M. Dent, 1996), p. 22.

39 Though noted as a vigorous leader, David Crouch argues, "His policy was simply to build on his natural affinity in the west country, to grab territorial power, and beat down any local rivals." Crouch notes that Robert "set the pattern of regional political disintegration that plagued England between 1138 and 1154": David Crouch, "Robert, first Earl of Gloucester (*b.* before 1100, *d.* 1147)," *Oxford Dictionary of National Biography* (Oxford University Press, 2004), www.oxforddnb.com/view/article/23716/ (accessed April 1, 2021).

40 Gransden, *Historical Writing in England*, p. 18.

41 N.J. Higham, *The Kingdom of Northumbria, AD 350–1100* (Wolfboro Falls, NH: A. Sutton, 1993), p. 232.

42 *The Ecclesiastical History of Orderic Vitalis*, 6 vols., ed. and trans. Marjorie Chibnall (Clarendon Press, 1969), VI, pp. 94–95.

43 See Ann Williams and G.H. Martin, eds., *The Domesday Book: A Complete Translation* (London: Penguin, 1992), pp. 785–881. *The Domesday Book* of 1086 notes roughly 800 vills, nearly 50 percent of all vills) in Yorkshire as being waste or partly waste. For a study of "waste" entries in *Domesday Book*,

see the essays in *The Domesday Geography of Northern England*, ed. H.C. Darby and I.S. Maxwell (Cambridge University Press, 1978), esp. pp. 59–70.
44 William illustrates, in one of many examples, the Northumbrians' inherent independence when he speaks of Earl Tostig's expulsion from Northumbria by its natives in 1065. William recounts the Northumbrians' defense made again Harold Godwin after his brother's overthrow: "The Northumbrians... defended what they had done before him, maintaining that, being born and bred as free men, they could not brook harsh treatment from any superior; freedom or death was their tradition" (*Nothanimbri, licet non inferiores numero essent, tamen quieti consulentes factum apud eum excusant: se homines libere natos, libere educatos, nullius ducis ferotiam pati posse; a maioribus didicisse aut libertatem aut mortem*) *GR*, I, pp. 364–65.
45 Orderic Vitalis, *Ecclesiastical History*, IV, pp. 231–33.
46 Translation is taken from Simeon of Durham, *A History of the Kings of England*, trans. J. Stephenson (Dyfed: Llanerch Enterprises, 1987), p. 137. Latin text is taken from *Symeonis Monachi Opera Omnia*. vol. II, *Historia Regum*. ed. Thomas Arnold (Longmans & Co., 1885), p. 188.
47 William of Malmesbury may have known Symeon's text. See Donald Matthew, "Durham and the Anglo-Norman World," *Anglo-Norman Durham 1093–1193*, ed. David Rollason, M. Harvey, and M. Prestwich (Woodbridge, 1994), pp. 1–22. Matthew suggests that Williams employs Symeon's *Libellus de exordio atque procurse istius hoc est Dunelmensis ecclesie* as a source for parts of Book II of *the Gesta Pontificum* (*GP*, I, 266–76). See also Thomson's note on Book I.61.4 in William of Malmesbury, *Gesta Regum Anglorum: General Introduction and Commentary Vol. 2*, 2 vols., ed. R.M. Thomson (Oxford University Press, 1998), p. 52.
48 See note 39 above.
49 John Gillingham, "Civilizing the English: The English Histories of William of Malmesbury and David Hume," *Historical Research* 74 (2001): 21.
50 Ibid., 32–34. See also Gillingham's *The English in the Twelfth Century: Imperialism, National Identity, and Political Values* (Boydell Press, 2000), esp. pp. 41–58.
51 William Kynan-Wilson, "Mira Romanorum artifitia: William of Malmesbury and the Romano-British Remains at Carlisle," *Essays in Medieval Studies* 28 (2012): 39.
52 Thomson, *William of Malmesbury*, p. 73.
53 See Kynan-Wilson, "Mira Romanorum artifitia," p. 43. Kynan-Wilson points out that William derives this Marius' identity from Caesar's *De bello Gallico* (I.40) and, perhaps, from *Orosius' Historiarum adversum paganos libri VII* (V.16). The Roman general Marius pursued the Germanic *Cimbri* from Italy across the English Channel into Britain where he won a victory in 101 BCE.
54 Fenton, *Gender, Nation, and Conquest*, p. 93.
55 David Garrard, "William of Malmesbury and Civic Virtue," in *Discovering William of Malmesbury*, p. 34.

56 Fenton, *Gender, Nation, and Conquest*, p. 93.
57 Garrard, "William of Malmesbury and Civic Virtue," p. 34.
58 Ibid., p. 36.
59 See Sønnesyn's discussion of William's presentation of William II and Henry I in book IV of the *Gesta Regum Anglorum*; *William of Malmesbury and the Ethics of History*, pp. 214–27.
60 *GR*, I, pp. 612–13. William, in fact, quotes the *Aeneid* here, as he cites Hildebert, in his description of noble Romans of the past, "lords of the world, those who the toga wore" (*Romanis olim rerum dominis genteque togata*) that contrast with the "inactive men" of Rome's present. See *Aeneid* I. 282.
61 Kynan-Wilson, "Mira Romanorum artifitia," p. 44.
62 Thomson, *William of Malmesbury*, p. 30.
63 Ibid.
64 Ibid.
65 C. Stephen Jaeger, "Charismatic Body – Charismatic Text," *Exemplaria* 9 (1997): p. 119.
66 "*Sed non erat ei tantum studii uel otii ut liteteras um quam audiret ... immo calor mentis ingenitus et conscia uirtus*" (*GR*, I, pp. 566–67); *GR*, I, pp. 563–67.
67 *Eadmeri Historia Novorum in Anglia, et Opuscula Duo De Vita Sancti Anselmi et Quibusdam Miraculis Ejus*, ed. Martin Rule (Wiesbaden, DE: n.p., 1965), p. 116.
68 John Gillingham, "The Ironies of History: William of Malmesbury's Views of William II and Henry I," in *Discovering William of Malmesbury*, p. 38.
69 Bjorn Weiler, "William of Malmesbury on Kingship," *History* 90 (2005): 7–8.
70 Sønnesyn, *William of Malmesbury and the Ethics of History*, pp. 214–17.
71 Jacob Burckhardt, *The Civilization of the Renaissance in Italy*, trans. S.G.C. Middlemore (Macmillan, 1904), p. 177, n.1.
72 Jennifer Summit, "Topgraphy as Historiography: Petrarch, Chaucer, and the Making of Medieval Rome," *Journal of Medieval and Early Modern Studies* 30, no. 2 (2000): 212–13.
73 Summit, "Topography as Historiography," p. 214.
74 Ibid.

3 The North–South Divide in the Medieval English Universities

1 Sønnesyn, *William of Malmesbury and the Ethics of History*, p. 106.
2 Ruddick, *English Identity and Political Culture*, p. 123.
3 Turville-Petre, *England the Nation*, p. 17.
4 See Robert Bartlett extensive discussion of these terms in "Medieval and Modern Concepts of Race and Ethnicity," *Journal of Medieval and Early Modern Studies* 31 (2001): pp. 39–56.
5 Anthony Wood, *The history and Antiquities of the University of Oxford in Two Books, now first published in English from the original manuscript in the Bodleian Library by John Gutch* (John Gutch, 1792–96), I, p. 401.

6 Pearl Kibre, *The Nations in the Mediaeval Universities* (Medieval Academy of America, 1948), pp. 4–5. The definition of one's nation by their common tongue occurs specifically in 1497 when statutes of the German nation at Bologna define those of its body as scholars who share the German language as their native tongue. Though during the Middle Ages, a student's principle place of residence rarely superseded his place of birth, by the early sixteenth century at the University of Padua, it had become the common determinant of one's nation.

7 See also William J. Courtenay, *Religion and Community in the Medieval University of Paris* (Notre Dame University Press, 2018). Courtenay explains the imitative nature of university nations to religious confraternities as well. These bodies of laypersons, as Courtenay explains, prove "somewhat parallel to medieval artisan guilds and sometimes connected with them" (p. 48). One important difference, Courtenay points out, "Members of urban confraternities were permanent residents in the town and joined voluntarily," whereas, "For students and masters at the university, one joined a nation automatically ... so that participation in the confraternal practices of a nation was obligatory, not voluntary, and attendance at its religious services was expected and sometimes forced" (p. 50).

8 Ibid., 5. For an explanation of the genesis of these two bodies, see Hastings Rashdall, *The Universities of Europe in the Middle Ages*, 3 vols. ed. F. M. Powicke and A. B. Emden (Oxford University Press, 1936), I, pp. 154-57.

9 Rashdall, *Universities of Europe* in the Middle Ages, 3 vols. Ed. F. M. Powicke and A. B. Emden (Oxford University Press, 1936), I, 184; see also Robert S. Rait, *Life in the Medieval University* (Cambridge University Press, 1918), n. p., chapter 2.

10 Kibre, *The Nations in the Mediaeval Universities*, pp. 9–11. If a student's nation was not specifically represented in the composition of nations at the university, he would go to the nation whose region was closest to his own.

11 Ibid., pp. 16–17.

12 Students beneath the masters (regent masters in art) could not vote or take part in faculty deliberations, nor those of the nations. As Kibre explains, "Their only relationship to the nation or the university was through their own masters" (p. 15).

13 Courtenay, *Religion and Community*, p. 37

14 Ibid., p. 37–38.

15 Ibid.

16 Ibid., pp. 43–44. This church was, according to Courtenay, in the rue de la Harpe, and presently serves as Librairie Gibert-Joseph on boulevard Saint-Michel.

17 Kibre, *The Nations in the Mediaeval Universities*, p. 1.

18 Rashdall, *Universities*, I, pp. 158–59.

19 Steven J. Overman, "Sporting and Recreational Activities of Students in the Medieval Universities," *Facta Universitatis* 1 (1999): p. 26.

20 Courtenay, *Religion and Community*, p. 38.

21 Jacobus de Vitriaco, *Historia occididentalis, Bk. 2,* Ch. 7, in *Translations and Reprints from the Original Sources of European history* (Philadelphia, PA: published for the Dept. of History of the University of Pennsylvania by the University of Pennsylvania Press, 1897–1907) II, 7, pp. 19–20.
22 Daron Burrows, "*Le Chastiement des clers: A Dit* concerning the Nations of the University of Paris, Edited from Paris, Bibliothèque Nationale, MS. F. FR. 837," *Medium Ævum* 69 (2000): 211–26.
23 Ibid., pp. 214–15.
24 F.M. Powicke, "Some Problems in the History of the Medieval University," *Transactions of the Royal Historical Society 4th Series, 17* (London: Royal Historical Society, 1934), pp. 4–5.
25 Kibre, *The Nations in the Mediaeval Universities*, p. 21.
26 Ibid., p. 163.
27 A.B. Emden, "Northerners and Southerners in the Organization of the University to 1509," in *Oxford Studies Presented to Daniel Callus* (Clarendon Press for the Oxford Historical Society, 1964), 1. See also *Statuta Antiqua Universitatis Oxoniensis*, ed. Strickland Gibson (Clarendon Press, 1931), lxxiv.
28 Emden, "Northerners and Southerners," p. 1.
29 Rashdall, *Universities*, III, p. 56.
30 See Allan Cobban, *The Medieval English Universities: Oxford and Cambridge to c.1500* (Scolar, 1988), pp. 103–4; see also Kibre, *The Nations in the Mediaeval Universities*, pp. 160–66.
31 Rashdall, notably, makes this claim. See *Universities*, III, p. 57.
32 Emden, "Northerners and Southerners," pp. 4–7. Emden makes this argument based on his study of the provenance of northern proctors from the mid-fourteenth century to the early sixteenth century. Most of these officials can be traced to "Lincoln diocese, the country of Lincoln, or, in three cases, more precisely, to Bottesford, Leicestershire, to Northampton and to Collyweston, Northamptonshire, all in Lincoln diocese," which is "not compatible with the acceptance of the Trent as the boundary" (pp. 4–5) because the diocese itself fell completely below the River Trent, which actually marked the diocese's northwest border. Emden further argues that "the line of the Nene was related far more nearly to the regional and linguistic diversities that promoted this fierce sense of locality among the young men who resorted to the schools of Oxford in the thirteenth century" (p. 7).
33 Cobban, *The Medieval English Universities*, 103–4; see also Hackett, *The Original Statutes of Cambridge University* (Cambridge University Press, 1970), p. 154. As I will discuss later, much of Cambridge's documents from the thirteenth century were lost in a fire that resulted, fittingly, from a large battle between northern and southern scholars there in 1261.
34 Emden, "Northerners and Southerners," pp. 10–11.
35 Ibid., p. 12. Like Wykham, Magdalen's founder, the Bishop of Waynflete, required the college to admit students from counties wherein the college held

property, and so the college had a typical ratio of three-fifths southern students and two-fifths northern students.
36 John Balliol and Lady Dervoguilla were the parents of King John I of Scotland (r.1292–1296).
37 Emden, "Northerners and Southerners," p. 10–12.
38 Charles Edward Mallet, *A History of the University of Oxford*, vol. I, *The Mediaeval University and the Colleges Founded in the Middle Ages* (Methuen and Co., Ltd., 1924), pp. 28–29.
39 Ibid.
40 Overman, "Sporting and Recreational Activities," p. 28; see also Leo Moulin, *La Vie de Etudiants au Moyen Age* (Albin Michel, 1991) and F.P. Magoun, "Football in Medieval England and in Medieval English Literature," *American Historical Review* 25 (1929): pp. 33–45.
41 Mallet, *A History of the University of Oxford*, p. 148.
42 Emden, "Northerners and Southerners," pp. 2–4.
43 J. E. Thorold Rogers, ed., *Oxford City Documents: Financial and Judicial 1268–1665* (Clarendon Press, 1891), p. 169.
44 Kibre, *The Nations in the Mediaeval Universities*, p. 164. See also Wood, *The history and Antiquities of the University of Oxford*, pp. 258–59.
45 Wood, *The history and Antiquities of the University of Oxford*, pp. 257–58; see also Jan Morris, ed., *The Oxford Book of Oxford* (Oxford University Press, 1978), pp. 11–12.
46 Owing to the understanding that the arming of students often provoked violence, a 1313 edict in Oxford states that students may only arm themselves when leaving the town. See C.R.L. Fletcher, ed., *Collectanea* 1 (Clarendon Press, 1885), p. 13.
47 Rashdall, *Universities* III, p. 58. See also Mallet, *A History of the University of Oxford*, p. 41.
48 Rashdall, *Universities*, III, p. 58.
49 John Fletcher, "University Migrations in the Late-Middle Ages, with Particular Reference to the Stamford Secession," in *Rebirth, Reform, Resilience: Universities in Transition, 1300–1700*, ed. James Kittelson and Pamela Transhue (Ohio State University Press, 1985), pp. 181–82.
50 Courtenay, *Religion and Community*, p. 39.
51 Rashdall, *Universities*, I, pp. 169–71. See also the discussion in Kibre, *The Nations in the Mediaeval Universities*, pp. 6–7.
52 Kibre, *The Nations in the Mediaeval Universities*, p. 8.
53 Fletcher, "University Migrations," p. 179. Fletcher explains, for example, the migration of Bolognese students to Arezzo in 1215 and to Vercelli in 1228, yet neither school found sustained success.
54 As Kibre points out, "It is this destruction of university archives together with similar acts of violence in 1322 and 1381, that probably explains in large part the obscurity surrounding the development of the Cambridge *studium generale* during the thirteenth and even fourteenth centuries" (p. 167).

55 See Cobban, *Medieval English Universities*, pp. 29–30. Northampton had been the site of a *studium generale* late in the reign of Henry II and into the reign of Richard I. Northampton might rival Oxford attraction of students from the West of England if only for its location, while it was less of a threat to Cambridge's recruiting grounds. Cobban claims that although Northampton had granted Oxford primacy by the end of the twelfth century, a college of some sort remained there. In addition to the 1260 migrations, Oxford scholars are said to have moved there, as well, in 1238.
56 See Katherine Walsh, *A Fourteenth-Century Scholar and Primate. Richard Fitzralph in Oxford, Avignon and Armagh* (Clarendon Press, 1981), pp. 74–84. Walsh summarizes the various reasons. Wood suggests that Merton College refused admission of several northern scholars. *The history and Antiquities of the University of Oxford*, p. 426.
57 Wood, *History and Antiquities of the University of Oxford*, p. 426.
58 Francis Peck, *Academia Tertia Anglicana, or the Antiquarian Annals of Stanford* [sic] *in Lincoln, Rutland, and Northampton Shires in XIV Books* (printed for James Bettenham, 1727), VI, p. 9.
59 Falconer Madan, "Brasenose College," *The Colleges of Oxford: Their Histories and Traditions*, ed. Andrew Clark (Methuen and Co., 1891), p. 253.
60 The petition can be found in Cotton MS Vesp. E. xxi, fo. 62
61 Peck, *Academia Tertia Anglicana*, VI, pp. 16–17; original French taken from *Collectanea*, I, p. 4.
62 Emden, "Northerners and Southerners," p. 5.
63 See George C. Broderick, *Memorial of Merton College, with Biographical Notices of the Wardens and Fellows* (Clarendon Press, 1885), pp. 188, 197. Broderick lists both a William de Barnaby and a John de Twislington, who Broderick claims was "among those who lectured at Stamford in 1335" (p. 197).
64 Peck's translation; *Academia Tertia Anlgicana*, p. 9; see also W. Harrod, *The Antiquities of Stamford and St Martins compiled chiefly from the Annals of the Rev. Francis Peck*, Vol. 1 (London, 1785). p. 51.
65 Ancient tradition held that the Bretonic King Bladud (*c*.863 BC), mentioned in Geoffrey of Monmouth's *Historia*, perhaps the father of Lear, and famously the creator of the hot springs at Bath, is said to have created a university at Stamford that flourished until the coming of Augustine, after which it was dispersed for its heretical practices: *Collectanea*, I, p. 2.
66 Wood, *History and Antiquities of the University of Oxford*, p. 432.
67 Fletcher, *Collectanea*, I, p. 4.
68 See Emden, "Northerners and Southerners," p. 7. Emden adds a further note to their Stamford migration, that the town itself lay just a short distance above the River Nene, the dividing line in the university's eyes between the North and the South.
69 Fletcher, *Collectanea*, I, p. 4.
70 H.E. Salter, "The Stamford Schism," *English Historical Review* 37 (1922): 249. I would like to thank the staff at the British Library for their assistance in my study of Royal MS. 12. D. xi for this chapter.

71 Salter, "The Stamford Schism," p. 251.
72 Emden, "Northerners and Southerners," p. 5.
73 My translation. The Latin text of the poem can be found in Salter, "The Stamford Schism," pp. 252–53.
74 Salter, "The Stamford Schism," suggests a date of 1332 or 1333 for the poem. This is based in part on the allusion to Hereford, and Salter offers that this could be Thomas de Hereford, who was an Oxford beadle (part of this office was to police the students against crime and violence). Salter also finds Rogerus le Bedel in 1332, and an Edward de Wyke, elected proctor in 1333, each of whom may be the men referred to in the poem (p. 252).
75 Fitzralph had already walked into an ongoing struggle between the university and the absentee archdeacon of Oxford, Cardinal Gailard Lamotte, who continually sought to extend his authority over the university among other places. The cardinal attempted legislation against the university at Avignon, and during Fitzralph's tenure the university was forced to send a proctor, in this instance Simon Bredon, to the papal curia to stand for the university. While this minor crisis would continue for some ten years more following Fitzralph's chancellorship, the university faced its own internal crisis one year after Fitzralph's election.
76 Michael Dunne, "Richard Fitzralph's *Lectura* on the *Sentences*," in *Medieval Commentaries on the Sentences of Peter Lombard*, ed. Phillipp Rosemann (Brill, 2010), pp. 405–6.
77 Salter, "The Stamford Schism," p. 249.
78 Ibid., p. 250. Salter claims attributes the suggestion to his colleague A. G. Little.
79 My translation, Latin text taken from Salter, "The Stamford Schism," p. 251.
80 Margaret Owens, *Stages of Dismemberment: The Fragmented Body in Late-Medieval and Early Modern Drama* (University of Delaware Press, 2005), p. 145. See also Jeffrey Jerome Cohen's discussion of decapitation as an act that establishes nation in *Of Giants: Sex, Monsters, and the Middle Ages* (Minneapolis, MN: University of Minnesota Press, 1999). Cohen offers several examples of the defeat of giants and other monsters, often through Davidic acts of decapitation, that form the "mythology of nation building" (p. 54).
81 Owens, *Stages of Dismemberment*, p. 145.
82 Fletcher, *Collectanea*, I, p. 4.
83 The text of the letter is found in Fletcher, *Collectanea*, I, p. 8.
84 Juliet Vale, "Philippa of Hainault," *Oxford Dictionary of National Biography* (Oxford University Press, 2008), www.oxforddnb.com/view/10.1093/ref: odnb/9780198614128.001.0001/odnb-9780198614128-e-22110 (Accessed May 4, 2020). Queen Philippa would grant the college a small hospital and lands in Southampton that, later, generated significant revenue for Queen's in the nineteenth and twentieth centuries, as the Southampton docks and surrounding areas were developed. Though it is perhaps ironic that while Philippa was called upon to advocate for the University against the northern

students who fled to Stamford, Queen's College would focus its admission on students from Cumberland and Westmorland. See "A Brief History," *Queen's College*. Oxford University. www.queens.ox.ac.uk/history (Accessed May 4, 2020).
85 See Alan B. Cobban, *The King's Hall Within the University of Cambridge in the Later Middle Ages* (Cambridge University Press, 1969).
86 French text taken from Fletcher, *Collectanea*, I, p. 8.
87 Translation from Peck, *Academia Tertia Anlgicana*, p. 11; Latin letter taken from Fletcher, *Collectanea*, I, p. 11.
88 Fletcher, "University Migrations," p. 186.
89 *Calendar of Close Rolls, Edward III, 1333–37* (London, 1898), p. 332.
90 See Wood, *History and Antiquities of the University of Oxford*, p. 427.
91 Fletcher, "University Migrations," p. 169.
92 Wood, *History and Antiquities of the University of Oxford*, p. 427.
93 A letter either from late 1334 or early 1335, from the University to the King attempts to explain the violence at Oxford of which the students complain. The chancellor asserts that the cause of strife is that the mayor of Oxford and his baillifs do not prosecute violence perpetrated by the students for the fact that they fear the commons reaction (*qe Meire et bailiffs de la ville avandite soi unt devant se shores escuse qil ne osasent, pour pour de la leur commune, entremettre de prendre les maufesours et les destourbours de la pees*). Again, it seems Edward solicits response to these charges, which he receives from William de Spersholt, the sheriff of Oxford. The sheriff complains that his jail is full and that the Chancellor of the University consistently sends him incorrigible students, committed by the Chancellor's own court, to the jail where they are held at the Chancellor's pleasure and as long as he (the Chancellor) deems fit. The Sheriff reiterates that he fears the commons, though he is specific that he worries over the clerks themselves who might endanger his castle and person if they are provoked (a summary of the Sheriff's letter is found in Montagu Burrows, ed., *Collectanea III* (Clarendon Press, 1896), p. 134). Following a second letter from the University on local disturbances in Oxford and soliciting his help, Edward issues a proclamation in June 1335 prohibiting the Oxford students wearing or possessing any arms in order to curb the violence there. The crown affords the sheriff of Oxford monies to repair Oxford castle "by view of testimony of Master Robert de Stratford." (entry for 10 February 1338, see also the entry for 10 March 1337 in *Calendar of Close Rolls, Edward III, 1337–39* (London, 1900, p. 23). A March 10, 1338 entry concerning orders to Geoffrey le Scrop and his fellows, which alludes to the chancellors "cognisance of trespasses in the suburbs of Oxford University outside the walls of the town, and within the walls, where a clerk was one of the parties, except please concerning the death of a man, and of mayhem, and that those passing through the town of Oxford should answer before the chancellor concerning contracts and trespasses made with scholars" (*Calendar of Close Rolls, Edward III, 1337–39*, p. 318).
94 *Calendar of Close Rolls, Edward III, 1333–37*, p. 330.

95 Peck, Antiquities of Stamford, p. 52.
96 See Fletcher, *Collectanea*, I, p. 15.
97 Kibre, *The Nations in the Mediaeval Universities*, p. 166. See also Wood, *History and Antiquities of the University of Oxford*, pp. 519–21.
98 David C. Fowler, *The Life and Times of John Trevisa, Medieval Scholar* (University of Washington Press, 1995), p. 28.
99 Higden and Trevisa, *Polychronicon*, p. 162.
100 See Ralph Hanna III, "Sir Thomas Berkeley and His Patronage," *Speculum* 64 (1989): pp. 878–916.

4 Chaucer's Northern Consciousness in the *Reeve's Tale*

1 Turville-Petre, *England the* Nation. p. 143.
2 Ibid.
3 Barrett, Jr., *Against All England*, p. 15.
4 Ibid., p. 1.
5 Ralph Hanna, *London Literature 1300–1380* (Cambridge University Press, 2005), pp. 2–3.
6 Robert Epstein, "'Fer in the North; I kan nat telle where': Dialect, Regionalism, and Philologism," *Studies in the Age of Chaucer* 30 (2008), p. 106.
7 David Wallace, *Chaucerian Polity: Absolutist Lineages and Associational Forms in England and Italy* (Stanford University Press, 1997), pp. 156–81.
8 J.R.R. Tolkien, "Chaucer as Philologist: *The Reeve's Tale*" Transactions of the *Philological Society* (1934), pp. 2–3. By 1934, Tolkien can already claim that the tale's northern speech is "so well known that it is taken for granted" (p. 3). See also A. C. Spearing, *The Reeve's Prologue and Tale, with the Cook's Prologue and the Fragment of his tale from the Canterbury Tales* (Cambridge University Press, 1979). Spearing calls the tale's dialect a "consistent realism" (p. 3); In addition, see Derek Pearsall, *The Canterbury Tales* (Allen and Unwin, 1985). Pearsall terms the clerks mere "rustic buffoons" (p. 188).
9 Recent work by scholars suggests that the northern long /a/ was actually shifting even in the late fourteenth century to a fronted /ɛ/; for example, Hengwrt has "hem" ("home") whereas Ellesmere has "ham." See John Burrow, "A Northern Pronunciation in Chaucer, Skelton, and Spenser," *Notes and Queries* 63, no. 2 (2016): pp. 191–94; and Jeremy Smith, "The Great Vowel Shift in the North of England, and Some Forms in Chaucer's *Reeve's Tale*" *Neophilologische Mitteilungen*, 96 (1995), pp. 433–37.
10 Epstein, "Fer in the North," p. 114. Epstein refers to Edward Said's description of the Orientalist in Said's *Orientalism* (Vintage Books, 1979), p. 160.
11 John M. Bowers, "Chaucer After Smithfield: From Postcolonial Writer to Imperialist Author," in *The Postcolonial Middle Ages*, ed. Jeffrey J. Cohen (St Martins, 2000), p. 57.

12 The three other tales I consider as explicitly taking place in England are those of the Miller, Cook, the canon's yeomen and arguably the Wife of Bath (with its Arthurian setting). Although its setting is not specified, we can argue that the *Nun's Priest Tale* take place in England given the reference to the martyred St Kenelm of Mercia (VII, 4301–2).
13 Wales, *Northern English*, pp. 72–75.
14 Ibid.
15 Butterfield, *The Familiar Enemy*, esp. pp. 8–10. Butterfield offers insightful critiques of critical claims about Chaucer's vernacularity and, thus, his Englishness as "retrospectivism," that is, the argument is shaped by England's later emergence as a national language rather than by attention to the everyday linguistic life the Chaucer himself lived. Butterfield argues, instead, that we see Chaucer's "Europeanness." Marion Turner's biography, *Chaucer: A European Life*, speaks further to Butterfield's linguistic argument. See also Susan Nakely's discussion in *Living in the Future*, esp. pp. 3–44.
16 Rose, *Kings in the North*. Rose notes that Gaunt was "[a] Londoner with lands in the Midlands and the South (but only one barony and Dunstanburgh Castle in Northumberland), Gaunt could not grasp the peculiar Northern social-cultural features like the virtually institutionalised banditry, a booty based economy and the clientage between the old intermarried Border dynasties and the gentry" (p. 328). See also, Tuck, "Richard II and the Border Magnates," *Northern History* 3 (1968): 39–40.
17 Turner, *Chaucer: A European Life* (Princeton University Press, 2019), p. 429.
18 Jewell, *The North–South Divide*, pp. 42–44.
19 John M. Bowers, *The Politics of Pearl: Court Poetry in the Age of Richard II* (Cambridge: D. S. Brewer, 2001), p. 73. Bowers discusses at length Richard's obsession with Cheshire, his surrounding himself with Chesire men, and his rumoured intent to "make Cheshire the inner citadel of the nation, a central bastion from whih to rule Wales and Ireland as well as England" (p. 74). Such a revelation only heightens the anxieties of Londoners like Chaucer who aimed both to declare and maintain the capital as England's hegemonic center.
20 See Britton J. Harwood, "Psychoanalytic Politics: Chaucer and Two Peasants," *ELH*, 68 (2001): pp. 2–27. Harwood suggests that Chaucer has in mind various historical figures and events, including the Peasant's Revolt, when he writes the *Reeve's Tale*. Important here is Harwood's assertion that Edmund de la Pole, who owned a water mill at Trumpington from 1372 and was the brother of the former chancellor of England Michael de la Pole, is the "signified" for Symkyn's mill in this tale of overtly political imperatives. Harwood correlates various figures, including Chaucer himself, with the tale's characters (some multiple times – Chaucer is both Symkyn and the clerks), and suggests that the clerks' northern dialect is one of many ways Pole's identity is "displaced," since the Poles "for three generations came from Hull and Yorkshire" (p. 10).
21 Parker, *Expositions on the Book of Psalms by S. Augustine*, p. 289.

22 See Parker, *Expositions on the Book of Psalms*, p. 289; Augustine explains "The mountain hath joined in itself two mountains; one house there is, and two houses; two, because coming from different sides; one, because of the Corner Stone, wherein both are joined together. Hear also this, *the mountains of Sion: the sides of the North are the city of the great King* . . . the sides of the North are joined to the city of the great King" (editor's emphasis).

23 As an instrument of God, the fiend finds an apt parallel in the Pardoner, who similarly claims "Yet kan I maken oother folk to twynne / From avarice and soore to repente" (VI, 430–31).

24 For a discussion of Bede's story, see Chapter 1 of this study. Chaucer would have found brief allusions to Bede's story in Higden and Trevisa, II, p. 507. Bede is, however, often cited as a possible source for Chaucer's list of works in his *Retraction* as well as for the form of the retraction itself. Bede deploys a list of works in both his *Historia Ecclesiastica Gentis Anglorum* and in his *Retractatio in Actus Apostolorum*. Bede is also alluded to as one example of the humility *topos* we find in Chaucer. See Anita Obermeier, "Chaucer's Retraction," in *Sources and Analogues of the Canterbury Tales*, vol. II, ed. Robert M. Correale and Mary Hamel (Bordell and Brewer, 2005), pp. 778–79.

25 See Robert Correale, "The Man of Law's Prologue and Tale," in *Sources and Analogues of the Canterbury Tales*, vol. II, pp. 282–83. Correale suggests that either Oxford, Bodleian, Rawlinson B.178 or Paris, Bibl. Nationale, franc, 9687 is closest to the version of Trevet's *Les Chroniques* that Chaucer would have known.

26 Quotations from John Gower are taken from G. C. Macaulay, ed., *The Complete Works of John Gower*, 4 vols. (Oxford, 1899–1902).

27 See Peter Nicholson, "Chaucer Borrows From Gower: The Sources of the *Man of Law's Tale*," in *Chaucer and Gower: Difference, Mutuality, Exchange*, ed. R.F. Yeager (English Literary Studies, 1991), pp. 85–99. Nicholson has argued that Chaucer relies significantly on Gower's version for its reduction of Trevet's longer narrative. Chaucer only uses Trevet in direct fashion for approximately 200 lines of the *Man of Law's Tale*.

28 Trevet's Constance is also more precise in her linguistic acumen, as she immediately speaks to the castellan in a Saxon tongue (*Et [ele] lui respoundi en Sessoneis, qe fu langage Olda, come cele / q'estoit aprise en diverses langages* [pp. 129–30]). In the *Man of Law's Tale*, however, Constance attempts to communicate with her pagan British interlocutors through "A maner Layn corrupt" (II, 519), and while the language she speaks here is not quite clear to contemporary scholars, neither was it likely clear to Chaucer's contemporaries. See Jonathan Hsy, "Translation Failure: The TARDIS, Cross-Temporal Language Contact, and Medieval Travel Narrative," in *The Language of Doctor Who From Shakespeare to Alien Tongues*, ed. Jason Barr and Camille D.G. Mustachio (London: Rowman and Littlefield, 2014), pp. 109–23. Hsy finds of this linguistic hinderance, "the fact that Constance must struggle with her language conveys the sense of the radical alterity of a past Britain – a world

distinctly 'foreign' to a contemporary audience" (p. 117); see also Hsy's discussion of Constance in Chaucer's *Man of Law's Tale* and John Gower's *Confessio Amantis*, Book II, in his book, *Trading Tongues: Merchants, Multilingualism, and Medieval Literature* (Ohio State University Press, 2013), esp. 65–72.
29 Suzanne Conklin Akbari, "Orientation and Nation in Chaucer's *Canterbury Tales*," in *Chaucer's Cultural Geography*, ed. Kathryn Lynch (Routledge, 2002), p. 121; see also Lavezzo, Angels on the Edge of the World. Lavezzo explains a similar if much earlier instance of this kind of narrative appropriation of the North. Analyzing Ælfric's account of the slave-children from the northern kingdom of Deira, whose beauty and mystery prompt the future Pope Gregory I to send the missionary Augustine to Britain in 597, Lavezzo claims, "The synechdocal role of Deira as a sign of the whole of England in the slave-boy homily ... imaginatively resolves the separation of Northumbria from England during Ælfric's lifetime" (p. 41). Ælfric's recapitulation, then, incorporation of a region, is "regressive" in its resistance to the institutional Anglo-Saxon church (p. 41).
30 Lavezzo, *Angels on the Edge of the World*, p. 96 and p. 102.
31 R. James Goldstein, "'To Scotland-Ward His Foomen for to Seke': Chaucer, the Scots, and the *Man of Law's Tale*," *Chaucer Review* 33 (1998): 35.
32 Ruth J. Dean, "Cultural Relations in the Middle Ages: Nicholas Trevet and Nicholas of Prato," *Studies in Philology* 45 (1948): 554; see also Ruth J. Dean, "Nicholas Trevet, Historian," in *Medieval Learning and Literature: Essays presented to Richard William Hunt*, ed. J.J.G. Alexander and M.T. Gibson (Clarendon Press, 1976), pp. 328–52.
33 Quotations from Trevet in both the original French and in English translation are taken from Correale, "The Man of Law's Prologue and Tale," p. 303.
34 See J.R. Maddicott, *Thomas of Lancaster 1307–1322, A Study in the Reign of Edward II* (Oxford University Press, 1970); and Gwilym Dodd, "Parliament and Political Legitimacy in the Reign of Edward II," in *The Reign of Edward II: New Perspectives*, ed. Gwilym Dodd and Anthony Munson (York: York Medieval Press, 2006), 165–89; on Harcla, see Henry Summerson, "Harclay, Andrew, Earl of Carlisle (c.1270–1323)." *Oxford Dictionary of National Biography*, Oxford University Press, 2008, www.oxforddnb.com/view/article/12235 (Accessed March 17, 2020); and Henry Summerson, '*Medieval Carlisle: The City and the Borders from the Late Eleventh to the Mid-Sixteenth Century.*' Vol. 1 (The Cumberland and Westmorland Antiquarian and Archaeological Society, 1993) esp. pp. 211–56.
35 Anthony Goodman, *John of Gaunt: The Exercise of Princely Power in Fourteenth-Century Europe*, 2nd ed. (Routledge, 2013), p. 332.
36 Goldstein, "To Scotland-Ward," p. 36.
37 Turner, *Chaucer: A European Life*, pp. 431–32.
38 Ibid., p. 431.
39 Tim William Machan, *English in the Middle Ages* (Oxford University Press, 2003), p. 125.

40 Thomas Garbáty, "Satire and Regionalism in the *Reeve's Tale*," *Chaucer Review* 8 (1972), pp. 2–3, p. 6; on specific attributes of Norfolk dialect in the Reeve's speech, see Simon Horobin, "Chaucer's Norfolk Reeve," *Neophilologus* 86 (2002), pp. 609–12; and Richard Beadle, "Prolegomena to a Literary Geography of Later-medieval Norfolk," in *Regionalism in Late Medieval Manuscripts and Texts: Essays Celebrating the Publication of A Linguistic Atlas of Late Meiaeval English*, ed. Felicity Riddy (Brewer, 1991), 89–108, especially 93–94; Phillip Knox has recently suggested that aspects of the Reeve's speech as definitively East Anglian might be exaggerated, see Phillip Knox, "The Dialect of Chaucer's Reeve," *Chaucer Review* 49 (2014): pp. 102–24.

41 Derek Pearsall, "Strangers in Late-Fourteenth Century London," in *The Stranger in Medieval Society*, ed. F. R. P. Akehurst and Stephanie Cain Van D'Elden (University of Minnesota Press, 1997), p. 51. For a thorough account of immigrant migration to London in the fourteenth century, see Eilert Ekwall, *Studies on the Population of Medieval London* (Lund, 1956).

42 Derek Pearsall explains three terms often used to refer to non-citizens of London. "Strangers" are those people from other parts of England who immigrated to London. "Aliens" are those people from overseas who came to the city. "Foreigners" are residents of London, but, as with the city's strangers and aliens, they were not freemen or citizens; rather, they were unenfranchised ("Strangers," pp. 48–49).

43 I take the term "intimate stranger" here from Jeffrey Jerome Cohen's study, *Of Giants*.

44 I use the term "uncanny" here in light of Sigmund Freud's extensive exploration of the term in his 1919 essay "The Uncanny," found in *The Standard Edition of the Complete Psychological Works of Sigmund Freud*, vol. XVII, ed. James Strachey with Anna Freud, trans. James Strachey (The Hogarth Press and the Institute of Psychoanalysis, 1955), pp. 217–52; Ingham, *Sovereign Fantasies*, p. 208, gestures, here, towards the interplay of the uncanny and issues of political nationhood, of national ideology, and foreignness in the work of Homi K. Bhabha and Julia Kristeva (notably *Strangers to Ourselves*, trans. Leon S. Roudiez (Columbia University Press, 1991)).

45 Homi K. Bhabha, *The Location of Culture* (New York: Routledge, 1994), p. 122.

46 Scholars have often attempted to locate "Strother." Long ago, Walter Skeat, and later John Matthews Manly, proposed a connection with the Strother family and Strother Castle near the Cheviot Hills in Northumberland. J.A.W. Bennett noted several northern toponyms using "strother." More recently, Andrew Breeze has pointed to the Scottish border location of Westruther, a location within the purview of Berwickshire and Berwick Castle, which was generally in English hands in the late fourteenth century. That the English would have domain over Westruther is significant because two aspirant clerks would have attended the English university of Cambridge rather Paris or Orleans, where Scots students sought their education. The Scots would have

supported the Pope at Avignon due to their French alliance. See Andrew Breeze, "Strother and Berwickshire," *Notes and Queries* 56, no. 1: pp. 21–23.
47 Cobban, *The King's Hall*, pp. 157–59). Only the county of Norfolk provided a greater number of students. As Cobban finds, from the period 1317–1443, the two counties provide one-quarter of the 203 scholars whose geographic origins might be identified by surnames, which is remarkable given that scholars over this period arrive from thirty-six different counties.
48 Derek Brewer, "*The Reeve's Tale* and the King's Hall, Cambridge," *Chaucer Review*, 5 (1971), pp. 311–12.
49 Cobban, *The King's Hall*, p. 16.
50 Wallace, *Chaucerian Polity*, p. 167.
51 Craig Bertolet, "Dressing Symkyn's Wife: Chaucer's *Reeve's Tale* and Bad Taste," *Chaucer Review* 52 (2017): 475.
52 Ibid.
53 On the tenuous relationship of King's Hall with local food producers, such as those in Trumpington, see Jaybe Elisabeth Archer, Richard Marggraf Turley, and Howard Thomas, "'Soper at oure aller cost': The Politics of Food Supply in the *Canterbury Tales*," *Chaucer Review* 50 (2015): 1–29; especially pp. 24–29.
54 See, for example, the work of William F. Woods, notably his recent book, *Chaucerian Spaces: Spatial Poetics in Chaucer's Opening Tales* (SUNY Press, 2008); Elizabeth Edwards, "The Economics of Justice in Chaucer's *Miller's* and *Reeve's Tales*," *The Dalhousie Review* 82 (2002), pp. 91–112; Alcuin Blamires, "Chaucer the Reactionary: Ideology and The General Prologue to the *Canterbury Tales*," *Review of English Studies* 51 (2000), pp. 523–39; Lee Patterson, *Chaucer and the Subject of History* (Univ. of Wisconsin Press, 1991). For Patterson, the Reeve subverts the Miller's "peasant consciousness" by revealing the "disunity within the peasant class itself" (p. 274).
55 In his seminal study of the French influence on Chaucer, Charles Muscatine finds the literature of the bourgeois tradition, within which he includes *fabliau*, to be "'realistic' or 'naturalistic'" in the sense that it "[deals] with life directly, with something of life's natural shape and vitality"; it is, further, "full of exaggeration, of caricature ad grotesque imagination" that "finds its easiest subject in low life": Muscatine, *Chaucer and the French Tradition* (University of California Press, 1957), p. 59. Benson echoes Muscatine in his introduction to the *Miller's Tale* in the *Riverside Chaucer*, where he describes the *fabliaux* as "a lively image of everyday life among the middle and lower classes" (p. 7). In his admittedly "elephantine description," Erik Hertog defines the *fabliau* as "a stylized short narrative in a predominantly materialist semantic register, involving mostly stock bourgeois, lower-class and clerical characters in rigidly programmed plots of far-fetched, humourous and often sexual deceptions and retaliations, governed by local space and clock-time, and often concluded with a moral": Hertog, *Chaucer's Fabliaux As Analogues* (Leuven University Press, 1991), p. 3.

56 V.A. Kolve, *Chaucer and the Imagery of Narrative: The First Five Canterbury Tales* (Stanford University Press, 1984), p. 224.
57 Ingham, *Sovereign Fantasies*, p. 9.
58 Heng, *Empire of Magic*, p. 3.
59 In his seminal study of *Les Fabliaux* (Geneva: Droz, 1971) Per Nykrog famously illustrates the proximity, at times overlap, of romance and fabliau: the fabliau as a "caricature burlesque" of the courtly romance. What I hope this essay demonstrates is that the *fabliau* aspires to more than simple parody; rather, that more pressing concerns of the local and national might underlie the explicit comedy of the *fabliau*.
60 William F. Woods, *Chaucerian Spaces*, p. 16.
61 Ibid., p. 20.
62 For further analysis of this impulse in the *Canterbury Tales*, see John Flyer, "Domesticating the Exotic in the *Squire's Tale*," *ELH* 55 (1988): p. 1–26.
63 Homi K. Bhabha, "DissemiNation: Time, Narrative, and the Margins of the Modern Nation," in *Nation and Narration*, ed. Homi K. Bhabha (Routledge, 1990), p. 297. Though vernacular *fabliaux* had not caught on in Chaucer's England by the late fourteenth century, the genre threw a large shadow in European literature of the later Middle Ages. Of *fabliau* narratives and the genre broadly, Hertog clarifies, "whatever form they took, it was always a dominant, 'official' literary form ... never a marginal or trivial one, neither formally, nor thematically, or functionally" (*Chaucer's Fabliaux as Analogues*, p. 3). Viewing the *fabliaux* in this way, as a popular and dominant literary form, connotes the potential for power and persuasion latent in their construction. What better vehicle for Chaucer's own national consciousness than such a popular literature?
64 See Michael W. Twomey and Scott D. Stull, "Architectural Satire in the Tales of the Miller and the Reeve," *Chaucer Review* 51 (2016): esp. 330–32.
65 Nicholas Royle, *The Uncanny* (Routledge, 2003), p. 108. In his famous essay, Freud performs an analysis on various German lexicons for the terms *heimlich* (homely) and *unheimlich* (unhomely), revealing ultimately that the definitions of these seeming opposite terms blur together across reference works.
66 Susan Yager, "'A Whit Thyng In Hir Ye': Perception and Error in the *Reeve's Tale*," *Chaucer Review* 28 (1994): 393; Helen Cooper, *Oxford Guides to Chaucer: The Canterbury Tales*, 2nd ed. (Oxford University Press, 1996), p. 115.
67 Elizabeth Scala, *Desire in the Canterbury Tales* (Ohio State University Press, 2016), p. 89.
68 Woods, *Chaucerian Spaces*, p. 59.
69 Ibid., p. 53.
70 Daniel F. Pigg, "Performing the Perverse: The Abuse of Masculine Power in the *Reeve's Tale*," in *Masculinities in Chaucer: Approaches to Maleness in the Canterbury Tales and Troilus and Criseyde*, ed. Peter Beidler (D.S. Brewer, 1998), p. 59.

71 See *The Literary Context of Chaucer's Fabliaux*, ed. Larry D. Benson and Theodore M. Andersson (Bobbs-Merril Company, Inc., 1971).
72 Long ago, R.E. Kaske refuted sympathetic readings of the Miller's daughter, suggesting instead that the parting speeches between Malyne and Aleyn were parodies of the *aube* or dawn-song, parodies that inform the lowliness of both the clerk's and the daughter's characters. His essay offers a brilliant comparative reading of the *Reeve's Tale's aube* with the medieval tradition of the dawn-song, yet Kaske does not study the lines preceding the night of sex, the lines of Aleyn's approaching Malyne, which I think are essential to interpreting the entirety of the scene's intentions: Kaske, "An Aube in the *Reeve's Tale*," *ELH* 26 (1959): 295–310.
73 Pigg, "Performing the Perverse," p. 8. Elaine Tuttle Hansen contends that although Malyne and her mother "do seem to enjoy sex" the *Reeve's Tale* argues that "women are literally as well as metaphorically dangerous, wittingly or unwittingly": Hansen, *Chaucer and the Fictions of Gender* (Berkeley, CA: Univ. of California Press, 1992), p. 242; Tamarah Kohanski, "In Search of Malyne," *Chaucer Review* 27 (1993): 228–38.
74 Nicole Nolan Sidhu, "'To Late for to Crie': Female Desire, Fabliau Politics, and Classical Legend in Chaucer's *Reeve's Tale*," *Exemplaria* 21 (2009): 8–12.
75 Scala, *Desire in the Canterbury Tales*, p. 89.
76 Freud, *Standard Edition*, p. 235.
77 See Scala, *Desire in the Canterbury Tales*, p. 88. Scala explains that misreading characterizes the very structure of the *Reeve's Tale*. In the Reeve's mean-spirited reply to the Miller, Chaucer "dramatizes more than a competitive reply to the Miller's story in the Reeve's fabliau; he stages a crucial scene of misreading and misrecognition that disables any widespread deployment of a dramatic principle from the very start."
78 Bhabha, *The Location of Culture*, p. 89.
79 Gila Aloni, "Extimacy in the *Miller's Tale*," *Chaucer Review* 41 (2006): 175–76.
80 Garbáty, "Satire and Regionalism," 6–7; E.T. Donaldson, *Chaucer's Poetry: An Anthology for the Modern Reader*, 2nd ed. (Scott, Foresman, and Co., 1975), p. 1071.

5 Centralization, Resistance, and the North of England in a *Gest of Robyn Hode*

1 Qtd in A.S.G. Edwards "*The Canterbury Tales* and *Gamelyn*," in *Medieval Latin and Middle English Literature, Essays in Honour of Jill Mann*, edited by Christopher Canon and Maura Nolan (Brewer, 2011), pp. 76–90, 85.
2 Masa Ikegami, "The Language and the Date of *A Gest of Robyn Hode*," *Neuphilologische Mitteilungen* 96 (1995): 271–82.
3 All quotations of the early ballads of Robin Hood, *The Tale of Gamelyn*, and Walter Bower's continuation of the *Scottichronicon* are taken from *Robin Hood*

and Other Outlaw Tales, ed. Stephen Knight and Thomas Ohlgren (Medieval Institute Publications, 2000).
4 R.B. Dobson and J. Taylor, *Rymes of Robyn Hood: An Introduction to the English Outlaw* (University of Pittsburgh Press, 1976), p. 25.
5 Although Dobson and Taylor among other critics hold that the text was probably compiled in the early fifteenth century (p. 74), David Fowler long ago suggested a date "well after 1400" (*A Literary History of the Popular Ballad* (Duke University Press, 1968), p. 79). More recently, J.C. Holt has concurred, offering a date of 1450. Stephen Knight dates the *Gest* near the time of its extant printed copies, during the reign of Edward IV in the second half of the fifteenth century. Holt, "Robin Hood: The Origins of the Legend," in *Robin Hood: The Many Faces of that Celebrated English Outlaw*, ed. Kevin Carpenter (Bibliotheks-und Enformationssystem der Universität Oldenburg, 1995), p. 30; Knight, *Robin Hood: A Complete Study of the English Outlaw* (Blackwell, 1994), p. 75.
6 See Rosemary Horrox, "England: Kingship and Political Community, 1377–c.1500," in *A Companion to Britain in the Later Middle Ages*, ed. S. H. Rigby (Blackwell, 2003), pp. 234–35. Horrox offers a concise definition of centralization in the fifteenth century as the "deliberate effort by the king to draw the threads of government into his own hands," a development led to "the emergence of the royal court as the principal source of political influence, with advancement sought in the king's service rather than in the possession of territorial power blocs." This consolidation was aided, as Helen Jewell points out, by three accessions to the throne over the course of the fifteenth century. Henry IV's usurpation of Richard II in 1399 ultimately fused the duchy of Lancaster, with its vast northern holdings, to the crown forevermore. Edward IV's accession in 1461 did the same for his Yorkist estates, while Richard III's rise to the throne brought with it the northern lands he acquired from the Earl of Warwick's demise in 1471. Jewell, *The North–South Divide*, explains, "when Henry [Tudor] defeated Richard at Bosworth in 1485 a dangerous northern independence was averted" (p. 57).
7 See Musgrove, *North of England*, p. 157. Speaking specifically of the northern marches, he claims, "By the fifteenth century England's perimeter was the home of very wealthy, well-connected, and interrelated families which could provide an entirely credible and even constitutionally legitimate alternative to the men at the centre, including the king."
8 Ingham, *Sovereign Fantasies*, p. 187-88.
9 Ibid.
10 Randy P. Schiff, "Borderland Subversions: Anti-imperial Energies in *The Awntyrs off Arthure* and *Golagros and Gawane*," *Speculum* 84 (2009): p. 613. In *Golagros*, Arthur and his army, en route to the Holy Land, come upon a majestic castle near the Rhone. Arthur seeks to know of the castle's lord "quham of is he haldand" (259), and is shocked to learn that this lord "haldis of nane leid ... / Bot everlasting but legiance, to his leving" (262–63). Arthur vows to bring the place under his own governance, and, upon returning from

Jerusalem, besieges the castle and its lord, Golagros. Like Galleroun in the *Awntyrs*, Golagros is defeated by Gawain in combat, but in the end Arthur, witnessing Golagros's humble fidelity, releases him from allegiance. Schiff finds that the poem's conclusion ultimately concerns a "critical compact between two lords" (Golagros and Gawain), and that the text speaks not from the "'national' perspectives" implied by Arthur and his army but to the military spaces of the Anglo-Scottish border and their local lordship in the later fifteenth century. Quotations of *Golagros* are taken from Ralph Hanna, ed. *The Knightly Tale of Golagros and Gawane* (Boydell Press for the Scottish Texts Society, 2008). See also Rose, *Kings in the North*, pp. 466–70.

11 A.J. Pollard, *The Wars of the Roses* (Macmillan, 1988), p. 48.
12 See Norman McCord and Richard Thompson, *The Northern Counties from AD 1000* (Longman, 1998). McCord and Thompson explain that during the fourteenth century "there was a reversal of the previous trend for the North to be absorbed into normal royal administration" (p. 70).
13 Richard Lomas, *North-East England in the Middle Ages* (John Donald Publishers, 1992), p. 86.
14 One of the clearest examples of the crown's encroachment on northern autonomy was the rise of Richard of Gloucester, the future Richard III, following the Wars of the Roses. In 1471, when Edward IV transferred the estates and offices of the Earl of Warwick (the "Kingmaker") to his brother Richard, he did not define Gloucester's power against that of the restored Earl of Northumberland, Henry Percy. We can assume, however, as Charles Ross suggests, that Edward's move "represented an effort to bring the north under some sort of supervision and control ultimately derived from the king" (*Edward IV* (University of California Press, 1974), p. 199). Clarity in the relationship between Percy and Gloucester seems evident a few years later when in July 1474 Percy became an indentured retainer to Gloucester. See Michael Weiss, "A Power in the North? The Percys in the Fifteenth Century," *The Historical Journal* 19 (1976): pp. 507–8; see also Musgrove, *North of England*, p. 172.
15 R.R. Reid, *The King's Council in the North* (Longman, Green and Co., 1921), p. 165.
16 James Simpson, *The Oxford English Literary History, Vol. II: Reformation and Cultural Revolution 1350–1547* (Oxford University Press, 2002), 1. Kathleen Davis, citing Simpson's study, further views "sixteenth-century politics (rather than fourteenth- or fifteenth-century humanism) ... as critical to medieval/early modern periodization in its predominant form" (*Periodization and Sovereignty: How Ideas of Feudalism and Secularization Govern the Politics of Time* (University of Pennsylvania Press, 2008), p. 17).
17 Centralization's effect was substantial because of the unique situation of the region's governance, the exceptional manner by which the North remained a province within the realm of England yet, at the same time, worked as though another country altogether. The palatinates of Chester, Lancaster, and Durham placed some or all responsibilities for local government in the hands

of private individuals, for instance the Bishop of Durham, rather than the crown. The palatinates were, then, as Lomas explains, "a decentralizing institution that diminished the authority of central government" (*North-East England*, p. 75).

18 Ralph Hanna, in his edition, *The Awntyrs off Arthure at the Terne Wathelyn* (Manchester, UK, 1974), dates that poem roughly between 1400 and 1430. Hanna, further, claims that *Golagros* might have been composed any time after the *Awntyrs* – which he cites as a significant source text – but likely not before the mid-fifteenth century (*Golagros and Gawain*, xxiv–xxv).

19 Whether through romance or not, Robin Hood was a character of significant interest to England's kings. Edward III staged a faux-ambush by a body of foresters all dressed in green for his prisoner, King John of France, as the latter made his way from Winchester to London in 1357. In 1510, a young Henry VIII and some of his nobles infiltrated the Queen's chamber dressed in green with hoods, bows, and arrows; and in 1515, King Henry and Queen Catherine were entertained at Shooter's Hill by "tall yomen, clothed all in grene with grene whodes & bowes & arroes, to the number of. ii. C." and led by one "which called him selfe Robyn hood" (*Hall's Chronicle, containing the history of England, during the reign of Henry the Fourth, and the succeeding monarchs, to the end of the reign of Henry the Eighth, in which are particularly described the manners and customs of those periods. Carefully collated with the editions of 1548 and 1550* (London, 1809), pp. 513 and 582).

20 J.C. Holt, *Robin Hood* (Thames and Hudson, 1982), p. 110.
21 Fowler, *Literary History*, p. 8.
22 The Abbot sends his cellarer to hold a meeting ("grete mote") with various London lawyers who might be willing to draw up a writ transferring Sir Richard's lands to the Abbot's control.
23 Christine Chism, "Robin Hood: Thinking Globally, Acting Locally in the Fifteenth-Century Ballads," in *The Letter of the Law: Legla Practice and Literary Production in Medieval England*, ed. Candace Barrington and Emily Steiner (Cornell University Press, 2002), p. 13.
24 Gerald Harriss, *Shaping the Nation: England, 1360–1461* (Clarendon Press, 2005), pp. 154–64.
25 Ibid. p. 164.
26 McCord and Thompson, *Northern Counties*, p. 78.
27 Ibid., p. 120.
28 Knight, *Robin Hood*, p. 15.
29 Peter Stallybrass, "'Drunk with the Cup of Liberty': Robin Hood, the Carnivalesque and the Rhetoric of Violence in Early Modern England," in *The Violence of Representation: Literature and the History of Violence*, ed. Nancy Armstrong and Leonard Tennenhouse (Routledge, 1989), p. 51.
30 Douglas Gray, "The Robin Hood Ballads," *Poetica* 18 (1982): p. 37.
31 Maurice Keen, *The Outlaws of Medieval Legend*, rev. ed. (Routledge, 1987), pp. 9-10.

32 Giorgio Agamben, *Homo Sacer: Sovereign Power and the Bare Life*, trans. Daniel Heller-Roazen (Stanford University Press, 1998), p. 105.
33 Ibid., p. 9.
34 Bracton's authorship is questionable at best, but for the purpose of clarity regarding further quotations, notably those of Kantorowicz, I will refer to him as author. As M.T. Clanchy notes, Bracton most likely inherited the text from his own law masters, later contributing additions as its final editor. See M.T. Clanchy, *From Memory to Written Record: England 1066–1307*, 2nd ed. (Blackwell, 1993), pp. 107–8; J.L. Barton, "The Authorship of Bracton: Again," *Journal of Legal History* 30 (2009): pp. 117–74; see also Samuel Thorne's introduction to volume three of Henry de Bracton, *De legibus et consuetudinibus Angliae*, ed. G.E. Woodbine, and S. E. Thorne, trans. by S.E. Thorne, 4 vols. (Harvard University Press, 1968 and 1977).
35 Ernst H. Kantorowicz, *The King's Two Bodies: A Study in Medieval Political Theology* (Princeton University Press, 1957), p. 151.
36 F.H. Hinsley, *Sovereignty*, 2nd ed. (Cambridge University Press, 1986), pp. 91-2.
37 See, for example, William E. Brynteson, "Roman Law and Legislation in the Middle Ages," *Speculum* 41 (1966): 420 *De legibus et consuetudinibus Angliae*, ed. G.E. Woodbine, and S. E. Thorne, trans. by S.E. Thorne, 4 vols. (Harvard University Press, 1968 and 1977), p. 37. Brynteson clarifies that what was viewed as law in the early Middle Ages "was not the result of a positive action on the part of the organs of the state but existed prior to those organs" (p. 420). He points out that, although natural and positive law are far more complexly related in the twelfth and early thirteenth centuries than is typically understood, legists of this period still "took pains to establish that 'lex' [positive law] must be in accord with the principles of the natural law" (p. 433).
38 Kantorowicz, *The King's Two Bodies*, pp. 148-49.
39 Elshtain, *Sovereignty: God, State, and Self* (Basic Books, 2008), p. 15.
40 Ibid., p. 21.
41 Ibid., p. 35.
42 Keen, *The Outlaws of Medieval Legend* (Basic Books). p. 99 200810.
43 Chism, "Robin Hood: Thinking Globally," p. 20.
44 See Daan Asser, "'Audi et alteram partem': A Limit to Judicial Activity," in *The Roman Law Tradition*, ed. A.D.E. Lewis and David J. Ibbetson (Cambridge University Press, 1994), pp. 209–23.
45 Carl Schmitt, *Political Theology: Four Chapters on the Concept of Sovereignty*, trans. George Schwab (MIT Press, 1988), p. 5.
46 Michael Wilks, *The Problem of Sovereignty in the Late Middle Ages: The Papal Monarchy with Augustinus Triumphus and the Publicists* (Cambridge University Press, 1963), p. 217.
47 I use the term "constitutional dictatorship" from Agamben's discussion of the "state of exception" in the work of political theorists Carl J. Friedrich and Clinton L. Rossiter, as well as Schmitt. See Agamben, *State of Exception*, trans. Kevin Attell (University of Chicago Press, 2005), p. 8.

48 Agamben uses the term "polis" as it is found in Aristotle's *Politics*. Aristotle, here, refers to the city-state, comprised of households and villages, which aims to "satisfy all the needs of man" and which is founded on man's "natural impulse towards political association" (Benjamin Jowett, ed. *Aristotle's Politics* (Random House, 1943), p. 31).
49 Hinsley, *Sovereignty*, p. 92.
50 Ibid., p. 94.
51 Wilkes, *Problem of Sovereignty*, pp. 212–13.
52 Elshtain, *Sovereignty*, p. 40.
53 Agamben, *Homo Sacer*, p. 106.
54 See Holt's discussion of the physical setting of the stories, *Robin Hood*, pp. 86–88.
55 Gray, "Robin Hood Ballads," p. 37.
56 Steve DeCaroli, "Boundary Stones: Giorgio Agamben and the Field of Sovereignty," in *Giorgio Agamben: Sovereignty and Life*, eds. Matthew Calarco and Steve DeCaroli (Stanford University Press, 2007), p. 47.
57 See Elizabeth Walsh, "King in Disguise," *Folklore* 86 (1975): pp. 3–24. Centering her discussion on the fifteenth-century Scottish romance, *The Taill of Rauf Coilyear how he harbreit King Charlis*, Walsh provides a thorough survey of "King and Subject" or "King in Disguise" texts in European literature from, arguably, the earliest analogue, "Alfred and the Cakes" – a humorous story from the twelfth-century *Annals of St Neots*, in which a peasant woman scolds King Alfred for burning pastries – to the sixteenth-century "Der Kohler und Kaiser Maximilian II," which, echoing *King Edward and the Shepherd*, relates Holy Roman Emperor Maximilian II's rustic meal at a peasant's forest home. Later in the text, the emperor, like King Edward, invites the collier to court both for amusement and reward.
58 Thomas Ohlgren, *Robin Hood: The Early Poems, 1465–1560: Texts, Contexts, and Ideology* (University of Delaware Press, 2007), p. 149.
59 All quotations of *King Edward and the Shepherd* are taken from *Middle English Metrical Romances*, ed. Walter Hoyt French and Charles Brockway Hale (Russell and Russell, 1964), pp. 949–85.
60 As Adrian Ailes explains, livery not only signified one's membership in a lord's larger retinue but also "adherence to the cause of that person or house" ("Heraldry in Medieval England: Symbols of Politics and Propaganda," in *Heraldry, Pageantry and Social Display in Medieval England*, ed. Peter R. Coss and Maurice Keen (Boydell Press, 2002): p. 95).
61 M.E. James, "The Murder at Cocklodge," *The Durham University Journal* 57 (1965): 80–87.
62 Reid, *King"s Council in the North*, pp. 75-77.
63 James, "Murder at Cocklodge," p. 83.
64 "Upon the Doulorous Dethe and Much Lamentable Chaunce of the Most Honorable Erle of Northumberland," *The Poetical Works of John Skelton: Principally According to the edition of Rev. Alexander Dice* (Scholarly Publishing Office, University of Michigan Library, 2005), pp. 8–17.

6 The Towneley Plays, the Pilgrimage of Grace, and Northern Messianism

1 The text of the letter appears in *Records of Early English Drama, York, vol. II, Appendixes, Translations, End-notes, Glossaries, Indexes*, edited by Alexandra F. Johnston and Margaret Rogerson (Manchester University Press, 1979), p. 649. The letter also appears in Richard Steele, ed., *King's Letters: from the early Tudors* (London: De la More Press, 1904), 238; as well as in James Orchard Halliwell, ed., *Letters of the Kings of England* (Henry Colburn, 1848), p. 354.
2 Steele, *King's Letters*, p. 238. The date appears in a parenthetical prior to the text of the letter.
3 Musgrove, *North of England*, p. 201.
4 C.S.L. Davies, "Popular Religion and the Pilgrimage of Grace," in *Order and Disorder in Early Modern England*, edited by Anthony Fletcher and John Stevenson (Cambridge University Press, 1985), p. 68.
5 Halliwell, *Letters of the King*, p. 354 n.1.
6 Quotations from the Sykes *Thomas* play are taken from Richard Beadle, ed., *The York Plays: A Critical Edition of the York Corpus Christi Play as recorded in British Library Additional MS 35290*, vol. II (Oxford University Press, 2013).
7 Beadle, *York Plays*, p. 397. As Beadle points out in his notes to the York play, the York version uses "boldly" instead of the Sykes MS' "bodeley," but the latter seems appropriate here.
8 Patricia Badir, "'The Whole Past, the Whole Time': Untimely Matter and the Playing Spaces of York" in *Performing Environments: Site Specificity in Medieval and Early Modern English Drama*, eds. Susan Bennett and Mary Polito (New York: Palgrave, 2014).
9 Thomas' words recall the moment Jesus appears to the disciples in *Luke 37*: "But they being troubled and frightened, supposed that they saw a spirit" (*conturbati vero et conterriti existimabant se spiritum videre*).
10 A.C. Cawley, "The Sykes Manuscript of the York Scriveners" Play," *Leeds Studies in English* 7 (1952): 69. Cawley repeatedly muses on the "magnificent economy" of the York versions versus Towneley (p. 70).
11 Duffey, *Stripping the Altars*, pp. 91–95.
12 Pamela M. King, *The York Mystery Cycle and the Worship of the City* (D.S. Brewer, 2006), p. 29. See also Sarah Beckwith, *Signifying God: Social Relation and Symbolic Act in the York Corpus Christi Plays* (University of Chicago Press, 2001), which imagines the ritual of the Blessed Sacrament signified in the York plays as "the social world of York … as a process of relation" (p. 54).
13 Paul Whitfield White, "Reforming Mysteries' End: A New Look at Protestant Intervention in English Provincial Drama," *Journal of Medieval and Early Modern Studies* 29, no. 1 (1999): 140.
14 See Arthur C. Cawley and Jean Forrester, "References to the Corpus Christi Play in the Wakefield Burgess Court Rolls: The Originals Rediscovered," *Leeds Studies in English* 19 (1988): 85–104; see also Barbara Palmer,

"'Towneley Plays' or 'Wakefield Cycle' Revisited," *Comparative Drama* 21 (1987): 318–48.

15 William Farrer, ed., *The Registers of the Parish Church of Burnley in the County of Lancaster: Christenings, Weddings, and Burials 1562–1653* (Aldine Press, 1899), p. 170.

16 See the description of the manuscript for auction in *Bibliotheca Towneleiana: A Catalogue of the Curious and Extensive Library of the Late John Towneley, Esq.* Part 1 (W. Bulmer and Co., 1814), p. 45. On Charles Towneley's habits, see Gerald Vaughn, "An eighteenth-century classicist's medievalism: The case of Charles Towneley," in *Reading Texts and Images: Essays on Medieval and Renaissance Art and Patronage in Honour of Margaret M. Manion* edited by Bernard J. Muir (Exeter University Press, 2002), p. 308; see also J. Payne Collier, *The History of English Dramatic Poetry to the Time of Shakespeare and the Annals of the Stage to the Restoration* (George Bell and Sons, 1879), who comments extensively on plays in what he terms the "Widkirk Collection," and includes a footnote on Douce's own comments on the manuscript (p. 147 n.1).

17 Meg Twycross, "'They Did Not Come Out of An Abbey in Lancashire: Francis Douce and the Manuscript of the Towneley Plays," in *"The best pairt of our play": Essays Presented to John J. McGavin*, eds. Sarah Carpenter, Pamela M. King, Meg Twycross, and Greg Walker (D.S. Brewer, 2015), pp. 149–65.

18 Barbara D. Palmer, "Recycling "The Wakefield Cycle": 108; Garrett P.J. Epp, "The Towneley Plays, or the Hazards of Cycling": 121–50.

19 Palmer, "Recycling," p. 97. See also Barbara D. Palmer, "Corpus Christi Cycles in Yorkshire: The Surviving Records," *Comparative Drama* 27 (1993): 218–31. Beverly played a major role in the 1536 rebellion. As late as 1519–20, the Beverly plays were undergoing change at the hands of the Earl of Northumberland's secretary, William Peeris, who was paid by the town's governors to make review and alter a Corpus Christi play. P.J.P. Goldberg, "Performing the Word of God: Corpus Christi Drama in the Northern Province," in *Life and Thought in the Northern Church c. 1100–1700: Essays in Honour of Claire Cross*, ed. Dana Wood (The Boydell Press, 1999), pp. 145–170, points out that "not only was the borough council … directly and personally intervening … but … it may have been using a professional author, whose prestige would lie in his employer's status rather than any critical appraisal of his own literary efforts, to mount a thorough revision of the Play cycle" (p. 155).

20 White, "Reforming," p. 127.

21 Palmer, "Recycling," p. 96.

22 Ibid., pp. 88–9.

23 See also Martin Stevens, "Language as Theme in the Wakefield Plays," *Speculum* 52 (1977): 100. Stevens calls him a "reviser who brought a particular point of view to the body of plays on which he worked; see also Epp, "Hazards," pp. 126–30, who further calls into question the editorial practices of the Wakefield editor, as well as the ascription of "Master."

24 Peter Happe, *The Towneley Cycle: Unity and Diversity* (University of Wales Press, 2007), p. 83.
25 P.J.P. Goldberg, "Performing the Word of God," pp. 148–49. This is not to say that drama broadly in the late medieval and early fifteenth century was clearly demarcated by regional lines. See Barbara Palmer, "Early Entertainment Patterns in Northern England," *Bulletin of the John Rylands University Library* 74 (1992): 175–87.
26 For an overview of the Statute of Uses and its context, see David. T. Smith, "The Statute of Uses: A Look at Its Historical Evolution and Demise," *Case Western Law Review* 18 (1966): 40–63.
27 *Letters and Papers, Foreign and Domestic, Henry VIII*, vol. XI, ed. Jaimes Gairdner (HM Stationery Office, 1888), p. 705 (entry 1). Subsequent references to vol. XI will be listed "volume, page, entry."
28 *Letters and Papers*, XI, 705, 1.
29 R.W. Hoyle, *The Pilgrimage of Grace and the Politics of the 1530s* (Oxford University Press, 2001), p. 49.
30 See Christopher Tyerman, *England and the Crusades, 1095–1588* (University of Chicago Press, 1996), pp. 343–44. The badges the pilgrims adopted were found at Pontefract in the keeping of Lord Darcy.
31 Hoyle, *Pilgrimage of Grace*, p. 206.
32 See "Sermon Preached Before the Convocation of the Clergy." *Sermons of Hugh Latimer*. Project Canterbury. http://anglicanhistory.org/reformation/latimer/sermons/index.html (accessed November 23, 2021).; See also Duffey, *Stripping the Altars*, pp. 389–391.
33 Michael Bush, *The Pilgrimage of Grace: A Study of the Rebel Armies 1536* (Manchester University Press, 1996), p. 89.
34 Items 15 and 23 from the Pontefract Articles. Quotations of the articles are taken from appendices in Michael Bush, *The Pilgrim's Complaint: A Study of Popular Thought in the Early Tudor North* (Ashgate, 2009), pp. 269–70.
35 Mary Bateson, "Aske's Examination" *English Historical Review* 5 (1890): 561–62.
36 Mary Bateson, "The Pilgrimage of Grace," *English Historical Review* 5 (1890): p. 336.
37 James Gairdner, ed., *Letters and Papers, Foreign and Domestic, Henry VIII*, vol. XII (HM Stationery Office, 1890), pp. 462–63 (1021); subsequent references to vol. XII will be listed "volume, page, entry."
38 Quotations of "O Faithful People" are taken from the appendices of Bush's *Pilgrim's Complaint*, pp. 257–62.
39 *Letters and Papers*, XII, 502,1088.
40 *Letters and Papers*, XII, 461,1019.
41 Susan E. James, "'Against them all for to fight': Friar John Pickering and the Pilgrimage of Grace," *Bulletin of the John Rylands Library* 85 (2003): 49.
42 Ethan Shagan, *Popular Politics and the English Reformation* (Cambridge University Press, 2003), p. 93
43 James, "Against them all," p. 50.

44 Michael Bush and David Bownes, *The Pilgrimage of Grace: A Study of the Postpardon Revolts of December 1536 to March 1537 and Their Effect* (University of Hull Press, 1999), pp. 221–22.
45 Reid, *King's Council in the North*, p. 126.
46 Bush, *Pilgrim's Complaint*, pp. 177–79; p. 185.
47 Ibid., p. 168; p. 178.
48 *Letters and Papers*, XI, 311, 804.
49 *Letter and Papers*, XI, 511, 1251.
50 *Letters and Papers*, XII, 9, 6; this text also appears in Bateson, "The Pilgrimage of Grace," pp. 343–44.
51 William Shannon, "The Last Abbot of Whalley and the First Large-Scale Maps from Lancashire and Cheshire," *Northern History* 53 (2016): pp. 56–7. See also *Letters and Papers*, XII, 461, 1020; see also XII, 294, 668: on 17 March, in a letter to Sussex and Derby, Henry writes, that he thinks that "as the house has been so corrupt, it were better taken into the king's hands."
52 The inventory taken by the Earl of Sussex on 24 March 1537 is found in *The Coucher Book, or Chartulary, of Whalley Abbey*, edited by W.A. Hulton (Manchester: Charles Simms and Co., for the Chetham Society, 1849), 1255–65. The abbey's vestments are listed on 1264–65. For detail of images on the vestments, see Palmer's appendix in "Recycling" p. 129.
53 For an extensive discussion of these vestments, see Lisa Monnas, "Opus Anglicanum and Renaissance Velvet: The Whalley Abbey Vestments," *Textile History* 25 (Spring 1994): 3–27. Sir John passed his first son Richard, a Protestant, over for his grandson Sir Richard.
54 *Letters and Papers*, XI, 305, 786, item 3; Gerald Brenan and Edward Phillips Statham, *The House of Howard* (Hutchinson and Co., 1907), p.196 n.3., offer the erroneous ascription to the St Mary's monks.
55 Dodds and Dodds, *The Pilgrimage of Grace, 1536–37*, and the Exeter Conspiracy, 1538 (Cambridge University Press, 1915), p. 261.
56 Quotations of the "Sawley Ballad" are taken from Bush, *Pilgrim's Complaint*, pp. 263–66.
57 Jaroslav Pelikan and Hilton C. Oswald, eds. *Luther's Works*, vol. XVII (Concordia Publishing House, 1969), pp. 140–41.
58 Clarence Steinberg, "Kemp Towne in the Towneley *Herod* Play," *Neophilologische Mitteilungen* 71 (1970): pp. 253–60, also suggests that the "kemptown" reference in the *Magnus Herodes* (l. 69) might allude to Kemp Field in West Riding, Yorkshire.
59 Kellogg, "Satan, Langland, and the North," pp. 413–414.
60 Editor's emphasis. Parker, *Expositions on the Book of Psalms by S. Augustine*, p. 290.
61 Norma Kroll, "The Towneley and Chester Plays of the Shepherds: The Dynamic Interweaving of Power, Conflict, and Destiny," *Studies in Philology* 100 (2003): 316.
62 J.C. Cox, *William Stapleton and the Pilgrimage of Grace* (A. Brown and Sons, Ltd., 1902), p. 4.

63 Bush, *Pilgrim's Complaint*, p. 193.
64 Steven G. Ellis, "Civilizing Northumberland: Representations of Englishness in the Tudor State," *Journal of Historical Sociology* 12 (1999): 116.
65 Bush, *Pilgrim's Complaint*, p. 256.
66 Ruth Nisse, *Defining Acts:* Drama and the Politics of Interpretation in Late-Medieval England (University of Notre Dame Press, 2005), p. 86.
67 Kroll, "Dynamic Interweaving," p. 326.
68 In the York play of the *Offering of the Shepherds*, III Pastor speaks to the coming of God's son: "I have herde say, by that same light / The childre of Israell shulde be made free, / The force of the feende to felle in fighte, / And all his pouer excluded shulde be" (pp. 29–32).
69 The play author inverts the lines from their original sequence in Virgil's *Eclogue IV*; translation from Loeb edition of *Virgil's Eclogues, Georgics, Aenied, Books 1–6*, revised edition, translated by H.R. Fairclough (Harvard University Press, 1999), pp. 48–49.
70 Nisse, *Defining Acts*, p. 79, notes how the Wakefield Master "draws attention to the similarities between Virgil"s rustics and his own," and certainly the complaints the politic complaints of a centralized authority sweeping away the rights of agrarian peasants from *Eclogues I* remain compelling in sixteenth-century England.
71 See A.C. Cawley and Martin Stevens, *The Towneley Manuscript: A Facsimile of Huntington MS HM 1* (Huntington Library Press, 1976), viii. Another of the more worn pages that illustrates touching up is the first leaf of *The Purification of Mary* play. Also, on F. 69v and 70, wherein the scene of the Last Supper occurs, the pages are worn. Also, the crown of thorns scene in the *Buffeting* play.
72 Nisse, *Defining Acts*, p. 79.
73 Lisa Kiser, "'Mak's Heirs': Sheep and Humans in the Pastoral Ecology of the Towneley *First* and *Second Shepherds; Plays*," *JEGP* 108 (2009): 339. This is critical commonplace when reading the shepherds plays, such as we see, for example, in E.B. Fryde, *Peasants and Landlords in Later Medieval England* (St Martins' Press, 1996), pp. 145–168.
74 *Letters and Papers*, XI, 465, 1155.
75 Bush, *Pilgrim's Complaint*, p. 269. Item 13 in the Pontefract Articles.
76 *Letters and Papers, Foreign and Domestic, Henry VIII*, vol. VIII, p. 338 (entry 863).
77 The most prominent argument on Mak as antichrist is William Manly's "Shepherds and Prophets: Religious Unity in the Towneley *Secunda Pastorum*," *PMLA* 78 (1963): 151–55. See also Jeffrey Helterman's discussion in "Satan as Everyshepherd: Comic Metamorphosis in the Second Shepherds' Play," *Texas Studies in Literature and Language* 12 (1971): 515–30.
78 Robert S. Sturges, "'Nerehand Nothynd to Pay or to Take': Poverty, Labor, and Money in Four Towneley Plays," in *Money, Morality, and Culture in Late Medieval and Early Modern Europe*, eds. Juliann M. Vitullo and Diane Wolfthal (Ashgate, 2010), p. 21.

79 On the shepherds' light punishment for Mak, see Susan E. Deskis, "Canvassed, or Tossed in a Blanket: Tracing a Motif from the *Second Shepherd's Play* Through the Seventeenth Century," *Notes and Queries* 54 (2007): 325–28.
80 Nisse, *Defining*, pp. 77–8. See also Ann Middleton, "The Audience and Public of 'Piers Plowman,'" in *Middle English Alliterative Poetry and Its Literary Background*, edited by David Lawton (D.S. Brewer, 1982), pp. 102–23.
81 "'Now,' quod he thos, 'cast up thyn eye; / See yonder, lo, the Galaxye, / Which men clepeth the Milky Way, / For it is whyt: and some parfey / Callen it Watlinge Strete'" (pp. 935–39). Larry D. Benson, ed. *The Riverside Chaucer.*
82 Edward Baines, *History, Directory, and Gazetteer of the County of York* (London, 1822), iv. J. Hewitt, *The History and Topography of the Parish of Wakefield* (Wakefield, 1864), p. 258, claims that Watling Street ran through Wakefield. A.C. Cawley, ed., *The Wakefield Pageants in the Towneley Cycle* (Manchester University Press, 1958), xiv, n. 8., refers to Hewitt's study.
83 Johnston and Rogerson, *Records of Early English Drama: York*, pp. 270–275.
84 Badir, "The Whole Past," p. 21.
85 Bush, *Pilgrim's Complaint*, p. 268.
86 Cawley and Stevens, *The Towneley Plays*, vol. II, p. 639, note on line 311 of the *Judgment* play.
87 Juanita Wood, *Wooden Images: Misericords and Medieval England* (Farleigh Dickinson University Press, 1999), p. 44.
88 Martin Stevens, *Four Middle English Mystery Cycles: Textual, Contextual, and Critical Interpretations* (Princeton University Press, 1987), p. 165.
89 James, "Against them all," p. 42.
90 Diarmaid MacCulloch, *Thomas Cranmer: A Life* (Yale University Press, 1998) pp. 154–55.
91 Cawley and Stevens, *The Towneley Plays*, vol. II, p. 651.
92 Pamela M. King, "The End of the World in Medieval English Religious Drama," *Literature and Theology* 26 (2012): 394.
93 See Rosemary Woolf, *The English Mystery Plays* (Berkeley, CA: University of California Press, 1972), pp. 227–32. See Edward J. Gallagher, "The *Visio Lazari*, the Cult, and the Old French Life of Saint Lazarus: An Overview," *Neuphilologische Mitteilungen* 90 (1989): 331–39.
94 Murray McGillivray, "The Towneley Manuscript and Performance: Tudor Recycling?," in *Editing, Performance, Texts: New Practices in Medieval and Early Modern English Drama*, eds Jacqueline Jenkins and Julie Sanders (Palgrave-Macmillan, 2014), p. 59.
95 Garrett Epp, "Re-Editing Towneley," *Yearbook in English Studies* 42 (2013): 95. In his recent TEAMS edition of the Towneley Plays, however, Epp moves the *Lazarus* play up in the order, after the *John the Baptist* play and prior to the *Conspiracy*. Garrett Epp, ed. *The Towneley Plays* (Medieval Institute Publications, 2018).

96 J.W. Earl, "The Shape of Old Testament History in the Towneley Plays," *Studies in Philology* 69 (1972): 452.
97 Theresa Coletti and Gail McMurray Gibson. "Tudor Origins of Medieval Drama," in *A Companion to Tudor Literature*, ed. Kent Cartwright (Wiley-Blackwell, 2010), pp. 242–43.
98 Barbara Gusick, "Time and Unredemption: Perceptions of Christ's Work in the Towneley *Lazarus*," *Fifteenth Century Studies* 22 (1996): 19.
99 King, "The End of the World," p. 396.
100 Ibid., pp. 394–95.
101 Agamben offers a compelling explanation of the linguistic figure of the example in *The Coming Community*, trans. Michael Hardt (Minneapolis, MN: University of Minnesota Press, 1993), p. 10: "Neither particular or universal, the example is a singular object that presents itself as such, that *shows* its singularity . . . . Hence the proper place of the example is always beside itself, in the empty space in which its undefinable and unforgettable life unfolds. This life is purely a linguistic life."
102 G.R. Owst, *Literature and the Pulpit in Medieval England* (Cambridge University Press, 1933), p. 487.
103 Epp, "Re-editing Towneley," p. 102.
104 Coletti and Gibson, "Tudor Origins of Medieval Drama," pp. 242–43.
105 Quotations of "The Cock in the North" are taken from Sharon L. Jansen, *Political Protest and Prophecy Under Henry VIII* (Boydell Press, 1991), pp. 101–4.
106 Jansen, *Political Protest and Prophecy*, p. 98.
107 *Letters and Papers*, XII, 558, 1212. The references to Henry as mole in the context of the prophecy is seen long before the Pilgrimage of Grace. In 1533, the Mistress Amadas explains of various prophecies she's reviewed that "the King's grace is called . . . the Mouldwarp, and is cursed with God's own mouth," and, further, "That a religious man living in an island, called 'the dead man,' shall keep a parliament in the Tower, called the parliament of peace"; see *Letters and Papers, Foreign and Domestic, Henry VIII*, vol. VI, , pp. 399–400 (entry 923).
108 Jansen, *Political Protest and Prophecy*, p. 99.
109 *Bibliotheca Towneleiana*, p. 45.
110 Alexandra Johnston, "The Politics of Civic Drama and Ceremony in Late Medieval and Early-Modern Britain," in *The Idea of the City: Early Modern, Modern, and Post-Modern Locations and Communities*, ed. Joan Fitzpatrick (Cambridge Scholars Publishing, 1999), pp. 25–26.
111 McGillivray, "The Towneley Manuscript and Performance," p. 63.
112 Louis Wann, "A New Examination of the Manuscript of the Towneley Plays," *PMLA* 43 (1928): 137–52.
113 Walter Benjamin, "Theses on the Philosophy of History," in *Selected Writings, vol. IV, 1938–1940*, ed. Howard Eiland and Michael W. Jennings, trans. Edmund Jephcott (Belknap Press, 2006), p. 392.
114 Palmer, "'Wakefield Cycle' Revisited," p. 341.

7 Conclusion: A Medieval and Modern North–South Divide

1. William Wordsworth, *The White Doe of Rylstone, or, The Fate of the Nortons* (Longman, Brown, Green Longmans, and Roberts, 1859).
2. Reid, *King's Council in the North*, p. 184.
3. *Calendar of State Papers Domestic: Elizabeth, Addenda, 1566–79*, ed. Mary Anne Everett Green (London, 1871), p. 135.
4. R.R. Reid, "The Rebellion of the Northern Earls, 1569," *Transactions of the Royal Historical Society* 20 (1906): 174.
5. Reid, "Rebellion of the Northern Earls," p. 147
6. See Maureen M. Meikle, "A Goodly Rogue: The Career of Sir John Forster, An Elizabeth Border Warden," *Northern History* 28 (1992): 126-63.
7. William Palmer, "High Officeholding, Foreign Policy, and the British Dimension in the Tudor Far North, 1525–1563," *Albion* 29, no. 4 (1997): 581.
8. As Meikle, "A Goodly Rogue," pp. 142–43, shows, John Forster's legal battles with Percys continues into the 1590s.
9. The polemicist Thomas Norton's 1569 treatise characterizes Percy's fallen state: "The one you see hardly beareth the contenance of his estate with his small portion of thath which his ancesters sometime had and lost." To the Queen's Majesty's Poor Deceived Subjects of the North Country, Drawn into Rebellion by the Earls of Northumberland and Westmorland (London: Imprinted by Henry Bynneman, for Lucas Harrison, 1569), p. 23.
10. Eamon Duffy, *A People's Tragedy: Studies in Reformation* (London: Bloomsbury, 2021), p. 58.
11. Anthony Wood, *Athenae Oxonienses, An Exact History of All the Writers and Bishops Who have Had Their Education in the University of Oxford, 3rd ed. Vol. 1* (London, 1813), p. 449; see also Mary Anne Everett Green, ed., *Life of Mr. William Whittingham, Dean of Durham, from a MS in Antony Wood's Collection, Bodleian Library, Oxford* (Camden Society, 1870), p. 33.
12. Reid, "Rebellion of the Northern Earls," pp. 177–78, notes that Elizabeth forced Percy to resign his wardenship of the East and Middle Marches, rendered him secondary and powerless as High Steward of the Queen's Lands in Richmond, and claimed lucrative copper mines found on his estate for the crown.
13. K.J. Kesselring, *The Northern Rebellion of 1569: Faith, Politics, and Protest in Elizabethan England* (New York: Palgrave, 2007), p. 21.
14. See *Calendar of State Papers Domestic: Elizabeth, Addenda, 1566–79*, p. 403. Percy explains to Hunsdon during his interrogation following his return to England in 1572 that "the Bishop of Ross came and fed my humour that the Queen would marry another, not the Duke." He further claims to have written, in a letter, "how her marriage with the Duke was misliked, he being counted a Protestant, and if she looked to recover her estate, it must be by advancing the Catholic religion; but that if the Duke were a Catholic, I would rejoice at the match." See also Kesselring's extended discussion of scholarly

disputes regarding Percy's disposition toward the marriage of Norfolk and Mary, p. 50.
15 "Rome: 1569, July–December," in *Calendar of State Papers Relating To English Affairs in the Vatican Archives, Volume 1, 1558–1571,* ed J. M. Rigg (London, 1916), pp. 310–19.
16 Kesselring, *Northern Rebellion,* p. 214.
17 Duffy, *A People's Tragedy,* p. 53.
18 Kesselring, *Northern Rebellion,* pp. 113–14.
19 *Memorials of the Rebellion of* 1569 (John Bowyer Nicholas and Son, 1810), p. 121.
20 *State Papers and Letters of Sir Ralph Sadler, Vol. II,* ed. Arthur Clifford (James Ballantyne and Co., 1809), p. 95.
21 *Calendar of State Papers Domestic: Elizabeth, Addenda, 1566–79,* pp. 186.
22 *Memorials of the Rebellion,* p. 160.
23 George Bowes' letter to his cousin Ralph Bowes is dated January 23 (*Memorials of the Rebellion,* p. 163).
24 Sussex's letter is dated January 10 (*Memorials of the Rebellion,* p. 144).
25 Kesselring, *Northern Rebellion,* p. 218.
26 *Calendar of State Papers Domestic: Elizabeth, Addenda, 1566–79,* p. 166.
27 Sussex writes to Cecil 1 January 1570 (*Memorials of the Rebellion,* p. 132).
28 *Calendar of State Papers Foreign: Elizabeth, Volume 9, 1569–1571,* ed. Allan James Crosby (London, 1874), p. 159.
29 See Herbert Maxwell, *A History of the House of Douglas, Vol. II* (Freemantle and Co., 1902), p. 160–61; under examination on 29 November 1571, John Lesley, the Bishop of Ross and a chief intimate of Mary Queen of Scots, famously testifies to a letter shown him by Ridolphi with the revelation that the Pope sent 12,000 crowns "for the English rebels" after many of these men had sent letters soliciting monies.
30 A.L. Rowse, *The England of Elizabeth,* 2nd edition (Palgrave, 2003), p. 499.
31 Qtd in Sally Badham, "Kneeling in Prayer: English Commemorative Art 1330–1670," *British Art Journal* 16, no. 1 (2015): 58–72, 58.
32 Rowse, *England of Elizabeth,* p. 501.
33 Kesselring, *Northern Rebellion,* p. 114.
34 Musgrove, *North of England,* p. 215.
35 For examples of the poems, see "The North–South Divide in Verse," *BBC News Magazine Online,* Feb. 16, 2009 http://news.bbc.co.uk/2/hi/uk_news/magazine/7892644.stm (accessed March 22, 2020).
36 Both Church's and Ashford's poems are found at "Poems on the North-South Divide," *BBC News Magazine,* February 17, 2009 http://news.bbc.co.uk/2/hi/uk_news/magazine/7894529.stm (accessed March 22, 2020).
37 The early Hovis television ads depict scenes of the working-class in post-war Britain. The 1974 ad, "Bike Ride" was directed by northerner Ridley Scott (*Alien, Blade Runner, Gladiator*) and has been voted the most popular television ad of all time in Britain. What explains Ashford's "anthem" line, however, is the fact that two of these early ads, "Northern" (1973) and

"Runaway" (1979) depict working-class folk speaking in very distinct northern dialect and colloquialisms. The company itself began in the Cheshire East town of Macclesfield in 1887 and its slogan states of the product: "It's as good for you today as it's always been."

38 Bill Bryson, *Notes From A Small Island* (Black Swan, 1996), p. 212.
39 The nineteenth-century librarian and antiquary William E. A. Axon discusses various iterations of the story in his folklore study, *Cheshire Gleanings* (Manchester: Tubbs, Brook, and Chrystal, 1884), pp. 56–68.
40 See Hilary Gatti, "Giordano Bruno: The Texts in the Library of the Ninth Earl of Northumberland," *Journal of the Warburg and Courtauld Institutes* 46 (1983): 63–77; as Gattii notes, Francis Bacon names the Earl, along with, for example, the astronomer and mathematican Thomas Harriot, as "possible allies in his great project for the development of experimental science" (p. 63).
41 Stuart Rawnsley, "Constructing 'the North': Space and a Sense of Places," in *Northern Identities: Historical Interpretations of "The North" and "Northernness,"* ed. Neville Kirk (Ashgate, 2000), p. 3.
42 Wales, *Northern English*, p. 10.
43 Simon Armitage, *All Points North* (Penguin, 1998), 17.
44 Daniel Dorling and Bethan Thomas, *People and Places: A 2001 Census Atlas of the UK* (Bristol: Policy, 2004).
45 Phillip Bond, "My five-point plan to fix the North–South divide," *Telegraph*, November 16, 2019 www.telegraph.co.uk/politics/2019/11/16/five-point-plan-fix-north-south-divide/ (accessed May 19, 2020).
46 Melvyn Bragg and Norman Davies, "The Nation-State," *In Our Time*, BBC Radio 4, London, UK, 14 October 1999.
47 The UK's most popular television series in 2018, *Game of Thrones*, further shows the pervasive nature of the North–South divide. American fantasy author George R.R. Martin admits that the fifteenth-century Wars of the Roses, in part, inspired his book series *A Song of Fire and Ice*, on which the television series is based. Near the conclusion of the first book in the series (titled *A Game of Thrones*) the heir to the lands of the North and their citadel at Winterfell, Robb Stark, is declared "King in the North" emphatically by his bannermen, including the regional lord Jon Umber (Humber) (George R.R. Martin, *A Game of Thrones: Book One of A Song of Fire and Ice* (Bantam Books, 2011 reprint; orig. pub. 1996), p. 797). Robb Stark proceeds to administer war against the southerly monarch – the youthful Joffrey Baratheon and his family – based in the southern port city of King's Landing. ABC News' Julia Macfarlane notes that "U.K fans in particular look at the show as deeply intertwined with both British history, and the travails of modern Britain" (Julia Macfarlane, "Why the UK takes "Game of Thrones" so seriously," ABC News April 15, 2019 www.abcnews.go.com/International/game-thrones-important-uk/story?id=62403834 (accessed May 29, 2020).

48 Kirsty Major, "Why the North of England Will Regret Voting For Brexit," *The Independent*, June 24, 2016 www.independent.co.uk/voices/why-the-north-of-england-will-regret-voting-for-brexit-a7101321.html (accessed October 20, 2019).
49 Simon Armitage, "Magnetic Fields: Simon Armitage on the Pull of Marsden," *The Guardian* March 7, 2020, www.theguardian.com/books/2020/mar/07/magnetic-field-simon-armitage-poet-collection (accessed May 19, 2020).

Works Cited

Ælfric. *Catholic Homilies: Second Series*. Ed. Malcolm Godden. EETS SS 5. Oxford University Press, 1979.
Agamben, Giorgio. *State of Exception*. Trans. Kevin Attell. University of Chicago Press, 2005.
  Homo Sacer: Sovereign Power and the Bare Life. Trans. Daniel Heller-Roazen. Stanford University Press, 1998.
  The Coming Community. Trans. Michael Hardt. Minneapolis, MN: University of Minnesota Press, 1993.
Ailes, Adrian. "Heraldry in Medieval England: Symbols of Politics and Propaganda." *Heraldry, Pageantry and Social Display in Medieval England*. Eds. Peter R. Coss and Maurice Keen. Woodbridge, UK: Boydell Press, 2002. pp. 83–104.
Akbari, Suzanne Conklin. "Orientation and Nation in Chaucer's *Canterbury Tales*." *Chaucer's Cultural Geography*. Ed. Kathryn Lynch. New York: Routledge, 2002. pp. 102–34.
Aloni, Gila. "Extimacy in the Miller's Tale." *Chaucer Review* 41 (2006): 163–84.
Archer, Jaybe Elisabeth, Richard Marggraf Turley, and Howard Thomas. "'Soper at oure aller cost': The Politics of Food Supply in the Canterbury Tales." *Chaucer Review* 50 (2015): 1–29.
Armitage, Simon. *All Points North*. London: Penguin, 1998.
Asser, Daan "'Audi et alteram partem': A Limit to Judicial Activity." *The Roman Law Tradition*. Eds. A. D. E. Lewis and David J. Ibbetson. Cambridge University Press, 1994. pp. 209–23.
Axon, William E. A. *Cheshire Gleanings*. Manchester: Tubbs, Brook, and Chrystal, 1884.
Badham, Sally. "Kneeling in Prayer: English Commemorative Art 1330–1670." *British Art Journal* 16 (2015): 58–72.
Badir, Patricia. "'The Whole Past, the Whole Time': Untimely Matter and the Playing Spaces of York." *Performing Environments: Site Specificity in Medieval and Early Modern English Drama*. Eds. Susan Bennett and Mary Polito. New York: Palgrave, 2014. pp. 17–35.
Baines, Edward. *History, Directory, and Gazetteer of the County of York*. London, 1822.

Barrett, Jr., Robert W. *Against All England: Regional Identity and Cheshire Writing, 1195–1656*. Notre Dame, IN: University of Notre Dame Press, 2008.
Bartlett, Robert. *Why Can the Dead Do Such Great Things? Saints and Worshipers from the Martyrs to the Reformation*. Princeton, NJ: Princeton University Press, 2013.
"Medieval and Modern Concepts of Race and Ethnicity." *Journal of Medieval and Early Modern Studies* 31 (2001): pp. 39–56.
Barton, J.L. "The Authorship of Bracton: Again." *Journal of Legal History* 30 (2009): 117–174.
Bateson, Mary. "Aske's Examination." *English Historical Review* 5 (1890): 561–62.
"The Pilgrimage of Grace." *English Historical Review* 5 (1890): 330–45.
Beadle, Richard, ed. *The York Plays: A Critical Edition of the York Corpus Christi Play as recorded in British Library Additional MS 35290, Vol. II*. Oxford: Oxford University Press, 2013.
Beadle, Richard. "Prolegomena to a Literary Geography of Later-medieval Norfolk." *Regionalism in Late Medieval Manuscripts and Texts: Essays Celebrating the Publication of A Linguistic Atlas of Late Mediaeval English*. Ed. Felicity Riddy. Cambridge: D.S. Brewer, 1991. pp. 89–108.
Beckwith, Sarah. *Signifying God: Social Relation and Symbolic Act in the York Corpus Christi Plays*. Chicago: University of Chicago Press, 2001.
Bede. *Ecclesiastical History of the English People*. Ed. Bertram Colgrave and R.A. B. Mynors. Oxford: Clarendon Press, 1969.
Benjamin, Walter. *Selected Writings, Vol. IV, 1938–1940*. Eds. Howard Eiland and Michael W. Jennings. Trans. Edmund Jephcott. Boston, MA: Belknap Press, 2006.
Benson, Larry D. ed. *The Riverside Chaucer*. Boston, MA: Houghton–Mifflin, 1987.
Benson, Larry D. and Theodore M. Andersson, eds. *The Literary Context of Chaucer's Fabliaux*. New York: Bobbs–Merril Company, Inc., 1971.
Berkhofer III, Robert F. "The Canterbury Forgeries Revisited." *Haskins Society Journal* 18 (2006): 36–50.
Bertolet, Craig. "Dressing Symkyn's Wife: Chaucer's Reeve's Tale and Bad Taste." *Chaucer Review* 52 (2017): 456–75.
Bhabha, Homi K. *The Location of Culture*. New York: Routledge, 1994.
"DissemiNation: Time, Narrative, and the Margins of the Modern Nation." *Nation and Narration*. Ed. Homi K. Bhabha. New York: Routledge, 1990. pp. 291–322.
Bhabha, Homi K. and Kristeva, Julia. *Notably Strangers to Ourselves*. Trans. Leon S. Roudiez. New York: Columbia University Press, 1991.
Bibliotheca Towneleiana: A Catalogue of the Curious and Extensive Library of the Late John Towneley, Esq. Part 1. London: W. Bulmer and Co., 1814.
Birkholz, Daniel. *The King's Two Maps: Cartography and Culture in Thirteenth Century England*. New York: Routledge, 2004.
Blamires, Alcuin. "Chaucer the Reactionary: Ideology and The General Prologue to the Canterbury Tales." *Review of English Studies* 51 (2000): 523–39.

Bowers, John. *The Politics of Pearl: Court Poetry in the Age of Richard II*. Cambridge: D.S. Brewer, 2001.
Bowers, John M. "Chaucer After Smithfield: From Postcolonial Writer to Imperialist Author." *The Postcolonial Middle Ages*. Ed. Jeffrey J. Cohen. New York: Palgrave, 2000. pp. 53–66.
de Bracton, Henry. *De legibus et consuetudinibus Angliae*. Eds. G.E. Woodbine, and S.E. Thorne. Trans. by S.E. Thorne. 4 vols. Cambridge, MA: Harvard University Press, 1968 and 1977.
Breeze, Andrew. "Strother and Berwickshire." *Notes and Queries* 56 (2009): 21–23.
Brenan, Gerald and Edward Phillips Statham. *The House of Howard*. London: Hutchinson and Co., 1907.
Brewer, Derek. "The Reeve's Tale and the King s Hall, Cambridge." *Chaucer Review* 5 (1971): 311–17.
Broderick, George C. *Memorial of Merton College, with Biographical Notices of the Wardens and Fellows*. Oxford: Clarendon Press, 1885.
Bruce, Mark P., and Katherine H. Terrell. "Introduction: Writing Across the Borders." *The Anglo–Scottish Border and the Shaping of Identity, 1300–1600*. Eds. Mark P. Bruce and Katherine H. Terrell. New York: Palgrave-MacMillan, 2012. pp. 1–14.
Bryson, Bill. *Notes From A Small Island*. London: Black Swan, 1996.
Brynteson, William E. "Roman Law and Legislation in the Middle Ages." *Speculum* 41 (1966): 420–37.
Burckhardt, Jacob. *The Civilization of the Renaissance in Italy*. Trans. S.G.C. Middlemore. New York: Macmillan, 1904.
Burrow, John. "A Northern Pronunciation in Chaucer, Skelton, and Spenser." *Notes and Queries* 63 (2016): 191–94.
Burrows, Daron. "Le Chastiement des clers: A Dit concerning the Nations of the University of Paris, Edited from Paris, Bibliothèque Nationale, MS. F. FR. 837." *Medium Ævum* 69 (2000): 211–26.
Burrows, Montagu, ed. *Collectanea III*. Oxford: Clarendon Press, 1896.
Burton, Janet. *The Monastic Order in Yorkshire, 1069–1215*. Cambridge University Press, 2009.
Bush, Michael. *The Pilgrim's Complaint: A Study of Popular Thought in the Early Tudor North*. Surrey, UK: Ashgate, 2009.
The Pilgrimage of Grace: A Study of the Rebel Armies 1536. Manchester University Press, 1996.
Bush, Michael and David Bownes. *The Pilgrimage of Grace: A Study of the Postpardon Revolts of December 1536 to March 1537 and Their Effect*. University of Hull Press, 1999.
Butterfield, Ardis. *The Familiar Enemy: Chaucer, Language and Nation in the Hundred Years War*. Oxford University Press, 2009.
Calendar of Close Rolls, Edward III, 1333–37 . London, 1898.
Calendar of State Papers Relating To English Affairs in the Vatican Archives, Volume 1, 1558–1571. Ed J.M. Rigg. London, 1916.

Calendar of State Papers Foreign: Elizabeth, Volume 9, 1569–1571. Ed. Allan James Crosby. London, 1874.
Calendar of State Papers Domestic: Elizabeth, Addenda, 1566–79. Ed. Mary Anne Everett Green. London, 1871.
Campbell, Bruce M.S. "North–South Dichotomies, 1066–1550," *Geographies of England: The North–South Divide, Material and Imagined*. Eds. Alan R. Baker and Mark Billinge. Cambridge: Cambridge University Press, 2004. pp. 145–74.
Casey, Edward. *Remembering: A Phenomenological Study*. Indiana, IN: University of Indiana Press, 1987.
Cawley, A.C., ed. *The Wakefield Pageants in the Towneley Cycle*. Manchester: Manchester University Press, 1958.
Cawley, A.C., "The Sykes Manuscript of the York Scriveners' Play." *Leeds Studies in English* 7 (1952): 45–80.
Cawley, Arthur C. and Jean Forrester. "References to the Corpus Christi Play in the Wakefield Burgess Court Rolls: The Originals Rediscovered." *Leeds Studies in English* 19 (1988): 85–104.
Cawley, A.C. and Martin Stevens, eds. *The Towneley Plays, 2 vols*. Oxford: E.E.T.S. and Oxford University Press, 1994.
Cawley, A.C. and Martin Stevens, The Towneley Cycle. A Facsimile of Huntington MS HM 1. With an Introduction by A. C. Cawley and Martin Stevens. (Leeds Texts and Monographs, Medieval Drama Facsimiles, II.) Leeds: The University of Leeds, School of English. San Marino, CA: The Huntington Library, 1976.
Chism, Christine. "Robin Hood: Thinking Globally, Acting Locally in the Fifteenth-Century Ballads." *The Letter of the Law: Legla Practice and Literary Production in Medieval England*. Ed. Candace Barrington and Emily Steiner. Ithaca, NY: Cornell University Press, 2002. pp. 12–39.
Clanchy, M.T. *From Memory to Written Record: England 1066–1307*, 2nd ed. Oxford: Blackwell, 1993.
Cobban, Allan. *The Medieval English Universities: Oxford and Cambridge to c.1500*. Aldershot: Scolar, 1988.
The King's Hall Within the University of Cambridge in the Later Middle Ages. Cambridge: Cambridge University Press, 1969.
Cohen, Jeffrey Jerome. *Hybridity, Identity, and Monstrosity in Medieval Britain: On Difficult Middles*. New York: Palgrave Macmillan, 2006.
Of Giants: Sex, Monsters, and the Middle Ages. Minneapolis, MN: University of Minnesota Press, 1999.
Coletti, Theresa, and Gail McMurray Gibson. "Tudor Origins of Medieval Drama." *A Companion to Tudor Literature*. Ed. Kent Cartwright. Oxford: Wiley-Blackwell, 2010. pp. 228–45.
Collier, J. Payne. *The History of English Dramatic Poetry to the Time of Shakespeare and the Annals of the Stage to the Restoration*. London: George Bell and Sons, 1879.

Collin, Dorothy W. "The Composition of Mrs. Gaskell's North and South." *Bulletin of the John Rylands Library* 54 (1971): 67–98.
Cooper, Helen. *Oxford Guides to Chaucer: The Canterbury Tales*, 2nd ed. Oxford University Press, 1996.
Correale, Robert. "The Man of Law's Prologue and Tale." *Sources and Analogues of the Canterbury Tales*, vol. II, Eds. Robert M. Correale and Mary Hamel. Woodbridge, Suffolk: Boydell and Brewer, 2005. pp. 277–350.
Courtenay, William J. *Religion and Community in the Medieval University of Paris*. Notre Dame, IN: Notre Dame University Press, 2018.
Cox, J.C. (ed). "*William Stapleton and the Pilgrimage of Grace*." *Transactions of the East Riding Antiquarian Society* 10 (1903).
Crouch, David. "Robert, first Earl of Gloucester (*b.* before 1100, *d.* 1147)," *Oxford Dictionary of National Biography* (Oxford: Oxford University Press, 2004), www.oxforddnb.com/view/article/23716/ (accessed April 1, 2021).
Damian-Grint, Peter. *The New Historians of the Twelfth-Century Renaissance: Inventing Vernacular Authority*. Woodbridge Suffolk: Boydell Press, 1999.
Davies, C.S.L. "Popular Religion and the Pilgrimage of Grace." *Order and Disorder in Early Modern England*. Eds. Anthony Fletcher and John Stevenson. Cambridge: Cambridge University Press, 1985. pp. 58–91.
Davies, R.R. "Nations and National Identities in the Medieval World: An Apologia." *Revue Belge D'Histoire Contemporaine* 34 (2004): 567–79.
Davis, Kathleen. *Periodization and Sovereignty: How Ideas of Feudalism and Secularization Govern the Politics of Time*. Philadelphia, PA: University of Pennsylvania Press, 2008.
Dean, Ruth J. "Nicholas Trevet, Historian." *Medieval Learning and Literature: Essays presented to Richard William Hunt*. Ed. J.J.G. Alexander and M.T. Gibson. Oxford: Clarendon Press, 1976. pp. 328–52.
"Cultural Relations in the Middle Ages: Nicholas Trevet and Nicholas of Prato." *Studies in Philology* 45 (1948): 541–64.
DeCaroli, Steve. "Boundary Stones: Giorgio Agamben and the Field of Sovereignty." *Giorgio Agamben: Sovereignty and Life*. Eds. Matthew Calarco and Steve DeCaroli. Stanford University Press, 2007, 43–69.
Deskis, Susan E. "Canvassed, or Tossed in a Blanket: Tracing a Motif from the Second Shepherd's Play Through the Seventeenth Century." *Notes and Queries* 54 (2007): 325–28.
de Vitriaco, Jacobus *Historia occidentalis, Bk. 2, Ch. 7. Translations and Reprints from the Original Sources of European History*. Philadelphia, PA: published for the Dept. of History of the University of Pennsylvania by the University of Pennsylvania Press, 1897–1907 II, 7, pp. 19–20.
Devizes, Richard. *The Chronicle of Richard Devizes of the Time of King Richard the First*. Ed. John T. Appleby. London: Thomas Nelson, 1963.
Dobson, R.B. *Church and Society in the Medieval North of England*. London: Hambledon Press, 1996.
Dobson, R.B. and J. Taylor. *Rymes of Robyn Hood: An Introduction to the English Outlaw*. Pittsburgh, PA: University of Pittsburgh Press, 1976.

Dodd, Gwilym. "Parliament and Political Legitimacy in the Reign of Edward II." *The Reign of Edward II: New Perspectives.* Eds. Gwilym Dodd and Anthony Munson. York Medieval Press, 2006. pp. 165–89.
Dodds, Madelaine Hope and Ruth Dodds. *The Pilgrimage of Grace, 1536–37, and the Exeter Conspiracy, 1538.* Cambridge: Cambridge University Press, 1915.
Doig, Allan. "Sacred Journeys/Sacred Spaces: The Cult of St Cuthbert." *Saints of North-East England 600–1500.* Eds. Margaret Coombe, Anne Mouron, and Christiana Whitehead. Turnhout, Belgium: Brepols, 2017. pp. 305–25.
Dolmans, Emily. *Writing Regional Identities in Medieval England: From the Gesta Herwardi to Richard Coer de Lyon.* Cambridge: D.S. Brewer, 2020.
Donaldson, E. Talbot, ed. *Chaucer's Poetry: An Anthology for the Modern Reader*, 2nd ed. Glenview, IL: Scott, Foresman, and Co., 1975.
Dorling, Daniel and Bethan Thomas. *People and Places: A 2001 Census Atlas of the UK.* Bristol: Policy, 2004.
Duffy, Eamon. *A People's Tragedy: Studies in Reformation.* London: Bloomsbury, 2021.
   Stripping the Altars: Traditional Religion in England, c.1400–c.1580. New Haven, CT: Yale University Press, 1992.
Dunne, Michael. "Richard Fitzralph's *Lectura* on the Sentences." *Medieval Commentaries on the Sentences of Peter Lombard.* Ed. Phillipp Rosemann. Leiden: Brill, 2010. pp. 405–437.
Earl, J.W. "The Shape of Old Testament History in the Towneley Plays." *Studies in Philology* 69 (1972): 434–52.
Edwards, A.S.G. *"The Canterbury Tales and Gamelyn." Medieval Latin and Middle English Literature, Essays in Honour of Jill Mann.* Eds. Christopher Canon and Maura Nolan. Cambridge: D.S. Brewer, 2011. pp. 76–90.
Edwards, Elizabeth. "The Economics of Justice in Chaucer's Miller's and Reeve's Tales." *Dalhousie Review* 82 (2002): 91–112.
Ekwall, Eilert. *Studies on the Population of Medieval London.* Stockholm: Lund, 1956.
Ellis, Steven G. "Civilizing Northumberland: Representations of Englishness in the Tudor State." *Journal of Historical Sociology* 12 (1999): 103–27.
Elshtain, Jean Bethke. *Sovereignty: God, State, and Self.* Philadelphia, PA: Basic Books, 2008.
Emden, A.B. "Northerners and Southerners in the Organization of the University to 1509." *Oxford Studies Presented to Daniel Cullus.* Oxford: Clarendon Press for the Oxford Historical Society, 1964. pp. 1–30.
Epp, Garrett, ed. *The Towneley Plays.* Kalamazoo, MI: Medieval Institute Publications, 2018.
Epp, Garrett, "Re–Editing Towneley." *Yearbook in English Studies* 42 (2013): 87–104.
   "The Towneley Plays, or the Hazards of Cycling," *Research Opportunities in Renaissance Drama* 32 (1993): 121–50.
Epstein, Robert. "'Fer in the North; I kan nat telle where': Dialect, Regionalism, and Philologism." *Studies in the Age of Chaucer* 30 (2008): 95–124.

Fairclough, H.R., trans. *Virgil's Eclogues, Georgics, Aenied, Books 1–6*, revised ed. Cambridge, MA: Harvard University Press, 1999.

Farrer, William, ed. *The Registers of the Parish Church of Burnley in the County of Lancaster: Christenings, Weddings, and Burials 1562–1653*. Rochdale: Aldine Press, 1899.

Fenton, Kirsten. *Gender, Nation and Conquest in the Works of William of Malmesbury*. Cambridge: Boydell and Brewer Press, 2008.

Fletcher, C.R.L., ed. *Collectanea 1*. Oxford: Clarendon Press, 1885.

Fletcher, John. "University Migrations in the Late-Middle Ages, with Particular Reference to the Stamford Secession." *Rebirth, Reform, Resilience: Universities in Transition, 1300–1700*. Eds. James Kittelson and Pamela Transhue. Columbus, OH: Ohio State University Press, 1985. pp. 181–82.

Flyer, John. "Domesticating the Exotic in the Squire's Tale." *ELH* 55 (1988): 1–26.

Fowler, David C. *The Life and Times of John Trevisa, Medieval Scholar*. Seattle, WA: University of Washington Press, 1995.

A Literary History of the Popular Ballad. Durham, NC: Duke University Press, 1968.

Freeman, Elizabeth. "The Priory of Hampole and Its Literary Culture." *Parergon* 29 (2012): 1–25.

French, Walter Hoyt and Charles Brockway Hale, eds. *Middle English Metrical Romances*. New York: Russell and Russell, 1964.

Freud, Sigmund. "The Uncanny." *The Standard Edition of the Complete Psychological Works of Sigmund Freud*, vol. XVII. Ed. James Strachey with Anna Freud, Trans. James Strachey. London: The Hogarth Press and the Institute of Psychoanalysis, 1955. pp. 217–52.

Fryde, E.B. *Peasants and Landlords in Later Medieval England*. New York: St Martins Press, 1996.

Gallagher, Edward J. "The *Visio Lazari*, the Cult, and the Old French Life of Saint Lazarus: An Overview." *Neuphilologische Mitteilungen* 90 (1989): 331–39.

Gameson, Richard. *The Manuscripts of Early-Norman England (1066–1130)*. Oxford: Oxford University Press, 1999.

Garbáty, Thomas. "Satire and Regionalism in the Reeve's Tale," *Chaucer Review* 8 (1972): 1–8.

Garrard, David."William of Malmesbury and Civic Virtue," *Discovering William of Malmesbury*. Ed. Rodney M. Thomson, Emily Dolmans, and Emily Winkler. Cambridge: Boydell and Brewer Press, 2017. pp. 27–36.

Gatti, Hilary. "Giordano Bruno: The Texts in the Library of the Ninth Earl of Northumberland." *Journal of the Warburg and Courtauld Institutes* 46 (1983): 63–77.

Gibson, Strickland, ed. *Statuta Antiqua Universitatis Oxonsiensis*. Oxford: Clarendon Press, 1931.

Gillingham, John. "The Ironies of History: William of Malmesbury's Views of William II and Henry I." *Discovering William of Malmesbury*. Eds. Rodney

M. Thomson, Emily Dolmans, and Emily Winkler. Cambridge: Boydell and Brewer Press, 2017. pp. 37–48.

"Civilizing the English: The English Histories of William of Malmesbury and David Hume." *Historical Research* 74 (2001): 17–43.

The English in the Twelfth Century: Imperialism, National Identity, and Political Values. Woodbridge, Suffolk: Boydell Press, 2000.

Goldstein, R. James. "'To Scotland-Ward His Foomen for to Seke': Chaucer, the Scots, and the Man of Law's Tale." *Chaucer Review* 33 (1998): 31–42.

Goodman, Anthony. *John of Gaunt: The Exercise of Princely Power in Fourteenth-Century Europe*, 2nd ed. London: Routledge, 2013.

Green, Mary Anne Everett, ed. *Life of Mr. William Whittingham, Dean of Durham, from a MS in Antony Wood's Collection, Bodleian Library, Oxford*. Camden Society, 1870.

Gransden, Antonia. *Historical Writing in England, Vol. I*. London: Routledge, 1996.

Gray, Douglas. "The Robin Hood Ballads," *Poetica* 18 (1982): 1–39.

Goldberg, P.J.P. "Performing the Word of God: Corpus Christi Drama in the Northern Province." *Life and Thought in the Northern Church c. 1100–1700: Essays in Honour of Claire Cross*. Ed. Dana Wood. Woodbridge, Suffolk: Boydell Press, 1999. pp. 145–170.

Griscom, Acton, ed. *The Historia Regum Britanniae of Geoffrey of Monmouth*. London: Longmans, Green, and Co., 1929.

Gusick, Barbara. "Time and Unredemption: Perceptions of Christ's Work in the Towneley Lazarus." *Fifteenth Century Studies* 22 (1996): 19–41.

Hackett, M.B. *The Original Statutes of Cambridge University*. Cambridge University Press, 1970.

Hall, D.J. *English Medieval Pilgrimage*. London: Routledge, 2019.

Hall's Chronicle, containing the history of England, during the reign of Henry the Fourth, and the succeeding monarchs, to the end of the reign of Henry the Eighth, in which are particularly described the manners and customs of those periods. Carefully collated with the editions of 1548 and 1550. London, 1809.

Halliwell, James Orchard, ed., *Letters of the Kings of England*. London: Henry Colburn, 1848.

Hanna, Ralph. "Yorkshire and York." *Europe: A Literary History, Vol. I*. Ed. David Wallace. Oxford University Press, 2016. pp. 256–78.

"Lichfield." *Europe: A Literary History, Vol. I*. Ed. David Wallace. Oxford University Press, 2016. pp. 279–84.

"The Transmission of Richard Rolle's Latin Works." *Library* 14 (2013): 313–33.

Hanna, Ralph. ed. *The Knightly Tale of Golagros and Gawane*. Woodbridge, Suffolk: Boydell Press for the Scottish Texts Society, 2008.

London Literature 1300–1380. Cambridge: Cambridge University Press, 2005.

"Sir Thomas Berkeley and His Patronage." *Speculum* 64 (1989): 878–916.

ed. *The Awntyrs off Arthure at the Terne Wathelyn*. Manchester, UK: Manchester University Press, 1974.

Hansen, Elaine Tuttle. *Chaucer and the Fictions of Gender.* Berkeley, CA: University of California Press, 1992.
Happé, Peter. *The Towneley Cycle: Unity and Diversity.* Cardiff: University of Wales Press, 2007.
Hardy, Thomas Duffus and Charles Trice Martin, eds. *Lestorie des engles solum la translacion Maistre Geffrei Gaimar.* London, 1889.
Harriss, Gerald. *Shaping the Nation: England, 1360–1461.* Oxford: Clarendon Press, 2005.
  Chaucer and the Fictions of Gender. Berkeley, CA: University of California Press, 1992.
Harrod, W. *The Antiquities of Stamford and St Martins compiled chiefly from the Annals of the Rev. Francis Peck, Vol. 1.* London, 1785.
Harvey, David. *Cosmopolitanism and the Geographies of Freedom.* New York: Columbia University Press, 2009.
Harwood, Britton J. "Psychoanalytic Politics: Chaucer and Two Peasants." *English Literary History,* 68 (2001): 2–27.
Heidegger, Martin. *Being and Time.* Trans. Joan Stambaugh. Albany, NY: SUNY Press, 2010.
Helterman, Jeffrey. "Satan as Everyshepherd: Comic Metamorphosis in the Second Shepherds' Play." *Texas Studies in Literature and Language* 12 (1971): 515–30.
Heng, Geraldine. *The Invention of Race in the European Middle Ages.* Cambridge: Cambridge University Press, 2018.
  Empire of Magic: Medieval Romance and the Politics of Cultural Fantasy. New York: Columbia University Press, 2004.
Henry, Archdeacon of Huntingdon. *Historia Anglorum, The History of the English People.* Ed. Diana Greenway. Oxford: Clarendon Press, 1996.
Hertog, Erik. *Chaucer's Fabliaux As Analogues.* Belgium: Leuven University Press, 1991.
Hewitt, J. *The History and Topography of the Parish of Wakefield.* Wakefield, 1864.
Higden, Ranulph. *Polychronicon Ranulphi Higden, Monachi Cestrensis; Together with the English Translations of John Trevisa and of an Unknown Writer of the Fifteenth Century,* 2 vols. Ed. Churchill Babington. London: Longmans, Green, and Co., 1869.
Higgins, Charlotte, "Antony Gormley Drops 60-tonne load for monumental structure," *Guardian* August 27, 2010. www.theguardian.com/artandde sign/2010/aug/27/antony-gormley-exposure-sculpture (accessed November 25, 2021).
Higham, N.J. *Re–Reading Bede: The Ecclesiastical History in Context.* London: Routledge 2006.
Higham, N.J. *The Kingdom of Northumbria, AD 350–1100.* Wolfboro Falls, NH: A. Sutton, 1993.
Hinsley, F.H. *Sovereignty,* 2nd ed. Cambridge: Cambridge University Press, 1986.

"History of the Angel of the North," Gateshead Council (accessed November 23, 2021): www.gateshead.gov.uk/article/5303/The–history–of–the–Angel–of–the–North (accessed November 23, 2021).
"The Angel Has Landed," BBC News February 16, 1998. http://news.bbc.co.uk/2/hi/uk_news/56000.stm (accessed November 23, 2021).
Holford, Matthew. *"Durham: History, Culture and Identity," Borders and Loyalties: North-East England, c. 1200–c. 1400*. Eds. M.L. Holford and K.J. Stringer. Edinburgh University Press, 2010. pp. 17–57.
Hollister, Warren. *Henry I*. New Haven, CT: Yale University Press, 2003.
Holt, J.C. "Robin Hood: The Origins of the Legend." *Robin Hood: The Many Faces of that Celebrated English Outlaw*. Ed. Kevin Carpenter. Oldenburg: Bibliotheks-und Enformationssystem der Universität Oldenburg, 1995. pp. 27–34.
Holt, J.C. *Robin Hood*. London: Thames and Hudson, 1982.
Holt, J.C. *The Northerners: A Study in the Reign of King John*. Oxford University Press, 1961.
Horobin, Simon. "Chaucer's Norfolk Reeve." *Neophilologus* 86 (2002): 609–12.
Horrox, Rosemary. "England: Kingship and Political Community, 1377–c.1500." *A Companion to Britain in the Later Middle Ages*. Ed. S.H. Rigby. Oxford: Blackwell, 2003. pp. 224–41.
Hoyle, R.W. *The Pilgrimage of Grace and the Politics of the 1530s*. Oxford: Oxford University Press, 2001.
Hsy, Jonathan. "Translation Failure: The TARDIS, Cross-Temporal Language Contact, and Medieval Travel Narrative." *The Language of Doctor Who From Shakespeare to Alien Tongues*. Eds. Jason Barr and Camille D.G. Mustachio. London: Rowman and Littlefield, 2014. pp. 109–23
Trading Tongues: Merchants, Multilingualism, and Medieval Literature. Columbus, OH: Ohio State University Press, 2013.
Hudson, Alison. "St Cuthbert and the South: A North of England Saint and South of England Reformers in the Late Tenth and Early–Eleventh Centuries." *Saints of North-East England 600–1500*. Eds. Margaret Coombe, Anne Mouron, and Christiana Whitehead. Turnhout, Belgium: Brepols, 2017. pp. 111–32.
Hughes, Jonathan. *Pastors and Visionaries: Religion and Secular Life in Late Medieval Yorkshire*. Woodbridge: Boydell Press, 1988.
Hulton, W.A. *The Coucher Book, or Chartulary, of Whalley Abbey*. Manchester: Charles Simms and Co., for the Chetham Society, 1849.
Ikegami, Masa. "The Language and the Date of A Gest of Robyn Hode." *Neuphilologische Mitteilungen* 96 (1995): 271–82.
Ingham, Patricia Clare. *Sovereign Fantasies: Arthurian Romance and the Making of Britain*. Philadelphia: University of Pennsylvania Press, 2001.
Jaeger, C. Stephen. "Charismatic Body – Charismatic Text." *Exemplaria* 9 (1997): 117–37.
James, M.E. "The Murder at Cocklodge," *Durham University Journal* 57 (1965): 80–87.

James, Susan E. "'Against them all for to fight': Friar John Pickering and the Pilgrimage of Grace." *Bulletin of the John Rylands Library* 85 (2003): 38–46.
Jansen, Sharon L. *Political Protest and Prophecy Under Henry VIII*. Suffolk, UK: Boydell Press, 1991.
Jewell, Helen. *The North–South Divide: The Origins of Northern Consciousness in England*. Manchester: Manchester University. Press, 1994.
Johnston, Alexandra. "The Politics of Civic Drama and Ceremony in Late Medieval and Early-Modern Britain." *The Idea of the City: Early Modern, Modern, and Post-Modern Locations and Communities*. Ed. Joan Fitzpatrick. Newcastle, UK: Cambridge Scholars Publishing, 1999. pp. 21–38.
Johnston, Alexandra F. and Margaret Rogerson, Eds. *Records of Early English Drama, York, Vol. II, Appendixes, Translations, End–notes, Glossaries, Indexes*. Manchester: Manchester University Press, 1979.
Jones, Sarah Rees. *York: The Making of a City, 1086–1350*. Oxford: Oxford University Press, 2013.
Jowett, Benjamin, Ed. *Aristotle's Politics*. New York: Random House, 1943.
Kantorowicz, Ernst H. *The King's Two Bodies: A Study in Medieval Political Theology*. Princeton, NJ: Princeton University Press, 1957.
Kaske, R.E. "An Aube in the Reeve's Tale." *ELH* 26 (1959): 295–310.
Keen, Maurice. *The Outlaws of Medieval Legend*, Rev. Ed. London: Routledge, 1987.
Kellogg, Alfred L. "Satan, Langland, and the North." *Speculum* 24 (1949): 413–14.
Kesselring, K.J. *The Northern Rebellion of 1569: Faith, Politics, and Protest in Elizabethan England*. New York: Palgrave, 2007.
Kibre, Pearl. *The Nations in the Mediaeval Universities*. Cambridge, MA: Medieval Academy of America, 1948.
King, Pamela M. "The End of the World in Medieval English Religious Drama." *Literature and Theology* 26 (2012): 384–99.
 The York Mystery Cycle and the Worship of the City. Cambridge: D.S. Brewer, 2006.
Kirk, Neville, ed. *Northern Identities: Historical Interpretations of "The North" and 'Northernness'*. Aldershot, Hampshire: Ashgate, 2000.
Kiser, Lisa. ""Mak's Heirs": Sheep and Humans in the Pastoral Ecology of the Towneley First and Second Shepherds; Plays." *JEGP* 108 (2009): 336–59.
Knight, Stephen and Thomas Ohlgren, Eds. *Robin Hood and Other Outlaw Tales*. Kalamazoo, MI: Medieval Institute Publications, 2000.
Knight, Stephen. *Robin Hood: A Complete Study of the English Outlaw*. Oxford: Blackwell, 1994.
Knox, Phillip. "The Dialect of Chaucer's Reeve." *Chaucer Review* 49 (2014): 102–24.
Kohanski, Tamarah. "In Search of Malyne." *Chaucer Review* 27 (1993): 228–38.
Kolve, V.A. *Chaucer and the Imagery of Narrative: The First Five Canterbury Tales*. Stanford University Press, 1984.

Kroll, Norma. "The Towneley and Chester Plays of the Shepherds: The Dynamic Interweaving of Power, Conflict, and Destiny." *Studies in Philology* 100 (2003): 315–45.
Kynan-Wilson, William. "Mira Romanorum artifitia: William of Malmesbury and the Romano-British Remains at Carlisle." *Essays in Medieval Studies* 28 (2012): pp. 35–49.
Lavezzo, Kathy. *Angels on the Edge of the World*. Ithaca, NY: Cornell University Press, 2006.
Letter and Papers, Foreign and Domestic, Henry VIII, Vol. XII. Ed. Jaimes Gairdner. London: HM Stationery Office, 1890.
Letters and Papers, Foreign and Domestic, Henry VIII, Vol. XI. Ed. Jaimes Gairdner. London: HM Stationery Office, 1888.
Lomas, Richard. *The Fall of the House of Percy, 1368–1408*. Edinburgh: John Donald Publishers, 2007.
North–East England in the Middle Ages. Edinburgh: John Donald Publishers, 1992.
Macaulay, G.C. Ed., *The Complete Works of John Gower*, 4 vols. Oxford: Clarendon Press, 1899–1902.
MacCulloch, Diarmaid. *Thomas Cranmer: A Life*. New Haven, CT: Yale University Press, 1998.
Machan, Tim. *William. English in the Middle Ages*. Oxford University Press, 2003.
Madan, Falconer. "Brasenose College," *The Colleges of Oxford: Their Histories and Traditions*. Ed. Andrew Clark. London: Methuen and Co., 1891.
Maddicott, J. R. *Thomas of Lancaster 1307–1322, A Study in the Reign of Edward II*. Oxford: Oxford University Press, 1970.
Magoun, F.P. "Football in Medieval England and in Medieval English Literature." *American Historical Review* 25 (1929): 33–45.
Mallet, Charles Edward. *A History of the University of Oxford, vol. I, The Medieaval University and the Colleges Founded in the Middle Ages*. London: Methuen and Co., Ltd., 1924.
Manly, William. "Shepherds and Prophets: Religious Unity in the Towneley Secunda Pastorum." *Publications of the Modern Language Association* 78 (1963): 151–55.
Marner, Dominic. *St Cuthbert: His Life and Cult in Medieval Durham*. Toronto: University of Toronto Press, 2000.
Matthew, Donald. "Durham and the Anglo-Norman World." *Anglo-Norman Durham 1093–1193*. Ed. David Rollason, M. Harvey, and M. Prestwich. Woodbridge, Suffolk: Boydell and Brewer, 1994. pp. 1–22.
Mayhew, A.L. ed., *Promptorium Parvulorum: The First English-Latin Dictionary*. London: Kegan, Paul, Trench, Trübner and Co., 1908.
Maxwell, Herbert. *A History of the House of Douglas, Vol. II*. London: Freemantle and Co., 1902.
McCord, Norman and Richard Thompson. *The Northern Counties from AD 1000*. London: Longman, 1998.
McGillivray, Murray. "The Towneley Manuscript and Performance: Tudor Recycling?" *Editing, Performance, Texts: New Practices in Medieval and*

Early Modern English Drama. Eds. Jacqueline Jenkins and Julie Sanders. Boston: Palgrave-Macmillan, 2014. pp. 49–69.

McIlroy, Claire Elizabeth, Ed. *The English Prose Treatises of Richard Rolle.* Cambridge: D.S. Brewer 2004.

Meale, Carol M. "oft sipis with grete devotion I pought what I miȝt do pleysyng to go": The Early Ownership and Readership of Love's Mirror, with Special Reference to its Female Audience." *Nicholas Love at Waseda.* Eds. Shoichi Oguro, Richard Beadle, and *Michael G.* Sargent. Cambridge: D.S. Brewer, 1997. pp. 19–46.

Meikle, Maureen M. "A Goodly Rogue: The Career of Sir John Forster, An Elizabeth Border Warden," *Northern History* 28 (1992): 126–63.

Memorials of the Rebellion of 1569. London: John Bowyer Nicholas and Son, 1810.

Middleton, Ann. "The Audience and Public of "Piers Plowman." *Middle English Alliterative Poetry and Its Literary Background.* Ed. David Lawton. Cambridge: D.S. Brewer, 1982. pp. 102–23.

Monnas, Lisa. "Opus Anglicanum and Renaissance Velvet: The Whalley Abbey Vestments." *Textile History* 25 (1994): 3–27.

Morris, Jan, Ed. *The Oxford Book of Oxford.* Oxford: Oxford University Press, 1978.

Moulin, Leo. *La Vie de Etudiants au Moyen Age.* Paris: Albin Michel, 1991.

Muscatine, Charles. *Chaucer and the French Tradition.* Berkeley, CA: University of California Press, 1957.

Musgrove, Frank. *The North of England: A History From Roman Times to the Present.* London: Blackwell, 1990.

Nakely, Susan. *Living in the Future: Sovereignty and Internationalism in the Canterbury Tales.* Ann Arbor, MI: University of Michigan Press, 2017.

Neville, Cynthia. *Violence, Custom, and Law: The Anglo-Scottish Border Lands in the Later Middle Ages.* Edinburgh University Press, 1998.

Nicholson, Peter. "Chaucer Borrows From Gower: The Sources of the *Man of Law's Tale,*" *Chaucer and Gower: Difference, Mutuality, Exchange.* Ed. R.F. Yeager. Victoria, BC: English Literary Studies, 1991, pp. 85–99.

Nisse, Ruth. *Defining Acts: Drama and the Politics of Interpretation in Late-Medieval England.* Notre Dame, IN: University of Notre Dame Press, 2005.

Nykrog, Per. *Les Fabliaux.* Geneva: Droz, 1971.

Obermeier, Anita. "Chaucer's Retraction," in *Sources and Analogues of the Canterbury Tales,* vol. II. Eds. Robert M. Correale and Mary Hamel. Woodbridge: Boydell and Brewer, 2005. pp. 775–808.

Ohlgren, Thomas. *Robin Hood: The Early Poems, 1465–1560: Texts, Contexts, and Ideology.* Newark, DE: University of Delaware Press, 2007.

Ormrod, Mark. "Competing Capitals? York and London in the Fourteenth Century," in *Courts and Regions in Medieval Europe.* Eds. Sarah Rees Jones, Richard Marks, and A.J. Minnis. Woodbridge: Boydell and Brewer, 2000. pp. 75–98.

Orwell, George. *The Road to Wigan Pier.* London: Harcourt, 1958.

Overman, Steven J. "Sporting and Recreational Activities of Students in the Medieval Universities." *Facta Universitatis* 1 (1999): 25–33.
Owens, Margaret. *Stages of Dismemberment: The Fragmented Body in Late-Medieval and Early Modern Drama*. Newark, DE: University of Delaware Press, 2005.
Owst, G.R. *Literature and the Pulpit in Medieval England*. Cambridge: Cambridge University Press, 1933.
Palmer, Barbara D. "Recycling 'The Wakefield Cycle': The Records." *Research Opportunities in Renaissance Drama* 41 (2002): 88–130.
——— "Corpus Christi Cycles in Yorkshire: The Surviving Records." *Comparative Drama* 27 (1993): 218–31.
——— "Early Entertainment Patterns in Northern England." *Bulletin of the John Rylands University Library* 74 (1992): 175–87.
——— "'Towneley Plays' or 'Wakefield Cycle' Revisited." *Comparative Drama* 21 (1987): 318–48.
Palmer, William. "High Officeholding, Foreign Policy, and the British Dimension in the Tudor Far North, 1525–1563," *Albion* 29 (1997): 579–95.
Parker, John Henry, Ed. *Expositions on the Book of Psalms by S. Augustine, Bishop of Hippo, Translated with Notes and Indices in Six Volumes, Vol. II*. Oxford and London: John Henry Parker; F. and J. Rivington, 1848.
Patterson, Lee. *Chaucer and the Subject of History*. Madison, WI: University of Wisconsin Press, 1991.
Pearsall, Derek. "Strangers in Late-Fourteenth Century London." *The Stranger in Medieval Society*. Eds. F.R.P. Akehurst and Stephanie Cain Van D'Elden. Minneapolis, MN: University of Minnesota Press, 1997. pp. 46–62.
Pearsall, Derek. ed. *Piers Plowman: The C–Text*. Exeter: Exeter University Press, 1994.
——— *The Canterbury Tales*. London: Allen and Unwin, 1985.
Peck, Francis. *Academia Tertia Anglicana, or the Antiquarian Annals of Stanford [sic] in Lincoln, Rutland, and Northampton Shires in XIV Books*. London: printed for James Bettenham, 1727.
Pelikan, Jaroslav and Hilton C. Oswald, Eds. *Luther's Works, Vol. XVII*. St Louis, MO: Concordia Publishing House, 1969.
Penman, Michael A. "The Scots at the Battle of Neville's Cross, 17 October 1346," *Scottish Historical Review* 80 (October 2001): 157–180.
Perret, Xavier. "An Annotated Text of the 'Hunting of the Cheviot,' with a French Rendition." *English Studies* 86 (2005): 1–39.
Pigg, Daniel F. "Performing the Perverse: The Abuse of Masculine Power in the Reeve's Tale." *Masculinities in Chaucer: Approaches to Maleness in the Canterbury Tales and Troilus and Criseyde*. Ed. Peter Beidler. Cambridge: D.S. Brewer, 1998. pp. 52–62.
Pollard, A.J. *The Wars of the Roses*. London: Macmillan, 1988.
Powicke, F.M. "*Some Problems in the History of the Medieval University.*" *Transactions of the Royal Historical Society 4th Series, 17*. London: Royal Historical Society, 1934.

Rait, Robert S. *Life in the Medieval University*. Cambridge: Cambridge University Press, 1918. n.p.
Rashdall, Hastings. *The Universities of Europe in the Middle Ages,* 3 vols. Eds. F.M. Powicke and A.B. Emden. Oxford: Oxford University Press, 1936.
Rawnsley, Stuart. "Constructing 'the North': Space and a Sense of Places." *Northern Identities: Historical Interpretations of "The North" and "Northernness."* Ed. Neville Kirk. Aldershot, Hampshire: Ashgate, 2000. pp. 3–22.
Reid, R.R. *(Rachel) The King's Council in the North*. London: Longman, Green and Co., 1921.
——. "Office of Warden of the Marches: Its Origin and Early History." *English Historical Review* 32 (1917): 482–83.
——. "The Rebellion of the Northern Earls, 1569," *Transactions of the Royal Historical Society* 20 (1906): 171–203.
Renevey, Denis. "Northern Spirituality Travels South: Rolle's Middle English Encomium Oleum Nomen Tuum in Lincoln College Library, MS 91, and Dublin, Trinity College, MS 155." *Revisiting the Medieval North of England*. Eds. Anita Auer, Denis Revenevy, Camille Marshall, and Tino Oudesluijs. Cardiff: University of Wales Press, 2019. pp. 13–24.
Reynolds, Susan. *Kingdoms and Communities in Western Europe, 900–1300*. Oxford: Clarendon Press, 1984.
Roberts, Martin. *The Buildings of England: County Durham*. New Haven, CT: Yale University Press, 2021.
Rogers, J.E. Thorold, Ed. *Oxford City Documents: Financial and Judicial 1268–1665*. Oxford: Clarendon Press, 1891.
Rose, Alexander. *Kings in the North: The House of Percy in British History*. London: Weidenfeld and Nicolson, 2002.
Ross, Charles. *Edward IV*. Berkeley, CA: University of California Press, 1974.
Rowse, A.L. *The England of Elizabeth*, 2nd ed. London: Palgrave, 2003.
Royle, Nicholas. *The Uncanny*. New York: Routledge, 2003.
Ruddick, Andrea. *English Identity and Political Culture in the Fourteenth Century*. Cambridge: Cambridge University Press, 2013.
Rule, Martin, Ed. *Eadmeri Historia Novorum in Anglia, et Opuscula Duo De Vita Sancti Anselmi et Quibusdam Miraculis Ejus*. Wiesbaden, D, 1965. N.p.
Russell, Dave. *Looking North: Northern England and the National Imagination*. Manchester: Manchester University Press, 2004.
Said, Edward. *Orientalism*. New York: Vintage Books, 1979.
Salter, H.E. "The Stamford Schism," *English Historical Review* 37 (1922): 249–53.
Scala, Elizabeth. *Desire in the Canterbury Tales*. Columbus, OH: Ohio State University Press, 2016.
Schiff, Randy P. *Revivalist Fantasy: Alliterative Verse and Nationalist Literary History*. Columbus, OH: Ohio State University Press, 2011.
——. "Borderland Subversions: Anti-imperial Energies in The Awntyrs off Arthure and Golagros and Gawane." *Speculum* 84 (2009): 613–32.

Schmitt, Carl. *Political Theology: Four Chapters on the Concept of Sovereignty.* Trans. George Schwab. Cambridge, MA: MIT Press, 1988.
Shagan, Ethan. *Popular Politics and the English Reformation.* Cambridge University Press, 2003.
Shannon, William. "The Last Abbot of Whalley and the First Large-Scale Maps from Lancashire and Cheshire." *Northern History* 53 (2016): 56–66.
Shields, Rob. *Places on the Margin: Alternative Geographies of Modernity.* London: Routledge, 1991.
Sidhu, Nicole Nolan. "'To Late for to Crie": Female Desire, Fabliau Politics, and Classical Legend in Chaucer's Reeve's Tale," *Exemplaria* 21 (2009): 3–23.
Simeon of Durham. *A History of the Kings of England.* Trans. J. Stephenson. Dyfed: Llanerch Enterprises, 1987.
Simpson, James. *The Oxford English Literary History, Vol. II: Reformation and Cultural Revolution 1350–1547.* Oxford: Oxford University Press, 2002.
Skelton, John. "Upon the Doulorous Dethe and Much Lamentable Chaunce of the Most Honorable Erle of Northumberland." *The Poetical Works of John Skelton: Principally According to the edition of Rev. Alexander Dice.* Ann Arbor, MI: Scholarly Publishing Office, University of Michigan Library, 2005. pp. 8–17.
Smith, David. T. "The Statute of Uses: A Look at Its Historical Evolution and Demise." *Case Western Law Review* 18 (1966): 40–63.
Smith, Jeremy. "The Great Vowel Shift in the North of England, and Some Forms in Chaucer's *Reeve's Tale*." *Neophilologische Mitteilungen* 96 (1995): 433–37.
Smith, Katherine Allen. *Encountering War in the Scriptures and Liturgy.* Woodbridge: Boydell and Brewer, 2012.
Smyth, Alfred. "The Emergence of English Identity, 700–1000." *Studies in Ethnic Identity and National Perspectives in Medieval Europe.* Ed. Alfred Smyth. London: MacMillan, 1998. pp. 24–52.
Sønnesyn, Sigbjorn Olsen. *William of Malmesbury and the Ethics of History.* Cambridge: Boydell and Brewer, 2012.
Southern, R.W. "The Canterbury Forgeries," *English Historical Review* 73 (1958): 193–226.
Spearing, A.C. *The Reeve's Prologue and Tale, with the Cook's Prologue and the Fragment of his tale from the Canterbury Tales.* Cambridge University Press, 1979.
Staley, Lynn. *The Island Garden: England's Language of Nation from Gildas to Marvell.* University of Notre Dame Press, 2012.
Stallybrass, Peter. "'Drunk with the Cup of Liberty': Robin Hood, the Carnivalesque and the Rhetoric of Violence in Early Modern England." *The Violence of Representation: Literature and the History of Violence.* Eds. Nancy Armstrong and Leonard Tennenhouse. New York: Routledge, 1989. pp. 45–76.
Stamp, A.E. Ed, *Calendar of Inquisitions Miscellaneous (Chancery)*, Vol. III. London: His Majesty's stationary Office, 1937.

State Papers and Letters of Sir Ralph Sadler, Vol. II. Ed. Arthur Clifford. Edinburgh: James Ballantyne and Co., 1809.
Steele, Richard, Ed. *King's Letters: From the Early Tudors.* London: De la More Press, 1904.
Stein, Robert. *Reality Fictions: Romance, History, and Governmental Authority, 1025–1180.* Notre Dame, IN: University of Notre Dame Press, 2006.
Steinberg, Clarence. "Kemp Towne in the Towneley Herod Play." *Neophilologische Mitteilungen* 71 (1970): 253–60.
Stevens, Martin. *Four Middle English Mystery Cycles: Textual, Contextual, and Critical Interpretations.* Princeton, NJ: Princeton University Press, 1987.
"Language as Theme in the Wakefield Plays." *Speculum* 52 (1977): 100–117.
Sturges, Robert S. "'Nerehand Nothynd to Pay or to Take': Poverty, Labor, and Money in Four Towneley Plays." *Money, Morality, and Culture in Late Medieval and Early Modern Europe.* Eds Juliann M. Vitullo and Diane Wolfthal. Surrey: Ashgate, 2010. pp. 13–32.
Summerson, Henry. *Medieval Carlisle: The City and the Borders from the Late Eleventh to the Mid-Sixteenth Century. Vol. 1.* Cumberland and Westmorland Antiquarian and Archaeological Society, 1993.
"Responses to War: Carlisle and the West March in the Later-Fourteenth Century." *War and Border Societies in the Middle Ages.* Eds Anthony Goodman and Anthony Tuck. London: Routledge, 1992. pp. 155–77.
Summit, Jennifer. "Topgraphy as Historiography: Petrarch, Chaucer, and the Making of Medieval Rome." *Journal of Medieval and Early Modern Studies* 30 (2000): 211–46.
Swanton, M.J., trans. *The Anglo-Saxon Chronicle.* London: J.M. Dent, 1996.
Sweet, Henry, Ed. *King Alfred's West Saxon Version of Gregory's Pastoral Care.* EETS, o.s. 45, 50. Oxford: Oxford University Press, 1871–72.
Symeon of Durham. *Libellus de Exordio atque Procursu istius hoc est Dunhelmensis Ecclesie.* Ed. and Trans. David Rollason. Oxford University Press, 2000.
Symeonis Monachi Opera Omnia, Vol. II, Historia Regum. Ed. Thomas Arnold. London: Longmans & Co., 1885.
Thomas, Hugh M. *The English and the Normans: Ethnic Hostility, Assimilation and Identity.* Oxford: Oxford University Press, 2003.
Thomson, Rodney. *William of Malmesbury*, Rev. Ed. Woodbridge: Boydell Press, 2003.
"John of Salisbury and William of Malmesbury: Currents in Twelfth Century Humanism." *The World of John of Salisbury.* Ed. Michael Wilks. Oxford: Basil Blackwell, 1984. pp. 117–25.
To the Queen's Majesty's Poor Deceived Subjects of the North Country, Drawn into Rebellion by the Earls of Northumberland and Westmorland. London: Imprinted by Henry Bynneman, for Lucas Harrison, 1569.
Tolkien, J.R.R. "Chaucer as Philologist: The Reeve's Tale." *Transactions of the Philological Society* (1934): -29.
Tuck, J.A. "Northumbrian Society in the Fourteenth Century." *Northern History* 6 (1971): 22–39.

"Richard II and the Border Magnates." *Northern History* 3 (1968): 27–52.
Turner, Marion. *Chaucer: A European Life*. Princeton, NJ: Princeton University Press, 2019.
Turville-Petre, Thorlac. *England the Nation: Language, Literature, and National Identity, 1290–1340*. Oxford University Press, 1996.
Twomey, Michael W. and Scott D. Stull. "Architectural Satire in the Tales of the Miller and the Reeve." *Chaucer Review* 51 (2016): 310–37.
Twycross, Meg. "'They Did Not Come Out of An Abbey in Lancashire': Francis Douce and the Manuscript of the Towneley Plays." *"The best pairt of our play": Essays Presented to John J. McGavin*. Eds. Sarah Carpenter, Pamela M. King, Meg Twycross, and Greg Walker. Cambridge: D.S. Brewer, 2015. pp. 149–65.
Tyerman, Christopher. *England and the Crusades, 1095–1588*. Chicago: University of Chicago Press, 1996.
Vale, Juliet. "Philippa of Hainault." *Oxford Dictionary of National Biography*. Oxford: Oxford University Press, 2008.
Vaughn, Gerald. "An Eighteenth-Century Classicist's Medievalism: The case of Charles Towneley." *Reading Texts and Images: Essays on Medieval and Renaissance Art and Patronage in Honour of Margaret M. Manion*. Ed. Bernard J. Muir. Exeter: Exeter University Press, 2002. pp. 342–358.
Vitalis, Orderic. *The Ecclesiastical History of Orderic Vitalis*, 6 vols. Ed. and Trans. Marjorie Chibnall. Oxford: Clarendon Press, 1969.
Wales, Katie. *Northern English: A Social and Cultural History*. Cambridge: Cambridge University Press, 2006.
Wallace, David. *Chaucerian Polity: Absolutist Lineages and Associational Forms in England and Italy*. Stanford, CA: Stanford University Press, 1997.
Walsh, Elizabeth. "King in Disguise." *Folklore* 86 (1975): 3–24.
Walsh, Katherine. *A Fourteenth-Century Scholar and Primate. Richard Fitzralph in Oxford, Avignon and Armagh*. Oxford: Clarendon Press, 1981.
Walsingham, Thomas. *Historia Anglicana*. Ed. Henry T. Riley, 2 vols. London, 1864.
Wann, Louis. "A New Examination of the Manuscript of the Towneley Plays." *Publications of the Modern Language Association* 43 (1928): 137–52.
Ward, Emily Joan. "Verax Historicus Beda: William of Malmesbury, Bede and historia." *Discovering William of Malmesbury*. Eds. Rodney M. Thomson, Emily Dolmans, and Emily Winkler. Cambridge: Boydell and Brewer Press, 2017. pp. 175–88.
Warren, Michelle. *History on the Edge: Excalibur and the Borders of Britain, 1100–1300*. Minneapolis, MN: University of Minnesota Press, 2000.
Watson, Nicholas. *Richard Rolle and the Invention of Authority*. Cambridge: Cambridge University Press, 1991.
Weiler, Bjorn. "William of Malmesbury on Kingship." *History* 90 (2005): 3–22.
Weiss, Michael. "A Power in the North? The Percys in the Fifteenth Century." *The Historical Journal* 19 (1976): 507–08.

Westminster Chronicle, 1381, 1394. Eds. and Trans. L.C. Hector and Barbara F. Harvey. Oxford: Clarendon Press, 1982.

Whitaker, Cord. *Black Metaphors: How Modern Racism Emerged From Medieval Race-ThinkingI*. Philadelphia, PA: University of Pennsylvania Press, 2019.

White, Paul Whitfield. "Reforming Mysteries' End: A New Look at Protestant Intervention in English Provincial Drama." *Journal of Medieval and Early Modern Studies* 29 (1999): 121–47.

Wilks, Michael. *The Problem of Sovereignty in the Late Middle Ages: The Papal Monarchy with Augustinus Triumphus and the Publicists*. Cambridge: Cambridge University Press, 1963.

William of Malmesbury. *Gesta Regum Anglorum, Vol. I*. Ed. and Trans. R.A.B. Mynors, R.M. Thomson, and M. Winterbottom. Oxford: Oxford University Press, 1998.

William of Malmesbury. *Gesta Regum Anglorum: General Introduction and Commentary Vol. 2*. 2 vols. Ed. R.M. Thomson. Oxford: Oxford University Press, 1998.

William of Malmesbury. *Gestum Pontificum Anglorum, vol. I*, 2 vols. Ed. M. Winterbottom. Oxford: Oxford University Press, 2007.

Williams, Ann and G.H. Martin. *The Domesday Book: A Complete Translation*. London: Penguin, 1992.

Wood, Anthony. *Athenae Oxonienses, An Exact History of All the Writers and Bishops Who have Had Their Education in the University of Oxford*, 3rd ed. Vol. 1. London, 1813.
  The history and Antiquities of the University of Oxford in Two Books, now first published in English from the original manuscript in the Bodleian Library by John Gutch. Oxford: John Gutch, 1792–96.

Wood, Juanita. *Wooden Images: Misericords and Medieval England*. Cranbury, NJ: Farleigh Dickinson University Press, 1999.

Woods, William F. *Chaucerian Spaces: Spatial Poetics in Chaucer's Opening Tales*. Albany, NY: SUNY Press, 2008.

Woolf, Rosemary. *The English Mystery Plays*. Berkeley, CA: University of California Press, 1972.

Wordsworth, William. *The White Doe of Rylstone, or, The Fate of the Nortons*. London: Longman, Brown, Green Longmans, and Roberts, 1859.

Wright, Sarah Breckenridge. "The Soil's Holy Bodies: The Art of Chorography in William of Malmesbury's Gesta Ponitificum Anglorum." *Studies in Philology* 111 (2014): 654–55.

Yager, Susan. "'A Whit Thyng In Hir Ye': Perception and Error in the Reeve's Tale." *Chaucer Review* 28 (1994): 393–404.

Yeager, Patricia. "Introduction: Narrating Space." *The Geography of Identity*. Ed. Patricia Yeager. Ann Arbor, MI: University of Michigan Press, 1996.

Index

A Gest of Robyn Hode, 29, 113–15, 117–26, 129–36
   provenance of, 113, 117–18
Act of Suppression of the Lesser Monasteries (1536), 137
Act of Supremacy (1534), 137
Ælfric of Eynsham, 39–40
Æthelfrith, King of Northumbria, 39, 41–48
Agamben, Giorgio, 121–22
Ailred of Rievaulx, 32
Anderson, Benedict, 8–9
Angel of the North (sculpture), 1, 184
Anglo-Saxon Chronicle, 46
Anglo-Scottish Border, 16–18, 96–97, 115–16, 119–20, 147, 151, 157–58, 175–76, 179–82
   marcher law, 17–18
   Wardens of the March, 18–19, 92, 136, 158, 175–76
Aquinas, Thomas, 124, 129
Armitage, Simon, 187, 189
Aske, Robert, 145–47, 150–51, 153, 157–58, 175
Augustine of Hippo, 155–56
Awntyrs off Arthure at the Terne Wathelyn, 20, 115, 120

Barrett, Robert, 8, 11, 29, 89
Becket, Thomas, Archbishop of Canterbury, 5, 23, 89
Bede, 4, 22, 27, 32–33, 35–49, 52–53, 61, 63, 95, 183, 188
   Historia Ecclesiastica Gentis Anglorum, 4, 27, 32–33, 37–39, 41–45
   regionalism in, 35
   Vita Sancti Cuthberti, 22
Berwick, 1, 8, 18, 175, 181, 212
Berwick, Treaty of (1586), 182
Birkholz, Daniel, 11
FitzRalph, Richard (chancellor of Oxford), 80–83
Bodín, Jean, 117

Boleyn, Anne, Queen of England, 166
Bologna, University of
   election of officials, 69–70
   legal autonomy, 67–68
   nations (divisions of students), 65–66
   student secession, 75–76
Bracton, Henry, 123–24, 127–28
Burkhardt, Jacob, 61–62

Cambridge, University of
   King's College, 84, 100
   nations (divisions of students), 27–28, 64, 70–72
   student secession, 76
   student sport, 72–73
   violence between students and townspeople, 76
Canterbury, archbishops of
   Arundel, Thomas, 26
   Lanfrac (1070-89), 15
   Lanfranc, 60
   Stigand (1052-70), 15
Canterbury, see of
   Canterbury–York primacy controversy, 15, 19, 40, 55
Carlisle
   Roman ruins at, 53–55
Chaucer, Geoffrey, 12
   Canterbury Tales, 10, 14–29, 98
      Cook's Prologue, 100–1, 110
      Cook's Tale, 101, 113
      Friar's Tale, 3, 28–29, 91, 93–95, 113
      Knight's Tale, 102–5, 109
      Man of Law's Tale, 28–29, 91, 95–97, 110
      Miller's Tale, 73, 101–3
      Parson's Tale, 91
      Reeve's Prologue, 98–99
      Reeve's Tale, 12, 28–29, 65, 73–74, 88–91, 99–112
      Second Nun's Tale, 61
      Sir Thopas, 106
      Squire's Tale, 99

251

Index

Chaucer, Geoffrey (cont.)
   Summoner's Tale, 28–29, 91, 97
   Tale of Gamelyn, 113, 120
   knowledge of the North, 92–93
Cheshire (palatine), 8, 12
Chester Plays, 155
Cock of the North, The, 169–71
Cohen, Jeffrey Jerome, 32, 206, 212
Coletti, Theresa and Gayle McMurray Gibson, 167, 169
Cromwell, Thomas, 137, 145, 165–66, 170
Cuthbert, St., 5, 19, 104, 184
   banner of, 5, 23–24, 176
   body of, 23
   cult of, 24
   miracles of, 23, 25
Towneley, John (of Gray's Inn), 143–44, 181–82

Damien, Peter, 124
Dante Aligheria, 124
David I, King of Scotland, 40, 193
David II, King of Scotland, 5, 18, 84
Devizes, Richard, 17
Disraeli, Benjamin, 6
Durham (palatine), 8, 12, 18–20
Durham, bishops of
   Bek, Antony (1285–1311), 19
   Fordham, John (1382–88), 19–20

Edgar Ætheling, 4, 49
Edgar, King of England, 40
Edmund, King of England (the Elder), 40
Edward I, King of England, 19, 116
Edward II, King of England, 97, 100
Edward III, King of England, 78, 81, 83, 85–86, 100
Edward IV, King of England, 116
Eleanor, Queen of England (wife of Edward I), 19
Elizabeth I, Queen of England, 174–81
Elshtain, Jean Bethke, 124, 128
Epistola de obitu Bedae, 37

Freud, Sigmund, 105, 107

Gaimar, Geffrei, 32, 46
Gaskell, Elizabeth, 6
Geoffrey of Monmouth, 45–46
Godly Queen Hester, The (play), 165–66
Gormley, Antony, 1, 184

Hanna, Ralph, 15, 25–26, 89
Harcla, Andrew, Earl of Carlisle, 97

Harrying of the North (1069-70), 4, 22, 25, 49–53, 173, 179
Heng, Geraldine, 9, 102, 197
Henry IV, King of England, 96, 170
Henry of Huntingdon, 32, 36–37, 46
Henry V, King of England, 116
Henry VI, King of England, 116
Henry VII, King of England, 175
Henry VIII, King of England, 116–17, 137–38, 150, 154, 163–65, 169–71, 175
Hidgen, Ranulph (monk at Werburgh), 14, 16, 86–87
Hildebert of Lavardin, 56–58
Hobbes, Thomas, 117
House of Fame, 163
Hugh du Puiset, 23
Humber Estuary, 7–8, 13–14, 16, 22, 26, 34, 86, 95, 145, 151, 187
Hunting of the Cheviot, 20–21

Ingham, Patricia Clare, 8, 10, 99, 102, 115

Jewell, Helen, 13, 15, 92
John I, King of England, 4
John of Gaunt, Duke of Lancaster, 92, 97, 101

Kantorowicz, Ernst, 123–24
King and Subject poems (King in Disguise), 122, 130–31
   King Edward and the Barker, 130
   King Edward and the Shepherd, 130–33

Lancaster (palatine), 8, 12
Law
   Justinian Code, 126
   natural law and positive law, 126–28, 130
   Roman Law (*lex regia*), 124, 127–28, 130
Le Chasthement Des Clers, 68–69
Luther, Martin, 154

Magna Carta, 4
Margaret of Anjou, Queen of England, 170
Marsilius of Padua, 124
Mary I, Queen of England, 143, 175–76
Mary, Queen of Scotland (Scots), 177–79, 182
Musgrove, Frank, 40, 179

Neville's Cross, Battle of (1346), 5, 18, 23
North of England
   devotional culture, 4–5, 21–26
   dialect (northern English), 14–15
   effect of centralization on, 114–20
   magnates and wardens of the marches, 115–17, 119–20
   Northern Rebellion of 1569, 173–81

government centralization, 175–76
government retribution, 178–79
profiting from the rebellion, 179–80
Protestant authority in the North, 176–77
North-South divide
boundaries between North and South, 13–14
Brexit, 188
origins, 5–7
Northumbria, kingdom of, 13, 22, 32, 34–56, 64, 95–96, 188
Bernicia, 39
Deira, 39–41, 95–96
N-town Plays, 155

Orwell, George, 5, 7
Otterburn, Battle of (1388), 19–21, 96, 186
Oxford, University of
All Souls College, 72
Balliol College, 72, 80
election of officials, 73
Exeter College, 71
Lincoln College, 72
Magdalen College, 72
Merton College, 71, 76
nations (divisions of students), 27–28, 64–65, 70–72
New College, 71–72
Oriel College, 72, 84
Queen's College, 72
student secession, 74–76
student sport, 72–73
University College, 72, 80
violence between students, 64–65, 73–74, 86–87

Palmer, Barbara, 142–43, 171–72
Paris, University of
election of officials, 69–70
nations (divisions of students), 66–69
student secession, 75–76
violence between students, 69–70
Percy family, 4, 29, 116
Percy, Henry (Hotspur), 4, 19–21
Percy, Henry, fourth Earl of Northumberland, 135–36
Pickering, John
O, Faithful People, 148–50, 165–66
Piers Plowman, 2–3, 93, 110–11, 155–65
Pilgrimage of Grace, 29–30, 117, 141–46, 150–51, 160, 169–71
Pontefract Articles (24 articles), 146–47, 150, 160, 164–65
Durham rising (third phase), 150–51
Lincolnshire Articles, 151
Lincolnshire rising, 144–45

O Faithful People, See Pickering, John
Pontefract Articles (5 articles), 146
Yorkshire rising, 145–46
Polychronicon, 14
Promptorium Parvulorum, 16

Queen Matilda (wife of Henry I), 33

Richard II, King of England, 4, 98
Robert I, King of Scotland, 97
Robin Hood and the Monk, 130, 133
Rolle, Richard (hermit of Hampole), 5, 25–26
Royle, Nicholas, 105
Ruddick, Andrea, 9, 63

Sawley Abbey, 145, 153–54
Sawley Ballad, 153–54
Scala, Elizabeth, 105, 107
Schmitt, Carl, 126
Shepeards Kalendar (1506), 166
Shields, Rob, 6
Sønnesyn, Sigbjorn, 33–34, 59, 63
South English Legendary, 39
Stamford Schism, 28, 65, 76–86
appeals to Queen Philippa, 83–85
King Edward III's response, 80–81, 83, 85–86
previous schools at Stamford, 77–78
Schism poems in BL Royal MS 12.D.xi, 78–83
St Leonard's Priory, 77, 83
Swein II, King of the Danes, 4
Symeon of Durham, 37, 51–52

Ten Articles (1536), 138
Thomas Play (Sykes Manuscript), 138–39
Thomas, Earl of Lancaster, 97
Thomson, Rodney, 33, 53, 56
Towneley Hall
Whalley Abbey vestements, 153
Towneley Plays, 12, 29–30, 139–44
Buffeting, 167
Conspiracy, 167
Creation, 154–55
First Shepherds' Play, 156–59
Harrowing of Hell, 167
Judas, 166
Judgment, 162–66
Lazarus, 166–71
manuscript (Huntingdon MS HM 1), 139–44
Second Shepherd's Play, 159–62
Thomas of India, 139–41, 167
Towneley Manuscript (Huntingdon MS HM 1), 159, 168, 171–72
Towneley, Christopher, 142

Towneley, Sir John (d. 1540), 143
Treaty of Edinburgh (1328), 96
Trent (river), 13, 187
Trevet, Nicholas, 96–97
Trevisa, John, 14, 16, 86–87, 98, 189
Turner, Marion, 97–98
Turville-Petre, Thorlac, 64, 88–89

Valor Ecclesiasticus, 137
Vitalis, Orderic, 32–33, 51

Wakefield Plot (1541), 163
Wales, Katie, 91
Wars of the Roses, 114
Whalley Abbey, 142–43, 152–53
   execution of Abbot John Paslew, 152
   execution of monk William Haydock, 152
   occupation by rebels, 152
   vestements, 153, *See* Towneley Hall
William II, King of England (Rufus), 58–60
William of Malmesbury, 12, 15–16, 27, 63–64, 88–98
   birth, 33

Gesta Pontificum Anglorum, 14, 27, 33–34, 37–38, 49–50, 53–56
Gesta Regum Anglorum, 15, 27, 33–60
   influenced by Bede, 33, 36
William of Ockham, 124, 128
William of York, St, 19
Wordsworth, William, 173
Wyclif, John, 80, 164–65

York
   as temporary capital, 5, 15–16
York Plays, 155
   Doomsday, 163
   Judgment, 163
   Thomas, 138–39
York, archbishops of
   Ealdred (1060–69), 15
   Lee, Edward (1531–44), 145
   Thomas of Bayeux (1070–1100), 15
   Thurstan (1114–40), 15, 40
   Wickwane, William (1279–85), 19
   William le Zouche (1342–52), 5
York, see of
   Canterbury–York primacy controversy, 15, 19, 40, 55

CAMBRIDGE STUDIES IN MEDIEVAL LITERATURE

1 ROBIN KIRKPATRICK *Dante's Inferno: Difficulty and Dead Poetry*
2 JEREMY TAMBLING *Dante and Difference: Writing in the "Commedia"*
3 SIMON GAUNT *Troubadours and Irony*
4 WENDY SCASE *"Piers Plowman" and the New Anticlericalism*
5 JOSEPH J. DUGGAN *The "Cantar de mio Cid": Poetic Creation in its Economic and Social Contexts*
6 RODERICK BEATON *The Medieval Greek Romance*
7 KATHRYN KERBY-FULTON *Reformist Apocalypticism and "Piers Plowman"*
8 ALISON MORGAN *Dante and the Medieval Other World*
9 ECKEHARD SIMON (ed.) *The Theatre of Medieval Europe: New Research in Early Drama*
10 MARY CARRUTHERS *The Book of Memory: A Study of Memory in Medieval Culture*
11 RITA COPELAND *Rhetoric, Hermeneutics, and Translation in the Middle Ages: Academic Traditions and Vernacular Texts*
12 DONALD MADDOX *The Arthurian Romances of Chrétien de Troyes: Once and Future Fictions*
13 NICHOLAS WATSON *Richard Rolle and the Invention of Authority*
14 STEVEN F. KRUGER *Dreaming in the Middle Ages*
15 BARBARA NOLAN *Chaucer and the Tradition of the "Roman Antique"*
16 SYLVIA HUOT *The "Romance of the Rose" and its Medieval Readers: Interpretation, Reception, Manuscript Transmission*
17 CAROL M. MEALE (ed.) *Women and Literature in Britain, 1150–1500*
18 HENRY ANSGAR KELLY *Ideas and Forms of Tragedy from Aristotle to the Middle Ages*
19 MARTIN IRVINE *The Making of Textual Culture: 'Grammatica' and Literary Theory, 350–1100*
20 LARRY SCANLON *Narrative, Authority, and Power: The Medieval Exemplum and the Chaucerian Tradition*
21 ERIK KOOPER (ed.) *Medieval Dutch Literature in its European Context*
22 STEVEN BOTTERILL *Dante and the Mystical Tradition: Bernard of Clairvaux in the "Commedia"*
23 PETER BILLER AND ANNE HUDSON (eds) *Heresy and Literacy, 1000–1530*
24 CHRISTOPHER BASWELL *Virgil in Medieval England: Figuring the "Aeneid" from the Twelfth Century to Chaucer*
25 JAMES SIMPSON *Sciences and the Self in Medieval Poetry: Alan of Lille's 'Anticlaudianus' and John Gower's 'Confessio Amantis'*

26 JOYCE COLEMAN *Public Reading and the Reading Public in Late Medieval England and France*
27 SUZANNE REYNOLDS *Medieval Reading: Grammar, Rhetoric and the Classical Text*
28 CHARLOTTE BREWER *Editing 'Piers Plowman': The Evolution of the Text*
29 WALTER HAUG *Vernacular Literary Theory in the Middle Ages: The German Tradition, 800–1300, in its European Context*
30 SARAH SPENCE *Texts and the Self in the Twelfth Century*
31 EDWIN D. CRAUN *Lies, Slander and Obscenity in Medieval English Literature: Pastoral Rhetoric and the Deviant Speaker*
32 PATRICIA E. GRIEVE *"Floire and Blancheflor" and the European Romance*
33 HUW PRYCE (ed.) *Literacy in Medieval Celtic Societies*
34 MARY CARRUTHERS *The Craft of Thought: Meditation, Rhetoric, and the Making of Images, 400–1200*
35 BEATE SCHMOLKE-HASSELMANN *The Evolution of Arthurian Romance: The Verse Tradition from Chrétien to Froissart*
36 SIÂN ECHARD *Arthurian Narrative in the Latin Tradition*
37 FIONA SOMERSET *Clerical Discourse and Lay Audience in Late Medieval England*
38 FLORENCE PERCIVAL *Chaucer's Legendary Good Women*
39 CHRISTOPHER CANNON *The Making of Chaucer's English: A Study of Words*
40 ROSALIND BROWN-GRANT *Christine de Pizan and the Moral Defence of Women: Reading Beyond Gender*
41 RICHARD NEWHAUSER *The Early History of Greed: The Sin of Avarice in Early Medieval Thought and Literature*
42 MARGARET CLUNIES ROSS (ed.) *Old Icelandic Literature and Society*
43 DONALD MADDOX *Fictions of Identity in Medieval France*
44 RITA COPELAND *Pedagogy, Intellectuals, and Dissent in the Later Middle Ages: Lollardy and Ideas of Learning*
45 KANTIK GHOSH *The Wycliffite Heresy: Authority and the Interpretation of Texts*
46 MARY C. ERLER *Women, Reading, and Piety in Late Medieval England*
47 D. H. GREEN *The Beginnings of Medieval Romance: Fact and Fiction, 1150–1220*
48 J. A. BURROW *Gestures and Looks in Medieval Narrative*
49 ARDIS BUTTERFIELD *Poetry and Music in Medieval France: From Jean Renart to Guillaume de Machaut*
50 EMILY STEINER *Documentary Culture and the Making of Medieval English Literature*
51 WILLIAM E. BURGWINKLE *Sodomy, Masculinity, and Law in Medieval Literature: France and England, 1050–1230*
52 NICK HAVELY *Dante and the Franciscans: Poverty and the Papacy in the "Commedia"*

53 SIEGFRIED WENZEL *Latin Sermon Collections from Later Medieval England: Orthodox Preaching in the Age of Wyclif*
54 ANANYA JAHANARA KABIR AND DEANNE WILLIAMS (eds.) *Postcolonial Approaches to the European Middle Ages: Translating Cultures*
55 MARK MILLER *Philosophical Chaucer: Love, Sex, and Agency in the "Canterbury Tales"*
56 SIMON A. GILSON *Dante and Renaissance Florence*
57 RALPH HANNA *London Literature, 1300-1380*
58 MAURA NOLAN *John Lydgate and the Making of Public Culture*
59 NICOLETTE ZEEMAN *'Piers Plowman' and the Medieval Discourse of Desire*
60 ANTHONY BALE *The Jew in the Medieval Book: English Antisemitisms, 1350–1500*
61 ROBERT J. MEYER-LEE *Poets and Power from Chaucer to Wyatt*
62 ISABEL DAVIS *Writing Masculinity in the Later Middle Ages*
63 JOHN M. FYLER *Language and the Declining World in Chaucer, Dante, and Jean de Meun*
64 MATTHEW GIANCARLO *Parliament and Literature in Late Medieval England*
65 D. H. GREEN *Women Readers in the Middle Ages*
66 MARY DOVE *The First English Bible: The Text and Context of the Wycliffite Versions*
67 JENNI NUTTALL *The Creation of Lancastrian Kingship: Literature, Language and Politics in Late Medieval England*
68 LAURA ASHE *Fiction and History in England, 1066-1200*
69 J. A. BURROW *The Poetry of Praise*
70 MARY CARRUTHERS *The Book of Memory: A Study of Memory in Medieval Culture (Second Edition)*
71 ANDREW COLE *Literature and Heresy in the Age of Chaucer*
72 SUZANNE M. YEAGER *Jerusalem in Medieval Narrative*
73 NICOLE R. RICE *Lay Piety and Religious Discipline in Middle English Literature*
74 D. H. GREEN *Women and Marriage in German Medieval Romance*
75 PETER GODMAN *Paradoxes of Conscience in the High Middle Ages: Abelard, Heloise, and the Archpoet*
76 EDWIN D. CRAUN *Ethics and Power in Medieval English Reformist Writing*
77 DAVID MATTHEWS *Writing to the King: Nation, Kingship, and Literature in England, 1250-1350*
78 MARY CARRUTHERS (ed.) *Rhetoric Beyond Words: Delight and Persuasion in the Arts of the Middle Ages*
79 KATHARINE BREEN *Imagining an English Reading Public, 1150-1400*
80 ANTONY J. HASLER *Court Poetry in Late Medieval England and Scotland: Allegories of Authority*
81 SHANNON GAYK *Image, Text, and Religious Reform in Fifteenth-Century England*
82 LISA H. COOPER *Artisans and Narrative Craft in Late Medieval England*

83 ALISON CORNISH *Vernacular Translation in Dante's Italy: Illiterate Literature*
84 JANE GILBERT *Living Death in Medieval French and English Literature*
85 JESSICA ROSENFELD *Ethics and Enjoyment in Late Medieval Poetry: Love after Aristotle*
86 MICHAEL VAN DUSSEN *From England to Bohemia: Heresy and Communication in the Later Middle Ages*
87 MARTIN EISNER *Boccaccio and the Invention of Italian Literature: Dante, Petrarch, Cavalcanti, and the Authority of the Vernacular*
88 EMILY V. THORNBURY *Becoming a Poet in Anglo-Saxon England*
89 LAWRENCE WARNER *The Myth of "Piers Plowman": Constructing a Medieval Literary Archive*
90 LEE MANION *Narrating the Crusades: Loss and Recovery in Medieval and Early Modern English Literature*
91 DANIEL WAKELIN *Scribal Correction and Literary Craft: English Manuscripts 1375-1510*
92 JON WHITMAN (ed.) *Romance and History: Imagining Time from the Medieval to the Early Modern Period*
93 VIRGINIE GREENE *Logical Fictions in Medieval Literature and Philosophy*
94 MICHAEL JOHNSTON AND MICHAEL VAN DUSSEN (eds.) *The Medieval Manuscript Book: Cultural Approaches*
95 TIM WILLIAM MACHAN (ed.) *Imagining Medieval English: Language Structures and Theories, 500-1500*
96 ERIC WEISKOTT *English Alliterative Verse: Poetic Tradition and Literary History*
97 SARAH ELLIOTT NOVACICH *Shaping the Archive in Late Medieval England: History, Poetry, and Performance*
98 GEOFFREY RUSSOM *The Evolution of Verse Structure in Old and Middle English Poetry: From the Earliest Alliterative Poems to Iambic Pentameter*
99 IAN CORNELIUS *Reconstructing Alliterative Verse: The Pursuit of a Medieval Meter*
100 SARA HARRIS *The Linguistic Past in Twelfth-Century Britain*
101 ERIC KWAKKEL AND RODNEY THOMSON (eds.) *The European Book in the Twelfth Century*
102 IRINA DUMITRESCU *The Experience of Education in Anglo-Saxon Literature*
103 JONAS WELLENDORF *Gods and Humans in Medieval Scandinavia: Retying the Bonds*
104 THOMAS A. PRENDERGAST AND JESSICA ROSENFELD, (eds.) *Chaucer and the Subversion of Form*
105 KATIE L. WALTER, *Middle English Mouths: Late Medieval Medical, Religious and Literary Traditions*
106 LAWRENCE WARNER *Chaucer's Scribes: London Textual Production, 1384–1432*

107 GLENN D. BURGER AND HOLLY A. CROCKER, (eds.) *Medieval Affect, Feeling, and Emotion*
108 ROBERT J. MEYER-LEE *Literary Value and Social Identity in the Canterbury Tales*
109 ANDREW KRAEBEL *Biblical Commentary and Translation in Later Medieval England: Experiments in Interpretation*
110 GEORGE CORBETT *Dante's Christian Ethics: Purgatory and Its Moral Contexts*
111 JONATHAN MORTON AND MARCO NIEVERGELT (eds.) *The Roman de la Rose and Thirteenth-Century Thought*
112 ORIETTA DA ROLD *Paper in Medieval England: From Pulp to Fictions*
113 CHRISTIANIA WHITEHEAD *The Afterlife of St Cuthbert: Place, Texts and Ascetic Tradition, 690-1500*
114 RICHARD MATTHEW POLLARD *Imagining the Medieval Afterlife*
115 DAVID G. LUMMUS *The City of Poetry: Imagining the Civic Role of the Poet in Fourteenth-Century Italy*
116 ANDREW M. RICHMOND, *Landscapes in Middle English Romance: The Medieval Imagination and the Natural World*
117 MARK CHINCA AND CHRISTOPHER YOUNG *Literary Beginnings in the Middle Ages*
118 MARK FAULKNER *A New Literary History of the Long Twelfth Century: Language and Literature between Old and Middle English*
119 JOSEPH TAYLOR *Writing the North of England in the Middle Ages: Regionalism and Nationalism in Medieval English Literature*

For EU product safety concerns, contact us at Calle de José Abascal, 56–1°, 28003 Madrid, Spain or eugpsr@cambridge.org.